automotive
MAINTENANCE and
TROUBLE SHOOTING

FOURTH EDITION

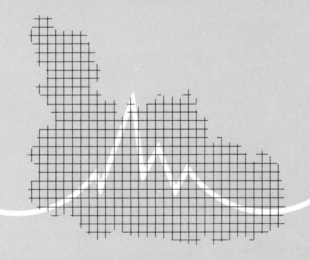

LESLIE F. GOINGS
*M. Ed., Instructor, Automotive Technology,
Henry Ford Community College, Dearborn,
Michigan. Member, American Vocational
Association.*

EDWARD D. SPICER
*Supervisor of Service Training and
Publications, Lincoln-Mercury Division of
Ford Motor Company. Formerly Body
Design Engineer; Aircraft Stress Engineer.*

AMERICAN TECHNICAL SOCIETY
CHICAGO   60637

Copyright ©, 1952, 1954, 1963, 1972, by
American Technical Society

Library of Congress Card Catalog No.: 78-181773
ISBN 0-8269-0102-6

FIRST EDITION
1st Printing 1952

SECOND EDITION
2nd Printing 1954
3rd Printing 1958
4th Printing 1960
5th Printing 1962

THIRD EDITION
6th Printing 1963
7th Printing 1964
8th Printing 1967
9th Printing 1970
10th Printing 1971

FOURTH EDITION
11th Printing 1972

PRINTED IN THE UNITED STATES OF AMERICA

FOREWORD

Most automotive troubles can be avoided. Periodic inspection, adjustment or replacement of those auto parts most likely to fail is a long step toward staying out of trouble. The basic procedures for such inspections and adjustments are presented throughout this book. However, even with reasonable periodic care some trouble must be expected. Thus, *Automotive Maintenance and Trouble Shooting* has three purposes: (1) to show how to prevent most troubles; (2) to find out how to quickly and accurately locate the cause of any trouble; and (3), once it is known what is wrong, to show how to restore the car to satisfactory operation.

In this new Fourth edition, the trouble shooting procedures, tests, and adjustments are arranged in twelve chapters. In each chapter the troubles common to a particular auto part or functional system are treated as separate units. Within the chapter the various topics are arranged for easy reference.

Throughout the text step-by-step diagnostic procedures and repair operations are given as solutions to specific problems. The basic *process* is emphasized rather than arbitrary rules of practice. Understanding *why* certain things are done in particular circumstances helps the student mechanic to apply similar logic to similar situations found when he is working in the auto shop.

Auto emission control equipment is thoroughly covered in the Fourth edition. A whole new chapter has been added on this vital subject. The introduction of transistorized electronic equipment to automotive circuitry has also added another aspect to circuit reading and trouble shooting. This too is covered in depth. To keep up with the ever-changing manufacturing improvements, new up-to-date illustrations and expanded diagrams have also been added.

Leslie F. Goings has joined efforts with Edward D. Spicer in updating *Automotive Maintenance and Trouble Shooting*. The combined efforts of these two automotive specialists should make this well-known text foremost in its contribution to vocational education.

The Publishers

CONTENTS

JOB OPPORTUNITIES

Service Manager
Parts Manager
Auto Mechanic
Automotive Technician
Alignment Specialist
Carburetor and Ignition Specialist
Auto Electrical Specialist
Brake Specialist
Radiator Specialist
Transmission Specialist
Auto Air Conditioning Specialist
Power System Specialist
Body and Fender Straightener
Auto Tune-Up Specialist
Auto Testing Specialist
Garage Manager
New and Used Car Dealer
Automobile Sales Manager
Used Car Manager
Salesman
Automotive Instructor
Auto Parts Dealer
Automotive Machinist
Service Station Operator
Truck Line Maintenance Supervisor
Automotive Claim Adjuster
Auto Painting Expert
Tool Engineer

CHAPTER 1

MAINTENANCE

The wide variety of makes and models of cars, trucks, and tractors, and the wide range of uses as well as the wide variation of climatic and road conditions over which these vehicles operate make it impossible to develop a maintenance procedure or schedule that would apply to all vehicles. The purpose of this chapter is to point out the considerations involved in planning a maintenance procedure for a specific vehicle or group of vehicles operating under a known set of conditions.

PLANNED MAINTENANCE

The driving public as a whole does not understand the involved mechanism of the modern automobile and, for this reason, is not in a position to request or demand specifically what is needed or desired. Generally, the request for service has to do with a desire either to maintain or restore the vehicle to its original high state of operation.

As a service specialist you should understand what the motivating forces were that prompted the original purchase of the vehicle. People buy automobiles for one or more of the following reasons: appearance, performance, economy, safety, comfort, and control. Any successful service business must be based on a sincere desire to establish or maintain these original qualities.

The thousands of parts of the modern automobile which fail or get out of adjustment do so by a gradual process. The process is speeded up by hard usage and neglect, and is slowed down by reasonable care and by periodic maintenance. Each time the brakes are applied a little of the lining wears off. Each time a spark fires across the electrodes of a spark plug a little of the electrode material erodes. Similar deterioration is constantly occurring in most of the parts of the vehicle. By knowing which parts are subject to deterioration and the factors that control the rate or degree of deterioration, and by adjusting or replacing these parts before actual failure occurs, an automotive vehicle can in theory be maintained in a completely troublefree state.

In practice, operations designed to maintain the vehicle vary considerably from the meager, entirely inadequate type of preventive maintenance opera-

SUMMER CHECK-UP	WINTER CHECK-UP
COOLING SYSTEM	COOLING SYSTEM
FUEL SYSTEM	FUEL SYSTEM
LUBRICATION SYSTEM	IGNITION SYSTEM
BRAKING SYSTEM	ELECTRICAL SYSTEM
TIRES	LIGHTING SYSTEM
IGNITION TUNE-UP	LUBRICATION SYSTEM
ELECTRICAL SYSTEM	BRAKING SYSTEM
EXHAUST SYSTEM	EXHAUST SYSTEM
ACCESSORIES	SUSPENSION SYSTEM
BODY CARE	ACCESSORIES
	BODY CARE

Fig. 1-1. Seasonal check-ups are needed to ensure safe driving.

tion offered to the public for a few dollars, to the elaborate type of preventive maintenance operation that may cost more than the trouble it is designed to prevent. Actually, no ideal can be established, since what would be ideal for one vehicle would not be for another.

Owners who place a high value on convenience, comfort, and time may want absolute assurance that no trouble will occur and are willing to pay for inspections, adjustments, and replacements if there is even the remotest possibility that trouble can be forestalled. Others will want to "get by" as economically as possible. Fig. 1-1.

It is almost impossible to work out a planned maintenance procedure for a large segment of owners. Generally, these people will bring a car to you only after trouble has developed or when they believe trouble is about to occur.

Some owners will place the car in your care and will expect you to advise them when they should bring it in for whatever maintenance operations you recommend. This is almost like having a signed blank check and it is your responsibility to see that you do not abuse the trust.

Many owners will not think of maintenance until they have plans for an ex-tended trip. At this time they will come to you for whatever is needed to eliminate the possibility of trouble during the trip. Most owners neglect ordinary maintenance until trouble or the threat of trouble develops. They will not have their car lubricated until a squeak, or something else that disturbs them, develops.

Regardless of how much experience or equipment you may have, many owners will be skeptical of your ability and some may even doubt your sincerity or honesty. Trouble shooting provides you with an opportunity to quickly demonstrate your ability and integrity. If an owner has experienced a performance trouble that has finally forced him to bring his vehicle to you, he may be wondering if you have the ability to correct the trouble and may have become reconciled to the necessity of spending a great deal of money. If you quickly locate the cause of the trouble and correct it, you will have demonstrated your ability to the owner. If the price you charge is lower than he expected, he will be convinced of your integrity. To such an owner you can point out that the trouble could have been avoided by regular inspections and adjustments. You have, therefore, an excellent opportunity to sell the idea of pe-

Fig. 1-2. A test center can determine correct operation of the engine. Sun Electric Corp.

riodic maintenance, and convert him to an enthusiastic regular customer. Fig. 1-2.

In trouble shooting you will often find a number of things out of adjustment. In this situation a tune up or some similar maintenance service should be sold rather than to continue with the trouble shooting.

Most automobile manufacturers have chosen lubrication service as a means of getting the auto back into the shop. This service is inexpensive enough so that an appeal can be made to all classes of owners. Once the auto comes in for lubrication, a trained operator can look for signs of maladjustment or approaching failure. Unfortunately, in many cases, the shop loses sight of its main objective and merely lubricates the auto, failing to make the inspections. A trained lubrication man can be the shop's best salesman.

TROUBLE SHOOTING

The words *analysis, diagnosis,* and *trouble shooting* each mean something

different and are commonly misused. These words should be in your vocabulary and an understanding of their specific meaning will permit you to use them correctly.

The dictionary defines analysis as:

ANALYSIS: Separation of anything, whether an object of the senses or of the intellect into constituent parts or elements.

Analysis clarifies rather than increases knowledge. In measuring the factors of performance or control and recording your findings, you are making an analysis.

On the other hand, the dictionary defines diagnosis as:

DIAGNOSIS: A conclusion arrived at through critical perception or scrutiny; hence, keen understanding of appearances.

A diagnosis includes a conclusion as to what has already happened or will happen, or a recommendation of what should be done. An easy way to remember the differences in these two words is to remember that an analysis involves finding out what you have to start with, while a diagnosis involves definite recommendations for changing what you find.

In this volume, and in general practice, the term *trouble shooting* is accepted as meaning:

TROUBLE SHOOTING: The discovery and elimination of causes of trouble and the correction of the trouble.

Just as a diagnosis includes an analysis, trouble shooting includes both an analysis and a diagnosis, plus correction. Trouble shooting is a more complete service than an analysis or a diagnosis, and for this reason this volume presents trouble shooting.

The things about which you are most interested are the ones that when in correct adjustment give good performance or when out of adjustment cause poor performance.

The ideal trouble shooter possesses an understanding of operating principles of each system in an automobile and the laws of physics on which operating principles are based. Such a person would need years of experience in which he had firsthand contact with automotive troubles. By this experience he would become acquainted with the things that can and do happen which would prove useful to him in locating troubles. In addition, he would need a high degree of ingenuity to devise and perform tests to prove or disprove a suspected condition. These things, plus the ability to apply logic to the circumstances, would be required of the trouble shooter to enable him to locate and correct every type of automotive trouble.

Obviously, few such men exist. Nevertheless, a large number of people not possessing these qualifications can successfully locate and correct any type of trouble that can happen. This can be accomplished in several ways.

As automobiles began to grow more complex, the job of training individuals on operating principles and locating causes of troubles appeared too complex for the people who had charge of training the nation's automobile mechanics. A plan evolved in which, regardless of the nature of trouble having to do with engine performance, the vehicle owner was sold an engine tune-up.

The performance of an engine tune-up is not trouble shooting, but in most instances it would correct the trouble regardless of where the trouble existed. In an engine tune-up, each of the more common factors having an effect on engine performance are tested and inspected and adjusted to restore them to a like-new condition.

The basic operations are performed first in an engine tune-up. For example, the ignition system is a system of considerable importance with regard to engine performance. In testing and re-establishing the ignition to a like-new state in an engine tune-up: (1) The battery, which represents the source, is tested first. (2) The battery cable connections are inspected. (3) The ignition primary circuit is inspected and, if it is worn or defective, restored to a like-new condition. (4) The distributor contacts are first cleaned and, if it should prove necessary, adjusted. (5) The distributor rotor and cap, or terminal plate, are inspected for cracks or evidence of leakage. (6) Finally, the quality of the spark at the end of each spark plug wire is determined.

By a study of the tune-up procedure, it becomes apparent that each portion of a system that can have an influence on other portions is tested and corrected before the portion affected by it is tested. By this method, any possible influence of a fault in the first portion of the system is eliminated in evaluating the results of tests of the second portion of the system.

If, in step No. 6 of the preceding series of operations, the quality of the spark from the end of the spark-plug wires was not good, the correction would be made in the ignition secondary circuit. If, however, the correct order of procedure had not been followed, the poor spark might be accounted for by any of the possible seats of trouble in the ignition secondary circuit, the primary circuit, or in the battery and its connections.

An engine tune up, or any similar operation, is a maintenance procedure; however, a maintenance procedure can be used to correct troubles. Nevertheless, it does not represent true trouble shooting.

The chief objection to selling a tune-up every time trouble is experienced is that many owners are unwilling to pay for a complete tune-up to correct a trouble that may turn out to be some simple, easily corrected fault. This objection to the

tune-up has resulted in the development of diagnostic test operations which follow the sequence and tests in the engine tune-up but do not provide for the correction of any faults uncovered.

This type of test will in many cases uncover the seat of trouble by indicating where the auto is below par in its operation. It is not trouble shooting in its strictest sense but a maintenance operation even though it can be used to uncover the more common troubles.

Such a test, since the nature and sequence of the separate steps of the operation are arbitrarily determined, and since it is uniform for all vehicles, does not indicate what should be done for a specific trouble. The same steps are performed every time no matter what the trouble may be.

While such test procedures are not trouble shooting, they are widely used, and many troubles are isolated and corrected. Such test procedures are known

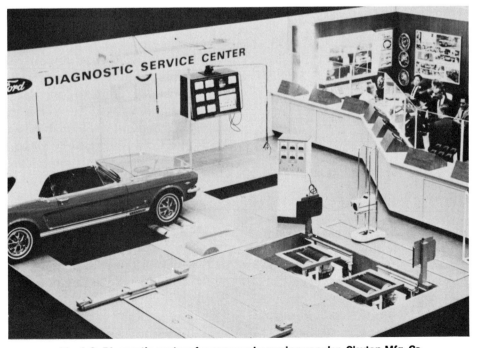

Fig. 1-3. Diagnostic centers for cars are becoming popular. Clayton Mfg. Co.

today by many names, such as "diagnosis check," "performance test," "performance analysis," "automotive clinic." Fig. 1-3.

This operation results in a lot of unnecessary steps where the object is to locate and correct an immediate trouble. A good example of this would be a complaint that an automobile "missed" on acceleration. In most standard automobiles, a miss on acceleration can be caused by: (1) an inadequate spark being delivered to the spark plugs; (2) incorrectly spaced or dirty spark plugs; (3) a disconnected carburetor accelerator pump, or a wrongly adjusted pump stroke; or (4) a faulty check valve on the accelerating pump system.

These are the four major considerations in a car that misses on acceleration. Of course, faulty valve action can account for a miss but the miss will appear at other times also. Likewise, an inadequate fuel supply being delivered to the carburetor could result in a miss on acceleration. However, if this were the only trouble, then the engine would lack power on a steady pull as well. So, the symptom of a miss on acceleration would have to be caused by one or more of the four things mentioned. Obviously, then, if a test containing all of the elements of an engine tune-up (without correction) were used to locate the cause of this trouble, at least 90 percent of the test operations performed would be of no value whatsoever in locating the trouble.

Many men are working in automotive service who lack an aptitude for this work, and many others do not possess the basic knowledge ordinarily considered as essential. In most instances, vehicle manufacturers, their dealers, garage owners, and equipment manufacturers cannot devote sufficient money or time to the training of men lacking these qualifications. Based on these premises, the man is

taught a test procedure such as that described. Under this plan, the student learns that, regardless of the nature of the trouble, the same test procedure is performed on each job. While this method of operation has achieved some admirable results, it also has some deficiencies.

When a test procedure or a tune-up is performed in an attempt to locate the cause of trouble, the procedure or tune-up will locate the cause in 85 to 90 percent of the cases. However, in 10 to 15 percent of the cases, such procedures may not locate the trouble. This is too high a percentage for anyone desiring to build confidence in his ability to shoot trouble.

Standard test procedures usually consume from $\frac{1}{2}$ to $1\frac{1}{2}$ hours. The length of time involved in making a series of tests and recording them makes it almost mandatory that these services be charged for. With 10 to 15 percent of the jobs resulting in failure to correct the trouble, you cannot establish yourself in your community as a competent trouble shooter. In instances where you charge but fail to correct the trouble, many of your customers may question your integrity.

The chief reason for the popularity of the test procedure for locating and correcting troubles is the fact that real trouble shooting requires considerable knowledge and a definite plan of action. Many persons who aspire to become trouble shooters or diagnosticians, or whatever name might be popular at the moment, are looking for some short cut that will eliminate the need for thinking. In fact, many of the people who purchase elaborate test equipment do so because they believe or hope this equipment will remove the necessity of learning how an automobile operates. Of course, no equipment can take the place of knowledge, and while equipment has a definite place in the scheme of things it must be run by

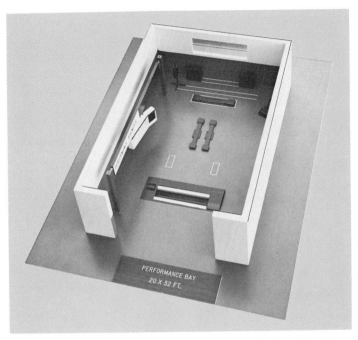

Fig. 1-4. A suggested layout for a test center. Clayton Mfg. Co.

people and the readings must be interpreted by people. The things to do and the things not to do under a set of circumstances must be established by people and not by a piece of equipment. No machine can think, and the major portion of trouble shooting is thinking. Fig. 1-4.

This volume is based on the assumption that you desire to become an expert trouble shooter and are willing to devote the time and effort required to achieve this end.

Consequently, this book has been designed to cover trouble shooting in its purest sense—for each trouble a definite procedure is presented that takes into account each of the factors that can account for that particular trouble. No consideration is given to, and no tests are made for, conditions that cannot account for the particular trouble being experienced.

In these trouble shooting procedures, the factors or possible causes of the particular trouble are arranged in the order of their probability or their accessibility. Generally, the procedure presents first the tests for the condition most likely to cause the trouble.

The trouble "engine misses on acceleration" may be used as an example. In the previous discussion, it was pointed out that a miss on acceleration can be caused by one of four things.

One of the four requires no test or adjustment of any kind but merely an observation as to whether or not the carburetor acceleration pump linkage is connected properly at the point that provides the correct stroke for the prevailing temperatures. While this is not the most likely cause of the trouble, it is a common cause that requires only observation to detect. On raising the hood, you look to determine if this possibility is the obvious cause of the trouble.

Second, the strength of the spark from

the end of each spark plug wire is tested. This test establishes quickly whether or not the trouble is in the ignition system. All of the tests performed in trouble shooting are made to establish whether or not a trouble exists in a particular unit or system. In every case, the test is made to determine which of two or more possibilities are true on that particular vehicle. If there were not at least two possibilities, then there would be no purpose for the test. In this case, the test is made to determine whether the ignition system is satisfactory or unsatisfactory. Obviously, if it is found to be unsatisfactory, the cause of the trouble is known to exist in the ignition system.

At this point it might be well to point out the different approach in trouble shooting as opposed to a maintenance operation such as a tune-up. In testing and adjusting the ignition system during a tune-up, the operation starts at the battery, and each unit that contributes to or influences the operation of additional units is tested and corrected before subsequent tests are made. This eliminates the units already tested and corrected from consideration where a test of a subsequent unit proves it to be below standard. In other words, in a maintenance procedure in each unit or system, you start at the source and work on through the system up to the point where you are checking the final result. In the case of the ignition tests and adjustments in the tune-up, you start at the battery and end up by testing the spark at the end of the plug wires. This is exactly opposite to the procedures in trouble shooting.

In trouble shooting, you desire to eliminate as quickly as possible all units or systems from further consideration and to definitely establish the trouble as being in a particular unit or system.

If, in the case of an engine missing on acceleration, the spark at the end of each spark plug was found to be satisfactory, you would have no reason to consider any other portion of the ignition system. By this one test, you have established that the ignition system is delivering a satisfactory spark to each spark plug every time. Since your main job is to find out why this engine misses, you can eliminate from further consideration the possibility of an ignition fault.

The next most likely cause of trouble is incorrectly spaced (gapped) or dirty spark plugs, so the next step is to remove the spark plugs from the engine. As they are removed, a quick glance at each will uncover such things as cracked or dirty porcelains, and it will be readily apparent whether or not either condition accounts for the engine missing on acceleration. To correct the trouble in this case, they must be cleaned and regapped. If, from the visual inspection, the plugs are found to be in good condition, then the spacing of the electrodes is checked and, if incorrect, adjusted to the original specifications.

If these procedures have failed to account for the engine missing on acceleration, the only remaining possibility is that the accelerating pump mechanism within the carburetor is not functioning correctly. This will involve at least a partial disassembly of the carburetor in order to locate the cause and to correct it.

Consider the difference between examining a carburetor for a fault that has been proven to exist as compared to the removal and cleaning of a carburetor during an engine tune-up where you have not established that anything is wrong with the carburetor. In the one case you know exactly what you are doing and what you are looking for, and in the other case you are working blindly.

This comparison of the two types of operations is presented to fix firmly in your mind the distinction between pure trouble shooting and any other type of operation. The following chapters of this book present pure trouble shooting procedures, each of which is designed to locate and correct specific trouble. Nothing is included in any of these operations that is not necessary or that cannot account for the immediate trouble.

Throughout the various trouble shooting procedures, tests and adjustments are called for. In some instances, a particular test or adjustment is called for in a number of separate trouble shooting procedures. Rather than repeat these instructions at each point where the operation is called for, instructions for these tests or adjustments are presented separately from the trouble shooting procedure. Detailed instructions on how each test or adjustment is performed are presented in the chapter dealing with that unit or system.

Some troubles can be caused by fault in any one of several systems, each of which may be presented in a different chapter. Where the real cause of the trouble lies in a different system, the trouble shooting procedure that fits the symptom will direct you to the correct chapter and symptom.

The trouble shooting procedures in most instances merely tell you what to do and the order in which to do it. This is based on the assumption that after some practice you will know how to make the various tests and adjustments called for. Likewise, after you have used these procedures several times, the details of the trouble shooting procedure will come back to you if you are reminded of the order of procedure.

Throughout the trouble shooting processes, the order of procedure is illustrated in flow charts with the instructions condensed to a few words. If, while reading the text of the procedures for the first time, it is difficult to keep in mind just what you have done or the logic involved, a glance at the flow chart will quickly make it all clear. After using the trouble shooting procedures and charts together a few times, you will find that the charts alone will, in most cases, be all the instruction or reminder that you need. Even so, the text will be a valuable reference when details of an individual test are forgotten.

To make the charts more usable, the various operations, tests, and adjustments are marked with a letter or number agreeing with the paragraph designation where the detailed instructions for that step of the procedure start.

TEST EQUIPMENT

The job of uncovering parts or systems that are causing trouble or are approaching failure and the job of adjusting or setting them to a specification require the use of several types of equipment. Equipment is of considerable importance in both maintenance operations and in trouble shooting since it provides you with the means of taking the necessary measurements. Equipment, however, does not take the place of knowledge, nor does it remove the necessity for a logical procedure to follow.

In most instances, the assembly in which a trouble lies can be established with a minimum of equipment. Modern test equipment, with its accurate gages, however, permits you to go further with the analysis.

As an example, in the case of a discharged battery, you can determine whether the generator, the generator regulator, or the battery is at fault by means of a jumper wire. But, having located the trouble in the generator you might be unable to establish whether the cause was in the field, armature, or brushes.

Before test equipment became commonplace, most of the things we do now were done but less efficiently because of the large number of manual operations and visual inspections that had to be performed. Now, through the use of instruments, the same analyses can be made in a fraction of the time formerly required, usually without disassembling the units involved.

A wide variety of makes and designs of equipment are in common use. Different ideas exist as to what is needed or desirable from an ideal point of view as compared to what is considered economically feasible. Other wide variations in the design of equipment are accounted for by what can be sold to the various service organizations needing equipment. Some of these differences and some of the reasoning behind the design of each should be appreciated by you.

PORTABLE AND STATIONARY UNITS

Some equipment is designed for bench work that is, for use with parts or assemblies that have been removed from the vehicle for testing or adjusting. In this category are generator test stands (Fig. 1-5), distributor test stands (Fig. 1-6), and a number of other units. In some instances, these units are made semiportable and are provided with casters so they can be moved easily from one part of the shop to the other. In general, it is more practical to take the small part to be tested or adjusted to the equipment rather than to move the equipment to the parts. An exception to this is where a number of similar parts have been assembled at one point.

Other equipment designed primarily for use in testing and adjusting the various systems or assemblies while they are still in the vehicle is portable, since it is usually more practical to roll or carry a piece of equipment to the vehicle than to

Fig. 1-5. A generator-alternator test unit. Sun Electric Corp.

move the vehicle to a piece of stationary equipment (Fig. 1-7).

Large equipment, such as a chassis dynamometer (Fig. 1-8), requires a firm installation and is always permanently mounted. In that case, the vehicle must be taken to the equipment.

Large wheel alignment machines

Fig. 1-6. A distributor test stand. Sun Electric Corp.

Fig. 1-7. Oscilloscope used for diagnosing ignition and other electrical problems. Allen Electric & Equip. Corp.

(Fig. 1-9) fall into this same category. However, the trend in recent years is toward portable wheel alignment equipment which can be taken to the vehicle (Fig. 1-10). Equipment of this nature is used in many cases where shops possess a large wheel alignment test stand used as permanently mounted equipment for correction and the portable equipment is used to determine whether or not corrections are required. More portable equipment is becoming available every day.

SEPARATE AND COMBINED UNITS

In test equipment designed to check engine and electrical system performance, two different approaches are used. In one, all of the devices considered necessary for all the separate tests are combined into a single test bench as shown in Fig. 1-11.

In another, separate units are designed to perform the tests involved for individual units of the vehicle. As an example, a separate unit might be provided for testing generator regulators, another unit might be an engine tachometer, and a third unit might be an ignition primary circuit tester. This type of test equipment

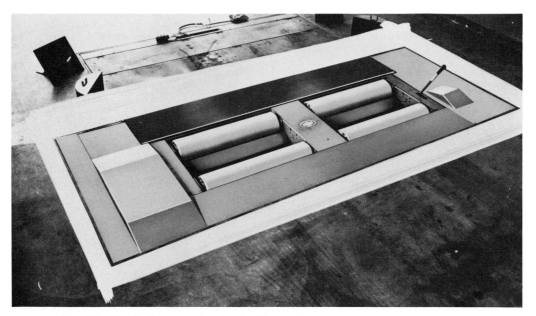

Fig. 1-8. Chassis dynamometer for checking engine performance. Clayton Mfg. Co.

Fig. 1-9. Permanent wheel alignment equipment in background.

has the advantage that it permits piece-meal purchase. The small, modestly equipped shop can purchase one unit at a time until eventually it has all the equipment that is necessary. As a rule, manufacturers design the separate units so they will fit into a master panel. When all of the separate units have been pur-chased, a complete set of test equipment is represented (Fig. 1-11).

One of the disadvantages of this sys-tem is that each of the separate units re-quires its own instruments. Therefore, after all the individual units have been bought, there will be duplication since equipment built into a single test bench

Fig. 1-11. A complete test stand composed of individual units. Snap-On Tools.

Fig. 1-10. Portable wheel alignment equipment. Enlarged view of gage is at the bottom. Bear Mfg. Co.

will have meters and test leads common to several different tests. This represents a saving in cost that generally is reflected in a lower price for the single unit complete test bench as compared to the multiple unit complete test bench.

STANDARD INSTRUMENTS

Standard instruments for the measurement of electrical and pressure values are incorporated in both types of test benches.

In the majority of tests in both maintenance and trouble shooting, several standard instruments will have identical results provided that the range and characteristics of the two instruments are comparable.

BUILT-IN TEST CIRCUITS

One advantage of complete test bench units over separate instruments is that it is possible to build test circuits into the complete unit. This can save considerable time in the testing process but it is always possible that the built-in test circuit may become obsolete with a change in automotive design.

Some units require complete test circuits, and the measurements desired cannot be obtained by the use of separate meters alone.

EQUIPMENT LIMITATIONS

Equipment can cost many hundreds of dollars, or it can be relatively simple.

In either case, you cannot accomplish an adequate job of diagnosis unless you have learned and remember the principles.

Regardless of the type of equipment you will be using, it is important that you realize that equipment by itself is powerless. What you know and your ability to interpret the readings that you obtain by the use of equipment are the things which determine whether or not you will be a successful trouble shooter or automotive expert.

ELECTRICAL TERMS

Some knowledge of the terms used and their relationship to one another are necessary for your understanding of the discussion of the various circuits.

Since electricity is generally carried through wires, the word *conductor,* as used here, refers to wires.

RESISTANCE

The resistance of a wire depends upon its material, its diameter, its length, and its temperature. For example, an iron wire has a resistance more than six times greater than a copper wire of the same diameter and length. A wire twenty feet long has twice the resistance of ten feet of the same wire. The thicker the wire the less its resistance. The longer the wire, the greater its resistance.

The resistance varies inversely as the cross-sectional area of the wires. A wire 0.020 in. in diameter has four times the resistance of a wire 0.040 in. in diameter since the resistance is controlled by the cross-sectional area rather than the diameter. Cross-sectional area would be determined by the formula:

$$\text{Area} = \pi R^2$$

In which
$$\pi = 3.1416$$
$$R = \text{radius}$$

Finding the cross-sectional area of round wires by this formula for the area of a circle is awkward, and often the results are difficult to express in inches. For this reason, diameters of wires are expressed in *mils*. One mil equals .001 in. Therefore, the diameter of No. 16 wire, instead of being read as 0.05082 in., is more simply read as 50.82 mils. Likewise, the diameter of the No. 0000 wire is 0.460 in., or 460 mils. To find the cross-sectional area of a wire in mils, square the diameter in mils. For example, 460 × 460 equals 211,600 mils. This 211,600 is called the circular mil area of a wire.

Table 1-1 shows a standard table for copper wire, giving gage numbers, diameters in circular mils (thousandths), and the resistance per thousand feet for several temperatures.

CONDUCTANCE

Conductance is the opposite of resistance. That is, resistance represents opposition or difficulty encountered when pushing current through a conductor, while conductance is the ease with which an electric current is sent through a conductor or circuit.

OHM'S LAW

Electrical measurements in established circuits are made to determine if changes have occurred. Changes are usually reflected in a change of resistance in the circuit. Changes can occur in several ways.

Added resistance can be the result of broken or frayed wires or cables, burned, pitted, or dirty electrical contacts, or loose connections. Lower than normal resistance usually indicates shorted wires or coils in the circuit. In these cases, a parallel path has been established that bypasses a portion of the current and lowers the resistance of the circuit.

TABLE 1-1 WIRE TABLE, STANDARD ANNEALED COPPER
American Wire Gage (B. & S.) English Units

Gage No.	Diameter in mills at 68° F	Cross section at 68° F.		Ohms per 1,000 Feet*			
		Circular Mils	Sq. Inches	0°C (32°F)	20°C (68°F)	50°C (122°F)	75°C (167°F)
0000	460.0	211600	0.1662	0.04516	0.04901	0.05479	0.05961
000	409.6	167800	.1318	.05695	.06180	.06909	.07516
00	364.8	133100	.1045	.07181	.07793	.08712	.09478
0	324.9	105500	.08289	.09055	.09827	.1099	.1195
1	289.3	83690	.06573	.1142	.1239	.1385	.1507
2	257.6	66370	.05213	.1440	.1563	.1747	.1900
3	229.4	52640	.04134	.1816	.1970	.2203	.2396
4	204.3	41740	.03278	.2289	.2485	.2778	.3022
5	181.9	33100	.02600	.2887	.3133	.3502	.3810
6	162.0	26250	.02062	.3640	.3951	.4416	.4805
7	144.3	20820	.01635	.4590	.4982	.5569	.6059
8	128.5	16510	.01297	.5788	.6282	.7023	.7640
9	114.4	13090	.01028	.7299	.7921	.8855	.9633
10	101.9	10380	.008155	.9203	.9989	1.117	1.215
11	90.74	8234	.006467	1.161	1.260	1.408	1.532
12	80.81	6530	.005129	1.463	1.588	1.775	1.931
13	71.96	5178	.004067	1.845	2.003	2.239	2.436
14	64.08	4107	.003225	2.327	2.525	2.823	3.071
15	57.07	3257	.002558	2.934	3.184	3.560	3.873
16	50.82	2583	.002028	3.700	4.016	4.489	4.884
17	45.26	2048	.001609	4.666	5.064	5.660	6.158
18	40.30	1624	.001276	5.883	6.385	7.138	7.765
19	35.89	1288	.001012	7.418	8.051	9.001	9.792
20	31.96	1022	.0008023	9.355	10.15	11.35	12.35
21	28.45	810.1	.0006363	11.80	12.80	14.31	15.57
22	25.35	642.4	.0005046	14.87	16.14	18.05	19.63
23	22.57	509.5	.0004002	18.76	20.36	22.76	24.76
24	20.10	404.0	.0003173	23.65	25.67	28.70	31.22
25	17.90	320.4	.0002517	29.82	32.37	36.18	39.36
26	15.94	254.1	.0001996	37.61	40.81	45.63	49.64
27	14.20	201.5	.0001583	47.42	51.47	57.53	62.59
28	12.64	159.8	.0001255	59.80	64.90	72.55	78.93
29	11.26	126.7	.00009953	75.40	81.83	91.48	99.52
30	10.03	100.5	.00007894	95.08	103.2	115.4	125.5
31	8.928	79.70	.00006260	119.9	130.1	145.5	158.2
32	7.950	63.21	.00004964	151.2	164.1	183.4	199.5
33	7.080	50.13	.00003937	190.6	206.9	231.3	251.6
34	6.305	39.75	.00003122	240.4	260.9	291.7	317.3
35	5.615	31.52	.00002476	303.1	329.0	367.8	400.1
36	5.000	25.00	.00001964	382.2	414.8	463.7	504.5
37	4.453	19.83	.00001557	482.0	523.1	584.8	636.2
38	3.965	15.72	.00001235	607.8	659.6	737.4	802.2
39	3.531	12.47	.000009793	766.4	831.8	929.8	1012
40	3.145	9.888	.000007766	966.5	1049	1173	1276

* Resistance at the slated tempertature of a wire whose length is 1,000 feet at 68° F

While the changes that occur are changes in resistance, the measurements taken usually are either in amperes or volts. Amperes, volts, and ohms all have a definite relationship to each other. This relationship is defined in Ohm's law.

OHM'S LAW: The quantity of an unvarying electrical current is directly proportional to the voltage and inversely proportional to the resistance of the circuit.

AMPERE: The current produced by one volt acting through a resistance of one ohm.

OHM: The resistance of a circuit in which a potential difference of one volt produces a current of one ampere.

VOLT: The amount of electromotive force which, when steadily applied to a conductor whose resistance is one ohm, will produce a current of one ampere.

With the letter *I* representing the strength of the current in amperes, *E* representing the electrical pressure in volts, and *R* representing the electrical resistance in ohms, the relationship of these three values can be expressed by the following equations:

$$\frac{E}{R} = I \text{ or } \frac{E}{I} = R \text{ or } I \times R = E$$

These equations indicate (1) voltage divided by resistance (ohms) equals strength of current (amperes), (2) voltage divided by strength of current (amperes) equals resistance (ohms), and (3) strength of current (amperes) times resistance (ohms) equals voltage.

For assistance in remembering Ohm's law, keep in mind the symbols arranged as follows:

$$\frac{E}{I \times R}$$

Cover the value to be determined. What remains is the formula for finding it.

EXAMPLE: To find voltage, cover E. What remains is I × R. To find amperage, cover I. What remains is E/R.

If you know any two of these values, it is an easy matter to determine the third one.

ELECTRICAL MEASUREMENTS

Most electrical measurements taken in automotive circuits are made with voltmeters and ammeters, and it is important that you understand the nature of these instruments, how to connect them, and how to evaluate the readings obtained. Likewise, it is necessary that you appreciate what these instruments can do for you and understand and appreciate their limitations as well.

Some units or systems are governed by alternating current principles and specially designed test circuits rather than meter connections are required to take the measurements needed. Test circuits also are used frequently in automotive practice to measure some mechanical adjustments and some chemical characteristics by electrical means.

CONCLUSIONS BASED ON ONE VALUE

Most automotive electrical circuits have a constant or nearly constant resistance peculiar to the particular circuit. In addition, most automotive vehicles have a twelve-volt battery. Based on the assumption that one or the other of these values is known, most electrical measurements are of one value only.

AMPERAGE. An ammeter installed in *series* in a circuit will show a higher than normal amperage if the resistance of the circuit is lower than normal, provided that the voltage is constant. If the current is being supplied by a battery of fairly constant voltage, generally it can be assumed that the resistance of the circuit is lower than normal when the amperage is higher than normal.

By the same reasoning, if an amperage reading lower than normal is obtained, it can be assumed that the resistance of the circuit is higher than normal.

VOLTAGE. A voltmeter installed *parallel* to either a complete circuit or any portion of a circuit (through which current is flowing) indicates the difference in pressure (voltage). Voltage readings are commonly referred to as *voltage drop*. If the characteristics of the circuit or unit are known and the source of electrical energy is constant, it is safe to assume that higher than normal voltage drop indicates higher than normal resistance. Likewise, lower than normal voltage drop indicates lower than normal resistance.

METER CONNECTIONS. In the previous explanation it should be noted that though the actual readings were in amperes or volts, the conclusion arrived at had to do with resistance. Likewise, it should be noted that the ammeter is installed in series in a circuit. Ammeters are *always* used in *series* with some resistance. Ammeters have, for all practical purposes, no resistance of their own. If an ammeter is connected to a battery without some resistance in series with it, the entire charge of the battery will try to "unload" through the ammeter at one time, damaging the meter.

It should be noted also that in the foregoing explanations the voltmeter is installed *parallel* to either a complete circuit or some portion of it. Voltmeters have extremely high resistance. If they are installed in series in a circuit, the entire nature of the circuit is changed and the reading has no particular value or significance.

EXAMPLE: Assume the resistance of a starting motor circuit to be 0.050 ohms and the voltage in the circuit to be constant at 8 volts. In such a case, the strength of the current would be 160 amperes. If a voltmeter having 10,000 ohms resistance were installed in series in this circuit, the total resistance of the circuit would then be 10,000.050 ohms and the amperage would be slightly less than 0.0008 (eight ten-thousandths) of an ampere.

To sum up: ammeters are connected in series with a resistance. Higher than normal readings indicate lower than normal resistance. Lower than normal readings indicate higher than normal resistance. Voltmeters are connected parallel to a resistance (a complete circuit or a portion of it). Lower than normal readings indicate lower than normal resistance. Higher than normal readings indicate higher than normal resistance.

METERS VARY IN CONSTRUCTION

Ammeters and voltmeters used for testing purposes can be identical insofar as their internal working parts are concerned. Starting with a basic meter, if a shunt is placed parallel to the meter, it becomes an ammeter. Resistance placed in series with the basic meter permits the meter to be used as a voltmeter.

A typical testing meter has the following basic characteristics: (1) one milliamp (0.001 ampere) full scale deflection; (2) 124 millivolt (0.124 volt) full scale deflection; (3) a resistance of 124 ohms; and a (4) sensitivity of 1,000 ohms per volt.

METER SHUNTS. This meter will read full scale (all the way across the dial) when 0.001 amperes flows through it. Making use of the fact that, when parallel paths exist, electricity divides itself between the

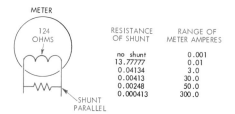

METER	RESISTANCE OF SHUNT	RANGE OF METER AMPERES
124 OHMS	no shunt	0.001
	13.77777	0.01
	0.04134	3.0
	0.00413	30.0
	0.00248	50.0
	0.000413	300.0

Fig. 1-12. Using a shunt in parallel to vary amperage readings.

two paths in proportion to the resistance of each, a parallel path is installed across the meter to by-pass a portion of the current.

Fig. 1-12 illustrates how shunts of different sizes may be used to change the range of the meter. In the case of the 0.000413 ohms shunt, the 300 amperes divides between the meter proper and the shunt. The shunt carries 299.999 amperes and the meter 0.001 ampere. Thus, if the meter dial is marked off so it indicates 300 amperes when 0.001 ampere flows through it, it becomes a 0 to 300 ampere meter when the 0.000413 ohm shunt is connected across it.

SERIES RESISTANCE. If, using this same basic meter, instead of placing a shunt parallel to the meter, resistance is added in series with it, the meter becomes a voltmeter. Fig. 1-13 illustrates resistance introduced in series with the meter to obtain various voltmeter ranges.

COMBINATION METERS. Some meters are built with either a shunt or a series

resistance incorporated in the meter case. In other instances, one meter is used as both a voltmeter and an ammeter, and either a switching arrangement or a choice of terminals is provided.

HOW TO USE METERS

To use electrical meters successfully, the circuit involved must be understood, and its relationship to other circuits must also be appreciated.

Fig. 1-14 is a schematic drawing of an ignition system primary circuit typical of most cars. Looking at this schematic drawing alone, it could be assumed that an ammeter placed in series anywhere in the circuit would give the primary ignition amperage.

Fig. 1-15 shows this same circuit and its relationship to other circuits. Portions of this circuit are also common to several other circuits. Most electrical gages or instruments are turned on by the ignition switch. The only place an ammeter can be installed in this circuit to obtain a true

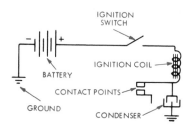

Fig. 1-14. Typical automotive ignition primary circuit.

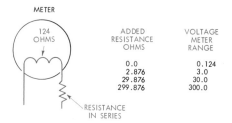

METER	ADDED RESISTANCE OHMS	VOLTAGE METER RANGE
124 OHMS	0.0	0.124
	2.876	3.0
	29.876	30.0
	299.876	300.0

Fig. 1-13. Using a shunt in series to vary the range of voltage readings.

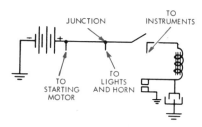

Fig. 1-15. Relation of ignition primary circuit to other circuits.

reading of the primary ignition amperage, therefore, is in that portion of the circuit that is exclusively primary ignition. In this case, the ammeter would have to be installed somewhere between the "cold" side of the ignition switch and the contact points.

Without taking the other circuits into account, it would appear that, by connecting an ammeter to the terminals of the ignition switch, the circuit would be completed through the ammeter without having to disconnect any wires. This, of course, is true, but in addition to the primary amperage the reading may include the current flowing to the instruments and such accessories (radio, heater, etc.) that may be tied into the ignition switch.

The safest practice is to install ammeters as far from the power source as possible. In this circuit, the primary terminal of the ignition coil is a safe place to disconnect the circuit and install the ammeter. Incidentally, no reading would be obtained if the contact points or the

ignition switch were open as shown. The engine would have to be cranked until the points closed. This would be indicated by a reading on the ammeter.

AMPERAGE. Each circuit has its own peculiar relationship to all other circuits in the car. In any circuit, the safest rule is to install the ammeter as far from the power source (battery) as possible.

VOLTAGE DROP. A voltmeter installed parallel to any resistance through which current is flowing will indicate the difference of the voltage at the two ends of the resistance. This difference is referred to as voltage drop. A voltmeter parallel to the source of current (no other current flowing) indicates the open circuit voltage or pressure available, as shown in Fig. 1-16(A). Usually such readings have little significance.

When current is being used in excess of the source's ability to supply it, the voltage at the source becomes less. When the starter switch in Fig. 1-16(B) is closed, the battery voltage drops.

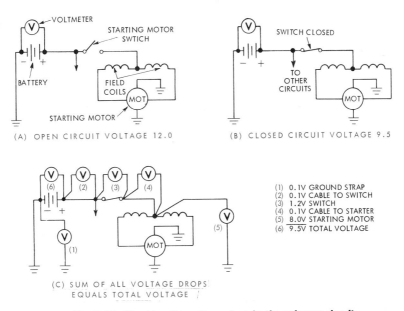

(A) OPEN CIRCUIT VOLTAGE 12.0

(B) CLOSED CIRCUIT VOLTAGE 9.5

(C) SUM OF ALL VOLTAGE DROPS EQUALS TOTAL VOLTAGE

(1) 0.1V GROUND STRAP
(2) 0.1V CABLE TO SWITCH
(3) 1.2V SWITCH
(4) 0.1V CABLE TO STARTER
(5) 8.0V STARTING MOTOR
(6) 9.5V TOTAL VOLTAGE

Fig. 1-16. Checking the voltage drop in the primary circuit.

The differences in closed circuit voltage drops for individual portions of the circuit indicate the differences in resistance. Fig. 1-16(C) indicates typical readings with the voltmeter parallel to different portions of the starting motor circuit. The sum of the voltage readings equals the total voltage available at the source ([1] + [2] + [3] + [4] + [5] = [6] Fig. 1-16 [C] or (0.1 + 0.1 + 1.2 + 0.1 + 8.0 = 9.5).

Since portions of all circuits are shared by other circuits, it is important that parallel circuits be turned off when checking voltage drop.

ACCURATE RESISTANCE MEASUREMENTS. In the previous discussions, only one reading was involved. Where accuracy is desired, it is necessary to take simultaneous readings of both voltage and amperage and divide the voltage by the amperage.

Fig. 1-17 shows a simple light circuit. To measure the resistance of the light switch in this circuit, the ammeter would be installed on the battery side of the light switch. The ampere reading would be the total current passing through the switch. The voltmeter would be installed parallel to the switch.

Notice that the ammeter is installed at the one point where all of the current flowing through the switch also flows through the meter. Likewise, current not flowing through the light switch does not flow through the meter. The voltmeter is parallel only to the particular resistance being measured.

EXAMPLE: 0.2 volts ÷ 10 amperes = 0.02 ohms resistance.

PARALLEL RESISTANCES. Where several resistances are in series with each other, the sum of all of the resistance controls the current. Where several resistances are in parallel to each other, the total resistance of the circuit is decreased.

With a voltmeter installed as shown in Fig. 1-18, it is parallel to everything else that is grounded. The voltage reading would be the voltage drop for the combination of the three branches of the circuit. The amperage would be the sum of the amperage of all three branches of the circuit. In the circuit illustrated, with a constant pressure of twelve volts, the amperage would be:

R.H. headlight 12 volts ÷ 1.5 ohms =
8 amperes

L.H. headlight 12 volts ÷ 1.5 ohms =
8 amperes

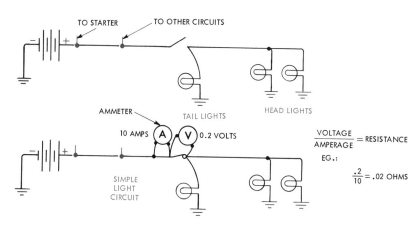

Fig. 1-17. Both voltage and amperage are used to obtain accurate resistance measurements.

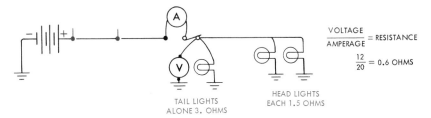

VOLTAGE / AMPERAGE = RESISTANCE

$$\frac{12}{20} = 0.6 \text{ OHMS}$$

Fig. 1-18. Measuring several resistances. The voltmeter is parallel to the resistance being measured.

Tail light 12 volts ÷ 3.0 ohms = 4 amperes

Total 20 amperes

By dividing the 12 volts by 20 amperes, we find that in parallel to each other the three resistances have a resistance of 0.6 ohms—considerably less than any of the resistances considered separately.

In the foregoing explanation, a pressure of 12 volts was assumed, but it could have been any voltage. Neither the voltage nor amperage is necessary to the problem. The problem can be indicated by the equation:

$$\frac{E}{\dfrac{E}{R} + \dfrac{E}{R} + \dfrac{E}{R}} = total\ resistance$$

The figure "1" can be substituted for E, since the actual value of the voltage has no influence on the problem. Any number of resistances may be added so long as each is divided into the voltage and added to the others. Using the three resistance values in Fig. 1-18, the equation now appears:

$$\frac{1}{\dfrac{1}{1.5} + \dfrac{1}{1.5} + \dfrac{1}{3}} = \frac{1}{\dfrac{2}{3} + \dfrac{2}{3} + \dfrac{1}{3}}$$

$$= \frac{1}{\dfrac{5}{3}} = \frac{1}{1\frac{2}{3}} = 0.6\ ohms$$

The 1⅔ equals the total amperage at 1 volt.

Low Resistance Circuits. While for nearly all practical considerations an ammeter is referred to as having no resistance, all ammeters do have some resistance. If introduced into a very low resistance circuit, they will change the characteristics of the circuit.

The resistance of a starting motor circuit under certain conditions can be as low as 0.01 ohms (one hundredth). The disturbing of the various connections and the placing of an ammeter in the circuit might double the resistance and reduce the amperage by half. To determine the amperage of such a circuit accurately, the substitute load method is employed. The equipment needed is a voltmeter, an ammeter of sufficient range, and a carbon pile rheostat. The rheostat must be able to carry as much as 300 amperes, which involves carbon disks two inches or more in diameter.

The voltmeter is connected in parallel with the battery as shown in Fig. 1-19. The ammeter and rheostat are placed in series with each other with the rheostat open so that no continuity exists. The ammeter and rheostat are also connected in parallel with the battery.

When the voltmeter was connected, an open circuit voltage reading of the battery was obtained. Close the starter switch and crank the engine. While the engine is cranking, observe the voltage reading

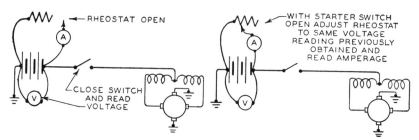

Fig. 1-19. Substitute load method for determining amperage in low resistance circuits.

which will now be considerably lower than the open circuit voltage reading previously obtained. This reading will be controlled by the condition of the battery (its ability to deliver high current) and the amperage of the circuit.

As soon as the voltage under starter load reading is obtained, open the starter switch. Adjust the rheostat immediately until the previous voltage reading is duplicated. This will occur when the amperage through the rheostat and the ammeter is exactly the same as the amperage through the starting motor. Read the starting motor circuit amperage on the ammeter and immediately break the circuit to avoid discharging the battery.

EQUIPMENT USED FOR SPECIAL TESTS

Some circuits are set up to measure certain mechanical adjustments and others some chemical characteristics by electrical means. Electrical instruments besides the voltmeter and the ammeter are used to measure various characteristics of circuits in an automobile.

WHEATSTONE BRIDGE. A Wheatstone bridge is a device for measuring or comparing resistances and is used for extremely fine measurements. Wheatstone bridges are commonly used in automotive work in electrically operated combustion analyzers and in expanded scale voltmeters.

The Wheatstone bridge generally is pictured as four resistors arranged in the shape of a diamond, with the current entering at one point of the diamond and leaving at the opposite point. A meter is connected across the center of the diamond, joining the other two points of the diamond as shown in Fig. 1-20.

Fig. 1-20 illustrates the circuit in the laboratory type Wheatstone bridge. The two upper resistances ($R1$ and $R2$) are of equal value. The resistance marked $R3$ is the resistance to be measured. Resistance $R4$ is a calibrated variable resistance. The arrow crossing resistance $R4$ at an angle is used to indicate that the resistance is adjustable. When $R4$ is adjusted to the point where no current

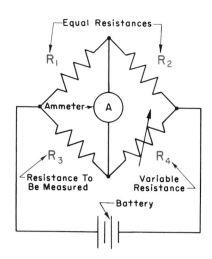

Fig. 1-20. A Wheatstone bridge.

flows through the meter, resistances $R4$ and $R3$ are known to be equal.

This type of Wheatstone bridge is not used in automotive service. However, some variations of this circuit are used.

CONDENSER TESTERS. The electrical values involved in an ignition condenser have to do with the ability of the condenser to hold extra electrons and its resistance to their movement. The ability to hold electrons is known as capacity and is measured in microfarads. Two different resistances are involved—series resistance, which should be low since it can limit the charge going into the condenser, and insulation resistance, which should be high since leakage will reduce the effective capacity of the condenser.

CAM ANGLE OR DWELL TESTERS. Distributor contacts close and open for each spark produced by the ignition system. It is important that the contacts remain closed long enough to permit an approach to magnetic saturation in the coil in order to obtain a satisfactory spark. At the same time, the contacts must be opened long enough to permit the coil and the condenser to complete their cycle and wide and fast enough to prevent the high primary voltages that occur during collapse of the magnetic field from discharging through the contacts to ground.

As engine speeds are increased, the time available for each spark cycle is reduced. Cam angle or dwell testers are designed to show the percentage of time the contacts are closed in each cycle.

In a cam angle tester, the reading obtained is the number of degrees the camshaft turns while the contacts are closed. In a dwell tester, the reading obtained is the percentage of time the contacts are closed.

OSCILLOSCOPES

Many manufacturers sell ignition oscilloscopes which can be a single unit or in combination with other types of test instruments. The oscilloscope is a valuable instrument when its operation is thoroughly understood. It is not, however, a replacement for the competent trouble shooter. The scope is merely another tool to speed up trouble shooting. The function of the scope is to display on a television-type screen the electrical operations of the ignition system. With an ability of showing all cylinders or individual cylinders, it is possible to rapidly determine the type of trouble and its location. When variations from a normal pattern appear, the operator must be able to interpret what the variations indicate and determine the steps to take to correct the defect. The scope is only as useful as the operator is capable of interpreting the scope patterns. The scope is particularly useful in determining quickly the overall condition of the ignition circuit components. Spark plugs, wires, coils, condensers, and contact point operation are readily observed with the scope.

ROAD SERVICE

It is possible, of course, that you may sometime be called upon to service a vehicle away from your shop. However, in nearly every instance (aside from calls for tire service), you will find that calls for road service have to do with vehicles that require starting or are inoperative and require towing.

Most vehicles today cannot be started by pushing. Towing a disabled vehicle with a chain or rope is considered to be an unsafe practice (and illegal in some places). If the vehicle being towed has power steering or power brakes it will be very difficult to control while being towed or pushed. When a vehicle cannot be started, it should be picked up and towed with a tow bar by a suitably equipped road service vehicle.

STARTING

When you are called upon to start a vehicle located away from the shop, you will need to take certain things with you. Generally the starting of the engine can be accomplished in several ways. Find out as much about the vehicle as you can before starting out on the call.

If the vehicle is sitting at a point handy to an electrical outlet, you may be able to start the engine by connecting a portable fast charger to the battery. If the vehicle is in a garage or driveway where it can be towed or pushed to start after it has been moved to the highway, you should know this before you start out. If the owner cranked the engine until the battery was discharged, but couldn't start it, a fully charged booster battery with the necessary cable connections or a fast charger should be taken along.

The road service procedure to follow on a road call to start an engine is presented in Chapter 2 under the trouble symptom in "Engine Does Not Crank."

TOWING

The same discussion presents the procedure to follow when towing or pushing to start is required. Special instructions are included for clutch equipped vehicles and for those that are equipped with automatic transmissions. Be sure to follow these instructions before attempting to tow or push a vehicle to start it.

If a collision, a broken part, or some other circumstance has rendered a vehicle inoperable or unsafe to drive, often you will be required to tow a vehicle to the shop. In this case, just how the vehicle is to be towed will be controlled by the nature of the fault. If rear axle or drive line trouble exists, you may want to raise the rear axle and tow the vehicle backward. Otherwise, the extent of the damage might be increased during the towing. In a different situation, you may want to raise the front of the vehicle and tow the vehicle forward. In other cases you will have to raise one end and place the other end on a dolly.

Be sure to check automatic transmission vehicles to see that the parking lock is released before towing, or the transmission may possibly be damaged. In many cars the steering wheel also locks when the ignition is turned off. Check the front wheels to make sure they are not locked or are locked in a straightforward position if the front end is not raised off the road.

TRADE COMPETENCY TEST

1. What is the value of periodic maintenance?
2. In automotive practice, what is the meaning of the words *analysis, diagnosis,* and *trouble shooting?*
3. Why are many owners unwilling to pay for a complete tune-up to correct an immediate trouble?
4. Why is equipment of great importance in maintenance operations and trouble shooting?
5. What advantage has the single, all-inclusive test bench over separate instruments?
6. What four things affect the electrical resistance of a conductor?

7. What two instruments are used to make most of the electrical measurements in automotive circuits?
8. When checking an automotive circuit of constant voltage, what is indicated when the amperage reading is lower than normal?
9. What term is used to describe the ability of a substance to hold electrons? What is the unit of measurement?
10. In answering a call for road service, why is it necessary to find out as much as possible about the vehicle before starting out?

CHAPTER 2

ELECTRICAL SYSTEMS

The automotive electrical system is very complex and interesting. This chapter will give you the necessary information with which troubles and problems can be readily diagnosed and remedied.

It is not possible to include all types of electrical faults nor is it possible to include all of the minor variations between models and manufacturers. However, if you approach the problems as indicated, virtually all charging, cranking, and battery problems can be handled with confidence.

The circuits discussed in this chapter are the ones which most frequently present problems to service technicians.

BASIC AUTOMOTIVE CIRCUITS

The electrical system of the modern automobile consists of seven basic circuits. This does not include the various accessories and optional equipment which have electrical circuits of their own. The seven circuits are: The Generating System; The Starting System; The Ignition System; The Lighting System; The Horn Circuit; The Instrument Circuits; and The Cigarette Lighter Cir-

cuit. The first five circuits are illustrated in Fig. 2-1 and show their relationship to one another. For the sake of convenience, the cigarette lighter circuit and the instrument circuits (other than the charge indicator and the headlight beam indicator) are not shown.

The ignition system provides the spark to operate the engine and is closely aligned with the other electrical systems. For this reason, ignition alone is considered in Chapter 4.

There are two types of generators used to produce electricity in automobiles. They are the old direct current generator, used for many years, and the rectified alternating current generator, commonly called the alternator. The practice is to call the DC generator a *generator* and the rectified AC generator an *alternator*. The text follows the industry usage, but keep in mind that both of them are generators and both of them deliver direct current to the car's electrical circuits. The generating system is a general term and refers to either type.

Some instruments are electrical, while others are mechanical. Trouble shooting procedures for all types of instruments,

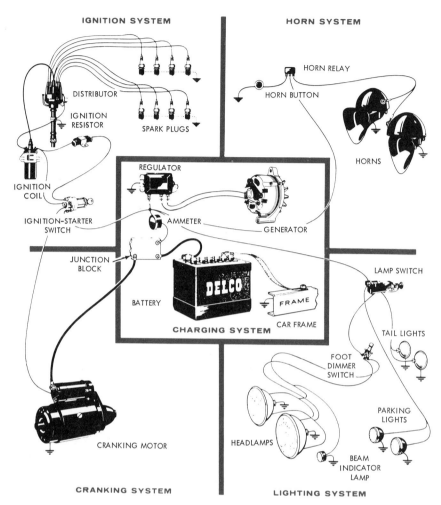

Fig. 2-1. Basic circuits of an automobile and their relation to one another. Delco-Remy Div. General Motors Corp.

electrical and mechanical, are presented separately in Chapter 8. The remaining electrical circuits (with the exception of the cigarette lighter circuit) are presented in this chapter. The cigarette lighter circuit is so simple that no formal trouble shooting procedures are included, and the brief discussion of that circuit will provide you with the information you need when trouble is encountered.

In electrical trouble shooting, it is important that you understand the differences that exist among the various makes and models of automobiles and trucks and be able to identify which particular type of circuit is used in the vehicle on which you are working. Likewise, you will find a surprising amount of similarity in all vehicles. In working with wiring diagrams, you will notice that the various manufacturers use different symbols and even those which all of them use appear with variations. The diagrams used in the text also use varying symbols but with everything labeled. It is unlikely that the industry will ever adopt standard symbols and you will have to depend on the labeling of the diagrams rather than on your knowledge of the symbols.

THE GENERATING SYSTEM CIRCUIT

The generating system is the source of current for all of the electrical requirements of the vehicle, and a part of this circuit is a part of each of the other circuits.

The portion of the generating system circuit that is a part of the starting motor circuit is composed of heavy cables to carry the current used in cranking the engine.

All of the current generated passes to the battery through a charge indicator. Formerly this indicator was built so that it would indicate the amount of current from the generator to the battery but would not show the amount of current which was being used from the battery in some circuits. Most automobiles today employ an indicator light which glows (usually red) when the battery is discharg-

ing and has no indication when the battery is being charged. In general, circuits used only intermittently (starting circuit, horn circuit) are connected into the generating circuit at some point between the battery and the charge indicator. In these cases, the current used by these circuits does not show on the charge indicator.

GENERATORS. Nearly all vehicles with a DC generator use a two-brush generator with a three-unit regulator. The differences (aside from capacity) among these various makes and models are that some systems have positive (+) ground, while some have negative (−) ground, and some generator fields are grounded internally (within the generator), while others have the field grounded externally. These differences account for the different circuits as shown in Figs. 2-2 and 2-3. Most vehicles today are negatively grounded.

All the major sources of generator trouble can be tabulated under three symptoms which appear as results of these troubles. Table 2-1 lists the symptoms with their sources of trouble. The sources

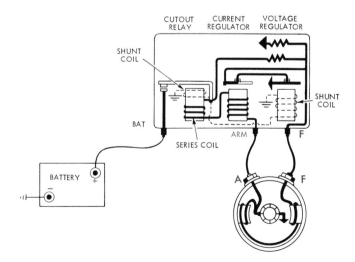

Fig. 2-2. Generator of the externally grounded field (Type A) circuit.

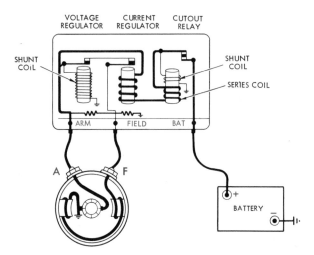

Fig. 2-3. Generator of the internally grounded field (Type B) circuit.

TABLE 2-1.   GENERATING SYSTEM-SOURCES OF TROUBLE AND ORDER OF CONSIDERATION

Sources	Symptom		
	Battery Low in Charge	Generator Output Low	High Charging Rate
Excessive Resistance in Battery to Ground Circuit	20	1	. . . .
Dirty Commutator	3	2	. . . .
Open Circuit -- Field	4	3	. . . .
Short Circuit -- Field	5	4	. . . .
Open Circuit -- Armature	6	5	. . . .
Short Circuit -- Armature	7	6	. . . .
Shorted Brush Holder	8	9	. . . .
Worn Generator Brushes	9	7	. . . .
Brushes Stuck in Holder	10	8	. . . .
Regulator Contact Stuck	12	. . . .	1
Loose or Worn Generator Belt	1	. . . .	. . . .
Battery Worn Out	2	. . . .	. . . .
Burned or Corroded Regulator Contacts	11	. . . .	. . . .
Cut-in Voltage High	13	. . . .	. . . .
Cut-in Voltage Low	14	. . . .	. . . .
Voltage Regulation High	. . . .	. . . .	2
Voltage Regulation Low	15	. . . .	. . . .
Current Limit Low	16	. . . .	. . . .
Regulator Not Grounded	17	. . . .	. . . .
Burned or Corroded Cut-out Contacts	18	. . . .	. . . .
Excessive Resistance in Armature to Battery Circuit . . .	19	. . . .	. . . .

are numbered to identify them by either the order of their probability or in the order that permits their speedy elimination from further consideration by testing. The table can also be used in reverse.

By knowing a source of trouble one or more symptoms can be predicted as a result.

ALTERNATORS. The modern automobile usually has many electrically oper-

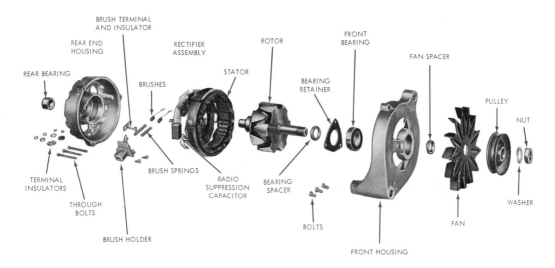

Fig. 2-4. Disassembled view of an alternator. Ford Div., Ford Motor Co.

ated accessories that result in a heavy electrical load upon the vehicle's battery and generator, particularly when the vehicle is driven at slow speeds. One of the characteristics of the old DC generator was that the voltage output was low at slow speeds. Specially designed generators with a very low cut-in speed provided a high output at slow speeds and were available as special equipment. However, these were usually too bulky and expensive for the average car.

Alternators have become standard equipment as a solution to this problem. Alternators are compact in design and have high output characteristics at slow speeds. However, the alternator should not be thought of as being the complete answer to all charging system requirements. Standard alternators are designed to provide greater slow speed output. For special requirements, such as two-way radio or other commercial equipment, either a heavy duty alternator or a heavy duty generator is recommended. An exploded view of a typical alternator is shown in Fig. 2-4. A schematic drawing

of an alternator system illustrating the alternator and the alternator regulator is shown in Fig. 2-5.

An understanding of basic electricity is essential to understand how an alternator works. The following paragraphs give a brief review of some basic facts about electricity and explain how an alternator is constructed and how it produces electrical current.

Magnetism. Electricity and magnetism are very closely related. Although magnetism is invisible, its effects are well known. A simple bar magnet has north and south magnetic poles and attracts iron filings. The space around the magnet, where iron filings arrange themselves in a pattern of lines, is called the "field of force" or magnetic field. The strength of this force varies with the strength of the magnet.

An electrical current (commonly called electrons) flows in an electrical circuit. When an electric current flows through a straight electric wire, a magnetic field is created around the wire. The greater the current that flows through the

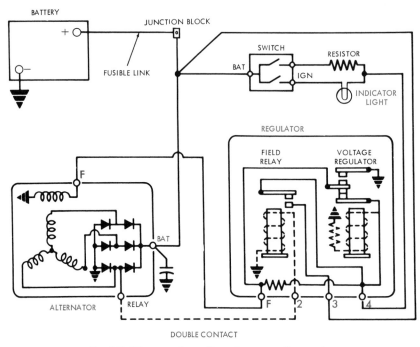

Fig. 2-5. Diagram of an alternator generating system.

wire, or conductor, the stronger the magnetic field produced and the larger the area affected.

Electromagnetic Fields. When a wire carrying current is formed into a loop, all the lines of magnetic force around the wire must pass through the loop. The lines of magnetic force outside the loop may dissipate in space. The lines of magnetic force inside the loop are confined and increase the lines of force per square inch of area. This creates a much stronger magnetic field with the same amount of current and establishes magnetic polarity. An electromagnet has a north and south pole similar to a simple, permanent bar magnet. Increasing the number of turns of wire in the current carrying loop or increasing the current flow increases the strength of the electromagnetic field. If an iron bar or core is placed in the center of the coil of wire, the magnetic field will

become even stronger because iron is a much better conductor of magnetic lines of force than air.

Electromagnetic Induction. A magnetic field, made up of lines of force, is created around a wire when electric current flows through it. When a conductor is moved past such a field so that it cuts across the magnetic lines of force, a voltage is induced in the conductor. *Induced Voltage* is the electrical pressure produced in a conductor by magnetic lines of force cutting across that conductor. If an electrical load is connected across the conductor to form a complete circuit, the induced voltage will cause a current to flow through the conductor and the circuit. This principle is called *Electromagnetic Induction* and is the fundamental operating principle of all generators. In a DC generator, the magnetic field produced by the field coils mounted in the housing is stationary, and the conductors in the armature are moved so they cut across the lines of magnetic force. As the armature rotates, the sides of the coil change position with respect to the magnetic field. This produces a current that alternates its direction of flow. However, the commutator rotates with the coil, and the segments change brushes at the same instant the current flow reverses in the coil. This results in a current that flows in one direction in the external circuit or a direct current.

In an alternator, the same principle of induced voltage is employed. However, in an alternator, the magnetic field is moved to cut across the conductors, which are stationary. The same principle of electromagnetic induction applies, but alternating current is produced.

Figure 2-6 shows a permanent magnet rotating inside a loop of wire (conductor) so that the lines of magnetic force produced by the magnet are cutting across the conductor. A voltage is induced in the conductor causing a current to flow through the completed circuit. With the north pole of the magnet at the top and the south pole at the bottom, the flow of current will be from A to B. When the magnet is rotated one-half turn (180°), the poles will have changed position, placing the north pole at the bottom and the south pole at the top. Movement of the armature magnet through one-half turn is termed one-half cycle. During the second half of the cycle, the lines of magnetic force will be cutting across the conductor in the opposite direction and the voltage induced will cause current to flow from B to A. When the north pole is again at the bottom, current will again flow from A to B. Current will flow through the conductor and circuit first in one direction and then in the opposite direction every half revolution. A full revolution is called a full cycle. The current employed in lighting most homes is called 60 cycle alternating current because it goes through a full cycle 60 times per second. This is accomplished with a multipole generator. Automotive alternators also have multi-poles as explained later.

Exciting An Electromagnetic Field. A

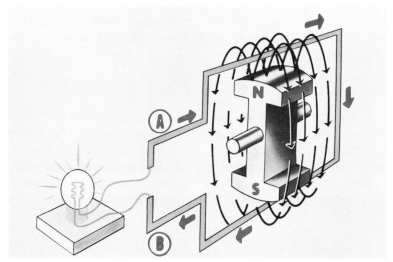

Fig. 2-6. Current is produced when a coil of wire cuts through a magnetic field.

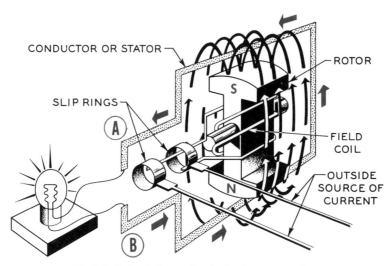

Fig. 2-7. A simple two pole, single phase generator.

generator may be either "internally" excited or "externally" excited. In an automotive DC generator, the field coils, which increase the strength of the electromagnetic field, receive electrical current from the generator brushes so they are termed "internally excited." In the alternator, the conductor is stationary, and the magnetic field is moved or rotated. Figure 2-7 illustrates a simplified version of an alternator and shows how a generator may receive its field current from an outside source. This is called an "externally excited" generator and is the principle used in most alternators. In an alternator, the field coil is wound on a rotor core or pole piece. The coil is connected to an external source of direct current through two slip rings and two brushes. The conductor (called a stator on alternators) is represented by the single loop of wire. Since the rotor pole piece is externally excited by direct current, as the poles change position, the current flow reverses. As the rotor revolves and the poles change position the current flow through the conductor or stator loop will reverse its direction every one-half revo-

lution. The simple alternator shown in Fig. 2-7 can be described as a two-pole externally excited, single phase, alternator. The rotor of an actual automotive alternator usually has twelve poles. Most automotive alternators have three sets of coil windings in the stator.

Three Phase AC Output. We have seen how an alternating voltage or AC current is generated by a simple single phase alternator. Before we go into the somewhat more complex problem of generating a three phase voltage output, we should review a few of the factors that affect the output of voltage and the control of that output.

1. Voltage will increase as the speed of the alternator rotor is increased.

2. Voltage will increase as the strength of the rotor's magnetic field is increased. The strength of this magnetic field is affected by:

a. The number of turns and the kind of wire used in the rotor windings.

b. The air gap between the rotor poles and the stator.

c. The voltage applied to the rotor

windings through the slip rings and brushes.

3. Voltage will increase as the number of turns of wire in the stator winding are increased because more conductors will be cut by the lines of magnetic force from the rotor.

4. Inductive reactance has an important bearing on alternator output. As current flow through a coil increases, lines of magnetic force will spread out and cut across the adjacent windings. The direction in which these lines of force cut the adjacent windings induces a voltage in the coils opposite to that which is being externally applied through the slip rings and brushes. This opposing voltage tends to limit the current flow through the coil windings. This induced resistance to current flow is called inductive reactance.

5. Magnetic fields are strongest at the poles. More voltage is induced when the rotor poles are passing close to the conductor or stator windings. As you can readily see, the induced voltage is constantly increasing and decreasing as the rotor revolves.

As we stated before, most automotive alternators have three sets of coil windings in the stator. In a typical stator winding arrangement, each of the windings has one end or terminal that is independent of the other two. The other end of each winding is connected to form a common junction called a "Y" connection. A single phase AC voltage is produced between any two of the independent terminals. Combined, these three single phases form a three phase "Y" connected stator.

Three phase circuit operation is shown in simplified form in Fig. 2-8. The curved overlapping lines at the top are called sine waves and are a graphical representation of the increase and decrease of current flow in the stator coils. The lines above the "O" current line indicate the positive current half cycle because the polarity of the voltage producing it is positive. The other half of the lines below the "O" current line are produced by

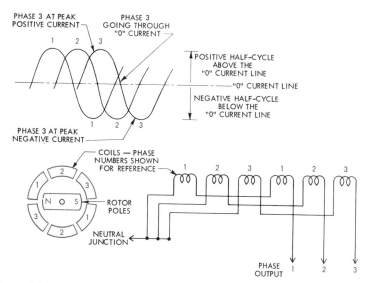

Fig. 2-8. Three phase operation, direct current. Current has a slight pulsation but does not alternate.

negative polarity voltage. An alternator is represented in simplified form in the lower part of Fig. 2-8 along with a simple wiring diagram of the unit. Stator coil positioning is not representative of actual coil windings, but it serves to illustrate the arrangement employed. In an actual alternator, the stator coils overlap as indicated by the overlapping sine waves. Phase numbers are assigned for reference. All three phases are connected at the "neutral" junction ("Y" connector in an actual alternator), and they are connected in series. Only two coils are shown in each phase to illustrate the method of connection. An actual alternator stator has twelve coils. Figure 2-9 shows the current flow in a three phase, full wave bridge rectifier circuit. Concern yourself with the current flow and not the rectification circuit which will be explained in subsequent paragraphs. Sine waves are shown

in the upper half of the illustration. Notice the dashed reference line that runs through them vertically. This line intersects each sine line at the instantaneous point of operation. Phase two is also shown as a dashed line in the sine waves. In this instantaneous position, phase one and phase three are near peak current flow, while phase two is at or near zero current flow. Notice, too, that phase one is positive, while phase three is negative. The important thing to remember is that two phases are always at or near peak output, while the other phase is at or near zero output. You may construct other instantaneous conditions of operation than the one shown by drawing a sine chart and then moving the reference line to the right along the zero line.

This brings us to the final stage of understanding alternator operation. Again refer to Fig. 2-9. Phase one is pro-

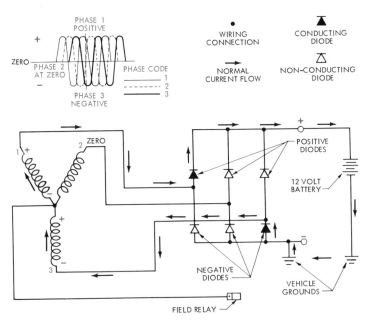

Fig. 2-9. Three phase current flow from an alternator. This system of rectifying uses all the current generated, not just the positive or negative.

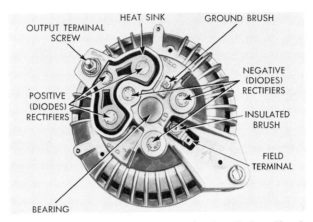

Fig. 2-10. View of end of alternator showing diodes. Chrysler Corp.

ducing positive polarity voltage. Phase two is producing zero voltage. Phase three is producing negative polarity voltage. Remember that we are attempting to produce electrical current to charge a positive polarity battery. Of the three phases shown in Fig. 2-9, only phase one is producing positive polarity voltage. The device employed to control current flow in an alternator is called a diode rectifier. You might describe a diode rectifier as a device which will allow current to flow in one direction only, similar to a check valve in a water or hydraulic system, which will allow fluid to flow in only one direction. In an alternator, six diode rectifiers are employed. Three are positive and three negative (See Fig. 2-10).

Refer once more to Fig. 2-9. Acquaint yourself with the symbols at the top of the illustration. For purposes of simplification, positive diodes allow current to flow from the alternator to the battery, and negative diodes allow current to flow from ground to complete the circuit. The diodes are the same. It is their position in the circuit that makes them positive or negative. In Fig. 2-9, current flows from the upper end of the phase one coil to the positive diode (black arrow). It flows through this diode to the positive alterna-tor terminal through the battery or other electrical load and then to ground. Current then flows from ground to the alternator housing and to the negative diode connected to the phase three stator coil, which has a negative voltage with respect to phase one voltage. No potential voltage difference exists between either of the other diodes and the negative alternator terminal. Therefore, no current can flow through these diodes. The positive diode connected to the phase three coil will not conduct or allow current to flow because the voltage across it is reversed (negative) in polarity which causes the diode to act as a check valve. As the alternator continues to rotate and the stator coils go from positive to negative and from zero output to peak output, there are many instantaneous circuit conditions, such as that shown in Fig. 2-9, that exist for only a split second. In each condition, the diodes control the current flow so that only positive direct current is flowing to the battery, even though the output from the stator coils to the rectifier diodes is alternating current.

Voltage Regulation. As previously explained, inductive reactance makes the alternator self limiting with respect to maximum output. However, this does

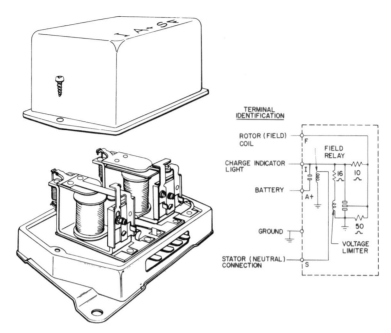

Fig. 2-11. An alternator regulator. This has only two units as the rectifier serves as a cutout.

not control voltage, so a voltage control or regulator is required. The only function of the regulator used with most alternators is to limit the DC voltage output, and it works much the same way as the voltage regulator used for DC generators. The two differences in the regulators are that a cutout is not needed with an alternator since the rectifier diodes will prevent the battery from discharging through the alternator, and alternator regulators have a field relay to control the flow of current to the field coil in the rotor. Fig. 2-11 shows a four terminal regulator for an alternator.

THE STARTING SYSTEM CIRCUIT

The battery and its cables, which are a part of the generating system circuit, are also a part of the starting system circuit.

The starting system is a low resistance circuit, since it must carry high amperage while the starter is cranking the engine. This involves the use of heavy conductors, heavy-duty connections, and a heavy-duty switch.

The cables generally used are B & S gage No. 00, No. 0, or No. 1. Gage No. 00 is 0.3648 in. in diameter and has a normal resistance of 0.07793 ohms per 1,000 feet. Gage No. 0 is 0.3249 in. in diameter and has a normal resistance of 0.09827 ohms per 1,000 feet. Gage No. 1 is 0.2893 in. in diameter and has a normal resistance of 0.1239 ohms per 1,000 feet.

The starter is electrically actuated through a remote control relay. Figs. 2-12, 2-13, and 2-14 show an ignition-switch operated, remote control relay. In these circuits, it should be noted that the relay circuit is grounded in the relay. The electrical energy required to actuate the relay

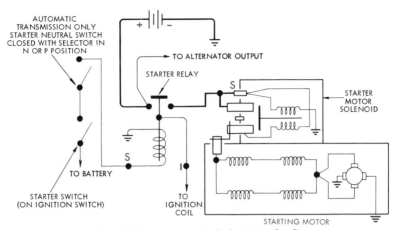

Fig. 2-12. A relay controlled starter circuit.

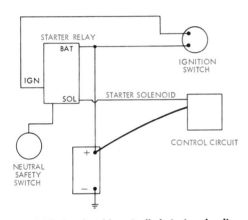

Fig. 2-13. A solenoid controlled starter circuit.

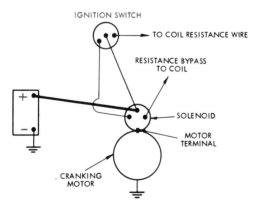

Fig. 2-14. A cranking circuit operated by a solenoid.

solenoid is taken from the ignition circuit. When the ignition switch is turned on, electrical energy is made available to a spring-loaded switch actuated by turning the ignition key past the "on" position.

Remember the differences in these two remote control relays, as they will have considerable influence in several of the starting motor-circuit test procedures covered in this chapter.

Starting motors generally have four brushes—two ground brushes and two field brushes and may have two, three, or four coils. Some variation in the internal circuits of starting motors exists. While all starting motors have their field coils connected in series between the connector bar and the insulated brush, some have a shunt coil (parallel connection) between the insulated sides of the circuit and ground. The shunt coil assists in controlling the speed of the motor.

In cranking the engine, the starting motor uses between 150 and 500 amperes depending upon the speed of the motor. The faster the motor runs the higher its resistance and the less current it uses. Anything that causes a reduction of starting motor speed lowers the electrical resistance and results in higher current flow. These facts are summed up in the statement "the current is inversely proportional to the speed."

Battery voltage drops during the time the starting motor is cranking the engine. At extremely slow starting motor speeds, battery voltage may drop to a point where the ignition system does not operate efficiently and the engine is difficult to start.

More service calls are made for failure to start than for any other reason. However, often the trouble lies elsewhere than in the starting system. The battery, the starter switch, the starter drive, the starting motor itself, and all of the wires or cables (including the ground circuit) involved are all a part of the starting system. The various procedures presented in this chapter are designed to determine, first of all, if the trouble lies in one of these units or in some other circuit or system; then, where the trouble is found to be in one of these units, to quickly locate which one.

THE IGNITION SYSTEM

The ignition system connects into the battery generator circuit between the ammeter and the generator. When the generator is not charging, the current used by the ignition system is indicated as discharge on the ammeter. The ignition circuit is completed through distributor contact points which interrupt the circuit while the engine is running. Ignition troubles are not covered here but in Chapter 4. However, a portion of the ignition circuit is common to other circuits, and for this reason the nature of this circuit must be understood.

The electrical instrument circuits and, usually, the electrical accessory circuits are connected into the ignition circuit on the coil (cold) side of the ignition switch. These circuits are automatically turned off when the ignition switch is turned off; otherwise, it would be necessary to turn off each accessory separately to avoid discharging the battery when the vehicle was not in use.

THE LIGHTING SYSTEM

The lighting system receives its current from the battery-generator circuit at a point between the ammeter and the generator. When the generator is not charging or is charging less than the current being used by the lights, current for the lighting system comes from the battery, and the ammeter shows discharge. If the generator is charging more than enough to supply all of the electrical needs, including the lights, the excess current flows to the battery.

Since the light circuit is connected into the battery-generator circuit between the charge indicator and the generator, the battery and its ground connection and the portion of the battery-generator circuit through the charge indicator (including the indicator) are all a part of the lighting system.

The lighting system consists of a number of parallel circuits, each of which is provided with at least one switch. Each of the separate lighting circuits has a portion of its circuit in common with all of the other lighting circuits. The general practice is to branch off from the main lighting circuit at whatever point is the most convenient.

The lamps used in an automotive vehicle vary considerably in the strength of current used. In general, the headlamp circuit is the main circuit and generally uses B & S gage No. 12 wire. Branches of this main circuit may use No. 12, No. 14, or No. 16 wire.

The diameter of No. 12 wire is 0.08081 in., and its normal resistance is 1.588 ohms per 1,000 feet, or 0.001588 ohms per foot (approx. 1.6 times the resistance of No. 10 wire). The diameter of No. 14 wire is 0.06408 in., and its normal resistance is 2.525 ohms per 1,000 feet, or 0.002525 ohms per foot (approx. 2½ times the resistance of No. 10 wire). The diameter of No. 6 wire is 0.05082 in., and its normal resistance is 4.016 ohms per 1,000 feet, or 0.004016 ohms per foot (approx. 4 times the resistance of No. 10 wire).

If larger than normal wires are used in the headlamp circuit, the life of the lamp bulbs will be materially reduced. Most headlamp circuits are designed to have a voltage drop of about 0.7 volts, and the length of the wires involved in some instances determines what gage wire is used. Usually, the circuit voltage (parallel to the lamp bulb) should be about 13.2 volts. Under this condition, the candle power will be normal, and the bulb life will be normal (about 460 hours). If, by use of larger wires or the installation of a relay in the circuit, the socket voltage is raised, the candle power would increase but bulb life would be reduced.

The lighting system circuits are protected from overload by means of a safety device. This may be a fuse, vibrating circuit breaker, thermal circuit breaker, or a combination of these units. These protective devices are actuated by high amperage. They do not protect the lamp bulb from high voltage.

The headlight circuit is the main circuit and carries the most load. This circuit usually runs along one side of the vehicle to one headlight. Just before it reaches this one light, a parallel or branch circuit runs to the other light.

All headlight systems have a *high* and a *low* beam. The low beam generally branches off the main headlight circuit at a dimmer switch. As the switch is depressed, the one headlight circuit is switched off and the other is switched on.

The fuse or other protecting device is in a part of the circuit common to these two branches of the main lighting circuit. If, through a defect in the dimmer switch, there is a short circuit, the safety device will be overloaded and shut off the current.

Nearly all vehicles use a three-position light switch mounted on the instrument panel. When this switch is all the way in, the lights are out. When the switch is pulled out to the first position, the parking lights, the tail lights, and the license plate lights are on. Both of these are separate circuits parallel to the main headlight circuit. Each of these has two or more parallel branches. Fig. 2-15 illustrates the elements of a lighting system circuit as established up to this point. This same illustration, likewise, shows the relationship to the six other main electrical circuits of the vehicle. This drawing is not for any particular car but represents what you will find in any of them.

THE HORN

As shown in Fig. 2-15, the horn circuit on most vehicles takes current from the battery-generator circuit at a point between the battery and the ammeter. The current used by the horn is not indicated on the ammeter.

Horns are illustrated as a vibrator, Fig. 2-16. The circuit is closed by a spring-loaded switch. This switch may be installed in series with the horn, or a relay may be in series with the horn, the spring-loaded switch for the relay being parallel to the horn.

Either one or two horns may be used. Where two horns are used, each has a different pitch which blends with the other, resulting in a pleasing tone.

Fig. 2-17 is a sectional drawing of a typical diaphragm type horn showing the vibrator adjustment.

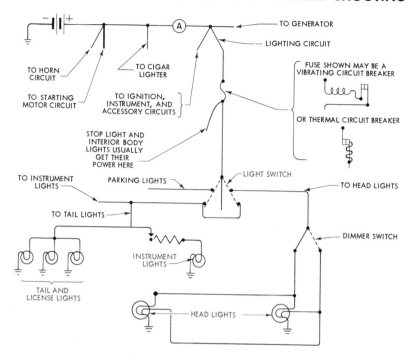

Fig. 2-15. The lighting circuit and its relation to the other circuits.

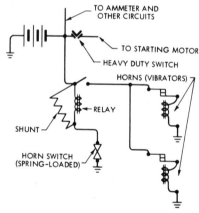

Fig. 2-16. A horn circuit with relay. The switch completes the circuit by grounding it.

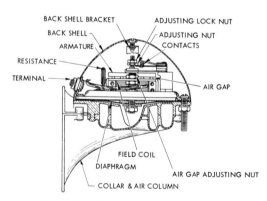

Fig. 2-17. Diaphragm type horn. The contacts and air gap are adjustable.

Fig. 2-16 shows a typical horn circuit using a relay. Generally, when no relay is employed, the horn button is between the horn and ground. It is important that you understand this difference and be able to recognize it, as it has a bearing on the trouble shooting procedures.

As a rule, in horn circuits without a relay, only one horn is used. Most vehicles use a relay in the horn circuit whether one or two horns are used. Many horn circuit relays include a shunt resistor parallel to the relay coil as shown in Fig. 2-16. When the magnetic field of the relay collapses, a high voltage is induced in the horn switch circuit. This high voltage can cause a disagreeable electric shock. The purpose of the shunt is to provide a path for this current, thus eliminating the possibility of an electric shock from this source. Usually the shunt consists of a short length of very fine wire.

THE INSTRUMENTS

As shown in Fig. 2-15, most electrical instruments are connected into the ignition circuit. The instrument circuits are connected to the cold side of the ignition switch so that, when the ignition switch is turned off, the instruments are likewise off. An exception to this is the ammeter which, as has been explained previously, is in series in the generator-to-battery circuit.

THE CIGARETTE LIGHTER

The cigarette lighter circuit receives current from a point between the ammeter and the battery in the battery-generator circuit. The current used does not show as discharge on the ammeter. Of course, remotely located lighters are connected to the nearest "live" circuit, which, in turn, may receive its current from a point between the ammeter and the generator. In that case, the lighter current would show as discharge on the ammeter.

The circuits for all lighters are completed by grounding the center of the spiral heater wire against a spring load that tends to break the ground contact once the pressure is released. The "pop out" type lighter maintains the ground until the heater wire is hot.

A short in a lighter circuit connected between the battery and the ammeter will discharge the battery but will not show on the ammeter. Since the wiring involved is quite heavy, a short in this circuit can cause fire. Fuses or circuit breakers may be employed in the circuit.

Intermittent shorts are located by tracing the wire from the lighter socket to the point where it connects into the battery-generator circuit. Look particularly at portions of the wire which pass near or over sharp edges.

Generally failure to operate is caused by the circuit to ground being incomplete. In most cases, you will find that the heater wire has burned out.

BATTERY CHARGE LOW

The discharged battery is the most frequently encountered trouble in the electrical system. The mere charging of the battery corrects the immediate trouble but does not uncover the cause of the failure, and usually the battery will again become discharged. You can do more to establish yourself as a trouble shooter in these cases by finding the real trouble.

Batteries become discharged because of the following reasons: (1) battery is worn out (under capacity); (2) more current is used than is supplied by the generating system; (3) battery solution allowed to become low, thus effectively reducing plate area; (4) accidental discharge of the battery such as when lights, accessories, or ignition are left turned on when generating system was not charging; (5) need for an engine tune-up (more than normal cranking time required); and (6) engine oil too stiff for the prevailing temperatures (slow cranking speed and consequent higher current consumption).

The most common cause of a discharged battery, however, is more current being used than is supplied by the generating system. This may be due to lack of capacity of the generating system, improper regulation, faults in the circuit, unwise use of electrical equipment, or insufficient highway operation to permit replacement of the current used for starting.

As a part of trouble shooting where the battery is discharged, determine from the owner as much about how the battery became discharged as you can. If the operation is such that there is no possibility of the system keeping the battery charged, you may have to recommend a higher capacity generator or alternator, a smaller generator or alternator pulley, a higher regulator setting or, accepting the discharge as inevitable, recommend recharging the battery periodically. In any case you will want to make sure that all of the units and the wiring in the battery-generating circuit are normal before making any kind of recommendation.

TROUBLE SHOOTING PROCEDURE

Before starting the steps of this procedure, confirm the symptom by checking the state of charge of the battery. Likewise, check the drive belt adjustment and condition. If the belt is missing or too loose, replacement or adjustment might be all that is needed. The procedure, in abbreviated form, is shown in Fig. 2-18.

RECHARGE AND TEST BATTERY. Since the battery is discharged, it must be brought to a fully charged condition before you can judge its ability to take and hold sufficient charge. After this has been done, test the battery capacity under a high discharge rate to determine whether or not it will take and hold a charge. If

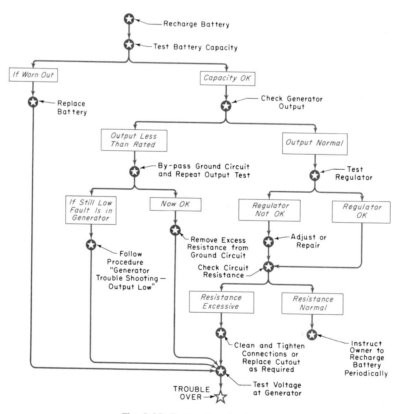

Fig. 2-18. Battery low in charge.

the battery is worn out or deteriorated, it will not be able to hold enough charge to supply the large current required by the starting system. If it is badly sulphated, as from internal discharge, it probably will not even accept a charge because of its high resistance. Replace the battery if the high discharge rate test indicates it is worn out or under capacity. Battery tests and servicing are covered later in this chapter.

If the battery is worn out, its condition may have been the only cause of the "battery low" symptom.

If the battery tests O.K. after change, proceed as follows:

CHECK GENERATING SYSTEM. After the battery has been eliminated as a possible source of trouble, the next most logical unit to check is the generating system since it is the source of energy for charging the battery.

Test the generating system output to determine if the system is at fault. Proceed as follows after determining the output:

(1) *Output Low.* If the current output of the generating system does not reach the rated output, connect a heavy jumper wire from the battery ground post to the generator or alternator ground terminal. You are substituting a known good ground for the existing ground path in the vehicle. Repeat the generating system output test.

If the output is still less than rated, the generator or alternator is at fault. If the output now reaches normal, the generator, the alternator, or the battery is not properly grounded to the engine or frame.

Install a new battery-to-ground cable if the existing cable is corroded or partially broken. Clean the cable connections at the battery and engine, and tighten connections. Make sure any engine ground straps are making good contact at both ends. Repeat the output test without the parallel jumper wire ground. If it now shows normal, you have corrected the trouble.

If the output is still low, the generator or alternator itself will have to be better grounded. Remove and scrape or sand the paint or dirt from the inner surface of the bracket strap and the corresponding surface of the frame. Remove the mounting bracket from the engine and scrape or sand the paint and dirt from the bracket-to-engine mating surfaces. Replace the bracket and generator or alternator and adjust the belt.

The fact that a separate ground wire from a generator to its regulator is provided does not remove the necessity of providing a good ground path from the battery to the generator. This ground wire is provided to assure a ground for the cutout shunt coil, without which the cutout contact points will not close. If, when the vehicle comes in off the road, this ground wire (generator to regulator) feels hot to the touch, the condition may be considered as an almost positive indication that a poor ground exists either between the engine and the generator or between the engine and the body or frame.

(2) *Output Normal.* If the generating system output tests normal, it can be eliminated from further consideration, and the next unit to consider is the regulator or control device. The regulator can be improperly adjusted, defective, or damaged. Since it controls output, it can be holding the output low enough to prevent full charge of the battery, thus accounting for the discharged condition.

CHECK GENERATOR SYSTEM REGULATOR. Test the regulator to determine if it is properly adjusted or in need of repair.

(1) *Regulator Inoperative.* If, during this test, any of the regulator units are

found to be improperly adjusted or in need of repair, make the necessary repairs or adjustment. (See "Generator Regulator Tests" and "Alternator Regulator Test," this chapter).

(2) *Regulator Operative.* If the regulator tested O.K., the trouble lies in the circuit connecting the generating system units together. Broken or high resistance wires, corroded or loose connections, and burned or corroded contacts can all cause a decrease in the available output of the system. Check the external circuit to determine if it has excessive resistance. (See "Generator Circuit Resistance Tests" and "Alternator Circuit Resistance Tests," this chapter).

(a) *Resistance Normal.* If the resistance (voltage drop) is equal to or less than specified in the test, the battery was low in charge due to unusual operational requirements of the owner. Excessive night driving or use of accessories, accidental discharge of battery (lights, ignition, radio, left on overnight), improper starting procedure (flooding engine, not using choke properly, etc.), or engine oil too heavy (high SAE number) could account for more current being taken from the battery than the generating system can replace. Vehicles not used every day, or used in such a manner as not to provide enough generator charging time to permit replenishment of the current used in starting, will have to be periodically recharged. Instruct the owner along these lines so he will no longer expect to use more current from the battery than the generating system can put into it.

(b) *Resistance Excessive.* If, in the resistance test of the circuit, the resistance (voltage drop) is greater than specified, locate the exact part of the circuit with the excessive resistance and eliminate the excess resistance.

Clean and tighten all wire and cable connections that were parallel to the volt-

meter when the excessive voltage drop was evidenced. Recheck the voltage drop. If it is still excessive, replace the wire or cable involved.

If the excessive resistance is at the regulator or cutout, remove the cover from the regulator. Disconnect the "BAT" wire from the regulator terminal. If the cutout contact points are badly burned or built up, replace or dress them. Remove oil and dirt from the cutout contact surfaces by pulling a piece of clean, bond paper or other lint-free substance between the contact surfaces while holding the contact closed on the paper. Examine soldered connections to see that they are in good condition. Recheck the voltage drop. If it is still excessive, replace the cutout contacts. If the contacts are not replaceable, replace the cutout or regulator.

TEST GENERATOR OR ALTERNATOR VOLTAGE. With the battery fully charged, the generator or alternator known to have full capacity, the regulator properly adjusted, and the circuit (including ground) resistance not excessive, the circuit should perform satisfactorily. Nevertheless, a quickly performed over-all check of generator voltage should be made before releasing the vehicle.

GENERATOR TROUBLE SHOOTING

The two sources of trouble in the battery-generator circuit are a low or nonexistent charging rate and an excessive charging rate. These can be caused by either a faulty generator or generator regulator.

OUTPUT LOW

Usually this symptom is uncovered when testing generator output. Low generator output can be the result of a dirty commutator; open or short circuit in the field, armature, brushes, or brush hold-

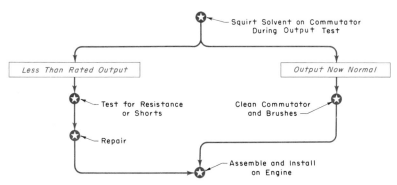

Fig. 2-19. Generator output low.

ers; or the brushes can be worn and not making good contact with the commutator.

The procedure to follow is illustrated in Fig. 2-19. The steps of this procedure should be followed at the time the generator output is tested in those instances where the generator output is found to be low.

COMMUTATOR CHECK. While testing the generator output, squirt carbon tetrachloride on the commutator through the generator frame ventilating slots to determine if the commutator is oily or dirty. The carbon tetrachloride will momentarily dissolve the dirt or oil on the commutator and permit the brushes to make better electrical contact. Observe the generator output. If the output is normal, proceed as follows:

(1) *Output Normal.* Remove the generator from the car and disassemble it. Do not remove the field pole shoes or field windings. Clean the commutator surface with fine sandpaper (not emery cloth or emery paper), and scrape out the slots between the commutator segments to remove dirt and carbon particles.

If the surface of the commutator is rough or more than 0.001 in. out of round, turn it down in a lathe or with a turning and undercutting tool (Fig. 2-20).

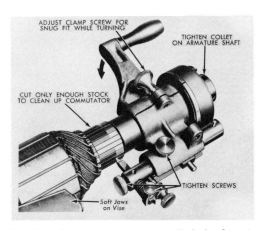

Fig. 2-20. Turning a commutator. Pad vise jaws to avoid damage to the wires. Chrysler Corp.

Remove no more copper than necessary to clean up the commutator.

After the commutator is turned down, undercut the mica between the bars $\frac{1}{32}$ in. below the copper, using a hacksaw blade or an undercutting tool (Fig. 2-21). Fig. 2-22 illustrates samples of proper and improper undercutting. Polish the commutator with 00 or 000 sandpaper to remove all burrs.

NOTE: Brush out all particles of copper from the mica insulation between the commutator segments.

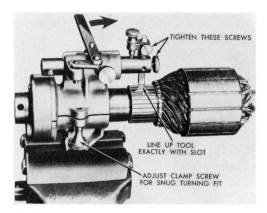

Fig. 2.21. Undercutting a commutator. Polish with fine sandpaper to remove burrs caused by undercutting. Ford Motor Co.

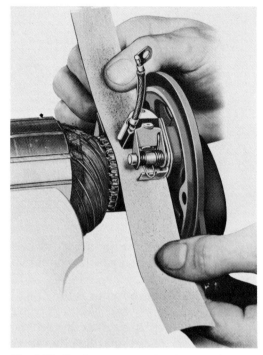

Fig. 2-23. Seating generator brushes on the commutator. Ford Motor Co.

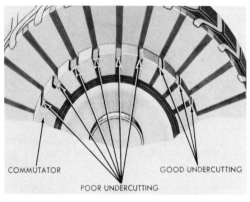

Fig. 2-22. Correct undercutting of a commutator. Ford Motor Co.

Clean the brushes or, if necessary, replace them.

Reassemble the generator. Whether new brushes have been installed or you are reusing the old brushes, they should be seated on the commutator. This is accomplished as shown in Fig. 2-23.

Mount the generator on the engine and adjust the generator belt to the proper tension.

(2) *Output Still Low.* If, during the generator output test, the output does not increase to the rated amperes when solvent is squirted on the commutator, test the generator on the engine for open or shorted circuits in the field, armature, or brushes.

(a) *Field Open or Shorted.* To test for an open or shorted field, disconnect the external field wire if a separate field terminal is provided. If no external field terminal is provided, insulate the field brush from the commutator.

Connect an ammeter between the battery and the field terminal (or brush). Divide the amperage reading obtained by the system's voltage. If the resistance value obtained is too high, look for a poor connection in the field, particularly at ground. If the resistance value obtained is low, one or several of the field coils are shorted. If the test of the field shows the field has an open or short circuit, remove the generator, disassemble it, and repair the condition, if possible. If no repairs can be made, replace the field coils and reassemble the generator. Mount the generator on the engine, and adjust the generator belt tension.

(b) *Armature Open or Shorted.* With the field disconnected and an ammeter connected from the battery to the armature terminal of the generator, the amperage reading, as each segment passes under the brush, will indicate continuity or shorts. In many generators, the normal amperage reading will be approximately the normal maximum amperage of that particular model of generator. High readings indicate shorts. Low readings indicate opens or resistance.

Press down on the armature brush to make sure it is making good contact with each segment. Look for poorly soldered connections to the commutator.

If the armature test shows the armature circuit to have an open or short, remove the generator, disassemble it, and repair the condition, if possible.

(c) *Brushes Open or Shorted.* If the preceding tests show the brushes to be open or shorted, remove the generator, disassemble it, and repair the condition, if possible. Clean or turn the commutator (Fig. 2-20) and replace or reseat the brushes (Fig. 2-23). If the brushes are stuck in the holder, replace the end plate and brushes. Replace the brushes if they are worn. If the armature brush holder is shorted to ground, repair the insulation, if possible. If not, replace the end plate and reassemble the generator.

Make sure the ground brush is making good contact with the commutator and is grounded properly.

Mount the generator on the engine and adjust the generator belt tension.

CHARGING RATE HIGH

Indications that point to this symptom are generator, lights (see Table 2-2), or radio tubes burning out prematurely, battery requiring filling too frequently, and burned ignition contacts. The most common cause of these troubles is high voltage, and the first step of trouble shooting is to correct possible high voltage regulation. In cases where the generator itself burns out in addition to the high voltage, a high setting of the current limiter could account for the failure.

A generator can charge at an excessive rate if it is the externally grounded field

TABLE 2-2. LIGHT BULB LIFE AT VARIOUS APPLIED VOLTAGES

Voltage		Candlepower (% of Normal)	Life	
At Socket	At Source		(% of Normal)	Hours
5.0	5.7	40	1,700	7,800
5.2	5.9	47	1,100	5,060
5.4	6.1	54	720	3,300
5.6	6.3	62	450	2,060
5.8	6.5	70	310	1,425
6.0	6.7	79	220	1,010
6.2	6.9	89	140	645
6.4	7.1	100	100	460
6.6	7.3	111	70	322
6.8	7.5	123	50	230
7.0	7.7	135	35	160
7.2	7.9	148	25	115
7.4	8.1	162	19	87
7.6	8.3	178	13	60

type and there is a grounded field in the generator. Disconnecting the field wire should cause the output to drop to zero. If it doesn't, the generator is at fault.

In certain instances, the owner may believe the charging rate is high. However, he may be relying only on the position of a charge indicator. This instrument tells the direction of current flow (to the battery—charge; from the battery —discharge) and cannot be relied on to show accurately the amount of current flow.

Make sure the battery is fully charged. If it is not, test the generator circuit.

CHECK VOLTAGE. Connect a voltmeter from the regulator "ARM" terminal to ground. Run the engine at 1,500 rpm.

Allow the generator to charge long enough to replace the current used for starting the engine. This will make certain that the battery is charged and will impart a surface charge to the battery plates. This will give assurance that the voltage limiter will work.

Generally, a maximum voltage of not over 15.2 volts is specified. If the reading is higher than this, adjust the regulator. (See "Generator Regulator Tests)

If the voltage reading is high, remove the regulator cover and depress the voltage regulator armature to see if the points are stuck and will not open. Check the contacts and replace them if they are burned or oxidized. On some regulators, the contacts are not replaceable. The regulator must be replaced if the contacts are in poor condition.

If the points are not sticking and are in good condition, adjust the voltage regulation to the specified limits. Recheck the setting with the cover in place.

ALTERNATOR TROUBLE SHOOTING

Diagnosing trouble in an alternator charging system is similar to diagnosing trouble in a generator charging system. Most problems start with an indication of trouble from the battery. The trouble shooting starts with the battery to determine whether or not it is capable of accepting a charge; then, the other units in the system are eliminated one by one until the problem is located. Most of the tests are made on the car. It is necessary to remove the alternator and disassemble it to make continuity tests of the stator or rotor windings or to test the diode rectifiers. The most commonly encountered problems with alternators are outlined here, with a method for determining the possible causes. One thing to remember is that the battery is tested in the same manner as with a regular DC generator.

OUTPUT LOW

A low or nonexistent charging rate can be caused by trouble in the alternator, the alternator circuit, or the alternator regulator. Follow the steps in the procedure given until the difficulty is overcome.

1. Check for a loose or broken alternator drive belt.

2. Clean and tighten the battery terminals.

3. Clean and tighten the ground leads and connections for both the alternator and the battery.

4. Check the brushes and slip rings for excessive wear, and replace any defective parts.

5. Perform a current output test on the alternator, and repair any defects discovered in the test. (See "Alternator Output Test," this chapter.) If the output test shows the alternator to be defective, remove it from the engine, and test the diode rectifiers for opens or shorts and the stator and rotor windings for high resistance or opens. (See "Alternator Bench Tests," this chapter.)

6. Check the regulator output and make any needed adjustments or repairs (See "Alternator Regulator Tests," this chapter).

7. If the alternator and the regulator are performing normally, check the circuit for high resistance. (See "Alternator Circuit Resistance Tests," this chapter.)

HIGH CHARGING RATE

Invariably the cause for this problem lies in the alternator regulator. It might be that the regulator is set too high or the regulator contacts may be stuck. The regulator voltage winding may be open, or the regulator base may be improperly grounded. In any event, perform a complete test of the voltage regulator, and adjust or replace as necessary.

NOISY ALTERNATOR

This problem may be caused either externally or internally.

1. Check for a loose alternator mounting.

2. Check for a loose or frayed drive belt.

3. Remove the alternator from the car, and disassemble it in order to check for the following things:

a. Worn bearings.

b. Interference between the rotor fan and the stator leads or rectifiers.

c. Rotor or rotor fan damaged.

d. Opens or shorts in the diode rectifiers.

e. Open or shorted windings in stator.

ENGINE DOES NOT CRANK

In most cases, the owner will have discharged his battery before calling for assistance and is more interested in getting his engine started quickly than in knowing why he had the trouble. In every case, when answering a service call away from the shop, take along either a fully charged battery with two heavy leads six to eight feet long having suitable connectors or a portable fast charger capable of delivering from 80 to 100 amperes.

A more complete diagnosis can be made after the vehicle is in the shop. If neither a booster battery nor a portable fast charger is available, follow the procedure starting with "Trouble Shooting Procedure." This procedure is illustrated in Fig. 2-24. Whenever a starting failure is experienced, it is a good plan to discuss with the owner the several points brought out in "Maintenance Precautions."

ROAD SERVICE PROCEDURE

Failure to start may have been the result of excessive choking by the operator, and the engine may start normally by the time you arrive. If the engine does not start, follow the procedure presented under the heading "Fast Charger" or "Booster Battery," whichever suits the equipment you have with you. If you have neither, you will have to follow the procedure outlined under "Towing or Pushing."

FAST CHARGER. If a suitable electric outlet is available, plug in the fast charger. Make sure all of the electrical accessories on the vehicle, particularly the radio, are turned off. Connect the charging leads to the battery, and gradually set the charging rate to maximum. If the power line fuse burns out, put in a larger fuse, but be sure to replace the correct fuse before leaving.

NOTE: Serious damage can be caused in the radio if it is left on while charging the battery at a high rate.

When charging the battery of a car with an alternator, connect the charger leads positive to positive and negative to negative. If the charger leads are reversed, damage to the alternator wiring and diodes can occur.

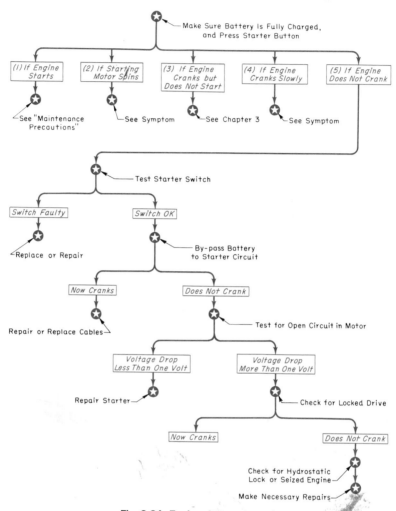

Fig. 2-24. Engine does not crank.

In most instances you will be able to crank the engine as soon as the charger starts. If not, leave the charger on and try it again after ten minutes of charging.

If the starting motor spins, the starter drive is at fault. Follow the procedure under the heading "Starting Motor Spins." If the engine cranks but does not start, refer to Chapter 3, and follow the procedure for this symptom. If the engine does not crank, trouble exists either in the engine or in the starting circuit. Fol-

low whatever portion of "Diagnosis Procedure" applies.

BOOSTER BATTERY. Turn on the ignition switch, and pull out the choke. Connect a fully charged battery to the battery in the car, and operate the starter switch. The starting motor should start cranking the engine.

If the engine starts now, check battery condition, and recharge or replace as required. Follow instructions given under heading "Trouble Shooting Procedure" to prevent future failure. If the starting motor spins, the starting motor drive is at fault. Follow the procedure under the heading "Starting Motor Spins." If the engine now cranks but does not start, the trouble is in the engine and not in the starting circuit. Refer to Chapter 3, and follow the procedure for this symptom.

TOWING OR PUSHING. When towing or pushing a vehicle to start it, there is always the possibility of a hydrostatic lock in the cylinders that could result in breaking the pistons. In general, a hydrostatic lock is the result of a leaking cylinder head gasket. If you have any reason to suspect the presence of water in the cylinders, rather than take the chance of damaging the engine remove the spark plugs and turn the engine over several times to expel the water before attempting to start the engine by either pushing or towing.

Even when you have no reason to suspect water in the cylinders, slip the clutch carefully during the starting process until you are sure the engine has made at least two complete revolutions. Usually fluid couplings and torque converters permit enough slippage to avoid damage to the engine.

(1) *Manual Clutch.* If the vehicle to be started is equipped with a clutch, little or no slippage will occur. Place the transmission in direct drive. Turn on the ignition switch. Tow or push the vehicle, holding down the clutch pedal until a speed of at least 5 miles per hour is reached. Then slip the clutch gradually until you feel the engine has turned over several times. If the engine starts to turn but stops suddenly, a hydrostatic lock exists which must be relieved before any further attempts to start are made. If the engine turns over satisfactorily, increase the towing speed to 20 or 25 miles per hour. If the engine does not start, follow the steps given under the heading "Trouble Shooting Procedure."

(2) *Automatic Transmission.* Fluid couplings and torque converters have considerable slippage at low speeds when the wheels are driving the engine. For this reason, in order to get high cranking speeds for starting, the selector lever is placed in the lowest speed range. Most manufacturers recommend that the vehicle be pushed in neutral until a speed of 20 or 25 mph is reached. Then, with the ignition turned on, move the selector lever to the low-speed position.

Whenever pushing a car with an automatic transmission or clutch, be sure to check the manufacturer's recommended procedure, or you may cause serious damage to the car. Many cars with automatic transmissions cannot be started by pushing or towing because the transmission has no pump driven by the propeller shaft and no power is transmitted to the engine.

TROUBLE SHOOTING PROCEDURE

Check the condition of the battery. Recharge or replace the battery if it is low in charge or capacity. Make sure the battery connections are clean and tight. Operate the starter switch. One of the following five things will be true. Follow the instructions given for whichever one applies:

1. ENGINE STARTS. If the engine starts now, discuss with the owner the points covered in the next section, "Maintenance Precautions."

2. STARTING MOTOR SPINS. If the starting motor spins but the engine does not crank, the starting motor drive or flywheel gear is at fault.

3. ENGINE CRANKS AT NORMAL SPEEDS. If the engine cranks at normal speed but does not start, the trouble is in the engine and not in the starting circuit. Follow

the procedure for this symptom in Chapter 3.

4. ENGINE CRANKS SLOWLY. If it has been determined that the battery is in satisfactory condition, follow the procedure under this heading later in the chapter. *NOTE: If this condition exists in sub-zero weather, it is advisable to check the viscosity of the engine oil and dilute, if necessary, as described in the next section "Maintenance Precautions."*

5. ENGINE STILL DOES NOT CRANK. If, with the battery known to be good and fully charged, the engine still does not crank, the procedure to follow consists of six steps: (1) test starter switch; (2) by-pass battery to starter circuit; (3) test for open circuit in starting motor; (4) check for locked starter drive; (5) check for hydrostatic lock or seized engine; and (6) test starting motor.

HYDROSTATIC LOCK: Since liquids (water, oil, or fuel) cannot be compressed, their presence in the cylinder will keep the piston from going all the way up on its compression stroke. This is referred to as hydrostatic lock.

Follow these steps in the order given until the cause of the trouble is located and corrected.

(1) *Test Starter Switch.* The procedure to follow in testing the starter switch is determined by the type of starter switch employed. If a starter relay is used, proceed as follows:

(a) *Starter Relay.* If a starter relay is employed, note whether or not the relay clicks when the starting switch is operated. If the vehicle is equipped with an automatic transmission or a transmission starter lockout switch, make sure the transmission is in neutral or park.

If a click is heard, use a battery cable or No. 2 wire as a jumper and connect it across the relay terminals. If the engine now cranks, replace the relay. If the engine still does not crank, follow the pro-

cedure under the heading "Test Relay to Starter Cable."

If no click is heard, proceed to the next step.

Ignition Switch Remote-Control Relay. It should be noted that the relay in Fig. 2-25 is grounded internally. In all automatic transmissions, and some manually shifted transmissions, the remote-control circuit is broken at all times except when the shift lever is in the neutral position. In these cases, several additional connections and an additional switch that might be a source of trouble must be taken into account. The circuit involved is shown in Fig. 2-25.

Connect a jumper wire from the battery to the small wire terminal of the relay. If the engine now cranks, leave one end of the jumper connected to the battery, and touch each terminal of the remote control circuit with the other end of the jumper wire. Start with the terminal nearest the relay. If at one position the engine no longer cranks, the fault lies between that point and the point where the engine last cranked. Repair or replace the switch or wire involved.

If, after following the procedures just presented, the engine does not crank, use a battery cable or a No. 2 wire as a jumper

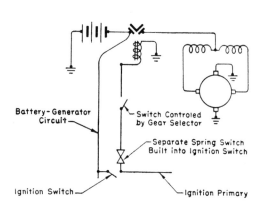

Fig. 2-25. Starting motor circuit.

and connect it across the relay terminals. If the engine now cranks, replace the relay. If the engine still does not crank, follow the procedure under "Test Relay to Starter Cable."

(1) *Mechanical Switch.* If the vehicle is equipped with a mechanical starter switch, connect a jumper wire (made from battery cable) across the starter switch. If the engine now cranks, replace the starter switch. If the engine still does not crank, proceed as follows:

(2) *Test Relay to Starter Cable.* Using a battery cable or a No. 2 wire as a jumper, connect it to the "hot" or ungrounded terminal of the battery and directly to the starting motor terminal. If the engine now cranks, replace or tighten the cable leading from the starter relay to the starting motor. If the engine still does not crank, proceed as follows:

(3) *Test for Open Circuit in Starting Motor.* Connect a voltmeter across the battery terminals. Press the starter switch and observe the voltage reading. If the voltage drop is less than one volt, an open circuit exists in the starting motor. Remove and repair or replace the starting motor. If the voltage reading at the battery drops more than one volt when the starter button is pressed, proceed as follows:

(4) *Check for Locked Starter Drive.* Put the manual transmission in high gear, and attempt to push the vehicle forward. If the vehicle will not move forward, probably the starter drive gear is locked. Rock the vehicle back and forth. Usually the backward motion will release the gear. Loosening the bolts which secure the starting motor to the engine will also release the gear. If the starter drive gear is not locked and the engine still does not crank, proceed as follows:

(5) *Check for Hydrostatic Lock or Seized Engine.* Remove the spark plugs and again attempt to crank the engine

with the starting motor. If the engine now cranks, it is usually an indication that water is leaking into the cylinders. Remove the cylinder head, and inspect the gasket or head for cracks. Also examine the cylinder block for cracks, particularly around the valve ports. Make the necessary repairs, and install the cylinder head. If the engine still does not crank, proceed as follows:

(6) *Test Starting Motor.* Remove the starting motor, and connect it to a fully charged battery. If the starting motor does not run, repair or replace it. If the starting motor runs satisfactorily, the engine is seized and must be disassembled and any faulty parts replaced.

MAINTENANCE PRECAUTIONS

Several precautions and recommendations which will help to prevent future starting failures can be given to the owner.

If the battery was low in charge, advise him to have the battery checked regularly, recharging it as required. Advise him to hold down the clutch pedal when starting the engine. Recommend oils of correct viscosity for engine, transmission, and differential. Show him how to choke the carburetor properly and how to overcome flooding by cranking the engine with the throttle open to exhaust the rich gases. Where temperatures from $-10°F$ to $-65°F$ prevail, use the oil recommended by the engine manufacturer.

STARTING MOTOR SPINS

If the starting motor spins and does not engage with the flywheel gear, remove the starting motor and either clean or replace the starter drive and worn or damaged parts (including flywheel gear), as required.

CAUTION: Do not oil the starter drive.

Clean the starter drive with a dry rag. It should work freely when dry. Small quantities of dust from the clutch or flywheel are thrown onto the starter drive where any oil or grease will hold it. This oil and dust may prevent free movement of the starter drive.

ENGINE CRANKS SLOWLY

Make certain that the viscosity of the engine oil also is correct for the prevailing temperature. If recent major repairs have been made, the engine may be tight.

Test the state of charge and condition of the battery. Replace or recharge the battery if necessary. If the battery is satisfactory and both ends of both cables are clean and tight, remove the cable from one side of the starter switch or relay, and contact the loose end of the cable against the terminal on the other side of the relay or starter switch. If cranking speed is now normal, replace the starter switch or relay. If confirmation of the fact that the switch relay is necessary, perform starter switch resistance test. (See "Starter Switch and Relay Tests," this chapter.)

If the cranking speed is still slow, check the condition of the wires and connections in the starting circuit. Replace wires or tighten connections as required. If the engine still cranks slowly, replace or repair the starting motor.

LIGHTS FLICKER OR DO NOT LIGHT

If all of the lights flicker from bright to very dim, the overload circuit breaker is operating as a result of a grounded or shorted wire in that particular circuit.

HEADLIGHT TEST

Turn on the headlights, and observe the reaction as you switch from high to low beam with the beam control switch. If the lights flicker when on low beam, the short is in that circuit. Likewise, the short is in the high beam circuit if the lights flicker on high beam.

UPPER BEAM FLICKERS. If the lights flicker only when the beam control switch is in the upper beam position, the short is in the upper beam circuit from the beam control switch to the headlights.

LOWER BEAM FLICKERS. If the lights flicker only when the beam control switch is in the lower beam position, the short is in the lower beam circuit from the beam control switch in the headlights.

BOTH BEAMS FLICKER. If the lights flicker in both high and low beam, set the headlight switch to the parking light position.

(1) *Lights Still Flicker.* If the parking lights flicker, a short exists in the tail light circuit.

(2) *Lights No Longer Flicker.* If the lights no longer flicker, a short exists between the headlight switch and the beam control switch.

LIGHTS DO NOT LIGHT

When one or several lights do not light and other lights do, usually the fault is in the bulb itself. Some light bulbs, of course, are easily replaced, while others are more difficult. The ease with which the particular bulb can be replaced determines the order of procedure. If the bulb is readily accessible, replace the bulb. If the new bulb still does not light, proceed as follows: If the bulb is difficult to replace, or if a new bulb was installed and still would not light, make sure the light is turned on. Then disconnect the wire nearest the bulb and momentarily ground it. If a spark occurs, proceed as follows:

SPARK OCCURS. If, when the wire is grounded, a spark occurs, the circuit up to that point can be dismissed from further consideration. Connect the wire and, unless this has already been done, replace the bulb at this time. Make sure the momentary shorting of the wire did not burn out the fuse. If the bulb still does not light, inspect the wiring that continues to the bulb from the point where it was momentarily grounded. Repair any broken or loose connections. If necessary, replace the bulb socket. Often the light fixture will be poorly grounded. Check for poor ground by using a jumper wire from the bulb socket to a good ground on the vehicle. If the bulb operates, clean the connections at the light fixture.

No Spark Occurs. If, when the wire was momentarily grounded, no spark occurred, an open circuit exists between the point that was grounded and the light switch.

LIGHTS BURN OUT REPEATEDLY

Lights burn out prematurely because of either high voltage or excessive vibration. The normal life of a bulb at a given voltage is shown in Table 2-2. Clean and tighten all electrical connections in the circuit involved, including the battery cable connections. Test the generator voltage regulator, and adjust or replace the regulator if required.

HORN MALFUNCTIONS

There are only two malfunctions of the horn; it does not sound or sounds continuously. In both cases, the owner may be the victim of vandalism, and you should always first check for those things which could have been caused deliberately before trying to trouble shoot the system.

DOES NOT SOUND

In cases where the horn does not sound, check to see if it has been disconnected by someone without the owner's

knowledge. The following procedure will eliminate this possibility from consideration:

Connect any wires that may have been disconnected at either the horn relay or at the bottom of the steering column. If the horn sounds when any of the wires are connected, follow the procedure outlined.

If a relay such as illustrated in Fig. 2-16 is used in the horn circuit, follow the steps of the procedure under the heading, "Relay." If the horn circuit you are working on does not have a relay, the circuit to ground is completed through the horn button or ring.

No Relay. If the horn does not sound when all of the wires are connected, press the horn ring or button. If the horn still does not sound, establish a good ground for the horn by means of a jumper wire. If the horn now sounds, the trouble is an open circuit in the horn button circuit (between the horn and ground).

If, in spite of these steps, the horn still does not sound, disconnect the main feed wire at the horn, and ground it momentarily. If no spark occurs, an open circuit exists between the end of the wire that was grounded and the battery. If a spark did occur as the wire was grounded, the circuit supplying current to the horn can be considered satisfactory. The trouble is within the horn itself.

Relay. Establish a good ground for the horn by means of a jumper wire. After grounding the horn with the jumper wire, press the horn ring or button. If the horn now sounds, the horn is not properly grounded. Remove the horn from its mounting bracket, and clean away rust or paint to assure a good ground.

If, in spite of the above steps, the horn still does not sound, disconnect the main feed wire at the horn relay, and ground it momentarily. Note whether or not a spark occurs as the wire is grounded. If no spark occurs, an open circuit exists between the end of the wire that was grounded and the battery. Make the necessary repairs to the circuit.

If a spark occurs when the feed wire is grounded, the circuit supplying current to that point can be considered satisfactory. Touch the feed wire to the horn terminal of the relay. If the horn now sounds, replace the horn relay. If the horn still does not sound, connect a jumper wire from the main feed wire to the terminal of the horn. If the horn now sounds, an open circuit exists between the relay and the horn.

If, when the main feed wire was connected through a jumper directly to the horn, it did not sound, the fault is in the horn itself. Repair or replace the horn.

SOUNDS CONTINUOUSLY

When a horn starts to sound continuously, the immediate problem is to make it stop sounding, after which you can locate and correct the cause more leisurely.

As previously explained, two types of horn circuits are in common use. By knowing which type of circuit is employed, often you can locate the cause of the trouble as you stop the horn from sounding.

Since stopping a horn from sounding is usually in the nature of an emergency service with exasperated or embarrassed people standing around, it is important that you know exactly what to do and that you do it quickly. Have a screw driver and a pair of side cutters in your hand when you raise the hood.

No RELAY. If no relay is used in the circuit, the trouble is a short in the ground circuit. This circuit runs from the horn up through the steering column to the horn ring or button which, when pressed, completes the circuit to ground.

If a connector is used in the horn to

steering column wire (usually near the bottom of the steering column), disconnect at this connector. If the horn stops sounding, the short (to ground) exists in the steering column horn wire or in the horn button itself.

If the horn still sounds, disconnect the ground wire at the horn. If this stops the sounding, this wire is shorted. If not, the horn is grounded internally. Disconnect the main feed wire at the horn. This, of course, will always stop the horn from sounding. Tape the end of this wire so it will not discharge the battery or start a fire if it should contact ground.

RELAY. In horn circuits using a relay, as shown in Fig. 2-16, continuous sounding of the horn can be the result of a short to ground in the relay-to-horn button or stuck contact points in the relay.

If a connector is used in the horn-button circuit near the bottom of the steering colum, disconnect the wire at this point. If the horn stops sounding, a short exists in the steering column horn wire or in the horn button or ring.

If the horn continues to sound, dis-

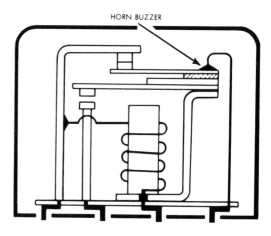

Fig. 2-26. Horn buzzer.

connect the horn-button wire at the relay. If this stops the sounding, the relay to steering column wire is grounded. If the horn still continues to sound, the relay contacts are stuck. Disconnect the main feed wire at the relay. This, of course, will stop the horn from sounding. Always wrap the end of the main feed wire with tape once it has been disconnected from the relay. This will remove the possibility of discharging the battery or starting a fire if this wire should become grounded.

Many cars are equipped with a buzzer warning system that sounds when a driver's door is opened with the key in the ignition switch. The buzzer is a modified horn relay as shown in Fig. 2-26. A typical wiring schematic is shown in Fig. 2-27. In cases where this system does not operate, check the door switch circuit for opens or a poor ground. The ignition key must be inserted fully for contact to take place in the switch. If the buzzer will not operate with a jumper from the number 4 terminal to ground and a supply jumper to the number 1 terminal, it is defective and should be replaced. Note that the relay-buzzer is an insulated device.

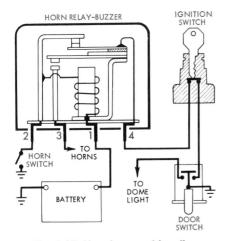

Fig. 2-27. Horn buzzer wiring diagram.

SERVICING ELECTRICAL SYSTEMS

As a part of the preceding trouble shooting procedures, a number of tests and adjustments in the electrical system are called for. In a number of instances, the same test or adjustment called for in one procedure is, likewise, called for in other trouble shooting procedures. To avoid the duplication which would result if these instructions were included in the trouble shooting procedures, these tests and adjustments are presented here. In some of these test or adjustment procedures, the method must be varied to suit the type of equipment available. These separate procedures are presented under descriptive subheadings under the general headings.

WIRING SYSTEM CHECK

A quick analysis of the entire electrical system to isolate the particular circuit causing trouble is made by determining if current is available at various points in the main circuit. Such an analysis is possible without leaving the driver's seat, and no equipment is required. Four operations and an observance of what occurs during each are involved as follows: (1) press horn button (momentarily); (2) turn starter switch (momentarily); (3) turn on ignition switch (15 seconds); (4) turn on headlights (momentarily).

Based on your observations of what happens during the above, the following analysis can be made:

HORN SOUNDS. If the horn sounds, the battery and the battery cables are O.K.

HORN DOES NOT SOUND. If the horn does not sound and all the other circuits operate satisfactorily, the trouble is in the horn circuit. (See "Horn Malfunctions," this chapter.)

STARTER ENGAGES. If the starter drive engages, the battery, cables, and starter switch or relay can be considered O.K.

STARTER DOES NOT ENGAGE. If the starter drive does not engage, but the horn sounds, follow the procedure in "Engine Does Not Crank."

INSTRUMENTS REGISTER. If the electrical instruments (except ammeter) register, the battery, cables, and the circuit to the overload circuit breaker or fuses, are O.K.

INSTRUMENTS DO NOT REGISTER. If none of the electrical instruments register and the lights do not light, the trouble is in the wire running from the starter switch or relay to the fuse or circuit breaker. If none of the instruments register but the lights light, the trouble is in the ignition switch or main feed wire to the instruments.

SOME INSTRUMENTS REGISTER. If some but not all of the electrical instruments register, follow the procedure for the faulty instrument in Chapter 8.

LIGHTS LIGHT. If the lights light, the battery, cables, and circuit breaker or fuse are all O.K.

LIGHTS DO NOT LIGHT. If the lights do not light, the battery cable is loose, the main feed wire is disconnected at the switch, or the wire is broken.

BATTERY STATE OF CHARGE TESTS

Battery failures are responsible for more road service calls than any other part or system in the vehicle. Battery state of charge can affect starting, lighting, and ignition, and the test of battery state of charge is called for in more trouble shooting procedures than any one other test.

Battery state of charge can be tested by means of a hydrometer (specific gravity) or by means of an open circuit voltage tester. Likewise high rate discharge testers can be used to determine the condition of a battery.

Aside from checking battery state of charge, several other things should be done when a battery is serviced.

(1) *Check Water Level.* Battery electrolyte should be checked and water added at 1,000 mile intervals or more often in hot weather. Remember, when servicing batteries, that the electrolyte is a strong solution of sulphuric acid which can damage wire or cable insulation and paint, can short out spark plugs, and can injure your eyes.

WARNING: Oxygen and hydrogen gases, which are a by-product of battery charging, are highly combustible. Don't permit smoking or an open flame near the vent openings of a battery that is being charged. An explosion might occur.

(2) *Clean Exterior.* As a part of battery service, battery acid can be neutralized and the battery and its cables can be cleaned with either ammonia or a soda solution (baking soda and water). After the foaming stops, flush off with clean water.

(2) *Tighten Cable Terminals.* Battery cable terminals should be clean and tight. A light film of petroleum jelly on the battery terminals will control corrosion. Battery hold-downs that are loose permit the battery to move around. If too tight, the battery case may crack.

Aside from the correction of an immediate trouble, the objective of battery service is to see that the customer obtains the maximum useful life from his battery. When the battery eventually approaches failure, the service should strive to predict the failure and replace the battery with a new one (fully charged) before a starting failure occurs.

In general, a battery should not be condemned as a result of a state of charge test. The usual practice is first to fully charge a battery; then to check its capacity before condemning it. Experience, however, has indicated that certain types of readings, particularly when a wide

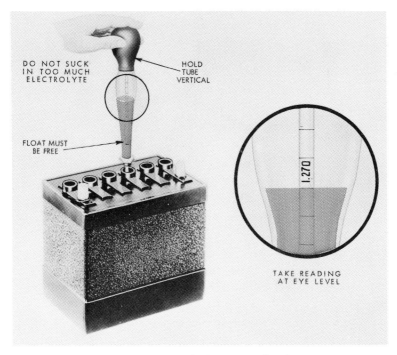

DO NOT SUCK
IN TOO MUCH
ELECTROLYTE

HOLD
TUBE
VERTICAL

FLOAT MUST
BE FREE

1.270

TAKE READING
AT EYE LEVEL

Fig. 2-28. Battery hydrometer and scale.

variation exists between cells, can be taken as an indication that the battery condition is bad (either interior shorts or loss of capacity).

SPECIFIC GRAVITY. When checking state of charge with a hydrometer (Fig. 2-28), never take the reading immediately after water has been added. At least a half hour of charging is necessary to mix the water with the electrolyte already in the battery. Moreover, specific gravity readings must be compensated for temperature.

Remove the battery vent plugs from the cells. Insert the rubber tube of the hydrometer through the opening into the electrolyte. Compress the bulb; then release until sufficient electrolyte is drawn into the hydrometer to cause the float to rise and float freely. Hold the hydrometer at eye level in a vertical position. Read the specific gravity on the scale of the float. Note the temperature of the electrolyte on the thermometer built into the hydrometer. This thermometer indicates the number of points that should be added to or subtracted from the specific gravity reading to compensate for the temperature of the battery.

Repeat this test for each cell. In general, readings of more than 1.250 are interpreted as a satisfactory state of charge. Variations of .050 points among the cells might indicate trouble in the low cell. If in doubt make a capacity test of the battery.

Specific gravities below 1.225 indicate the battery is low in charge and should be recharged before you arrive at any conclusion as to its suitability.

OPEN CIRCUIT VOLTAGE. The open circuit voltage ascertains the state of charge of a battery by measuring the voltage of the cells on open circuit (no current

Fig. 2-29. Cell tester for solid top batteries.

flowing). Fig. 2-29 illustrates a typical cell voltage tester. An expanded scale voltmeter is a voltmeter that either does not start at zero or one that starts at zero but has graduations that are closely spaced in the ranges where the voltmeter is not used and are expanded or stretched out in the range where it is useful. Usually these expanded scale voltmeters are graduated to $\frac{1}{100}$ of a volt and can be read to one-half this amount.

Some lack of uniformity exists among the various battery manufacturers as to just how far an open circuit voltage reading can be used to judge the internal faults of the battery. Some battery manufacturers use a 0.05 (five one-hundredths) of a volt variation between cells as indication that the battery is worn out and should be replaced. Others maintain that a battery should not be condemned in any instance until it has first been fully charged and then retested.

(1) *Surface Charge.* When a car comes in off the road, generally the car generator will have been charging the battery, and the voltage of the individual cells will be abnormally high due to what is termed a "surface charge." Some battery manufacturers have included in their recommendations for the use of the open circuit battery tester instructions to turn on the headlights for a definite period of time to dissipate this surface charge before the reading is taken. This reading can then be accurately used to judge the state of charge of the battery.

(2) *How to Make the Test.* The open circuit voltage is measured by placing the voltmeter probes into the filler openings of the cells. Start with the cell nearest to the positive terminal and proceed across the battery. Make sure the positive (+) probe is to the positive terminal. In most testers, the positive probe is painted red or the wire running to it is red. If the tester you are using indicates the time the headlights should be left on, turn on the

lights for that length of time before taking the reading. Battery cells with a voltage between 1.95 and 2.15 are fully charged. Voltages between 1.95 and 2.05 indicate a state of partial discharge. Readings below 1.95 volts indicate the battery charge is dangerously low and should be recharged. Batteries in good condition and fully charged will show little, if any, difference in cell voltages. Differences in cell voltages of 0.05 volt indicate probable trouble in the low reading cell. Such batteries should be recharged and given a capacity test as outlined in the next two sections.

CHARGING

Fast charging will safely charge batteries to 90 percent or more of full charge without damaging the battery, providing the temperature of the electrolyte is not permitted to exceed 125° F and violent gassing is avoided. Violent gassing can wash active material from the plates and lower the capacity of the battery.

NOTE: Every fast charge should be followed by at least 15 minutes of slow charging.

Before beginning either a slow charge or a fast charge, remove the battery filler caps and check the electrolyte level in the individual cells. If the electrolyte is less than ⅜ in. above the top of the plates, refill to that level with distilled water. One type of battery charger is shown in Fig. 2-30.

SLOW CHARGE. The slow charge is used when it is necessary to charge several batteries at one time and when the length of time required for the charging is not critical. A 12-volt battery with a specific gravity above 1.225 should be charged only by the slow charge method.

Connect the batteries in series, the charger positive (+) lead to the positive (+) terminal of one battery and the

Fig. 2-30. Portable battery charger. Sun Electric Co.

charger negative (−) lead to the negative (−) terminal of another battery. The intervening batteries are connected positive to negative. Turn on the charger and adjust it to the rate recommended by the charging equipment manufacturer. Charge the batteries for a sufficient length of time to bring them to a state of full charge and test the battery for capacity. Check the electrolyte level after charging and refill if necessary.

FAST CHARGE. The fast charge method is used when it is necessary to bring a battery quickly up to full charge to prevent tying up the customer's vehicle for an excessive period. Generally the battery can be charged in less than an hour without removing it from the vehicle.

Connect the charger to the battery. Adjust the charging control until the current is approximately 30 amperes, the maximum for 12-volt batteries. Check the charging voltage. If it is higher than 8.5 volts for 6-volt batteries and 15.5 volts for 12-volt batteries, reduce charging current until the voltage drops below this figure. *NOTE: When the charger is equipped with automatic thermostatic control, place the thermostat (connected to one of the charger leads) in the center cell electrolyte. The thermostat will shut off the charger when the electrolyte temperature reaches 125° F (safe limit of temperature).*

If the charger is controlled by a time clock, set the timer for the amount of time needed to charge the battery.

Until you become experienced in using this type charger, set the time according to the following table:

Check the state of charge, and reset the charger clock to the estimated time required to fully charge the battery. Test the battery (capacity after charge), and check the electrolyte level. Refill with distilled water if necessary.

BATTERY CAPACITY TEST

The battery capacity test or high-rate discharge test indicates the internal condition of the battery. The test is only conclusive if the battery is fully charged at the beginning of the test.

The test is made by discharging the battery at a rate approximately equal to the current drawn by the starter under load (approximately 180 amperes) and measuring the terminal voltage of the battery under this load.

NOTE: Most battery test equipment has the scale calibrated to show "good," "fair," and "worn out." Usually these scale readings are colored green, yellow, and red respectively to indicate battery condition.

Most testers provide a means of varying the discharge rate to suit batteries of different sizes. Some equipment provides a setting for each type of battery based on rated capacity. Others base the setting on the number of plates per cell. Still others further distinguish between plates and use a different setting for "high" or "low" plates. Each type of equipment carries full instructions in abbreviated form on the test panel.

Connect the heavy test clamps to the proper terminals of the battery. Adjust the tester to the ampere hour rating of the battery and read the battery condition on the scale. If the meter needle points to "good" (green portion) and holds steady, the battery capacity is satisfactory. If the needle will not hold steady in the green range and drops rapidly into the "fair" (yellow scale) range, or will not reach the green range, the battery condition is unsatisfactory. Early failure can be predicted (on the first cold morning for instance). If the needle points to "worn out" (red scale), the battery must be replaced.

A discharge rate of three times the amp-hour rating of the battery for 15 seconds is commonly used. If the voltage of the battery after 15 seconds is 9.6 volts or less, the battery is not dependable.

GENERATOR CIRCUIT RESISTANCE TEST

The difference between battery voltage and generator voltage, divided by the resistance of the generator circuit, establishes the charging rate of the battery. Voltage limiters, current limiters, and the speed of the generator, of course, are likewise limiting factors. Nevertheless, if the generator is being run at the speed at which it develops maximum charge, the generator voltage, less the battery voltage, divided by the resistance, establishes the charging rate.

Usually the generator circuit involves about 8 or 10 feet of No. 10 wire which has a resistance of 0.001 ohm per foot or a total resistance of from 0.008 to 0.010 ohm. The circuit includes the battery cables, the generator ground, and the cutout. Normally the total resistance of all of these units amounts to not more than about 0.025 ohm in most vehicles.

To measure accurately the resistance of any portion of the circuit, an ammeter of a range that permits reading the maximum output of the generator and a voltmeter graduated in hundredths of a volt are required. Normally none of the voltages involved will exceed 0.5 volt, so a one-volt meter will be ample.

Connect the ammeter in series at the generator armature terminal. (Where the cutout is mounted directly on the generator, connect the ammeter in series at the battery terminal of the cutout.) Start the engine, and increase the speed until a reading is obtained on the ammeter. Then connect the voltmeter parallel to the circuit from the generator armature terminal or armature brush to the hot side of the battery. Disconnect the voltmeter before you stop the engine.

Divide the voltage reading by the amperage reading to find the resistance of the circuits.

EXAMPLE: If the voltage reading is 0.4 volt at the time the amperage reading is 32, divide the voltage by the amperage.

$$\frac{0.4}{32} = \frac{0.1}{8} = 0.012 \text{ ohm}$$

The resistance of any portion of the circuit, including battery-to-ground and ground-to-generator, can be determined in this manner by connecting the voltmeter parallel to the portion of the circuit desired.

The most common point of high resistance is the battery ground. The second most common point of high resistance is the regulator. Similarly poor bonding or grounding of the engine to the frame is a common point of trouble.

GENERATOR OUTPUT TEST

First, determine the type of generator you are testing. Then turn to the heading that follows which describes that type of generator. The tests are all made with the generator mounted in the vehicle. In each case, the generator should produce rated wattage (amperes times volts) or slightly more. If not, check to locate the seat of the trouble within the generator.

Most 12-volt generators should charge at a 30-ampere rate and 6-volt generators at a 45-50 ampere rate.

FIELD GROUNDED EXTERNALLY. Disconnect the armature and field wires. Connect a grounded jumper to the field terminal. Start the engine, and let it idle. Connect a 0–50 ammeter (0–100 amperes if generator is rated at more than 50 amperes) to the generator and battery as shown in Fig. 2-31. Increase engine speed to 1,500 rpm (or specified speed), and observe the ammeter reading.

Slow the engine to idle speed; disconnect the ammeter immediately; then stop the engine. Remove test leads, and reconnect the generator wire.

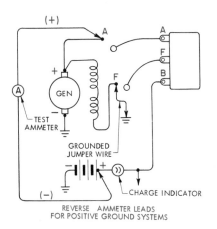

Fig. 2-31. Meter connections for testing output of generator.

FIELD GROUNDED INTERNALLY. Disconnect the armature and field wires. Connect a jumper wire from the generator armature terminal to the field terminal. Start the engine, and let it idle. Connect a 0–50 ammeter (0–100 amperes if generator is rated at more than 50 amperes) to the generator and battery as shown in Fig. 2-32. Increase engine speed, and observe the ammeter reading.

Slow the engine to idle speed; disconnect the ammeter immediately; then stop the engine.

GENERATOR BENCH TESTS. Generally generator test stands consist of some means of driving the generator plus the same instruments used in the preceding tests.

Most generator test stands are also generator regulator testers. However, insofar as the generator itself is concerned, all test stands fall into one of the following classifications: variable speed or constant speed.

(1) *Variable Speed.* In the variable speed generator test stand, a variable speed motor or a mechanical means of varying the generator speed is provided. This type of test stand permits checking performance at high speeds and permits tests to see if the armature coils will pull out of the armature slots due to centrifugal action at high speeds. In some cases, the test is made at as much as 8,000 rpm. Such tests always create the possibility that a satisfactory armature may be damaged by the test since the test is made at speeds never or rarely reached in normal use. Even though the armature meets the test, there is always the possibility that the centrifugal pull on the wires may have loosened the soldered connections at the commutator.

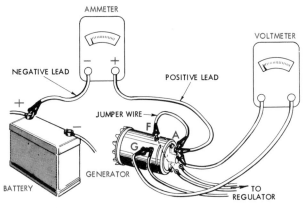

Fig. 2-32. Testing generator output for an internally grounded type.

The variable speed generator test stand is ideal for laboratory or instructional purposes since armature reaction and other things affected by speed can be studied or demonstrated.

(2) *Constant Speed*. Generally constant speed generator test stands are provided with a means of varying the generator field current. This permits the full speed range from zero to the speed at which the generator is driven to be simulated by adjustment of an external field rheostat. Such test stands use a single speed, AC motor to drive the generator.

GENERATOR REGULATOR TESTS

The following test procedures take into account different types of regulators. You may infrequently encounter variations of these regulators in the field. However, you can adapt one of these tests to suit the regulator, which differs from the average.

The separate equipment you will need to make all of the adjustments and tests presented here is a 0–50 ammeter, a 0–100 ammeter, a 0–10 voltmeter, a 0–50 ohm variable resistor (2 ampere rating), a ¾ ohm fixed resistor for six-volt systems and a 1.5 ohm fixed resistor for 12-volt systeams (15 ampere rating), a heavy-duty carbon pile variable resistor, and assorted connecting wires and test leads equipped with suitable connectors.

The test meters you use for checking regulators must be accurate instruments. Voltmeters must be accurate within 1 percent (0.1 volt) and ammeters within 2 percent (1 ampere) to be able to check and adjust regulator units to manufacturer's specifications. Handle your test meters with care and have them calibrated at least once a year against a standard voltmeter and ammeter.

Three-Unit Regulator. The three-unit generator regulator used with the two-brush generator is a widely used means of controlling generator output. It consists of a cutout, a voltage limiter, and a current limiter. It is important that you understand a few things about the operation of these devices before you attempt to test or adjust them.

The design of the various makes of three-unit regulators is changing constantly as engineers and service men attempt to solve field problems. Likewise factory instructions on testing and adjusting are often changed. In view of these things, it is well to go back to fundamentals and learn some of the general principles involved so that what you do is correct and will conform with any procedure soundly conceived.

Some of the testing and adjusting procedures are based on the availability of a specific combination of testing instruments that have been approved by the vehicle or regulator manufacturer. This equipment varies considerably in its completeness. All you have to have is: A voltmeter accurate to $\frac{1}{10}$ volt. This should be a 1.000 ohm per volt meter. The voltmeter range should be 50 percent greater than the rated voltage (12 volt: 18-volt voltmeter—24 volt: 36-volt voltmeter). A 0–50 ammeter accurate within one ampere. If you will be working on heavy-duty equipment, you will need ammeters that have a range of 50 percent greater than the rated amperage of the system and several jumper wires made up of No. 10 wire.

In the following test and adjusting instructions, the way these meters are connected and how the readings are interpreted are presented. Meter connections in a variety of battery generator circuits are illustrated, and these illustrations are referred to in the instructions. These illustrations show rheostats and resistors which have been introduced into the circuits. If you do not have these devices available, just ignore the fact that they appear in the illustration. The instructions presented here tell you how to make the tests with the meters and tell you what to do if you do not have this additional equipment as well as how the procedure is varied in case you do have it.

(1) *Cutout.* In the satisfactory operation of a generator cutout, the contacts must close at a definite voltage. They must open when the generator voltage drops below battery voltage, and the contacts must offer a minimum of resistance to the flow of current.

All cutouts are basically the same. Generally cutouts used with any type of voltage limiter are the same as the simple cutout used alone, except that in many regulators a means of temperature compensation is provided. Where the cutout used alone could be designed to close at any point from slightly over battery voltage to as much as 17 volts, the cutout used with a regulator must (at all temperatures) close at a voltage lower than the regulated voltage of the generator. Otherwise, the regulator would start to regulate first and the cutout would not close.

Since most regulators are located away from the generator, frequently the ground or return path back to the generator is a source of trouble. If the cutout shunt (voltage) coil is not grounded, the cutout will not close. Being grounded to the body or frame is not enough. The ground must be to the generator ground. Many vehicles provide a separate ground wire from the regulator to the generator frame.

Where a separate ground wire is not used, usually this return path is through the regulator mounting screws. From the mounting surface, it must flow to the generator but since engines and bodies usually are mounted on rubber a good path

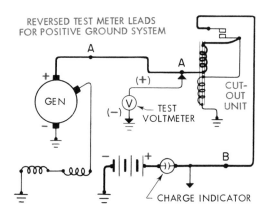

Fig. 2-33. Meter connections for testing closing voltage of the cutout.

is not provided. In many instances, the only ground is through the choke and throttle controls.

With a given cutout, the lower the cutout closing voltage the less tension on the cutout armature and the less positive the opening of the contacts.

(a) *Closing.* Connect a voltmeter from the generator or cutout armature terminal to ground (Fig. 2-33). If no armature terminal is provided or if the cutout is mounted directly on the generator so the armature terminal is not accessible, connect the voltmeter direcly to the armature brush. If a reading is obtained when this connection is made, the cutout points are closed when they should be open. This will cause the battery to run down.

Start the engine and observe the voltmeter while you gradually increase the speed of the engine. When the cutout points close, the voltage will drop back slightly. The highest reading just before the voltage dropped back is the cutout closing voltage.

In some test equipment, a field rheostat is provided. If you are using such equipment, remove the field lead at the regulator and connect the rheostat to the generator field and to the regulator field lead. In this case, the generator or engine speed is set at the speed of generator maximum output, and the output is controlled by adjusting the rheostat instead of varying the speed. If you have installed a rheostat in the field circuit, merely increase the field resistance where these instructions say to lower the engine speed. Where the instructions say increase speed, merely back off the rheostat, reducing the field circuit resistance.

Lower the generator speed until the voltage reading suddenly increases. This will indicate that the cutout contacts have opened. It is a good plan to repeat the test cycle several times to make sure that the cutout both opens and closes consistently. Generally this is the only cutout test required.

A variation of this test is made by disconnecting the battery wire from the cutout and installing a 1.5 ohm resistance from the cutout to ground. In this case, the counter emf (voltage) of the battery is eliminated and a more easily indication of cutout closing and opening voltage is obtained.

(b) Adjustment. Generally single-unit cutouts are sealed and often can be replaced more economically than adjusted. Most other cutouts can be adjusted. Some have replaceable contacts. Those that do not have replaceable contacts will have to be replaced as a unit if the contacts are badly burned.

Regardless of the cutout design, if the contacts show high resistance or if the closing voltage is incorrect, the cover must be removed to service them. Examine the contacts. If they are burned on one side, realign them by bending the parts controlling the alignment. If the contacts are burned or oxidized, either replace or dress and clean them. It is considered good practice to replace the generator regulator rather than attempt to clean oxidized points.

In all types, the cutout closing voltage

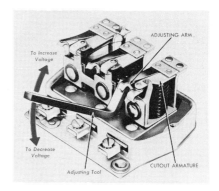

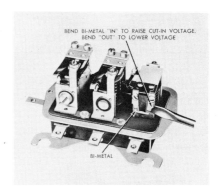

Fig. 2-34. Adjusting closing voltage in two types of cutout relays. Ford Motor Co.

is adjusted upward by increasing the spring tension on the contacts. Cutout closing voltage is reduced by decreasing the tension. Tension on the cutout contacts is accomplished in a number of ways. Some have small coil springs; others use flat springs. In most cases, with either type, a bendable part is provided that controls the tension. By bending this part to increase the tension, you will be increasing the closing voltage. Adjustments, of course, are made with the testing hookup intact so that you can check what you are doing. Fig. 2-34 shows how the adjustment is accomplished in two different cutouts, both employing flat springs for tension.

(c) Reverse Current Test. The previous test indicates the voltage at which the cutout closes and assures its opening.

However, in some types of operation where much idling of the engine is involved, the amperage that flows from the battery to the generator before the cutout opens is also a consideration. Door-to-door delivery units with a too slow idling speed and chauffeur driven cars that may wait at the curb for long periods with the engine running fall in this category.

Generally cutouts will open with three or four amperes of reverse current. Eight amperes are considered excessive. To measure reverse current, an ammeter must be installed in the charging circuit.

Since, during the opening and closing cycle of the cutout points, the direction of the current reverses, the ammeter must be installed so that it reads less than zero when the generator is charging. Then, as the engine speed is further reduced to the point where generator voltage is less than battery voltage, a reading will be obtained just before the points open. Continue to reduce the generator speed until the ammeter reading falls back to zero. This will occur when the points open. The last or highest reading obtained before the points open is the cutout reverse current. Repair or replace the cutout if the reading is eight amperes or more.

(2) Voltage Regulator. The voltage regulator, of course, does not control the generator voltage; it merely prevents it from exceeding the voltage to which the regulator is adjusted. Up to the voltage setting of the regulator, the voltage of the generator is controlled by the generator speed and the connected load. If the battery is discharged so that it will accept a large amount of current or if the connected electrical load is heavy, the generator voltage will be lower.

As the voltage regulator windings become heated, their resistance increases. This means that a higher voltage is required to open the contacts, and the voltage is then limited at a higher point. At the same time, the voltage of the heated battery is low so it provides a smaller counter emf to the generator. This combination of circumstances can permit considerable current to go into the battery after the battery is already fully charged.

The average resistance of a generating circuit is in the neighborhood of 0.025 ohm. The effective voltage of the circuit is equal to the generator voltage less the battery voltage. For each 0.1 volt difference, the generator will put 4 amperes of current into the battery. Thus, in a normal circuit, a 1.0 volt difference would provide a charging rate of 40 amperes. A 0.7 volt difference would provide a charging rate of 28 amperes.

When a battery is being charged at a high rate, the electrons are being pushed into the negative plates faster than the chemical processes of the battery can accept them. Likewise, electrons are taken from the positive plates faster than the chemical processes can provide them. This results temporarily in an abnormally high voltage, referred to as surface charge. To fully charge the battery, the voltage of the generator must be greater than this voltage.

To check voltage regulation with a minimum of equipment: (1) The regulator temperature should be normal. (2) The battery should be fully charged. (3) The generator must be in good condition. (4) The circuit resistance must not be excessive. (5) The generator must be driven at the speed at which maximum output is normally developed.

(a) Temperature. If the vehicle comes in off the highway, it can be assumed that its temperature is normal. Generally one-half hour operation is considered as the time required for a regulator to reach normal temperature. Some test equipment is designed to heat regulators before testing.

(b) Battery Charge. The voltage regulator is designed to reduce the field current and thereby reduce the generator voltage when full charge of the battery is reached. In order to make the voltage regulator work during a test where the battery is not fully charged, it may be necessary to install a rheostat in series with the battery or a fixed resistance (¾ ohm for 6-volt system, 1.5 ohm for 12-volt system) in place of the battery. Most test equipment has either one or the other or both of these devices built into them. If the battery is fully charged, neither of them is required. So, by charging the battery before testing voltage regulation, no equipment other than a voltmeter is required.

(c) Generator Condition. In order to test the regulator, it is necessary that the generator be able to attain the output to which it is to be regulated.

(d) Circuit Resistance. As previously mentioned, normally the resistance of the generator-battery circuit is 0.025 ohm or less. If, when testing or adjusting the regulator, an element of doubt exists as to the resistance of the circuit, two courses are open. Test and, if necessary, eliminate any points of excessive resistance before proceeding with the regulator test, or install parallel paths to both the ground and "hot" sides of the circuit.

(e) Speed. Starting from zero speed and zero output, the output of all generators increases. In the instructions presented here, an engine speed of 1,500 rpm is specified. However, some variation exists among generators. Where the test point for the particular generator is at some other speed, substitute that specified speed for the 1,500 rpm given.

When testing the generator or regulator on the vehicle, the engine speed can be varied to suit the generator. On generator and generator regulator test stands, the speed is varied by means of a variable speed motor or by means of a mechanically variable drive. Other test stands have a constant speed motor that will drive the generator fast enough to assure maximum output. On these machines, make sure the field rheostat is not connected.

(a) Testing. Connect a voltmeter into the armature-to-regulator circuit as shown in Figs. 2-35 and 2-36. If you are going to check the current limiter next, connect a 0–50 ammeter between the cutout and the battery as shown in the illustrations. These same illustrations show where a field rheostat, 1½ ohm resistor, and a carbon pile rheostat are installed.

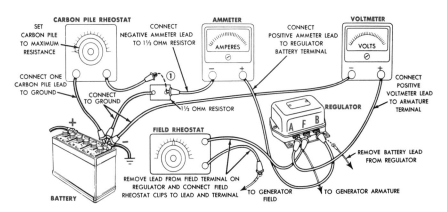

Fig. 2-35. Complete hook-up for checking regulator for internally grounded regulator.

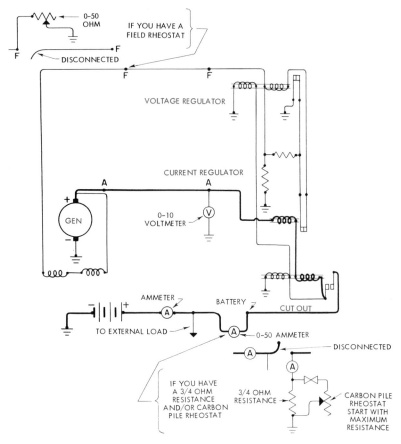

Fig. 2-36. Diagram for checking regulator for externally grounded generator.

If a field rheostat was installed for testing the cutout, it must be taken out of the circuit at this time and the field wire reconnected to the regulator.

Run the engine or generator at the speed at which maximum output is reached, and read the point of voltage regulation. If you are not using a $1\frac{1}{2}$ ohm resistance and if the battery is fully charged, the voltage will rise rapidly to the point of regulation also. If, however, the battery is discharged, you will have to introduce resistance into the circuit or fast charge the battery.

Observe the voltage at which the generator is being regulated. If you have the manufacturer's specifications, check your findings against these. If you do not have the manufacturer's specifications, a low limit of 14.8 volts and a high limit of 15.6 volts can be followed safely.

(b) Adjustment. As was true of the cutout closing voltage, voltage regulation is controlled by the spring tension on the contacts. This tension is adjustable in all regulators.

If any of the units of the regulator are at fault, it is necessary to remove the cover to service them. Once the cover is removed, examine all of the contacts. Realign them if they are contacting on one side. If they are burned or oxidized, the regulator must be replaced.

With the test circuit the same as out-

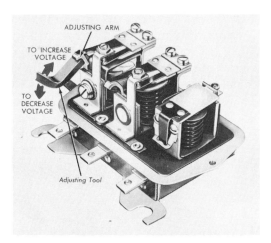

Fig. 2-37. Adjusting a voltage limiter. Ford Motor Co.

lined in the testing instructions, repeat the test. While the regulator is operating, increase the contact spring tension to increase the setting. Fig. 2-37 shows the bending arm being bent to change the voltage regulation point in one type of regulator.

(3) Current Limiter. The current limiter unit reduces the generator field current when the generator amperage reaches a pre-determined value. Since it is the nature of a two-brush generator to increase its output as its speed is increased, these generators will burn themselves out without regulation. Normally, the counter emf (voltage) of the battery establishes the generator voltage somewhere near the point of voltage regulation.

Where the battery is badly discharged, or where the connected electrical load is particularly heavy, the circuit voltage is lowered. Under these circumstances, the wattage produced can be enough to burn out the generator even though the voltage does not reach the point of voltage regulation. Three-unit regulators have a current sensitive vibrator, the contacts of which are in series with the voltage sensitive contacts of the voltage regulator.

Likewise most of the factors in testing and adjusting the voltage regulator are factors affecting the current limiter.

An ammeter (0–50 amps), of course, is required. The ammeter is installed as shown in Figs. 2-35 and 2-36. Unless the battery is badly discharged at the time of the test, it will be necessary to place a load on the circuit in order to make the current limiter operate. Of course, the current limiter, rather than the voltage regulator, must be working in order to determine its setting.

(a) Testing. Install a 0–50 ammeter in the circuit as shown in Figs. 2-35 and 2-36. If you have a carbon pile rheostat, connect it as shown. With the engine or generator running at the speed at which maximum output is reached, place a load on the circuit and observe the amperage. If the reading is low, continue to increase the load so long as the amperage increases. When you reach the maximum amperage, this is the current limiter setting.

If you have a heavy-duty carbon pile rheostat, connect it as shown in Figs. 2-35 and 2-36. This will permit you to adjust the load and, connected to ground as shown, eliminates the battery.

To apply the load, start gradually. If too great a load is placed on the circuit, since in this case there is no battery counter emf, the circuit voltage may drop so low that the field current is reduced. In this case, the generator output is reduced, and the current limiter will remain inoperative.

If you do not have a carbon pile rheostat, a load is imposed on the circuit by turning on the headlights and accessories to hold down the voltage.

If you know the manufacturer's specifications for current limiter setting, work to them. If not, but you know the generator rating in watts, divide the wattage by 7 or 14, as the case may be, and work to this amperage.

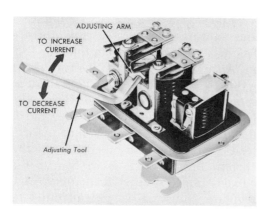

Fig. 2-38. Adjusting a current limiter. Ford Motor Company.

EXAMPLE: generator of 220 watts

$$\frac{220}{7} = 31 \text{ amperes or}$$

$$\frac{220}{14} = 15.7 \text{ amperes}$$

(b) Adjustment. If the current limiter is faulty, it is necessary, of course, to remove the cover to service it. If the contacts are mis-aligned, burned, or oxidized, replace the regulator.

Repeat the test procedure. During the test, increase the current limiter contact spring tension to raise the setting. Decrease the tension to lower the setting. Fig. 2-38 shows how the current limiter adjustment is made in one design.

ALTERNATOR SYSTEM TESTING

Because of the difference between alternator circuits and generator circuits, it is necessary to follow a completely different approach when alternator system complaints are encountered.

Basically, the various alternator circuits are identical, but manufacturers

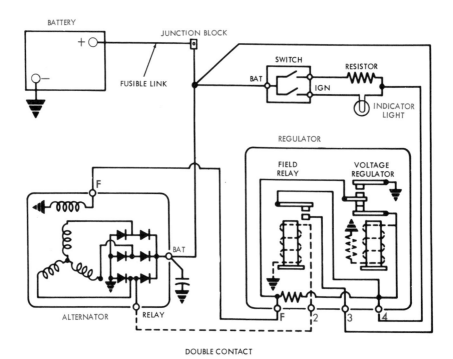

Fig. 2-39. An alternator voltage regulator.

design their components so that at first glance they appear to be different from the others. As an example, one company uses a regulator which has the terminals marked I, A+, S, F, while another uses F, 2, 3, 4. If you study the circuits

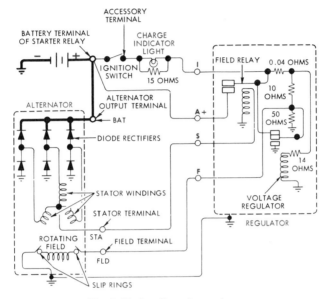

Fig. 2-40. An alternator system.

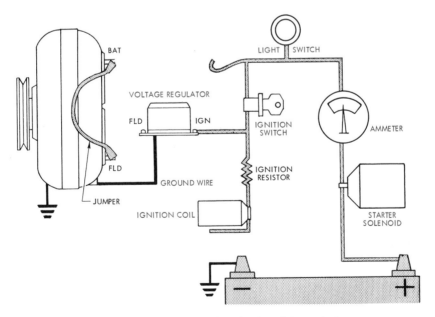

Fig. 2-41. Alternator charging circuit resistance test.

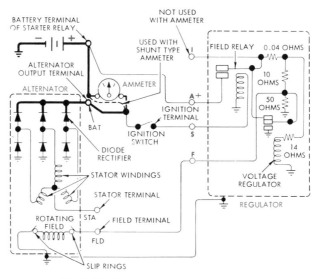

Fig. 2-42. Alternator charging circuit.

carefully, it becomes apparent that these designations are identical, but not interchangeable, except for the terminal names. Figs. 2-39 and 2-40 show two different circuits. Note that the stator and relay terminals are the same source. The I and 4 terminal is the indicator light terminal. The A+ and 3 terminal are "hot" at all times. One other manufacturer uses a slightly different arrangement as shown in Fig. 2-41. The basic circuit is the same but no field relay is used. These vehicles use a special ignition switch to energize the rotor (field) instead of a field relay.

Another difference is found between an ammeter equipped circuit and one which uses the indicator light only. Note this difference in Fig. 2-42. With these basics understood thoroughly, the procedures described will provide quick, accurate information about the various system components.

EQUIPMENT NEEDED. A voltmeter, ammeter, and carbon pile rheostat are necessary along with some jumper wires and a special battery post adapter such as the one shown in Fig. 2-43.

If this type of switch is not available, the ammeter can be inserted at the alternator output terminal.

Test Procedure: (1) Test battery, (2) Test alternator output, (3) Check circuit resistances, (4) Check regulator settings.

TEST BATTERY. As a first step in alternator trouble shooting, always check the

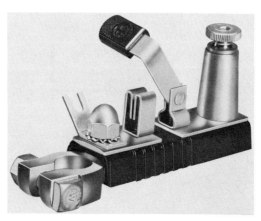

Fig. 2-43. Battery post adapter. Allen Electric Co.

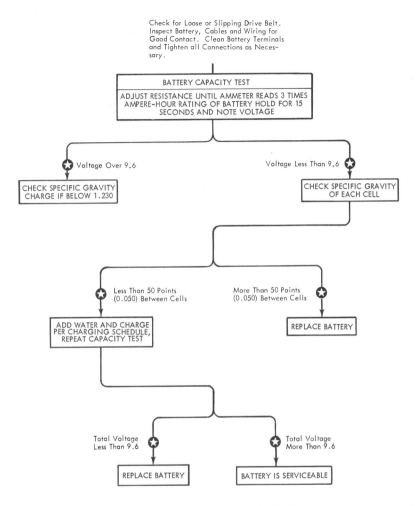

Check for Loose or Slipping Drive Belt. Inspect Battery, Cables and Wiring for Good Contact. Clean Battery Terminals and Tighten all Connections as Necessary.

BATTERY CAPACITY TEST
ADJUST RESISTANCE UNTIL AMMETER READS 3 TIMES AMPERE-HOUR RATING OF BATTERY HOLD FOR 15 SECONDS AND NOTE VOLTAGE

Voltage Over 9.6

Voltage Less Than 9.6

CHECK SPECIFIC GRAVITY CHARGE IF BELOW 1.230

CHECK SPECIFIC GRAVITY OF EACH CELL

Less Than 50 Points (0.050) Between Cells

More Than 50 Points (0.050) Between Cells

ADD WATER AND CHARGE PER CHARGING SCHEDULE, REPEAT CAPACITY TEST

REPLACE BATTERY

Total Voltage Less Than 9.6

Total Voltage More Than 9.6

REPLACE BATTERY

BATTERY IS SERVICEABLE

If The Owner Has Had Previous Difficulty With The Battery Running Down and Past History Does Not Indicate That The Problem is Due to Excessive Night Driving, Excessive Use of Accessories, Short Trips or Extended Periods of Idle. Then it is Suggested That The Complete Charging System Be Checked.

Fig. 2-44. Battery test diagram.

battery specific gravity and capacity. See Fig. 2-44. A typical schedule for battery charging is shown in Fig. 2-45. If the battery is fully charged, the alternator system is operating properly. Battery low in charge requires that the battery be fully charged and further checks made. Instead of waiting for a fully charged battery, a substitute battery of proper voltage can be used. Some test equipment can simulate a fully charged battery by placing a $\frac{1}{4}$ ohm resistance in the ammeter circuit.

Check drive belt and all wiring for loose or corroded connections. Make a battery drain test to determine if there is an unwanted load discharging the battery. To check battery drain, connect a voltmeter between the battery terminal post and the cable. With all circuits off, the meter should read zero. If a reading

ALLOWABLE BATTERY HIGH RATE CHARGE TIME SCHEDULE

Specific Gravity Reading	Charge Rate Amperes	40	45	55	65	70	80
				HIGH RATE CHARGING TIME			
1.125* to 1.150	35	1 Hr.	1 Hr. 5 Min.	1 Hr. 20 Min.	1 Hr. 35 Min.	1 Hr. 40 Min.	1 Hr. 55 Min.
1.150 to 1.175	35	45 Min.	50 Min.	1 Hr. 5 Min.	1 Hr. 15 Min.	1 Hr. 20 Min.	1 Hr. 35 Min.
1.175 to 1.200	35	35 Min.	40 Min.	50 Min.	1 Hr.	1 Hr.	1 Hr. 10 Min.
1.200 to 1.225	35	25 Min.	30 Min.	35 Min.	40 Min.	45 Min.	50 Min.
Above 1.225	5	NOTE: Charge at low rate only (5 amps) until specific gravity reaches—1.260 at 80°F (Standard Battery), 1.250 at 80°F (Sta-Ful Battery)					

*If the specific gravity is below 1.125, use the indicated high-rate charge, then use a low rate of charge (5 amperes) until the specific gravity reaches: 1.260 at 80°F (Standard Battery), 1.250 at 80°F (Sta-Ful Battery)

Fig. 2-45. Battery charging rate tables.

is indicated, determine what is discharging the battery by disconnecting major circuits. *Caution:* an electric clock or transistorized regulator will always be on. These units must be isolated to perform the drain test. Fig. 2-46 illustrates the drain test. Notice that the voltmeter is connected in series for the check.

ALTERNATOR OUTPUT TEST. The alternator output is checked with the ammeter installed as shown in Fig. 2-47. If a field rheostat is not available, a short jumper can be used. The alternator output is checked by supplying battery voltage to the field terminal of the alternator. Usually the regulator connector can be used. The jumper should be connected from the A+ to F openings (or 3 to F). Always disconnect the regulator when checking output.

Operate engine at medium speed (1,500-2,000 rpm), and note the amperage of the alternator. Use the carbon pile rheostat to hold the voltage to its speci-

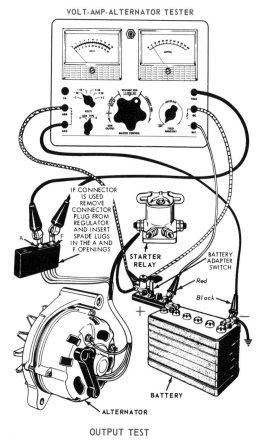

Fig. 2-47. Alternator output test.

VOLTMETER

Fig. 2-46. Battery drain test diagram.

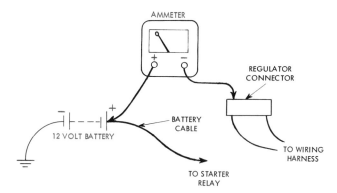

Fig. 2-48. Field current test connections.

fied value which normally will be 14 volts. Excessive, uncontrolled voltage can damage electrical components. Add 5 amps to this reading to account for field and ignition current. Compare this total output to specifications. If output is O.K., proceed to regulator tests and resistance checks. If output is 10 amps or less than rated output, the alternator is defective. If alternator fails the output test, an ammeter can be connected in series between the battery positive cable and the field opening at the regulator connector. See Fig. 2-48. This will determine if the rotor is open or shorted. A zero reading indicates an open field, while a higher than normal reading indicates a shorted field.

A defective alternator must be removed for bench tests or be exchanged for a rebuilt or new one if repairs are not possible. See bench test portion of this chapter.

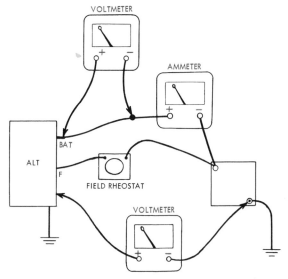

Fig. 2-49. Circuit resistance test connections. Upper voltmeter is insulated side. Lower voltmeter is grounded side.

CHECK CIRCUIT RESISTANCES. If the battery and alternator are O.K., the insulated and ground circuit resistances should be checked. Fig. 2-49 shows the connections for these tests. Usually the specifications will give a certain voltage drop with a certain amount of alternator output. A field rheostat can be used to control alternator output as shown in Fig. 2-49, or the lights and heater can be operated which will give approximately a 20-amp load for the alternator. Check

regulator can be checked. Connect the regulator and alternator. With the ammeter and voltmeter connected, operate the engine at medium speed. See Fig. 2-51. The amperage should be less than 5 amps with a fully charged battery. Note the voltage reading. Then turn on the headlights and heater and recheck the voltage reading. With the load of the lights, the regulator should be operating on its normal contacts. With low output (5 amps or less), the regulator is operating on its

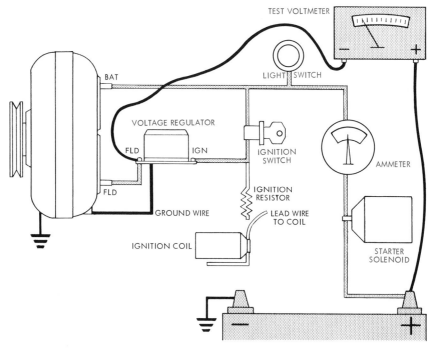

Fig. 2-50. Checking alternator field circuit resistance.

specifications to determine if the drops are excessive or not. If they are excessive, clean and tighten all appropriate connections. If there is no field relay, the field circuit resistance through the ignition switch and regulator can be checked also. This is shown in Fig. 2-50.

CHECK REGULATOR. If a defective component has not been discovered, the

"shorting" contacts. The difference between these two voltage readings should not be more than .7 volt. Fig. 2-52 shows the range of voltage settings and the ambient air temperatures. The voltage setting refers to the shorting contact operation since this will be the higher voltage.

If the regulator cannot be adjusted

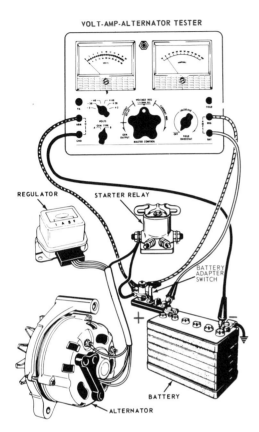

VOLT-AMP-ALTERNATOR TESTER

REGULATOR   STARTER RELAY

BATTERY ADAPTER SWITCH

ALTERNATOR

BATTERY

VOLTAGE LIMITER TEST

Fig. 2-51. Voltage limiter test.

Ambient Air Temperature °F	Voltage Regulator Setting (Volts)
25	14.4 – 15.0
50	14.3 – 14.9
75	14.1 – 14.7
100	13.9 – 14.5
125	13.8 – 14.4
150	13.6 – 14.2
175	13.5 – 14.1

Fig. 2-52. Voltage temperature range.

readily, most manufacturers require replacement as repairs are not to be attempted. Newer regulators are sealed, and the cover cannot be removed. Use your

good judgment as to your course of action.

Normally the field relay does not present any problem. However, it is possible to supply battery voltage to the field relay as indicated in Fig. 2-53. If the cover of the regulator can be removed, the field relay can be checked readily by merely observing if it closes when the ignition switch is turned on. If the relay closes, it is satisfactory.

The field circuit resistance test is made with a voltmeter.

To measure the resistance in the field circuit wiring, disconnect the ignition coil lead at the ballast resistor to prevent the flow of current in the ignition circuit and turn on the ignition switch. Use a voltmeter, and connect the positive lead to the positive battery post and the negative lead to the voltage regulator FIELD terminal. Rotate the voltmeter selector knob to low voltage, and read the meter.

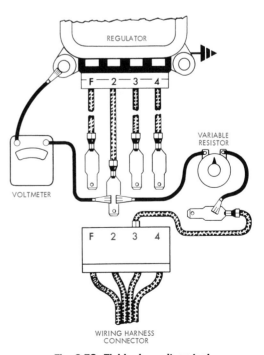

REGULATOR

F   2   3   4

VARIABLE RESISTOR

VOLTMETER

F   2   3   4

WIRING HARNESS CONNECTOR

Fig. 2-53. Field relay voltage test.

The voltage reading on the meter is the voltage drop of the field circuit between the battery and the regulator FIELD terminal. It should not exceed 0.3 volt. A voltage drop exceeding 0.3 volt indicates high resistance in the circuit. To locate the cause, move the negative voltmeter lead to each connection along the circuit toward the battery. A sudden drop in voltage indicates high resistance between that point and the last point tested. Clean and tighten all loose connections.

TRANSISTORIZED ALTERNATOR SYSTEM CHECKS. Two types of transistorized regulators are used. Some older cars and trucks will have a transistorized regulator similar to the unit shown in Fig. 2-54. Newer transistorized regulators are built into or attached to the alternator such as in Figs. 2-55 and 2-56.

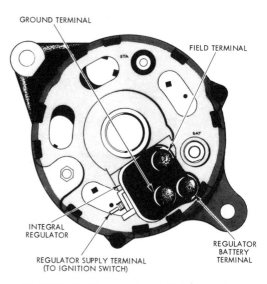

Fig. 2-55. An alternator transistorized regulator.

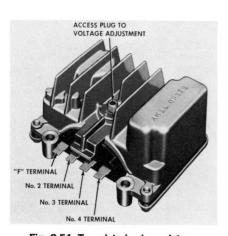

Fig. 2-54. Transistorized regulator.

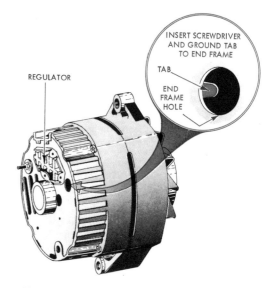

Fig. 2-56. Grounding a transistorized regulator.

The tests for these systems are much the same as the standard alternators. In particular, however, the alternator brush leads are insulated so that field current is grounded within the integral type regulator only. On these units, the field is externally grounded (type A). The output test does *not* use a jumper from battery to field. Instead, the field of the alternator is grounded as indicated in Fig. 2-56.

If the battery tests good and all connections are secured properly, the alternator output should be checked. With good output, the regulator is the source of

CONTACT HEAT SINK   CONTACT EACH TERMINAL

Fig. 2-57. Alternator diode test.

adjustment screw that will increase or decrease voltage by .3 volt. Maximum range is .6 volt. One final reminder is that the condition of the battery is the key to alternator system operation. Be absolutely certain about the condition of the battery. If the battery remains properly charged, there is no reason to suspect any charging system trouble.

ALTERNATOR BENCH TESTS

If the tests on the car indicate trouble internally with the alternator, it will be necessary to remove it from the car and disassemble it for further testing.

The stator coils and the rotor coils can be tested with a simple self-powered test lamp for both continuity and grounding or short circuiting. It is necessary to have a diode tester in order to test the diodes in the rectifier. Several good diode testers are available on the market. Whichever one is used, the hookup will be similar to that shown in Fig. 2-58. Follow the instructions for the diode tester you happen to be using.

In most instances, first the positive diodes, and then the negative diodes are tested. When two diodes are good and one is shorted, the reading taken at the good rectifiers will be low, and the reading taken at the shorted diode will be zero. When one rectifier is open, it will read approximately one ampere on the diode tester, and the two good diodes will read in the satisfactory range.

STARTER SWITCH AND RELAY TESTS

The circuits involved in the various types of starter switches are illustrated in Figs. 2-12 and 2-14. The normal tests of these switches and their remote control circuits are all covered under the trouble shooting procedures, "Engine Does Not Crank" and "Engine Cranks Slowly." Since no repairs generally are made on

trouble. Be certain that the supply voltage (Fig. 2-55) is present when the ignition switch is on. *Note:* The field is constantly "live" with a very small current. This small current flow will not discharge the battery over a long period since it is so small. The supply terminal fully energizes the regulator. No adjustments are possible on these regulators. They must be replaced if defective. The older type regulator shown in Fig. 2-54 does have a plug, which, when removed, exposes an these switches, and since the switches are inexpensive, these procedures merely locate the trouble in the switch and recommend their replacement. Where further confirmation of the need for replacement is required, the following test will prove the need.

Simple starter switches that are manually operated can have their contact surfaces burned so as to increase their resistance and in exceptional cases in some designs fail to make actual contact.

Remotely controlled relay types of starter switches can have these same troubles plus troubles in the remote control circuit or in the solenoid of the relay. While, as mentioned previously, it is unusual for a manually operated switch to fail to make actual contact, this trouble is more common with starter relays.

Tests of the starter switch or relay fall into two groups: those having to do with the starter switch itself in either the simple or relay type of switch and a second group having to do with the actuation of the relay. The tests in the trouble shooting procedure are all that are required of the remote control circuit. Likewise, open circuit in the starter switch is proven by the trouble shooting procedures.

Starter switches that have burned contacts will reduce the cranking speed and may be a factor in starting.

RESISTANCE. In normal warm weather, warm engine cranking amperage for a gasoline engine is about 150 amperes. At these amperages, a starter switch voltage drop of 0.1 volt (one-tenth), measured with an accurate voltmeter, would indicate a resistance of from 0.00062 (sixty-two hundred thousandths) ohm to 0.00058 ohm, which is not excessive. Actually, if the engine is cranking at a normal speed, a drop of 0.2 volt probably would be satisfactory. However, if the engine cranks slowly, observe the 0.1 volt

drop as the maximum permissible.

STARTING MOTOR TESTS

In the various trouble shooting procedures where the starting motor fails to run, the fault is either in the starting motor itself or in the unit which is preventing the starting motor from running. In these cases, either the starting motor runs or does not run. However, how efficiently the starting motor runs can be determined only by testing the starting motor itself.

CRANKING TEST. A cranking test is one in which the amperage draw of the starting motor is read while it is cranking the engine. It might be well to remember several things that apply specifically to starting motors and their circuits.

First, the resistance of the starting motor increases and the amperage decreases with speed. The faster the starting motor runs the less current it uses. Anything that slows the starting motor decreases the resistance and increases the amperage. In the previous test, it was pointed out that at idle amperage would be in the neighborhood of 60 amperes. This same starting motor, if held from turning (lock torque), would draw at least ten times this amount (600 amperes or more).

Second, the starting motor circuit has very little resistance (under some conditions as low as 0.01 ohm). The disturbing of the various connections and the placing of an ammeter or shunt in the circuit might double the resistance and reduce the amperage by half.

Two methods of testing under load that do not disturb the circuit are possible: the substitute load method described in Chapter 1 and the loop type ammeter described here. A third method involves the breaking of the circuit at one point and the installation of a shunt to which the meter is calibrated.

(1) Loop Ammeter. Ammeters operating on the same principles as the loop type ammeters used on the instrument panel of some cars are used to measure starter draw. These ammeters have from ten to fifteen times the capacity of the dash type meters and employ a spring type clip to hold the meter to the starter cable in place of the unbroken loop used on the dash units. The lines of force around the starter cable actuate the meter needle. The more the current (amperage) the greater the needle deflection.

Clip the meter to the starter cable, and observe the reading as the engine is cranked. This reading is the approximate cranking amperage.

(2) Remote Shunt. Some equipment manufacturers provide a meter shunt that is installed in series in the starter circuit. The meter is connected to the two ends of this shunt. Generally the shunt is calibrated to a particular meter, and the two must be together. This method eliminates the necessity of long leads capable of carrying the high amperage involved.

TRADE COMPETENCY TEST

1. What are the seven basic automotive circuits?
2. What are the three symptoms of generator trouble?
3. What are the advantages of using an alternator?
4. How is a generator "excited"?
5. Why is there no cutout in an alternator regulator?
6. What is the effect of reducing the resistance of lighting circuit?
7. Why do batteries become discharged?
8. What is one positive sign of a poor generator ground?
9. What are the causes of low generator output?
10. On a car equipped with an alternator, what is the first step in quick-charging the battery?
11. What is a hydrostatic lock?
12. What causes lights to burn out prematurely?
13. What is one sure way to shut off a horn?
14. What are the four steps of the "quick check of the wiring system"?
15. What is a surface charge?
16. What does a voltage "regulator" actually do?

CHAPTER 3

GASOLINE ENGINES

To the average owner, the automobile is divided chiefly into the steering mechanism, the braking mechanism, and the engine. If he has difficulty in steering, he attributes the trouble to the steering gear. If he hears a noise when he applies the brakes, he says the brakes are noisy. If the car runs sluggishly, he says the engine lacks power. Many things other than the engine itself could account for the lack of power. Just as a distorted rear axle housing could account for steering difficulty or loose steering connections be responsible for the noise when the brakes are applied, many things not usually associated with the engine could account for the apparent lack of power in the engine.

In the diagnosis and correction of engine troubles, often other units or systems closely associated with the engine are the seat of trouble that is brought to you as engine trouble. These are the ignition system, the fuel system, the starting system, and the cooling system, all of which are covered in other chapters. While many troubles are the result of faults in the engine itself, some troubles might have their source in one or more of the separate systems.

The trouble shooting procedures take gine speed governor, make sure that it

into account maladjustments and a wide variation in degree of deterioration. They are planned to provide for those things that can be anticipated logically. The thinking processes used in the procedures presented here will aid you in locating the cause of some of the things that logically should not occur.

POWER LOSS OR POOR ACCELERATION

Usually the causes of power loss, low top speed, or poor acceleration are the same, and generally the same procedure can be used for each. At least 90 percent of the time these troubles can be located by the quickly performed method explained under the heading "Simple Procedure." When it is apparent that the engine has been neglected, all of the factors of performance should be restored to normal. This is accomplished by an engine tune-up. (See "Tune Up," this chapter.)

Since lack of power, low top speed, or poor acceleration can be caused by any one or a combination of a wide variety of faults, usually the procedure is to determine quickly and correctly what work is to be performed so a repair order can be written. The simple procedure will accomplish this in at least 90 percent of

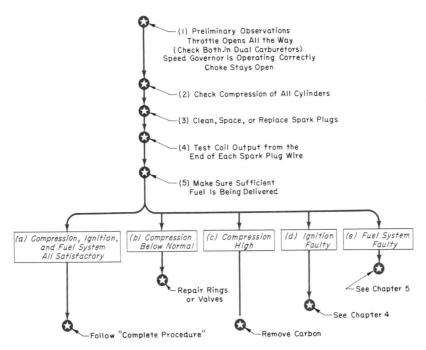

(1) Preliminary Observations
Throttle Opens All the Way
(Check Both in Dual Carburetors)
Speed Governor Is Operating Correctly
Choke Stays Open

(2) Check Compression of All Cylinders

(3) Clean, Space, or Replace Spark Plugs

(4) Test Coil Output from the
End of Each Spark Plug Wire

(5) Make Sure Sufficient
Fuel Is Being Delivered

(a) Compression, Ignition, and Fuel System All Satisfactory

(b) Compression Below Normal

(c) Compression High

(d) Ignition Faulty

(e) Fuel System Faulty

Repair Rings or Valves

See Chapter 5

See Chapter 4

Follow "Complete Procedure"

Remove Carbon

Fig. 3-1. Power loss or poor acceleration. Simple procedure.

the cases. You should also be familiar with the common contributing causes of this trouble.

SIMPLE PROCEDURE

Don't overlook the obvious. The correction of most troubles is simple if you are observant. The simple procedure for quickly locating the cause of lack of power, low top speed, or poor acceleration, illustrated in Fig. 3-1, requires some preliminary observations:

PRELIMINARY OBSERVATIONS. Make sure the throttle opens all the way when the accelerator pedal is pressed all the way down. Failure of the throttle to open fully may be all that is wrong. This is not uncommon and can result from tight, loose, or bent throttle linkage or throttle shaft, or bent butterfly valves. A twisted throttle shaft on dual carburetors would keep one throttle from opening fully.

If the engine is equipped with an en- is not restricting the engine at points below the governed speed. Likewise, a choke valve that does not open fully could account for this trouble. Four areas to check are:

(1) *Compression.* Check compression of all cylinders.

(2) *Spark Plugs.* Clean, space, or replace spark plugs.

(3) *Coil Output.* Test coil output from the end of each spark plug wire.

(4) *Fuel Supply.* Make sure sufficient fuel is being delivered to the carburetor, that there is no flooding, and that the mixture is not too lean.

CORRECTION. As a result of the last four operations, three of the following conditions will be found to exist: (1) compression below normal; (2) compression higher than normal; (3) ignition not satisfactory; (4) fuel system not functioning properly; (5) compression normal;

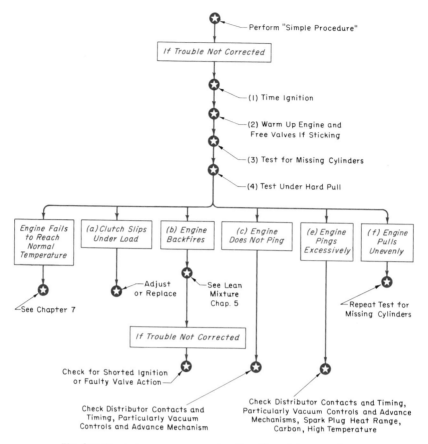

Fig. 3-2. Power loss or poor acceleration. Complete procedure.

(6) ignition satisfactory; and (7) fuel system functioning properly.

Determine which of these conditions is true for the engine being worked on, and proceed as follows, ignoring those paragraphs that do not apply.

(1) *Compression, Ignition, and Fuel System Satisfactory (Items 5, 6, and 7).* If compression is O.K. and the ignition and fuel systems are functioning properly, follow information under the heading, "Complete Procedure."

(2) *Compression Low.* If compression in one or more cylinders is found to be below normal, repeat the compression test after squirting oil on top of the pistons in the cylinders involved. If the compression is now normal, the trouble is blow-by past the rings. If, on the other hand, the oil fails to increase the compression, the trouble probably is in the valves. However, the pistons and rings may be in such a bad condition that the oil could not seal them.

(3) *Compression High.* If compression of a standard engine is higher than normal the condition can be accounted for only by the presence of carbon which will have to be removed from the combustion chamber.

(4) *Ignition Faulty.* If the ignition is unsatisfactory, the trouble lies in the ignition system. (See Chapter 4, "No Spark," "Spark At Some Wires," "Intermittent

Spark," and "Weak Spark.")

(5) *Fuel System Faulty*. If it is found that the fuel system is not right, see Chapter 5, *Gasoline Fuel Systems*, "Fuel Starvation," "Flooding," "Mixture Too Lean," and "Mixture Too Rich."

COMPLETE PROCEDURE. If the foregoing simple procedure has not located the cause of the trouble, proceed as follows (Fig. 3-2):

(1) *Check Ignition Timing*. Check and, if required, adjust the distributor contacts and reset the ignition timing.

(2) *Warm Up Engine*. Start the engine and allow it to idle until normal operating temperature is reached. If the valves are noisy, either the valve action is sluggish or the tappet-to-valve clearance or lash is too wide. Wide spacing changes valve timing which, of itself, could accoun valve timing which, of itself, could account for the trouble. With the engine idling, disconnect the air cleaner and slowly pour ¼ pint of light, gum-solvent oil into the carburetor throat. This same procedure should be followed if there is any evidence of sludge in the oil or if there are any indications of oil pumping or excessive carbon.

The engine speed will slow down as the oil is added. Don't pour the oil in so fast that the engine will stall. Usually this oil will free up the valve action at least temporarily and should reduce the valve noise. In addition, add gum solvent to the engine oil (replace the engine oil after 300 miles with a detergent oil).

(5) *Check for Lean Mixture*. If the foregoing inspections and tests do not locate the cause for lack of power, probably the trouble is a lean fuel mixture. (See "Mixture Too Lean" Chapter 5.) If the procedure in Chapter 5 does not correct the trouble, determine if any of the following causes apply.

OTHER CAUSES

Other conditions not provided for spe-

cifically in the foregoing procedures that can account for lack of power, lack of speed, and poor acceleration are shown in Fig. 3-3. All of these instructions are in addition to the various operations given in the "Simple Procedure" and in the "Complete Procedure."

COMMON AREAS OF TROUBLE. Practically everything on the car, truck, or tractor has an effect on power, speed, and acceleration. The more common contributing causes, all of which should be taken into account, are as follows:

(1) *Brakes and Tires*. Make sure that both the hand and service brakes are not dragging and that the tires are inflated to the specified pressure.

Make sure that the brake pedal has necessary free travel and that the brake master cylinder vent is not obstructed. If the vehicle is operated in mud or dust, the brake shoes may not be retracting properly. Clean and lubricate (sparingly) the points where unwanted friction might exist.

The owner may not have been releasing the hand brake fully, or some restriction of movement in either the shoes, band, or disk and the linkage, or the cable sticking in its conduit, may prevent complete release every time.

(2) *Exhaust*. Make sure the exhaust tail pipe has not been bent or plugged so as to cause restriction of the exhaust gases.

If it is suspected that there is excessive exhaust back pressure due to clogged muffler, sticking exhaust thermostat or heat control valve, clogged or bent tail pipe, etc., make a road test under load with the exhaust disconnected during the test. An intake manifold vacuum test would provide a clue to restricted exhaust if the restriction were serious enough to affect the engine idle. It is entirely possible, however, for a partial restriction to affect the engine idle. It is entirely possible, however, for a partial restriction to

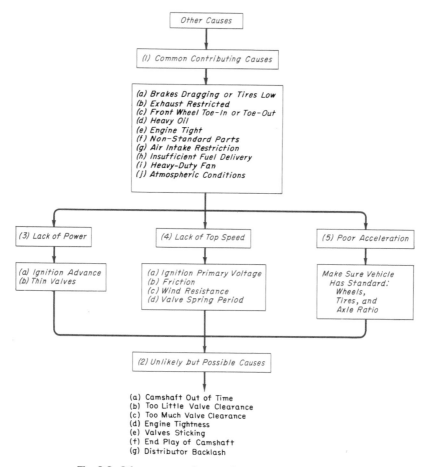

Fig. 3-3. Other causes of power loss or poor acceleration.

affect power under full load and yet not show up on the vacuum test.

NOTE: It is not uncommon for a vehicle to be backed into an embankment with the result that a nearly solid plug of mud or clay is forced into the exhaust tail pipe.

On engines with positive crankcase ventilation, clean the system if it is clogged.

If the engine is equipped with an exhaust thermostat, make sure it is not stuck in the closed position.

(3) Wheel Alignment. Observe the type of wear on the front tires to determine if the toe-in adjustment is incorrect.

Adjust the tie rod or rods, if the adjustment is incorrect. (See "Wheel Alignment," Chapter 9.)

(4) Oil. New engine oil or oil that is too heavy will noticeably reduce the power, top speed, and flexibility of the engine. Avoid changing oil unnecessarily. Don't change the oil just before making performance tests.

(5) Recent Repairs. If the engine has just received major repairs, it may be tight, and top speed and power will be reduced until the new parts are run in and normal working clearance have been established.

(6) Standard Equipment. Make sure the vehicle is equipped with the correct size tire, correct axle ratio, correct speedometer gear ratio, and the correct cylinder head.

(7) Air Cleaner. All types of intake air cleaners or silencers offer some restriction to incoming air, thus reducing the engine power. While in most cases the normal restriction is of little consequence, accumulations of dust and dirt or, in the case of the oil-bath-type air cleaner, too high an oil level will restrict the incoming air and reduce the engine power.

Improper assembly of some air cleaners will result in abnormally high restriction. Some air cleaners or silencers have a silencing pad that must be kept dry. If these pads are washed with the rest of the cleaner, they may sag and offer restriction.

Occasionally an air cleaner filter element, particularly when new, may shed some of the short hairs or fibers of which it is made. If these short hairs pass into the air stream and lodge in the carburetor, the fuel-air balance will be upset until the carburetor is cleaned.

Some carburetors do not provide a shoulder for the air cleaner to rest on and it is possible to push the cleaner too far onto the carburetor, reducing the air flow.

(8) Fuel Supply. Fuel supply that appears normal under no load conditions may be insufficient under maximum load. This could be accounted for by:

(a) Short Fuel Pump Stroke. A short fuel pump stroke can be caused by a worn camshaft eccentric, a worn fuel pump push rod or operating lever, or excessive lash in the fuel pump linkage.

(b) Restricted Air Vent in the Fuel Tank. Unless air is admitted to the fuel tank as rapidly as fuel is removed, the fuel pump must work against a partial vacuum and will be unable to deliver fuel to the carburetor in sufficient quantity.

(c) Retriction in the Fuel Lines. Pay particular attention to the flexible line. In some cases the inner linings have been known to loosen and collapse under vacuum. It is possible also for a small section of loosened lining to swing like a gate with the flow of fuel, almost entirely shutting off the fuel supply.

(d) Low Float Level. A low float level setting might not affect performance at part throttle operation but could seriously affect performance at wide-open throttle.

(e) Fuel Line Air Leak. The fuel line from the fuel tank to the inlet side of the fuel pump is under vacuum when the engine is running. If a small air leak exists, it will reduce the quantity of fuel being delivered to the fuel pump. A large leak of course, would shut off the fuel completely.

(9) Heavy-Duty Fan. Heavy-duty fans designed for extra cooling may reduce the net delivered power of the engine by ten to twenty horsepower. There is little that can be done about this loss of power if a large fan is needed.

(10) Atmospheric Conditions. Due to the reduction in the size of the fuel-air charge at lower atmospheric pressures, a loss of power at high elevations is normal. The loss of power can be lessened, but not eliminated, by installing smaller jets in the carburetor or cylinder heads that provide a higher compression ratio.

In addition to the effect of low atmospheric pressure, air temperature and humidity also affect engine power.

POSSIBLE AREAS OF TROUBLE. Other conditions can affect power, speed, and acceleration and, though not commonly encountered, are possible causes of trouble. If the trouble is not corrected by the usual procedure and if none of the common causes of trouble are found, one

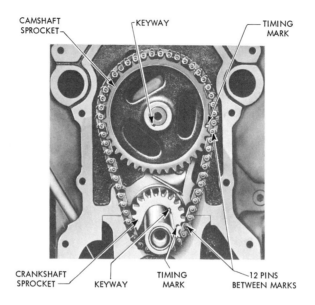

Fig. 3-4. Timing chain drive. Timing is set by the number of pins between the marks. Ford Motor Co.

Fig. 3-5. Timing gear drive. Marks must match up when the gears are in mesh.

of the following may be the cause:

(1) Camshaft Timing. If the camshaft is out of time, the ignition will be out of time. The camshaft might be out of time if the gear or chain has been replaced, major repairs have just been made, or if the main bearings have been replaced. (The crankshaft may have been dropped low enough to get the gears out of time.) Remove the valve cover or the gear or chain cover to make the inspection (Figs. 3-4 and 3-5). End play of the camshaft will

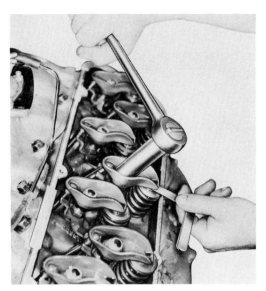

Fig. 3-6. Mechanical valve adjustment. Chevrolet Motor Div., General Motors Corp.

piston rings have been installed without sufficient end gap.

(4) Distributor. Distributor backlash can change ignition timing. Test for this condition. (See "Camshaft End Play" this chapter.)

(5) Ignition Advance. Lack of power at lower engine speeds might be the result of improper spark timing control. Failure to advance or faulty retarding of the spark could cause loss of power.

(6) Thin Valves. Improperly seated valves (valves that are seated too near the edge of the valve head) can cause trouble under sustained maximum loads. This is particularly true with thin headed valves. Such engines will show normal compression during the compression test, but at high temperatures developed under maximum compression the edges of the head distort upward slightly, in effect lessening

also change the ignition timing where helical gears are used. (See "Camshaft End Play" this chapter.)

(2) Valve Clearance. Too little valve tappet clearance results in valves not completely closing when hot. Remove the valve chamber cover to inspect the clearance and make the required corrections (Fig. 3-6).
NOTE: Ordinarily, this does not apply to engines with hydraulic valve lifters. However, even with these lifters the valves may be installed with too little clearance. When the lifter is collapsed, a clearance of at least 0.030 in. should exist.

Too much valve tappet clearance results in valves opening late and closing early. (Ordinarily this does not apply with hydraulic lifters.) Remove the valve cover for the inspection, and make the necessary corrections.

(3) Major Repairs. Wrong size parts may have been installed or parts installed incorrectly. This is particularly true if

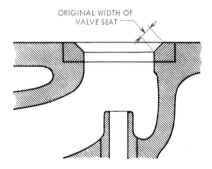

ORIGINAL WIDTH OF
VALVE SEAT

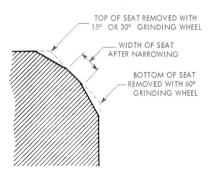

TOP OF SEAT REMOVED WITH
15° OR 30° GRINDING WHEEL

WIDTH OF SEAT
AFTER NARROWING

BOTTOM OF SEAT
REMOVED WITH 60°
GRINDING WHEEL

Fig. 3-7. Narrowing and centering valve seats to compensate for thin headed valves.

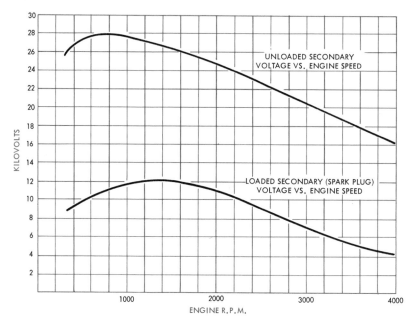

Fig. 3-8. Ignition voltage drop off at high speeds for loaded and unloaded voltages.

the valve tappet clearance. Reduce the diameter of the valve seat in the block or cylinder head (Fig. 3-7), or install valves with an oversize head diameter.

(7) Ignition Primary Voltage. Battery ignition systems have good low-speed characteristics, but their performance drops off at high speeds (Fig. 3-8). At high speeds, due to lower compression, ignition requirements are less. However, anything that reduces the ignition system performance can affect top speeds. If the generator is inoperative or the generator regulator voltage setting is too low, the ignition primary voltage will be correspondingly low. Likewise, a heavy electrical load (radio, heater, defroster, short circuit, etc.) will lower the ignition primary voltage.

(8) Friction. Any increase in speed increases the effect of the friction involved in the wheels rolling on the road. A road or deceleration test in neutral (see "Road

Tests" this chapter) will uncover not only excessive rolling friction but drive line friction as well. Both of these factors can affect top speed.

(9) Wind Resistance. Wind resistance is controlled by the design. However, car top carriers or anything the owner may have added to the outside of the vehicle can be a contributing factor to reduce top speed.

(10) Valve Spring Period. At certain speeds a valve spring will "dance" or surge and will not close the valve. The valve spring period in most cases is calculated carefully so that it does not happen at or near the normal top speed of the engine.

In some engines, the valve spring period is the limiting factor of top speed. In other engines, two separate springs, each having a different frequency, are used to avoid a noticeable valve spring period at attainable speeds.

CRANKS AND FAILS TO START

It is always a good plan in any trouble shooting to find out what you can from the owner or operator. Often a valuable clue that identifies immediately the reason for the trouble is uncovered, saving several unnecessary steps.

If the engine cranks but will not start, don't fail to consider what might obviously be the cause of the trouble: no fuel in the tank or the ignition switch not turned on.

SIMPLE PROCEDURE

Aside from the obvious reasons for the engine not starting, several other easily observed conditions might provide the clue needed to start the engine. See Fig. 3-9. Each of these conditions requires a different procedure as follows:

MOISTURE. If the engine is wet, wipe all moisture from the distributor terminal housing, cap, coil, spark plugs, and spark plug wires. It may save some time to wipe the spark plug porcelains dry and again attempt to start the engine. Often this will be all that is required.

NOTE: Carbon tetrachloride applied to wet parts will dry them almost immediately. Many mechanics on road calls to start wet engines take along an oil can full of carbon tetrachloride to squirt on spark plugs, distributor caps, wires, and other parts that may be wet and shorting the ignition. Be careful not to inhale fumes from carbon tetrachloride.

HEAT. If the engine is hot, either *vapor lock or percolation* might exist. If (on a down draft carburetor) gasoline is observed dripping out of the throttle body around the throttle shaft, it is a sure sign of percolation. However, percolation can exist without fuel leaking out at this point. Remove the air cleaner, and look for liquid fuel lying on top of the throttle plate. If the carburetor is still percolat-

ing, you will see liquid gasoline "spitting" out of the fuel discharge passages. Percolation causes flooding.

If the engine is hot the procedure to follow is the same regardless of whether the cause of the trouble is percolation or vapor lock. Hold down the accelerator pedal and crank the engine. This clears away either vapor lock or flooding which may be present. Don't pump the accelerator, or the accelerating pump may cause flooding.

PERCOLATION: Percolation occurs when gasoline in the passages of the carburetor vaporizes. These bubbles rise, pushing whatever liquid gasoline that lies above them into the carburetor throat. Percolation occurs only when the engine speed is reduced, as when stopping for red light or stop sign. Percolation cannot occur at highway speeds.

VAPOR LOCK: Vapor lock is when gasoline vaporizes before it reaches the carburetor. Vapor lock occurs under load and can slow down or completely stop the engine on the highway. While vapor lock and percolation are both caused by gas bubbles, if you have the operator explain just what happened, you can tell easily which is occurring by remembering under which condition each causes the engine to stop.

FLOODING. If the engine is flooded (due to repeated attempts to start while the carburetor was choked, to over-manipulation of the accelerator and accelerating pump, or to percolation), hold down the foot throttle (accelerator pedal). Crank the engine to exhaust the surplus fuel until the engine starts.

EXTREME COLD. If the engine is extremely cold, make certain the choke is working. If a manually operated choke button or control is provided, pull it out to the stop. Hold down the clutch pedal. With the ignition switch on, operate the starter.

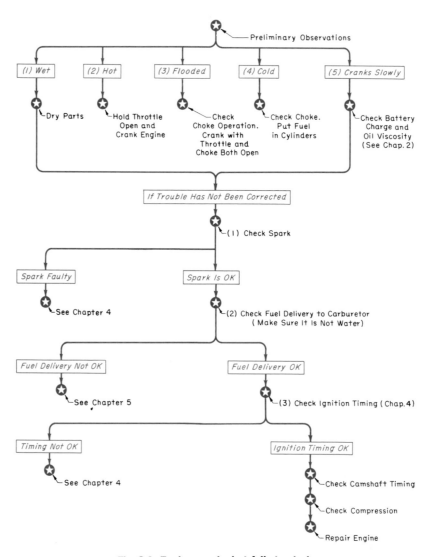

Fig. 3-9. Engine cranks but fails to start.

In subzero temperatures, sometimes it is difficult to get fuel into the cylinders, particularly where an updraft carburetor is used. With an updraft carburetor, it is necessary to lift the liquid (not vaporized) fuel into the cylinders. Three courses are open:

(1) Prime at Carburetor. If you are working outside on a downdraft carburetor, and use care, gasoline may be squirted directly into the carburetor from an oil can as the engine is cranked (ignition must be on), or with either updraft or downdraft carburetors petroleum ether, which vaporizes at extremely low temperatures, may be used. A good method is to pour a quantity of ether on a sponge and allow the carburetor to breathe the ether-laden air through the spronge as the engine is cranked. Highly volatile gas may be used in this manner. However, you cannot be as sure of va-

porization as you can with ether.

WARNING: When using these methods of getting gasoline into the cylinders, be careful not to get gasoline on your clothes or hands, as a backfire of the engine could cause a fire. Be sure that only a small quantity of inflammable fluid is used. These methods should not be used indoors.

(2) Prime at Cylinders. Remove the spark plugs, and put a small quantity of gas directly into the cylinders. Replace the plugs, and attempt to start the engine.

(3) Preheat Engine. Where neither ether nor gasoline is available to pour into the cylinders or carburetor, the fuel, in some instances, can be made to vaporize by pouring boiling water on the intake manifold.

Another effective method, although usually not practiced, is to remove all of the coolant from the engine and radiator and heat it. When the heated coolant is replaced in the engine, usually it will raise the temperature so the gasoline will vaporize. This method should not be employed if an inflammable antifreeze is used.

STIFFNESS. On engines equipped with a clutch pedal, always release the clutch when cranking the engine. If, with the clutch released, the engine cranks slowly, make sure the battery is not partially discharged and that the viscosity of the engine oil is correct for the prevailing temperature. If the cranking speed is still slow, there will be several things to check. (See "Engine Cranks Slowly" Chapter 2.)

COMPLETE PROCEDURE

If the engine still fails to start after the above observations have been made and the suggestions have been followed, proceed with the subsequent steps in the order given until the trouble has been corrected. (See Fig. 3-9.)

SPARK DELIVERY. Turn on the ignition switch. Remove the wire from any spark plug, and hold the wire terminal 3/16 in. from the cylinder head while the engine is being cranked. If a spark does not jump this gap, the ignition is at fault. (See "No Spark" Chapter 4.)

FUEL DELIVERY. Determine if fuel is being delivered to the carburetor either by looking for accelerator pump discharge or by loosening the float bowl drain plug, whichever method is the easier.

NOTE: Make sure that it is fuel and not water that is being delivered to the carburetor. Water in the fuel is not uncommon. Humid air cooled in a tank (either in the vehicle or in the gasoline station) will deposit its water in the tank. Water, since it is denser than gasoline, will go to the bottom of the tank. It is a good plan to keep tanks full, thus reducing the amount of air and condensation.

Alcohol added to the gasoline will pick up the water in the tank. This solution (alcohol and water) is combustible and usually the engine can be started.

On carburetors which have a drain plug, remove the plug from the carburetor float bowl. If fuel runs from the drain, it indicates fuel is being delivered to the carburetor. Proceed with the instructions under the next heading, "Ignition Timing." If fuel does not run out, there is fuel starvation. (See "Fuel Starvation" Chapter 5.)

On carburetors not equipped with a float bowl drain, or on engines on which it is easier to remove the carburetor air cleaner than to remove the drain plug, remove the cleaner, and observe if a spray of gasoline is coming from the accelerator pump spray nozzle (located inside the air throat of the carburetor) each time the throttle is opened fully. If a spray is observed, it indicates fuel is being delivered to the carburetor. Proceed with the instructions under "Ignition Timing." If a

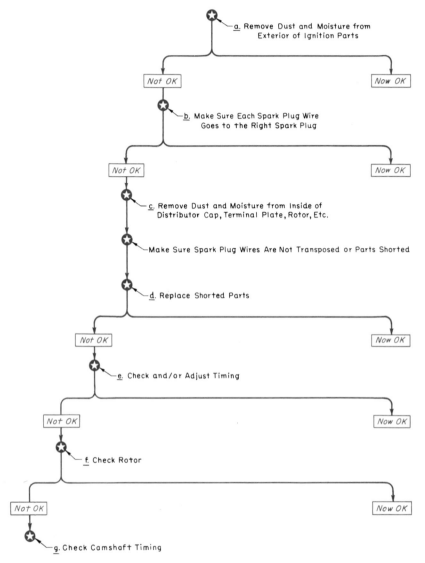

Fig. 3-10. Engine backfires but fails to start.

spray or stream of fuel is not observed, there is fuel starvation. (See "Fuel Starvation" Chapter 5.)

IGNITION TIMING. If the engine still does not start, check the timing of the ignition. Keep in mind that a degree or two would not keep the engine from starting.

On most engines with a timing mark that revolves with the crankshaft (either flywheel or vibration damper mark), it is possible for the ignition timing to be on the mark. Yet it may be off one crankshaft revolution (180 camshaft degrees). Make sure the spark plug wires are in the correct sockets at the distributor.

CAMSHAFT TIMING. If the engine still does not start, proceed as follows: (1) Remove No. 1 spark plug, reconnect the spark plug wire, and lay the plug on some metal part of the engine so that the gap is visible. (2) Connect a compression gage to the opening, and crank the engine. (3) If a spark occurs at the spark plug gap at a time other than when the cylinder is under compression, the camshaft is out of time. (4) If the cylinder registers no compression, proceed to the next step.

COMPRESSION. If, from the preceding tests, the ignition system, the fuel system and the timing are known to be not at fault, the trouble must lie in the engine itself. Test the compression at all of the cylinders. (See "Compression" this chapter.)

BACKFIRES AND FAILS TO START

This trouble or symptom nearly always is caused by the spark plugs not firing in the proper order. Usually this is the result of: (1) the high tension wires being shorted (if it has been raining or the car has just been washed, this is probably where the trouble lies); (2) the spark plug wires being transposed (one or several wires connected to the wrong spark plug or terminal in the distributor cap or terminal plate; (3) the distributor out of time; or (4) the ignition distributor rotor not keyed properly to the shaft.

TROUBLE SHOOTING PROCEDURE

The following procedure will locate the trouble and enable the engine to start. (See Fig. 3-10.)

CLEAN AND DRY IGNITION. Wipe all dust and moisture from the exterior of the distributor, coil, spark plugs, and spark plug wires and again attempt to start the engine.

CHECK SPARK PLUG WIRES. If the engine still fails to start, make sure each spark plug wire is attached and goes to the correct spark plug.

CHECK DISTRIBUTOR CAP. Make sure

the spark plug wires are installed at the correct terminals of the distributor cap or terminal plate and that the interior of the distributor is not wet.

REPLACE SHORTED PARTS. Replace the distributor cap or terminal plates if there is evidence of their being permanently shorted.

CHECK TIMING. Check the distributor timing and correct it if required.

CHECK ROTOR. Make sure the rotor is the correct one and is keyed properly to the shaft.

CORRECT CAMSHAFT TIMING. If the above procedure has not corrected the trouble, probably the camshaft is out of time. Remove the engine front cover, and correct the camshaft timing.

BACKFIRES AND RUNS UNEVENLY

This trouble is different from the preceding symptom, "Backfires and Fails to Start," in that here the engine runs, whereas in the other trouble it wouldn't start. This automatically eliminates several possibilities from further consideration. The same things, but in a lesser degree, cause this trouble. In addition to the causes shown in the procedure (see Fig. 3-11), this same trouble may be experienced if the valves are out of time.

(1) Ignition. Several, but not all, of the spark plug wires might be shorted (to each other) or transposed. The distributor terminal plate (or cap) or the rotor might be shorted in such a way that the spark can jump to the electrode or spark plug wire of some spark plug not under compression at that time.

(2) Fuel. This trouble is also characteristic of a lean fuel mixture.

(3) Cylinders. A blown or burned out cylinder head gasket, permitting flame from one cylinder to blow through to another cylinder, might account for this trouble.

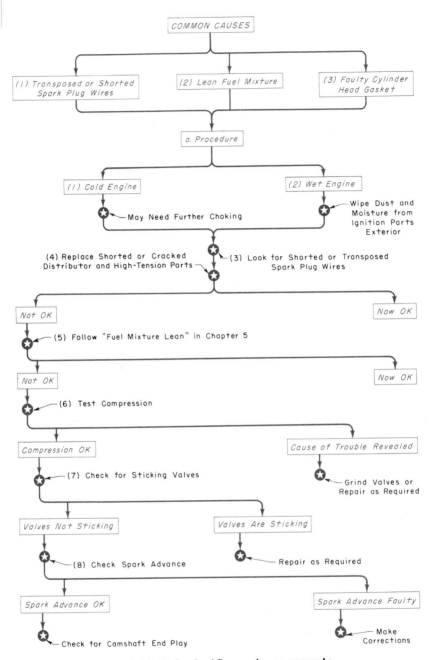

Fig. 3-11. Engine backfires and runs unevenly.

TROUBLE SHOOTING PROCEDURE

The first two steps cover the most common causes of this trouble. Perform these operations first. If they do not correct the trouble, proceed with the rest of the steps.

COLD ENGINE. If the engine is cold, the

carburetor may need further choking until the engine is warmed up.

WET ENGINE. Wipe all dust and moisture from the exterior of the distributor, coil, spark plugs, and spark plug wires.

SPARK PLUG WIRES. Check to determine if the spark plug wires are attached to the spark plugs and the distributor cap or terminal plates in their proper firing order.

DISTRIBUTOR CAP AND ROTOR. Replace the distributor cap or terminal plates if they are cracked or shorted.

FUEL MIXTURE. If the ignition is found not to be at fault, the fuel mixture may be too lean. (See "Mixture Too Lean" Chapter 5.)

COMPRESSION. Test the compression of each cylinder, and make the necessary corrections.

VALVES. Run the engine at idle speed and observe if any of the valves are noticeably noisy. Abnormally noisy valves indicate sluggish action, valve lash too wide, or a broken valve spring. Make the necessary corrections to the valves (adjust tappets).

NOTE: This does not apply to engines equipped with hydraulic valve lifters. Remove the valve chamber cover to check valve action.

SPARK ADVANCE. Check spark advance on the engine as outlined in Chapter 4. Repair the distributor spark advance mechanism if required. If the distributor spark advance mechanism is satisfactory, yet the advance is incorrect on the engine, make sure any vacuum lines or passages to the distributor are neither obstructed nor leaking. Also make sure that no binding of the spark advance mechanism is occurring on the engine.

CAMSHAFT AND DISTRIBUTOR. If the foregoing procedure has not corrected the trouble, either the distributor has excessive backlash or the camshaft has excessive end play. (See "Camshaft End Play" this chapter.)

STARTS AND QUITS

When the engine starts but fails to keep running, usually the trouble is caused by the fuel system failing to deliver fuel. Occasionally, however, the ignition system can suddenly fail. In most cases, the car will not be running when you get to it.

The condition or conditions that caused the engine to stop may have corrected themselves by the time you arrive. This will require some tact on your part. Most owners will at least slightly resent your getting in the driver's seat and attempting to start the engine which they have just told you wouldn't start. If you do and the engine starts easily, the owner always feels a little ridiculous unless he is prepared for this possibility by what you have told him.

Before attempting to start the engine, a good plan is to ask how much time has elapsed since he tried to start the engine. Whether it is a matter of a few minutes or several hours, be sure to tell him that quite often an engine that wouldn't start will start if the ignition is turned off and the car allowed to stand for a short time. This will prepare him for your attempt to start the engine and will remove some of the surprise in case the engine starts on the first try.

If the engine does start, determine why it wouldn't start before, and do whatever is indicated to prevent a similar failure later on.

TROUBLE SHOOTING PROCEDURE

The steps to be followed, if the engine starts but fails to keep running, are illustrated in Fig. 3-12. The procedure is as follows:

CHECK FUEL SUPPLY. Determine if fuel is being delivered to the carburetor.

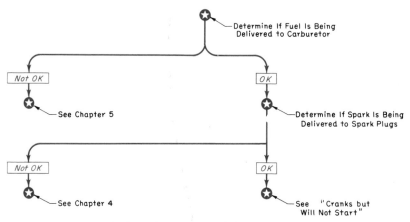

Fig. 3-12. Engine starts but fails to keep running.

If it is not being delivered, determine why not. (See "Fuel Starvation" Chapter 5.)

CHECK SPARK. If fuel is being delivered to the carburetor, determine if a satisfactory spark is being delivered to the spark plugs. (See "Spark Strength" Chapter 4.)

MISFIRES AT HIGH SPEED

This trouble should not be confused with a "flattening off" of power at high speeds and applies only when a definite miss occurs at high speed.

At high speeds, due to the reduced time available, the cylinder does not receive a full charge of fuel-air mixture. Consequently compression pressures are lower, thus reducing the ignition secondary voltage requirements. This is fortunate, since the performance characteristics of battery-coil ignition systems fall off at high speeds.

Since the ignition system is operating with a lower secondary voltage at high speed, the leakage factor becomes less significant, and "shorts" that would cause a miss at lower speed and maximum torque may not cause a miss at high speed. However, several other things do become factors that can account for missing at high speeds. These are:

(1) Distributor Contacts. Distributor contact bounce. Reduced contact dwell due to friction in the contact arm bearing or low contact spring pressure can cause a miss at high speed.

(2) Condenser. A faulty condenser or a dirty or loose ground connection for the condenser can cause a miss at high speeds. Replace the condenser if it should prove defective.

(3) Coil. All coils have a top output and some may not produce enough voltage at high speeds. They are not always uniform, and occasionally you will encounter a coil that performs perfectly at normal temperatures but will miss when hot, as might occur during sustained high-speed operation.

(4) Spark Plugs. Wide spark plug gaps can fire at low speeds under maximum compression but fail to fire under the lower compressions of high speed due to the rapid drop-off of secondary voltages as the limit of the ignition system's ability is approached.

(5) Valve Spring Tension. Valve springs having a different tension from the others in the same engine might cause those cylinders to miss at a particular speed. This may be due to warped, short, or crooked springs.

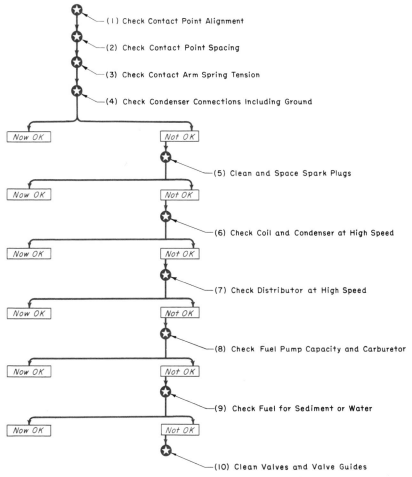

(1) Check Contact Point Alignment

(2) Check Contact Point Spacing

(3) Check Contact Arm Spring Tension

(4) Check Condenser Connections Including Ground

Now OK   Not OK

(5) Clean and Space Spark Plugs

Now OK   Not OK

(6) Check Coil and Condenser at High Speed

Now OK   Not OK

(7) Check Distributor at High Speed

Now OK   Not OK

(8) Check Fuel Pump Capacity and Carburetor

Now OK   Not OK

(9) Check Fuel for Sediment or Water

Now OK   Not OK

(10) Clean Valves and Valve Guides

Fig. 3-13. Engine misfires at high speeds.

TROUBLE SHOOTING PROCEDURE

Usually a high-speed miss is due to faulty ignition. However, the approach to the ignition is different in this case from most other troubles since here it is advisable to check first those things that can account for a high-speed miss. The sequence of operations shown in Fig. 3-13 should be followed until something is uncovered that will account for the trouble.

The full procedure consists of the checking and correcting (where required) of the following 10 factors in the order given until the cause of the trouble has been located and corrected:

(1) Contact point alignment.

(2) Contact point spacing.

(3) Contact arm spring tension.

(4) Condenser and connections, including ground.

(5) If the reason for the ignition miss has not been located by the first four steps and corrected, remove, clean, and space the spark plugs.

NOTE: While it is doubtful that anything unusual about the compression would be a factor in this trouble, it is good practice to check the compression of an engine at any time when all of the spark plugs are out. The removal and re-installation of the plugs represent about 90 percent of the work of a compression test, and you may uncover some additional need in the engine even though it has little bearing on the immediate fault.

(6) Check the coil and the condenser either together or separately, paying particular attention to their operation at high speed. (See "Coil Output" and "Condenser," Chapter 4.)

(7) Check the distributor on a test bench (see "Spark Advance" and "Contact Points" Chapter 4) paying particular attention to the action of the spark advance at high speed. Likewise, watch for any reduction of cam angle or dwell at speeds at which the missing occurs.

(8) Determine if any foreign matter is in the fuel that could intermittently hold open fuel pump valves or restrict fuel flow in the various carburetor passages.

(9) If solid material or water is found in the fuel, clean the carburetor, fuel pump, and fuel filter. (You may encounter some ceramic filters that lose grit into the fuel stream.)

Pay particular attention to the power supply system in the carburetor.

Blow out the fuel lines, and drain the fuel tank to remove the water or sediment. The straining of gasoline through chamois skin will remove both sediment and water.

CAUTION: Fuel tank drain plugs are heldom removed, and there is always the hazard of causing a fuel tank leak when attempting to remove a drain plug that has become badly corroded.

(10) If these procedures have not corrected the trouble, free the valves with a gum solvent through the carburetor. If this corrects the high-speed miss temporarily, the valves and their guides will have to be cleaned thoroughly to correct sluggish valve action at high speeds.

MISFIRES ON ACCELERATION OR HARD PULL

In about 75 percent of the engines misfiring on acceleration or hard pull, you will find the trouble in the ignition system. During acceleration or hard pulling, if the ignition system is unable to deliver the required voltage, if the spark plug gaps are too wide (thereby increasing the voltage requirements), or if the high-tension circuit insulation is unable to carry the high voltage, missing will result. (Likewise spark plugs of the wrong heat range could account for misfiring under load.)

In about 20 percent of the cases encountered, you will find the carburetor accelerating pump or "power" fuel supply system at fault.

In most of the remaining 5 percent of the cases, the cause will be sluggish valve action.

TROUBLE SHOOTING PROCEDURE

The separate steps of this procedure (Fig. 3-14) are presented in the order that can be most quickly performed. This is not necessarily in the order of probability. Perform the following operations in the order given until you encounter and correct the obvious cause of the trouble.

CHECK ACCELERATING PUMP LINK. Make sure the accelerating pump link is in the proper position for the prevailing temperature.

TEST SPARK. Test the quality of the spark at the end of each spark plug wire (see "Spark Strength," Chapter 4) and make the corrections indicated.

CHECK SPARK PLUGS. Clean and space spark plugs, or replace damaged or faulty plugs. Replace any spark plugs not of the correct heat range.

Check the engine compression, while

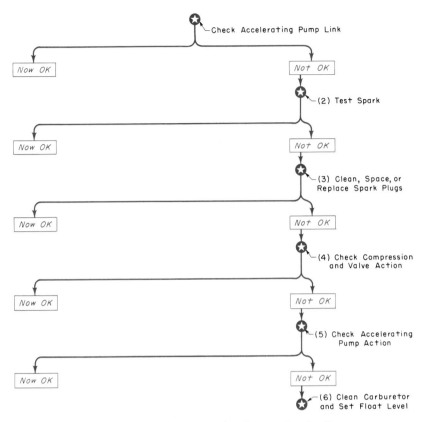

Fig. 3-14. Misfiring on acceleration or a hard pull.

the spark plugs are removed, to avoid the necessity of removing the spark plugs later.

CHECK COMPRESSION AND VALVE ACTION. Test the compression of each cylinder, and make corrections as required. Run the engine at idle speed, and observe if any of the valves are noticeably noisy. Abnormally noisy valves (except on engines equipped with hydraulic valve lifters) indicate sluggish valve action or the valve lash is too wide. Make the necessary corrections to the valves.

CHECK ACCELERATING PUMP ACTION. Remove the air cleaner, and observe if a spray of gasoline comes from the pump discharge nozzle (located inside the carburetor air throat) each time the throttle is opened fully. Repair or replace the carburetor if no spray or a very light spray is observed (carburetor accelerating pump mechanism or check valve is faulty).

CLEAN CARBURETOR. Remove and clean the carburetor thoroughly. Reset the float level if it is out of adjustment.

POOR IDLING

A number of conditions can account for failure of the engine to idle properly and at the same time also affect the operation under other speeds and loads. In this symptom, however, we are concerned primarily with those conditions that affect idling.

The first consideration is to be sure that a too severe standard is not expected. The trouble may be the result of someone trying to idle the engine at too slow a speed. Idle speeds which are too slow will introduce a number of conditions that place too many handicaps on the engine. At slow idle speeds, intake velocity is reduced, and distribution of the fuel air mixture is affected, with the result that the cylinders will not receive equal charges. The air-fuel ratio may be incorrect and, with compression low, combustion will be imperfect and the plugs will quickly foul.

NOTE: The fouling of the spark plugs is reduced by wider gaps, but the wide gaps may cause missing under load or high speed.

At low speeds the quantity of fuel and air entering through the carburetor is reduced, and at the same time the manifold vacuum is high. This increases the seriousness of any vacuum loss or leakage into the intake system at slow idle, but the effect drops off rapidly as the engine speed is increased.

In most engines, the spark does not start to advance until speeds of 600 to 800 rpm are reached. The engine will run smoother after the spark has started to advance.

At 600 rpm, with no load, the engine is running at approximately the same speed as it would with the car traveling at ten miles per hour without load in high gear. A load will reduce the speed of the engine to the neighborhood of seven miles per hour. This is as slow as a car should be expected to run in direct drive.

NOTE: A radio interference suppression condenser installed between the coil primary and the distributor will cause a low-speed miss and may cause the contacts to fail prematurely. These condensers must be installed on the battery side of the coil.

The procedure to follow to get the engine to idle properly is illustrated in abbreviated form in Fig. 3-15.

TROUBLE SHOOTING PROCEDURE

Perform the following operations in the order given until the engine idles smoothly:

NOTE: Don't expect any engine to idle smoothly without choking when it is cold. If the engine is cold and runs unevenly, inspect and correct any faults in the choke mechanism.

SET IDLE SPEED. Run the engine until normal operating temperature is reached. Set the idle speed to specified rpm.

ADJUST IDLE FUEL SUPPLY. Adjust the idle fuel supply jets on the carburetor. (See "Carburetor Tests and Adjustments," Chapter 5.) If this increases the idle speed above the specified rpm, reset the idle speed. If the engine does not run smoothly now, proceed as follows:

CLEAN AND ADJUST SPARK PLUGS. Remove, clean, and adjust the gaps of the spark plugs. Always test compression while you have the spark plugs out.

TEST IGNITION. Test the quality of the spark from the end of each spark plug. (See "Spark Strength," Chapter 4.)

CHECK TIMING. Check the timing at idle speed, and reset it if necessary.

TIGHTEN CONNECTIONS. Tighten all connections in the ignition primary circuit, including the condenser ground connection.

ADJUST CARBURETOR. If these operations have increased the engine speed above specified rpm, reduce the speed to proper rpm. If any of the operations reduced the speed, it is an indication that something is wrong, and you should perform that particular operation again and more carefully.

Set the carburetor idle screw for smoothest operation of the engine. (See "Carburetor Tests and Adjustments" Chapter 5.)

NOTE: Engines with emission controls

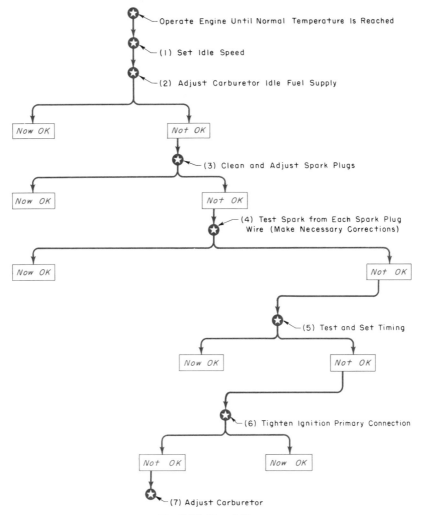

Fig. 3-15. Poor idling.

require a high idle speed and a lean idle mixture. Usually these engines have the ignition retarded at idle. On these engines a smooth idle should be obtained, but the engine may not run as smoothly as might be expected because of the emission modifications.

(1) Mixture Is Rich. If the mixture is too rich, even with the idle adjustment screw set lean all the way, one of the following is true: (1) The carburetor float level is high. This could be caused by incorrect adjustment, a leaking float

needle valve, or high fuel pump pressure. (2) The air bleed to the idle fuel system is obstructed or the accumulated deposits in the throttle body are so great that the throttle plate is held off position and fuel is being discharged from the second idle discharge hole. (3) In some carburetors, any leakage (within the carburetor) past the power jet (or economizer valve) will enrich the mixture.

NOTE: Usually, the idle fuel supply adjustment limits the fuel to one discharge hole only. If, due to the throttle being off position, fuel is being discharged from the second hole, you cannot control the quantity of fuel.

One or several of these conditions exist if the mixture is rich. Check the fuel pressure. (See "Fuel Pump Tests," Chapter 5.) Remove and clean the carburetor, scraping the barrel of the throttle body with a knife to remove the thin deposits that hold the throttle off position. Set the float and reassemble the carburetor, using new gaskets throughout. Readjust the carburetor.

(2) Mixture Is Lean. If the mixture is lean, make sure the idle tube or passages in the carburetor are not plugged. Tighten any vacuum connections, and tighten the intake manifold.

If this does not correct the trouble, use a vacuum gage or tachometer or, by observation, note any increase of engine speed or vacuum as you squirt oil on each point of possible vacuum leakage, including the intake manifold gaskets at both the carburetor and the cylinder block. If the vacuum or the speed increases, the point where the oil caused it to increase is leaking. Look for a cross-threaded connection or defective gasket.

After correcting vacuum leaks, re-adjust the carburetor, including the carburetor float setting if required.

NOTE: In intake manifolds heated by exhaust gases routed through passages in the manifold, the manifold casting may be faulty in such a way as to permit exhaust gas to enter the intake manifold. The result will be the same as a severe vacuum leak.

EXCESSIVE OIL CONSUMPTION

Excessive oil consumption is one of the most common troubles. As the parts wear, engines use more and more oil. Likewise new engines, or newly overhauled engines, can use excessive quantities of oil. New car and truck purchasers watch oil consumption carefully while the engine is in the warranty period so that if excessive oil consumption exists it will be corrected at the dealer's or manufacturer's expense.

Before getting into the procedure to follow when excessive oil consumption is encountered, a number of different considerations should be understood.

(1) New Engines. A small percentage of new or recently overhauled engines, regardless of make, will be oil consumers due to what is commonly referred to as the "human element." Some of the things that are encountered in such engines are: folded pan gaskets; improperly tightened oil pan cap screws (unevenly tightened or loose); defective oil seals at either end of the crankshaft; leakage at oil filter lines or connections; and tapered or grooved piston rings installed upside down.

If the cylinder bores in some engines are too smooth, a long period of operation is necessary before the rings seat enough to effectively stop the oil going past them. In such engines about 1,000 miles of operation are required before the rings seat. In extreme cases, as much as 6,000 or 7,000 miles of operation are required to seat the rings.

Loosely fitted intake valve guides permit excessive quantities of oil to be drawn through them into the cylinders. The looseness may be excessive clearance either between the valve stem and guide or between the guide and the cylinder block.

Even in cases where the valve guide clearance is not excessive, if oil baffles have been left out of the engine, or if they have been installed incorrectly, excessive oil consumption can result.

(2) Old Engines. Old engines can become oil consumers as a result of both wear and dirt. Oil consumption in an old

engine usually is due to one or several of the following: worn valve guides; worn or weak piston rings; worn ring grooves in the pistons; scored cylinders; and scored pistons that prevent normal movement of the piston rings.

Oil return slots in the oil control piston rings or the oil return or drain holes in the piston can become plugged, thus preventing the oil wiped off the cylinder walls from returning to the oil pan.

Loose crankpin or main bearings can result in excessive quantities of oil being thrown on the cylinder walls. If the piston rings are unable to effectively wipe off this extra oil, excessive oil consumption will result.

(3) Crankcase Dilution. Water, a by-product of combustion, blows past the pistons in vapor form and in cold weather condenses on cold surfaces in the engine. This water dilutes and adds to the quantity of liquid in the oil pan. Likewise, incompletely vaporized gasoline entering the cylinder even from normal choking, but especially from overchoking, runs past the piston rings into the crankcase, where it dilutes the oil and also adds to the quantity of liquid in the crankcase. These dilutions occur in cold weather when the engine is operated below normal operating temperatures.

Such an engine operated below normal temperatures will give every indication of having its full requirement of oil. However, if it is taken on a trip during which normal operating temperatures are maintained, first the gasoline and then the water in the oil pan will evaporate and pass out the crankcase breather. If the owner checked the level of what he thought was all oil before starting, and finds that after fifty miles of operation it was necessary to add three quarts of oil to re-establish the correct level, he will think that he used three quarts of oil in fifty miles. The evaporation of diluents

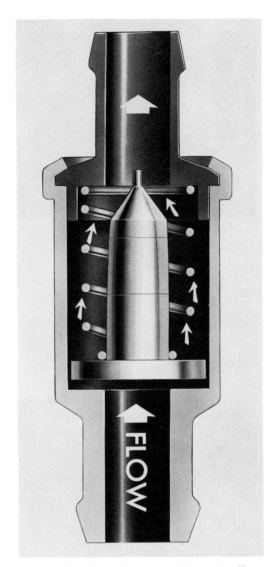

Fig. 3-16. Positive crankcase ventilation valve. Chevrolet Motor Div., General Motors Corp.

in the oil in a few miles of operation is not oil consumption.

Positive crankcase ventilation systems (PCV) systems) reduce considerably these dilution effects because they continually draw out vapors and condensation to promote cleaner operation and reduce crankcase emissions to the atmosphere. Figs. 3-16 and 3-17 show a PCV valve and its location on a typical engine.

Fig. 3-17. Installation of PCV valve.

(4) Oil Leakage. Most owners have heard so much about this or that piston ring and its ability to stop oil consumption that they are prone to think of piston rings when excessive oil consumption is first manifest. However, leakage runs a close second to dirty or worn piston rings as a cause of oil loss. Even though the owner of the vehicle asks for new rings, it is a good plan to check for oil leakage before proceeding with the work.

When in doubt as to whether or not the engine is using an excessive amount of oil, check the oil consumption. (See "Oil Consumption" this chapter.)

TROUBLE SHOOTING PROCEDURE

The procedure to follow covers the steps to be taken in the order of the amount of work involved with the most quickly performed steps presented first.

OIL LEVEL CHECK. Make sure the oil being used is of the correct viscosity and that the level of the oil in the engine oil pan is correct.

Engine manufacturers often change the shape of the oil pan. In some cases, a different bayonet type oil level gage is

required for each type of pan. Occasionally you will encounter an engine with the wrong bayonet gage. If in doubt, check the gage with one from another engine of the same model.

NOTE: In most engines, if the oil level is too high, the connecting rods may dip (or dip too deeply) and an excessive amount of oil is thrown on the cylinder walls where it will find its way past the rings.

LEAKAGE CHECK. Spread clean paper on the floor under the engine and transmission. Start the engine, and set the idle speed at 1,000 to 1,250 rpm (equal to about 20 to 25 mph). Allow the engine to run at this speed for several minutes after it has reached normal operating temperature. During this time, at about half-minute intervals, momentarily race the engine (wide-open throttle) and allow it to come back to the fast idle speed (as previously set) immediately. Any severe gasket leakage will result in oil dripping on the paper. If no oil drips on the paper, examine the underside of the engine, including the flywheel housing, for oil wetness. Remember that two minutes of operation are equal to less than one mile of operation on the road, and no great quantity of dripping oil is to be expected.

Accelerate the engine after operating at idle speed for a short time. Excessive oil burning will be indicated by blue-gray smoke from the exhaust.

MECHANICAL CHECK. If the preceding test did not uncover leakage as the cause of oil consumption or if, with the correct oil level, excessive smoking occurs, the cause of trouble is mechanical. Proceed as follows:

(1) Oil Pressure. If the oil pressure is low after several minutes of running as outlined above, and the viscosity of the oil is known to be correct, it can be assumed that the crankpin or main bearings or the camshaft bearings are loose, and

your recommendations should include replacement of bearings as required.

(2) Compression. Check the compression of all cylinders. (See "Compression," this chapter.)

As the spark plugs are removed for the compression test, look for oil on the plugs. Oil or heavy black carbon deposits on the plugs indicate that oil is getting into the combustion chamber. If the compression was low but was brought up to normal by sealing the rings with oil, the piston rings and the cylinder walls (either or both) are worn or scored, and major repairs are required. If the compression was normal, the oil may be going past either the piston rings or the valve guides.

(3) Positive Crankcase Ventilation. On engines with positive crankcase ventilation, inspect the system to make sure that it isn't clogged, and clean it if it is.

LOW OIL PRESSURE

Before getting into the procedure to follow, it may be well to review the nature of oil and some of the characteristics of the various oil pressure systems as they have a bearing on low oil pressure.

Engine oil pressure, or any hydraulic pressure, cannot exceed the pressure required to overcome the resistance to the movement of the oil that exists at the moment. The thicker (higher the viscosity) the oil the greater the resistance to movement. The tighter the bearings the greater the resistance to the movement. All engine oils are thicker when cold and the pressure required to move them is greater.

At subzero temperatures, the engine oil may become so thickened that it cannot be forced through the small spaces through which it returns to the oil pan. Since most oil pumps are positive displacement pumps, the pressure under such conditions would momentarily increase until either it was great enough to overcome the resistance or until the pump or something else broke.

POSITIVE DISPLACEMENT: Positive displacement, as the term is applied to oil pumps, means that for each cycle (complete revolution or stroke of the pumping members) a definite quantity of oil is forced into the oil lines.

To avoid breakage, all pressure lubricating systems are provided with an escape valve that opens at a predetermined pressure. These valves are referred to as *oil pressure regulators.* See Fig 3-18. Some systems employ two such regulators, one near the pump and a second at the far end of the oil gallery.

Positive displacement pumps are positive displacement only when an ample supply of new oil keeps the pump full at all times. The oil flows to the pump by a combination of gravity and atmospheric pressure. If the oil is so cold that it channels, it will not flow into the pump.

NOTE: When oil is extremely cold it has the consistency of cup grease. If you run your finger through a can of cup grease, a channel will be formed in the grease. When oil is so cold that it will not fill up the space behind a moving part, the oil is said to be channeling.

In most engines the oil pump is located above the level of the oil in the oil pan. This means that the pump first must remove the air from the intake tube or pipe, lowering the pressure (creating a vacuum) in it. Atmospheric pressure exerted on the surface of the oil in the pan pushes the oil into the intake and on up into the pump. Regardless of the pressure the pump can develop, the pressure that pushes the oil into the pump is atmospheric pressure (approximately 14.7 lbs per sq in. at sea level). Therefore, any restriction in the pump intake will reduce the supply of oil to the pump and will lower the pressure being delivered to the oil lines.

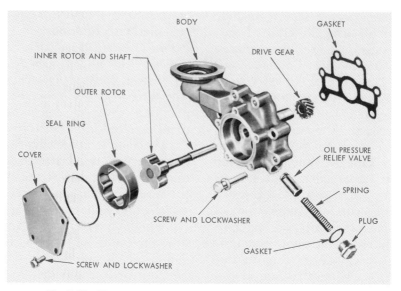

Fig. 3-18. Oil pump, disassembled. Plymouth Div., Chrysler Corp.

Oil pump screens become clogged and prevent the pump from getting an adequate supply of oil. Some oil pumps are so designed or become so worn that they will pump oil but not air. Such pumps must be primed in order to start them pumping.

TROUBLE SHOOTING PROCEDURE

Check the amount, viscosity, and degree of dilution of the engine oil. Usually, you will have to ask the owner what viscosity oil he has been buying. Place several drops of oil from the bayonet oil gage onto a sheet of clean, white paper to see how much dirt is in the oil. Rub a drop of oil between your thumb and finger. If it does not feel oily, or if it has a gasoline smell, replace the oil. Remember that these tests are not conclusive. However, equipment to make these tests scientifically is not available for service work. If you doubt the quality of oil, replace it with oil of known quality.

PRESSURE CHECK. Once it has been established that a sufficient quantity of good oil is in the engine oil pan, start the engine, and read the oil pressure gage on the instrument panel. On engines with an oil pressure warning light instead of a gage, connect a master gage at the engine.

If the pressure is normal, let the engine reach operating temperature and again read the gage. If the gage still reads normal, the trouble was due to dilution, low viscosity, or inadequate supply.

If the pressure is below normal, either when the engine was first started or after the engine is warm, the difficulty might be either mechanical trouble in the engine or a faulty gage.

NOTE: An oil filter without its cartridge will lower the effective level of the oil and may be a factor in low oil pressure.

PRESSURE GAGE CHECK. Some engines have a pipe plug that can be removed to permit the connection of a master gage. Connect a master gage, and again start the engine. Compare the master gage and instrument panel gage readings. If the two gages agree, the trouble is in the engine. If the master gage shows normal pressure and the instrument panel gage shows less than normal, replace the defective gage.

PRESSURE RELIEF VALVE CHECK. If the level and viscosity of the oil is known to be right and the oil pressure is proven low by a test with a master gage, check the oil relief valve (pressure regulator). Look particularly for anything that prevents the valve from seating. Check the pressure of the spring. If a means of adjustment is provided, adjust the relief valve. Most relief valves are not adjustable and are an integral part of the pump.

ENGINE CHECK. If the foregoing procedure has not corrected the low oil pressure, it will be necessary to remove the engine oil pan and pump to determine the cause of trouble. Look particularly for a dirty screen, worn pump, and/or loose crankpin, main, and camshaft bearings. Likewise, any point in the oil passages that might permit oil to escape must be made pressure-tight. Plastigage can be used to check bearing oil clearances.

ABNORMAL ENGINE NOISE

The diagnosis of engine noise involves an understanding of the various kinds of noise that will be encountered and the things that can account for or contribute to each. Once you have this knowledge, you are ready to isolate the noise.

Attempts to diagnose engine troubles from sound alone often do not turn out right. For this reason, it is well to remember that you can (and occasionally will) be wrong in your diagnosis.

KINDS OF NOISES. Mechanics, engineers, and others throughout the years have adopted a number of descriptive terms which they use in an endeavor to describe the various types of noises that are encountered. Among these the following terms are included: ping, click, rap, thump, whine, rattle, slap, chucking noise, and thud.

These terms are modified by descriptive or limiting terms like sharp, loud, faint, dull, irregular, regular, and intermittent. Often a term, either with or without modification, is supplemented by phrases such as when cold, when hot, under load, during acceleration, on deceleration, at idle, at high speed, when oil pressure is low, when oil pressure is high, and at a specific speed (of engine or vehicle).

Both the modifying term and the supplementary description are important in providing a clue to the probable cause of the trouble. If you have an opportunity to discuss the noise with the operator, determine under what conditions it occurs and how intense it is. While his definitions or description may not exactly fit one of the terms such as thud, rattle, or slap, suggest these terms when listening to his description. This will in a measure make up for the differences in your automotive vocabularies.

In the following discussions it must be appreciated that often words are ineffective in describing sounds. However, the descriptions and the conclusions presented have been reviewed by many people with long experience in diagnosing engine noises, and their comments have been incorporated.

PING. A ping is the term used to describe the noise that occurs when, under maximum load, improper combustion is developed. The trouble can be caused by early timing of the spark or by pre-ignition.

If, with the engine cold, the ping starts as soon as a load is imposed on it, probably it is safe to assume that the trouble is early timing. If, however, the ping does not develop for several minutes, it can be assumed that the trouble is pre-ignition.

At road speeds, the ping may occur so rapidly that the term "rattle" may more accurately describe it. Nevertheless, the term "rattle" usually is reserved for an entirely different condition.

(1) Early Timing. Early timing can be caused by (a) low octane fuel; (b) initial spark advance early; (c) automatic spark advance too rapid; or (d) compression ratio too high.

(a) Low Octane Fuel. Low octane fuel burns faster than high octane fuel, and, if it is to be used constantly in the particular engine involved, the basic or initial timing must be changed to suit the fuel. In some instances, the spark advance characteristics would have to be changed to suit the fuel. Since this would involve a basic change in the spark advance mechanism, it is more practical in most cases to change to a higher octane fuel.

(b) Early Spark Advance. In most ignition distributors, the breaker arm rubbing block wears down more rapidly than the points pound down. This results in reduction of the contact point spacing and retarding of the ignition timing. However, most contact point sets have one flat contact surface and one with a spherical radius. This is designed to permit a centered contact and perfect alignment once the spherical contact has pounded into the flat contact. In some cases this pounding in will develop more rapidly than the rubbing block wears. The result is that the contact spacing increases and the initial timing is advanced.

Set the ignition contacts to the correct dwell, cam angle, or spacing, and time the ignition. (See "Contact Points" and "Timing," Chapter 4.)

(c) Rapid Spark Advance. If the initial timing is correct, but the automatic spark advance is too rapid, the engine will ping on acceleration. If the distributor is provided with a vacuum retard, make sure it is operating. Check the spark advance characteristics of the distributor against the manufacturer's specifications

and repair or replace as required.

(d) High Compression Ratio. Occasionally you will encounter an engine on which someone has installed a cylinder head having a higher-than-standard compression ratio, either for high elevation operation or for some other reason. This will not be uncommon on so-called "hot rods" or cars that have been used at high elevations (such as Denver and Mexico City) and have been moved to low country. Several ways are used to increase the compression ratio of cylinder heads. These include removing metal from the gasket surface of the head, reducing the depth of the combustion space, or by adding material to partially fill in the combustion space. Check the cylinder heads against standard specifications.

In addition to the possibility of the engine having the wrong head, the compression ratio can be changed in some engines by the installation of the wrong pistons.

The most common condition encountered, however, is a change in the compression ratio due to the presence of carbon in the combustion chamber. Carbon, being a solid, will not compress. Thus, the volume of the combustion chamber is reduced and the compression ratio increased.

NOTE: In some cases the carbon deposits on both the piston and the head can build up until they contact each other, resulting in a slight click that later develops into a distinct knock.

(2) Pre-ignition. Pre-ignition occurs when the mixture in the cylinder is ignited prior to the time the spark occurs. It is caused by heat, and anything that causes overheating can cause pre-ignition. If the combustion chamber contains something that does not cool between power strokes, this hot surface or substance can, under compression, ignite the mixture, even with everything normal.

The most common cause of pre-ignition is carbon in the combustion chamber. The carbon is a poor heat conductor and, if permitted to become red hot, will cause pre-ignition as will valves with thin edges. Cylinder head gaskets reinforced with fine wire can cause pre-ignition if one or several strands of this wire are exposed to the heat of combustion. Spark plugs that are too hot (incorrect heat range for engine or type of operation) can cause it.

Engines running on pre-ignition will continue to run after the ignition is turned off. To stop such an engine, shut off the fuel or air to the carburetor or, with the throttle closed, place a load on the engine to stall it.

CLICK. A click is a distinct but not necessarily loud sound that can be caused by any one of a number of conditions such as (1) a nick on a timing or oil pump drive gear; (2) piston or top ring lightly touching a head gasket or cylinder ridge; or (3) excessive valve lash.

RAP. The term "rap" is used to describe a sound similar to that resulting when a hammer strikes a hard surface. In an engine low on oil, it is the sound the connecting rods make as the engine speed or load is increased.

THUMP. The term "thump" is used to describe a deep sound that you seem to feel as well as hear. A thump can be the result of any one of a large number of conditions such as loose main bearings (under load).

WHINE. A whine is a high-pitched sound that is continuous, although it is more pronounced at some speeds than at others. Such a sound can be caused by a fan belt, generator brushes or bearing, timing gears, or any number of things. Usually a whine heard only when the clutch is released is caused by the clutch release or clutch pilot bearing.

RATTLE. A rattle is the term used to describe a sound similar to that which results when a baby's rattle is shaken violently. A rattle can be caused by a number of conditions such as loose pistons or early ignition timing.

SLAP. Slap is a term used to describe a sound similar to a rap (hammer striking a hard surface) but not quite so sharp. Loose pistons either rattle or slap.

CHUCKING. A chucking noise is rather difficult to describe. However, the term is used to define the kind of noise that is caused by end play in a camshaft, but it can be caused by several other conditions. In some engines, oil pressure at one end of the camshaft can overcome the natural thrust of the camshaft gear helix. As the camshaft moves back and forth, a chucking noise is heard.

A similar noise can result from end play of the generator or starter armature shaft, the fan, or the crankshaft.

THUD. A thud is about the same as a thump except that the term "thump" is used to describe a sound that repeats every revolution or cycle, whereas the term "thud" is more often used to describe an intermittent sound. A loose flywheel or end play of the crankshaft could result in a thud.

TROUBLE SHOOTING PROCEDURE

Don't attempt to analyze the cause of an unusual noise in the engine merely from the sound. All engine noises fall into one of the following four classifications: (1) sound that occurs once every revolution; (2) sound that occurs once every cycle (two revolutions); (3) sound that occurs intermittently with no apparent relationship either to the revolution or cycle of the engine; and (4) continuous sound.

Operate the engine until normal temperatures are reached unless it is apparent from the noise of the engine that further damage might result by continued running. In this event, the entire following procedure should be omitted.

Set the engine speed at approximately 600 rpm, and observe the oil pressure. If the oil pressure is low, check the oil, and drain and refill, or add to it as required.

With the engine running at 600 rpm, place a neon type spark plug tester on one of the spark plugs, and note whether the engine noise occurs once or twice for each flash or if it seems to have no definite relationship to the flash.

OCCURS TWICE FOR EACH FLASH. If the noise occurs twice for each flash, the source is at some point driven by or driving the crankshaft, such as pistons, rings, pins, crankpins, or main journals. Of course, anything either driving or driven by the crankshaft can be the cause of the noise, and the nature of the noise should assist you in determining the probable cause.

OCCURS ONCE FOR EACH FLASH. If the noise occurs once for each flash, it means that the noise is occurring once each cycle of the engine. The camshaft makes but one revolution per cycle, and everything driven by or with it likewise operates once each cycle. Probably such noises are caused by valves or the valve-operating mechanism, fuel pump, oil pump, or distributor. Likewise a nicked camshaft gear tooth could cause a noise once each cycle (every other revolution).

OCCURS INTERMITTENTLY. If the noise occurs intermittently, (that is, neither once nor twice for every flash of the neon spark plug tester), the cause of the trouble is some movement not definitely tied into the rotation of either the camshaft or the crankshaft. End play of the camshaft, crankshaft, or the armatures in the shafts of the various engine accessories (generator, starter, distributor, etc.) may be the cause.

OCCURS CONTINUOUSLY. Generally a continuous sound such as a whine or rubbing sound is caused by a rotating rather than a reciprocating part.

A continuous whine probably is caused by the timing gears, although in some instances the oil pump or distributor drive or idler gears can cause a whine.

Often a rubbing sound is the result of the flywheel rubbing on its housing. Any rotating part rubbing, of course, could cause this kind of noise.

OCCURS IN A CYLINDER. Usually a further isolation of the noise can be made by shorting out the spark plug of each cylinder in turn. If the noise stops when one of the cylinders is thus shorted, the trouble is at that cylinder.

SERVICING GASOLINE ENGINES

Gasoline engine troubles can be the result of any one or several of a great number of faults not only in the engine proper but in the other units or systems not ordinarily considered as a part of the engine. Often, particularly when maintenance services are neglected, a trouble may be the result of a combination of neglected units. During a trouble shooting procedure where, after a few preliminary checks, you find several units or systems to be at fault, recommend an engine tune-up. This will permit you to restore all units to a good operating condition, thus correcting the trouble.

TUNE-UP

An engine tune-up operation is intended to restore an engine to normal operating condition. It is a correction procedure and not mere checking procedure. The engine tune-up has to do only with parts or units that influence engine performance and does not take into account the generating, starting, and lighting systems, or the horn and instruments.

If equipment for this purpose is available, make a combustion analysis while the vehicle owner is present so that he may observe the results of the analysis prior to the engine tune-up.

Lacking a combustion analyzer, a manifold vacuum test will give a good indication of the over-all performance of the engine. Likewise, an accurate fuel consumption road test may be used to demonstrate the over-all performance of the engine.

PROCEDURE. While there is some variation among different shops usually the engine tune-up provides for correction at no extra cost (except for parts) for all units except the engine proper. Extra charges are always made for corrections involving the removal of heads, manifolds, etc. Since this operation provides for correction, repair and cleaning of the carburetor, fuel pump, and distributor are included. The tune up procedure is given in Fig. 3-19.

(1) Compression. Since repairs of the engine proper are not provided for in engine tune-up, the procedure should start with a compression test. If the compression is not normal, it will not be possible to tune the engine. Therefore, test the compression first, preferably while the vehicle owner is present, so that additional work necessary can be authorized by the owner.

(2) Cylinder Head Nuts and Manifold Bolts. Where loose, tighten the manifold bolts and the cylinder head nuts to the specified torque.

(3) Spark Plugs. Visually examine the spark plugs. If the color of the firing end of the ceramic insulation is light brown, the plug is the right heat value and has been functioning properly. If the color is a dead white, the plug type is too hot or the engine is running too hot. If the plug is wet with oil, it has not been firing. If the plug has a black deposit on the firing

end of the ceramic insulation, the plug type is too cold for the engine. If the electrodes have eroded away or if the insulator is chipped or cracked, discard it, and install a new plug.

If the spark plugs are to be re-used, clean them thoroughly on a sand-blast-type spark plug cleaner. Set the spark plug electrode to the specified gap. This applies whether the plugs are new or old. Install spark plugs in the engine, and tighten to the required torque.

(4) Battery and Cables. Remove the battery cables from the battery. Clean the battery and cable connections. Inspect the battery case for cracks and leakage and the cables for worn insulation and deteriorated connectors. Replace or repair defective parts. Reinstall cables and tighten connectors.

NOTE: Ordinary baking soda and water is an excellent means of cleaning the battery and the surrounding areas where acid has splashed or run over.

(5) Battery Charge. Test the battery and recharge or replace it if it is defective.

(6) Distributor. Test and adjust the distributor on a distributor test fixture if available, making repairs or replacements as required. (See "Timing" and "Spark Advance," Chapter 4.)

(7) Ignition Timing. Time the ignition (see "Timing," Chapter 4).

(8) Distributor Cap. Clean and inspect the distributor cap and terminal plates, and replace them if they are cracked, carbon tracked, or otherwise damaged. Use carbon tetrachloride as a cleaner. (Lacquer thinner is a good substitute cleaner.)

(9) Ignition Primary Circuit. Check the primary circuit resistance, and visually inspect these wires for faulty insulation or poor connections.

(10) Spark. Determine if the spark from each spark plug wire will jump a satisfactory gap. If the spark is unsatisfactory at all spark plugs, trouble exists

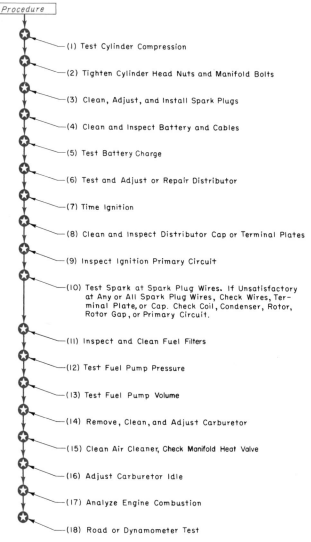

Procedure

(1) Test Cylinder Compression

(2) Tighten Cylinder Head Nuts and Manifold Bolts

(3) Clean, Adjust, and Install Spark Plugs

(4) Clean and Inspect Battery and Cables

(5) Test Battery Charge

(6) Test and Adjust or Repair Distributor

(7) Time Ignition

(8) Clean and Inspect Distributor Cap or Terminal Plates

(9) Inspect Ignition Primary Circuit

(10) Test Spark at Spark Plug Wires. If Unsatisfactory at Any or All Spark Plug Wires, Check Wires, Terminal Plate, or Cap. Check Coil, Condenser, Rotor, Rotor Gap, or Primary Circuit.

(11) Inspect and Clean Fuel Filters

(12) Test Fuel Pump Pressure

(13) Test Fuel Pump Volume

(14) Remove, Clean, and Adjust Carburetor

(15) Clean Air Cleaner, Check Manifold Heat Valve

(16) Adjust Carburetor Idle

(17) Analyze Engine Combustion

(18) Road or Dynamometer Test

Fig. 3-19. Tune-up. Complete procedure.

in the coil, condenser, rotor, rotor gap, or the primary circuit. Repair or replace defective parts.

If the spark is unsatisfactory at some, but not all, of the spark plug wires, the trouble is in the wire itself, the wire not seated in the terminal plate or cap, or the terminal plate is shorted.

(11) Fuel Filter. Clean or replace all fuel filters.

(12) Fuel Pump Pressure. Check the fuel pump pressure. If the pressure is not within specifications, remove and repair the pump.

(13) Fuel Pump Volume. Check the fuel pump volume. A good pump will deliver 1 pint of fuel in 30 seconds. If volume is low, check for restrictions in supply lines.

(14) Carburetor. Remove, disassemble, and clean the carburetor. Make sure to remove gum deposits from the throttle

Sun RASTRONIC ENGINE DIAGNOSIS

CARBURETION

IGNITION   COMPRESSION

CHARGING

STARTING

Order No. _____

Customer Name _____ Date _____

Address _____ Phone _____

Make _____ Model _____ Mileage _____ License No. _____

Customer Comments: _____

START

IDLE

CRUISE
(1000 RPM)

ACCELERATE

TURNPIKE
(2500 RPM)

Travel Sun's Diagnostic Highway!

TEST PROCEDURE	READ	TEST CONDITION OF:	SPECS.	RESULTS
Cranking Voltage	Voltmeter	Battery, Starting System		●
Cranking Coil Output	Scope (Display)	Coil, Ign. Primary Circuit		
Cranking Vacuum	Vacuum Gauge	Engine Mechanical		
PCV Test	Vacuum Gauge	Positive Crankcase Vent.		
Idle Speed	Tachometer	Idle Speed Adjustment		
Dwell	Dwell Meter	Breaker Point Setting		
Initial Timing	Timing Advance Unit	Spark Timing Setting		
Fuel Mixture	Combustion Eff. Tester	Carburetor Idle Circuit		
Manifold Vacuum	Vacuum Gauge	Engine Idle Efficiency		
Dwell Variation	Dwell Meter	Distributor Mechanical Cond.		
Coil Polarity	Scope (Superimposed)	Coil Installation, Sys. Polarity		
Cam Lobe Accuracy	Scope (Superimposed)	Distributor Breaker Cam		
Secondary Circuit Condition	Scope (Raster)	Plugs, Wires, Cap, Rotor Res.		
Coil and Condenser Condition	Scope (Raster)	Coil Windings, Cond. Leakage		
Breaker Point Condition	Scope (Raster)	Point close, bounce, open, arc		
Spark Plug Firing Voltage	Scope (Display)	Fuel Mix., Comp., Plug Rotor Gaps		
Fuel Mixture	Combustion Eff. Tester	Carb. Air Bleeds, Float level		
Electro Power Balance	E.P.B. & Vac. Gauge Scale	Individual Cyl. Comp. Factors		
Record RPM and Vac.	1	2	3	4	5	6	7	8
Spark Plugs Under Load	Scope (Display)	Worn or Fouled Spark Plugs		
Accelerator Pump Action	Combustion Eff. Tester	Carburetor Accelerator Pump		
Timing Advance	Timing Advance Unit	Dist. Mech. and Vac. Advance		
Maximum Coil Output	Scope (Display)	Coil, Condenser, Ign. Primary		
Secondary Circuit Insulation	Scope (Display)	High tension Wires, Cap, Rotor		
Charging Voltage	Voltmeter	Generator-Alternator, Volt. Reg.		●
Fuel Mixture	Combustion Eff. Tester	Air Cleaner, Carburetor		
Exhaust Restriction	Vacuum Gauge	Exhaust System		

STOP REVIEW TESTS RESULTS ... ➡

Fig. 3-20. A diagnostic check form. Sun Electric Co.

barrel. Make repairs and replacements as required. Set the float level, assemble, and install the carburetor.

(15) Air Cleaner. Clean the air cleaner, remove obstructions and dirt, and reinstall. On oil bath type cleaners, add the specified amount of oil. On other type cleaners, oil the mesh. On those using a paper cartridge, replace the cartridge.

(16) Carburetor Idle. Connect vacuum gage and correct any vacuum leaks at intake manifold, accessory, distributor, or power brake lines.

Check the positive crankcase ventilation valve (PCV) by observing if, when engine is idling and with oil filler cap removed, there is a noticeable vacuum at the opening. If valve is plugged instead of a vacuum, there will be a pressure. *NOTE: Usually an extra charge is made if it should become necessary to remove the manifold or for any work on power brake vacuum lines.*

Set the idle speed and the idle adjustment. (See "Carburetor Tests and Adjustments," Chapter 5.)

(17) Combustion. Test the engine combustion (air-fuel ratio) or engine vacuum and accelerator pump operation as a check on the work performed.

(18) Final Check. Road test the vehicle as a further check on work performed.

TUNE-UP TEST PROCEDURES. A variation of the tune-up in which a check is made of the various factors of performance has become increasingly popular. The procedures are similar to the tune-up but do not provide for correction. In each instance, an added charge is made for any correction required.

In some procedures, the correction is made (at extra charge) as each maladjustment is revealed. In other procedures, all units or factors of performance are checked and the findings recorded. From these findings, recommendation of repair or adjustment is made. In some types of operation, a flat charge is made for the checking operation plus a charge for correction. In other cases, the test operations are performed at no charge.

In a tune-up or a test procedure in which corrections are made as the need is revealed, factors of performance that influence units tested later are corrected so they cannot influence the subsequent readings.

Fig. 3-20 illustrates a typical form used for these operations. It will be noted that these forms are general enough in nature to permit their use on any make or model of car or truck and can be used as an outline and a means of recording the readings for either a tune-up or a test procedure. It should be noted also that tests of the generator and starter circuits, which normally are not considered a part of a tune-up operation, are provided for.

Fig. 3-21 shows a typical diagnostic

Fig. 3-21. A diagnostic testing center. Sun Electric Co.

machine which is used with the form shown in Fig. 3-20. These machines use electronic methods to check the various operations of the engine and car.

TESTS AND ADJUSTMENTS

Throughout the preceding sections, various tests and adjustments were indicated. To avoid repetition, the methods of making these tests and adjustments are presented here.

MISSING CYLINDERS. If one or several cylinders are obviously missing, some time can be saved by finding which are missing and concentrating on them. The test for missing cylinders consists of two steps.

(1) Determine Which Cylinder Is Missing. Most automotive engines fall into two groups. These are based on the number of cylinders and whether they employ a single or dual ignition system. The procedure for determining which cylinders are missing varies for each group of engines.

(a) Four or Six-Cylinder Engines. With the engine running, momentarily short out, in turn, each spark plug. If the shorting of a plug has no effect on the running of the engine, that particular cylinder is missing.

(b) V-8 Engines. Generally eight-cylinder engines will run on four cylinders. Short out every other cylinder in the firing order. The engine will run on four cylinders. Momentarily short out, in turn, each of the remaining four spark plugs. If the shorting of a plug has no effect on the running of the engine, that particular cylinder is missing. Repeat the procedure for the other four cylinders.

(c) Dual Ignition. Engines employing two coils should be run first on one coil; then on the other. Disconnect the primary low-tension lead from one coil, and start the engine. Momentarily short out, in turn, each of the four spark plugs that

work from the coil still connected. If shorting out a spark plug has no effect on the running of the engine, that cylinder is missing.

Reconnect the first coil, and disconnect the second coil. Repeat the procedure for the second four spark plugs.

(2) Determine Cause of Missing. Once it is established which cylinders are missing, your attention can be concentrated on those cylinders.

Test the strength of the spark from each of the spark plug wires. If a satisfactory spark is obtained from the end of the spark plug wire running to a missing cylinder, remove the spark plug. Check the compression of the cylinder, and clean and space or replace the spark plug as required.

NOTE: Missing cylinders are nearly always the result of faulty ignition (including the spark plugs) or a loss of compression. Occasionally an engine will be encountered with missing cylinders that have good compression and good ignition. In such cases, the cause of the miss is probably faulty distribution of the air-fuel mixture to the cylinder.

COMPRESSION. A test of the compression of each of the cylinders will uncover mechanical faults in the engine. Generally it is advisable to run the engine until normal operating temperatures are reached before attempting to test the compression, since in some instances the valves will "hang up" when hot but will perform satisfactorily when cold.

One of the first instruments that should be obtained for diagnosing engine troubles is a good compression gage. The use of the compression gage is as follows:

(1) Taking a Reading. Remove all spark plugs. (This will permit both a faster cranking speed and reduce the drain on the battery during the test.) Don't test any cylinders until all spark plugs are out. Remove the air cleaner

and block the carburetor throttle linkage in open position to assure a full charge of air in the cylinders. With the ignition switch off and the gage in place in one cylinder, crank the engine with the starter until the gage pointer no longer rises. (Usually about six or seven compression strokes are required.) Record the compression reading. Remove the gage and release the air from the gage by means of the bleeder valve.

Test and record the compression of the rest of the cylinders.

(2) Analysis of Reading. If the readings of all cylinders are within 25 percent of each other, usually the difference in compression will not be noticeable in the performance of the engine.

If the compression of any or all of the cylinders shows 25 percent or more variation, the heads should be removed and the carbon scraped from all surfaces of the combustion chamber (head, valves, and piston).

NOTES: The presence of carbon reduces the volume of the combustion chamber, thereby changing the compression ratio. This accounts for the higher-than-normal reading.

Any reading below normal indicates a loss of compression. Usually compression is lost past the valves, piston rings, or through a leaking gasket.

If below-normal readings are obtained on one, several, or all cylinders, squirt about two tablespoonfuls of oil on top of the piston in the cylinder that showed the lowest reading and repeat the compression test for that cylinder. If the reading is now normal, the loss of compression is probably past the piston rings. If the reading is still below normal, the loss of compression is probably past the valves.

NOTE: Neither of the above conclusions is entirely foolproof. Occasionally you will encounter deeply scored cylinders, pistons with a hole through them, and blown head gaskets, none of which will seal with oil, and valves slightly open that will seal themselves during a compression test with oil.

The correction of abnormal compression, either too high or too low, requires the removal of the cylinder heads in order to make a completely accurate analysis of the cause.

Loss of compression past the valves requires either a reseating of the valves or the freeing up of the valve operation. Loss of compression past the pistons requires freeing up or replacement of the rings, new pistons, reboring of the cylinders, or a combination of these.

CYLINDER LEAKAGE. Another method of checking cylinder compression and general condition is by making a cylinder air leakage test. This test is made by applying shop air pressure to a cylinder with a special fitting in the spark plug hole. Each cylinder is checked when the piston is at top center. In this position air introduced to the compression chamber should not leak out very rapidly. However, if a valve, gasket, or the rings are worn, the air leaking past can be heard in the tail pipe if an exhaust valve; carbu-

Fig. 3-22. Tester used to check cylinders with compressed air.

retor if an intake valve; and bubbles will be seen in the radiator if a head gasket leaks. Excessive air past the rings will be noticed by air coming from the oil filler opening. These testers have a gage which will show the percent leakage of the cylinder. A good cylinder should not leak more than 20 percent. Fig. 3-22 illustrates the leakage tester.

INTAKE MANIFOLD VACUUM. A reading of intake manifold vacuum is a valuable indication of engine efficiency if you understand the limitations of the reading. An intake manifold vacuum reading is used in three different ways: as a preliminary test before any corrections are made, as a final test after corrections have been made to prove their effectiveness, and to adjust the carburetor.

In all three uses, connect the vacuum gage to a convenient source, and start the engine.

(1) Preliminary Test. An intake manifold vacuum reading that is normal and steady is a fair indication that the engine has little, if anything, wrong with its operation at the particular speed and load at which the reading is obtained. A low or erratic reading indicates that something is wrong. It must be remembered that anything that affects the efficiency of the engine will affect the vacuum reading.

The things that can account for a low erratic reading are too many to permit interpretation until you have eliminated as many causes as possible from consideration.

A test made prior to making corrections is of value since a second test after the corrections will prove whether or not the corrections were effective.

(2) Final Test. An intake manifold vacuum test, like an exhaust analysis, is an over-all test of the engine efficiency. Any deficiency of ignition, carburetion, or valves will be reflected in the vacuum reading. It is assumed that you have completed the necessary tests and corrections and so have removed the ignition and carburetion from further consideration.

With the vacuum gage connected to the intake manifold, observe the vacuum as the engine runs at idle speed. With engine idling, normal vacuum reading is between 17 and 20.

The following interpretations apply to most engines.

Valve guide loss is indicated by a very fine, rapid tremor of the hand at slow idle speed. As the speed of the engine is increased, tremor disappears.

A valve not seating, such as caused by a burned valve, a stuck valve, or one with insufficient tappet clearance, should have been discovered during the compression test. On the vacuum gage it will register as a regular drop of the hand of one division or more, depending upon how far the valve remains open.

Observe the value of the vacuum reading while the engine is idling slowly.

Open the throttle, evenly and slowly building the engine speed up gradually to about 1,000 rpm. Just a little above the slow idling speed, the vacuum should increase from one-half to two divisions of the scale as the automatic spark advance cuts in. Watch the action of the spark advance by noting the engine speed at which it cuts in. This should be just above idling. Repeat this test several times.

Starting from an idle speed, build the engine speed gradually and evenly up to at least 3,000 rpm, observing the vacuum gage carefully during the build up in speed. A weak valve spring or gummy valve guide may permit the valve to close at the lower speeds, but as the engine speed is built up a point may be reached where the weak spring or gummy valve guide will prevent the valve closing. This will be reflected on the vacuum gage by sudden drops of the hand appearing when this point in speed is reached.

COMBUSTION. A combustion analysis, like an intake manifold vacuum test, is a measure of the engine efficiency at the speed and load at which it is operating at the time of the test. It must be remembered that readings of rich or lean do not necessarily mean faulty carburetion. Internal combustion engine operation is the result of the combustion process. If the combustion process is perfect, a definite percentage of the exhaust gases will be carbon dioxide. The combustion analyzer, or exhaust gas analyzer as it is sometimes called, indicates when the exhaust gas is unbalanced, denoting less than perfection.

This lack of perfection, in addition to faulty carburetion, can be caused by faulty compression, imperfect ignition, or ignition occurring either too early or too late. If you keep this in mind, you will find that a combustion analyzer is a valuable tool. If you fail to keep this in mind, and attempt to diagnose trouble from an exhaust gas analysis alone, you will be in trouble constantly since the reading does not provide you with enough information to make a diagnosis.

The combustion analysis is of value if a reading is taken before correction. Then, by taking a second reading after the correction, you can demonstrate the effectiveness of the corrections you have made. In both instances, the engine must be at normal operating temperature when the test is made.

In connection with a chassis dynamometer, which provides a means of placing any degree of load on the engine at various speeds, the combustion analysis becomes a valuable tool, providing specific rather than general information. Except where a chassis dynamometer is available, conditions of speed and load cannot be duplicated on the garage floor. This means that carburetor power jets cannot be made to operate in the shop.

Exhaust and intake restriction, likewise, cannot be duplicated.

Remember the limitations of the combustion analyzer and it becomes a valuable tool.

Most combustion analyzers are provided with a "balance" adjustment which must be set before the analyzer is connected to the exhaust. This adjustment is important. Follow the instruction procedure exactly for the particular equipment with which you are working.

TEST FOR STICKING VALVES. In most engines, valves that are sticking will be indicated by a regular or occasional valve noise while the engine is operating. Occasionally, however, you will encounter an engine in which the valves function perfectly at idle speed and the tendency to hang up is not revealed either by valve noise or a compression test. A road or dynamometer test under load, however, will result in a definite miss in the cylinders involved. This miss may or may not occur each cycle. In most instances, sticking valves are at least temporarily relieved by introducing a gum solvent oil into the carburetor throat while the engine is running.

If an engine that missed under load no longer misses after introduction of the gum solvent oil, it is safe to assume that the valves have been sticking and the gum solvent oil has temporarily corrected the condition. Permanent correction will require the removal and thorough cleaning of the parts involved or the use of a gum solvent in the engine oil, plus repeated applications of solvent through the carburetor until the condition is cleared up. *CAUTION: The use of a gum solvent oil in the crankcase will loosen sludge, gums, carbon, and other contaminants and keep them suspended in the engine oil. If the engine is particularly dirty, enough of this material may be circulated to clog the oil passages and the oil pump screen.*

CYLINDER HEADS AND MANIFOLDS. The tightening of cylinder heads and manifolds should be a part of every tune up and of most trouble shooting procedures.

(1) Cylinder Heads. Several methods of tightening cylinder head bolts are popular and are equally good. In all of these methods, the center bolt or screw is tightened first. From this point, the others are tightened one at a time. First on one side of the center, then on the other side. In all cases, after the first bolt or screw is tightened, each subsequent screw or bolt tightened is next to one bolt that has been tightened previously. This order is indicated by the numbers shown in Fig. 3-23.

All manufacturers specify a particular torque to which the cylinder bolts or screws should be tightened. This torque represents the maximum tension that can be placed on them without distortion of the cylinder bores or valve seats. Manufacturer's specifications for cylinder head bolt or screw torque must be rigidly followed.

(2) Intake Manifold. While the compression of an intake manifold gasket is not so great as a cylinder head gasket, these gaskets also take a "set." Intake manifold screws should be tightened or checked for tightness prior to any attempt to adjust the carburetor.

Air leakage into the intake manifold will make the fuel-air mixture lean. While in some instances it will be possible to compensate for this extra air by enriching the idle fuel adjustment, the mixture will be rich at greater engine speeds where the extra air becomes less of a factor.

Most engine manufacturers specify a torque to which intake manifold nuts should be tightened. Lacking such a specification, the manifold nuts can be tightened "firm."

At the time the intake manifold screws are tightened, all other points of possible air entry should be checked. Air leakage can occur at the carburetor-to-manifold gasket, and the nuts or screws should likewise be tightened. Most intake manifolds are provided with a vacuum connection for operation of vacuum accessories. All connections must be vacuum tight. A test of the effectiveness of the above tightening to eliminate vacuum leakage can be made by adjusting the carburetor until the engine runs smoothly. Then, with the engine running, squirt oil on the various vacuum connections or other points of possible air leakage. If the engine speed increases when oil is placed on one of these points, leakage is occurring at that point.

(3) Exhaust Manifold. Ordinarily, the tightening of exhaust manifold nuts is not a part of the various tune-up or trouble shooting procedure. However, if an observation of the manifold-to-cylinder-block connection indicates looseness or leakage, the manifold should be tightened to prevent exhaust manifold gasket failure.

CAMSHAFT END PLAY. Due to the helix of camshaft drive gear or distributor drive gear teeth, any fore-and-aft movement of the camshaft or up-and-down movement of the distributor shaft will result in a change of the ignition timing. If the engine flywheel, crankshaft pulley, or damper is provided with timing marks, end play of either the camshaft or distributor shaft that takes place during idle will result in a change in timing that can be observed with a timing light.

If these units are provided with marks indicating maximum spark advance, the advance at other speeds likewise can be checked with a timing light. If, with the engine running at a constant speed (and load), the timing mark appears to move when viewed with a timing light, it may be an indication of end play of either the camshaft or distributor shaft. Usually, a

Fig. 3-23. Tightening procedure for cylinder head bolts.

movement of one degree or less is not a serious factor.

In some engines, the end play of the camshaft can be checked with a feeler gage between the end of the shaft or the gear and the camshaft thrust surface.

End play of the distributor shaft on venturi vacuum advance distributors in which the cam is integral with the shaft usually can be detected by alternately raising or lowering the distributor cam to observe the amount of movement (end play). This method cannot be used on distributors with centrifugal advance.

ROAD TESTS. Road tests under load are a means of checking for ignition breakdown, early timing, pre-ignition, faulty power jet operation, or any other condition that affects performance under load.

If available, a hill should be used for the test. However, in flat country, a hill can be simulated by partial application of the brakes.

Attain the speed desired. Then gradually apply the brakes, at the same time pressing the accelerator all the way down and the brakes are holding the speed at the desired point.

Usually maximum compressions are reached at speeds between 30 and 45 mph

when the throttle is wide open. Ignition breakdown will cause missing in this range. In all vehicles, the carburetor power jet should be operating at any speed with the throttle wide open.

Pinging at all speeds under load indicates early timing. Either the basic timing is too early or the retard mechanism is not functioning. Pinging at one or several speeds, but not all speeds, usually indicates the spark advance is not following its curve.

(1) Dynamometer. A chassis dynamometer provides an excellent means of performing this test. In fact, it provides the only means of making the carburetor power jets function at any given speed without taking the vehicle out on the road.

(2) Top Speed. Very few locations provide a suitable place for a high-speed test. Not only must local ordinances be taken into account, but the safety of the operator and others must be considered.

(3) Acceleration. Select a strip of straight, smooth, and dry pavement for the test. With the car traveling 7 mph in high gear, press the accelerator all the way down, noting the number of seconds required to reach 25 mph.

Check the acceleration starting at 7

mph in high gear, noting the number of seconds required to reach 50 mph.

Repeat the tests, going in the opposite direction, and use the average time to compensate for the wind.

If you do not have acceleration data for the particular make and model of car, make a test of another car of the same make, model, and axle ratio, and compare the two readings to determine if the car is normal.

If you have manufacturer's specifications that indicate either a different starting or finishing speed, follow the manuturer's recommendations.

OIL CONSUMPTION. Before attempting to make an accurate test of oil consumption, make sure that the oil is not diluted and is the correct viscosity, that the oil level is correct, and that leakage does not exist.

Start the engine and allow it to run until normal operating temperatures are reached. Then stop the engine, and drain the oil into a clean container. Allow it to drain for five minutes. Weigh the oil and container. Put the oil back in the engine. *NOTE: If a scale is not available, measure the oil carefully.*

Make sure the car is level, and allow it to sit for five minutes to be sure the oil has time to run down into the oil pan. Mark the oil level on the oil level gage.

Make a run at the speed at which the owner claimed the consumption was high. If no particular speed is indicated, make the test at 50 mph. The test run can be for 10, 20, or 50 miles, depending on the degree of accuracy required.

After returning from the run, stop the engine at a place where the vehicle is level, and allow it to sit for at least five minutes. If absolute accuracy is required, as would be true on an official test, drain the oil into the container used originally. Allow the oil to drain for at least five minutes. Again weigh the oil and container. The difference between this weight and the original weight is the consumption for the number of miles driven at the test speed.

Usually, if the oil consumption test is merely to demonstrate the consumption to the owner, it may be satisfactory not to drain the oil either before or after the test. Merely make sure the oil in the engine is good quality and the correct viscosity and that the level is not too high. With the engine at normal temperature, allow the engine to sit for five minutes. Mark the level on the gage, make the run, and compare the level after the run.

TRADE COMPETENCY TEST

1. If below-normal compression is brought up to normal after squirting oil on the top of the pistons, what is indicated?

2. What causes higher than normal compression?

3. What effect does engine oil that is too heavy have on engine performance?

4. What is the effect of vapor lock?

5. What is the usual cause when the engine backfires and fails to start?

6. What are the two most common conditions which cause the engine to run unevenly and backfire through the carburetor?

7. If the engine starts but fails to keep running, what is usually the cause of the trouble?

8. If gum solvent added through the carburetor

temporarily corrects a highspeed miss, what permanent correction must be made?

9. Why do ignition faults not apparent under other conditions show up under acceleration or hard pull?

10. What are some of the hazards of setting the idle speed too low?

11. If an engine idles smoothly when warm, but runs unevenly when cold, what do you do first?

12. How can cold weather operation cause crankcase dilution?

13. In what way does too high an oil level affect oil consumption?

14. What is meant by a positive displacement oil pump?

15. How can you determine whether a ping is caused by early timing or pre-ignition?

16. If the piston or top ring touches the head-gasket lightly, what kind of sound can be heard?

17. When a noise accurs twice each cycle, what parts are involved?

18. What instruments can be used to quickly demonstrate the need of an engine tune-up?

19. Why should the compression test be the first step performed i n an engine tune-up?

20. How can you determine which cylinder is missing in a four- or six-cylinder engine?

21. What engine faults are disclosed by a compression test?

22. What is the purpose of an intake manifold vacuum test?

23. What things other than the fuel system have an influence on the combustion analyzer reading?

24. What hazards are involved when gum solvents or detergent oils are added to the crankcase oil?

25. Why must the cylinder heads not be tightened above the torque specified by the manufacturer?

26. In operation, under what conditions is maximum compression usually obtained?

CHAPTER 4

IGNITION SYSTEMS

The ignition system of the automobile is a unique one. It has not changed very much from its inception but it has benefited from year to year improvements. With these improved ignition systems less difficulty in starting and high-speed operation is encountered. The major emphasis now is on proper periodic maintenance to keep the ignition system operating at its optimum level and to reduce the possibility of troubles such as *can't start, missing,* or even *poor gasoline mileage.*

Ignition system troubles can be very disturbing to the driver. The service technician should spend a little extra time developing his understanding of the ignition trouble shooting procedures presented in this chapter as they are most important and will be frequently used. Proceedures are described for use with or without special test equipment such as an oscilloscope. In many cases the scope is not even necessary for the trouble shooting process. In other instances, the scope, if used, will reduce trouble shooting time immensely.

Regardless of the equipment, a trouble shooter must understand the system and whatever testing equipment he has available will be extremely helpful if properly used.

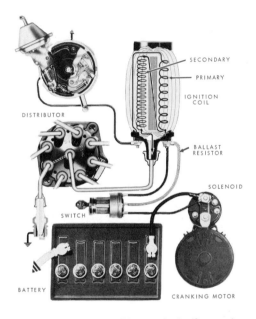

Fig. 4-1. A typical ignition and starting system. Pontiac Motor Div., General Motors Corp.

Troubles in the ignition system generally will come to you as engine troubles as covered in Chapter 3 of this volume or as "excessive fuel consumption" as presented in Chapter 5.

Wherever possible in ignition trouble shooting, as in all trouble shooting, the final result is checked rather than the source. The effectiveness of ignition sys-

127

tem operation is judged by the quality and regularity of the spark obtained at the end of each of the spark plug wires.

Most automotive engines use battery-coil ignition systems. The basic battery-coil ignition circuit which you will encounter is shown in Fig. 4-1. While it does

The third, combination of vacuum and centrifugal spark advance, is the one most commonly used.

Most distributors are equipped with one set of contact points. Some, however, use two sets of contact points. The circuit shown in Fig. 4-2 employs two sets of

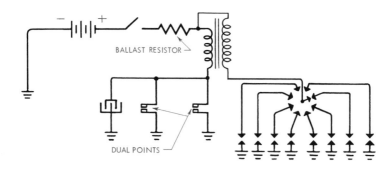

Fig. 4-2. Diagram of an ignition system with dual points.

not represent all of the possible combinations, all of the parts involved are shown.

Ballast resistors between the ignition switch and the coil primary terminal are shown in Figs. 4-1 and 4-2.

While you may never encounter a dual ignition system, you should be able to recognize it. Dual ignition systems provide two of everything, including two connections to the spark plug in each cylinder. Dual ignition systems are thought to provide better operational characteristics for racing engines and other heavy duty operations.

Ignition distributors are gear driven through the camshaft.

Distributors fall into three additional classifications, depending upon the type of spark advance mechanism employed:

1. Centrifugal,
2. Vacuum, and
3. Combination vacuum and centrifugal.

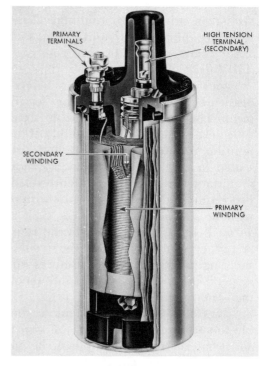

Fig. 4-3. View of ignition coil showing construction. Delco Remy Div., General Motors Corp.

contact points parallel to each other as shown. In this case, one set closes the circuit and the other opens it.

Most ignition systems employ the can type coils as shown in Fig. 4-3.

TROUBLE SHOOTING EQUIPMENT

The following procedures will use a voltmeter and a jumper wire. For most trouble shooting these items work very well. It is possible to use an oscilloscope to assist in ignition trouble shooting, if one is available. It should be used according to the instructions supplied by the manufacturer. Typical oscilloscope patterns are shown in Fig. 4-4. Each scope has some slight variations, but when you become familiar with a normal pattern, experience will help you to determine faults very quickly. The instruction booklets also give examples of abnormal patterns. Keep in mind that the scope is

no magic device. The operator must understand what he is doing for the scope to be useful.

TROUBLE SHOOTING PROCEDURE

The ignition circuit can be quickly checked to localize the areas that are working properly and those that are not. A lack of spark, or if the engine starts but stops when the ignition switch is released, indicates definite ignition problems.

ENGINE STARTS BUT STOPS

If the engine starts but stops when the switch is released the usual problem is an open resistor or resistance wire. When cranking the engine the resistor in the primary circuit is by-passed. It is possible that an open switch exists in the primary circuit from the ignition switch to the coil also.

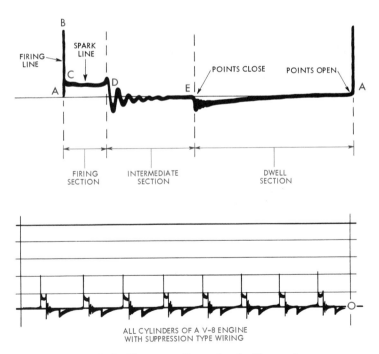

Fig. 4-4. Oscilloscope pattern of an ignition system.

NO SPARK

If an engine fails to start a check should be made to determine if spark is available. Fig. 4-5. This is done by removing a spark plug wire from a spark plug, holding the wire approximately ¼″ from the engine, and cranking the en-

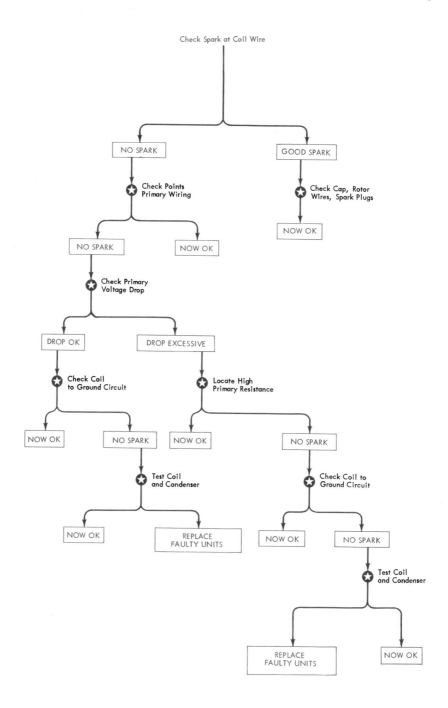

gine. Fig. 4-6. If a spark does exist and will jump the air gap it indicates that the ignition system is not at fault. If no spark occurs, the next step is to remove the coil high tension wire from the center of the distributor cap and hold it $\frac{1}{4}''$ from a good ground. Crank the engine again, briefly. If a good spark occurs, the ignition primary circuit is operating. Fig. 4-7. The ignition failure then must be in the secondary circuit. Check the wires, distributor cap, and rotor. It is also a

good idea to remove at least one spark plug to determine the condition of the plugs.

At this point it is wise to check inside the distributor. Remove the cap and rotor and observe whether the contact points are opening and closing. If they are not operating, they should be adjusted so they do open and close. When this is done, check for spark again at the high tension lead as in Fig. 4-7. If no spark occurs, replace the contact set. If the points are oxidized or if the rubbing block is worn excessively, replace the contacts. Be sure to lubricate the breaker cam. If no spark was delivered from the coil wire, the ignition primary circuit should now be checked.

To check the primary circuit, first test the battery to coil circuit. This can be done with a voltmeter connected from the battery positive terminal to the battery terminal of the coil. Crank the engine. The voltage drop should not be

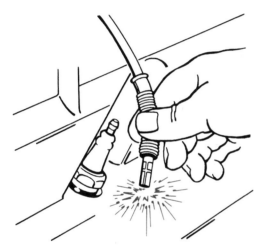

Fig. 4-6. Checking ignition wiring to see if a spark is produced.

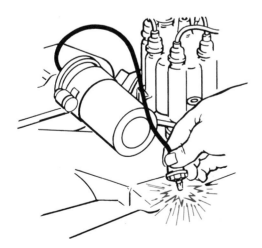

Fig. 4-7. Checking the primary circuit.

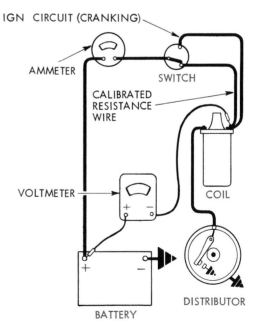

Fig. 4-8. Measuring battery to coil voltage drop.

greater than 1 volt. If it is less, the primary circuit so far is O.K. See Fig. 4-8.

The preceding test is by-passing the ignition switch "run" contacts and the ignition primary resistor. These can be checked by placing a jumper wire from the distributor terminal of the coil to ground as shown in Fig. 4-9. The voltage

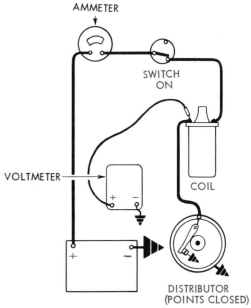

Fig. 4-10. Checking the coil to ground voltage drop.

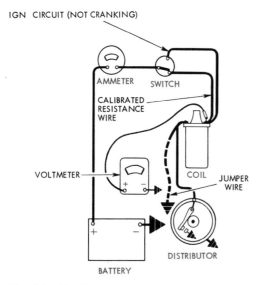

Fig. 4-9. Checking the primary circuit to coil voltage drop.

reading should be between five and eight volts. If it is, the primary circuit is good to the coil. If the voltage is too high, check the wiring, ignition switch, and resistor. If no spark occurs, the next step is to make a coil to ground test as shown in Fig. 4-10. With the contact points closed, ignition switch on, the voltage should read .1 volt or less. If the reading is too high, check the wiring from the coil to and through the distributor to ground. If there is still no spark the trouble is in the coil or condenser. These units can be tested on a special tester or a good coil or condenser may be substituted to determine which is at fault.

SPARK AT SOME WIRES

The procedure to be followed when a satisfactory spark is obtained from some but not all of the spark plug wires is illustrated in Fig. 4-11.

Test the spark from the end of each spark plug wire at idle speed of from 500 to 700 rpm as outlined later. A spark that fails to jump this gap regularly is considered a weak spark.

DEFINITION: A satisfactory spark is one that will, without missing, regularly jump a spark gap equivalent to the resistance offered by a correctly spaced spark plug under the compression pressure encountered in the operation of the engine. Usually, if the spark will regularly jump a 1/4 in. gap, it will fire under the compressions encountered in most engines.

The fact that a satisfactory spark is obtained from some spark plug wires eliminates from consideration those factors that affect equally the output of all of the spark plug wires. These factors are

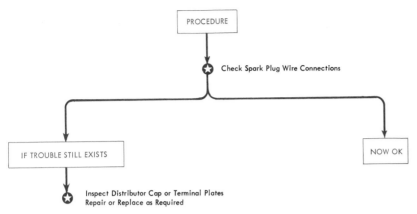

Fig. 4-11. Spark at some wires.

the entire primary circuit, including the contact points, the condenser, and the coil. Likewise, the rotor, as well as the coil-to-distributor high-tension circuit, can be considered as being satisfactory and eliminated from further consideration. The following procedure takes into account each of the factors that could account for this symptom in the order of its probability.

An unsatisfactory spark at some but not all of the spark plug wires indicates faulty insulation or series resistance (air gap) in the high-tension circuit.

TROUBLE SHOOTING PROCEDURE

The distributor ends of the spark plug wires are accessible from the outside of the distributor on some ignition systems and inaccessible on others. The order of the following can be varied to suit the particular ignition system being worked on.

CHECK SPARK PLUG WIRES. Replace spark plug wires if the insulation is damaged. Make sure all the spark plug wires are in good contact with their terminals. Make sure the spark plug wire terminals and the terminal sockets are free from corrosion and that the wires are firmly

seated in the distributor cap. An ohmmeter should be used to check the resistance of the suspected wire. Suppression type secondary wire should have a resistance of approximately 6-8,000 ohms per foot of length. If the foregoing procedure has not corrected the trouble, proceed as follows:

INSPECT DISTRIBUTOR CAP. Remove the distributor cap and clean with carbon tetrachloride. If the terminals, cap, or rotor electrodes are burned or cracked, or have carbon tracks replace the parts at fault (see "High Tension Insulation," this Chapter). Make sure the wires are firmly seated in the terminal sockets of the distributor cap.

INTERMITTENT SPARK

Test the spark from the end of each spark plug wire at idle speed with a 1/4 in. gap. A spark that does not consistently jump this gap is considered an intermittent spark.

When the spark delivered at the end of the spark plug wire is satisfactory but intermittent, the primary ignition circuit is logically given first consideration in the diagnosis procedure. The fact that between "misses" the spark is satisfactory precludes the possibility that the trouble is in the secondary circuit. The exception would be in relatively rare cases of intermittent breakdown of the insulation in the coil, or when moisture, oil, or foreign matter is allowed to accumulate on the distributor cap, or distributor rotor in sufficient quantities to short the high-tension circuit intermittently to ground.

TROUBLE SHOOTING PROCEDURE

The procedure to follow is illustrated in Fig. 4-12.

TIGHTEN CONNECTIONS. Make sure that all connections in the primary circuit are clean and tight, including both terminals of the condenser and both ends of both battery cables.

Make sure the coil-to-distributor high-tension wire is seated all the way in the high-tension terminal of the coil.

If the foregoing has not corrected the trouble, proceed as follows:

ADJUST CONTACT POINTS. Align and respace the distributor contact points (see "Contact Points," this chapter). Make sure the breaker arm is not binding on its bearing. Make sure the breaker arm

spring tension is within the specified limits.

Reset the timing, and again test the quality of the spark. If the spark is still intermittent, proceed as follows:

TEST COIL AND CONDENSER. Test the coil output and the condenser (see "Coil Output" and "Condenser," this chapter). If the coil and condenser were both found to be satisfactory, examine which might cause an intermittent leak of high-tension current to ground. Clean any of the parts in question and replace the parts having carbon runs embedded in the surface.

NOTE: A distributor rotor just starting to short through to the distributor shaft could cause an occasional miss under load. Eventually such a rotor will short every spark.

WEAK SPARK

A weak spark at all of the spark plug wires can only be the result of trouble in some unit or units that have an equal effect at all of the spark plug wires. The entire primary circuit, including the contact points, has an equal effect on all

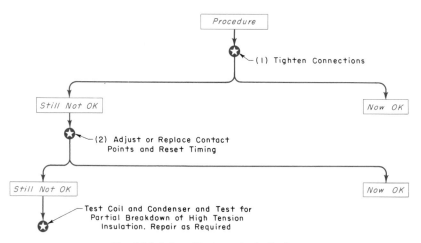

Fig. 4-12. Intermittent spark at all wires.

spark plug wires. The high-tension wire from the coil to the distributor also can influence the output of all of the spark plug wires. These represent the probable causes of weak spark.

It is possible for all of the spark plug wires or all of the terminals or distributor cap to leak. However, this is considered unlikely, and in the following procedure the more probable causes are considered first in the order of their accessibility.

TROUBLE SHOOTING PROCEDURE

Since the ignition secondary output is dependent on the primary voltage, the condition or state of charge of the battery is an important consideration. If the battery will not crank the engine, recharge or replace the battery. With the battery eliminated as a source of the trouble, the problem of locating the cause of the weak spark consists of two steps. These two steps are the elimination of unwanted resistances in the coil primary and tests of the units in the circuit. An outline of the complete procedure to follow is illustrated in Fig. 4-13.

REMOVE EXCESSIVE RESISTANCE. Resistance in the ignition primary circuit will lower the output of the coil secondary and can account for this symptom. The distributor contact points are the most common source of trouble in the primary circuit and for this reason are tested first. The battery-to-coil circuit is tested next.

(1) Test Contact Spacing, and Cam Angle. Measure the contact point spacing, dwell, or cam angle (see "Contact Points," this chapter). If with the contact point spacing, dwell, or cam angle within the manufacturer's specified limits, the spark is still weak, test the resistance of the circuit from the battery to the coil.

If the spacing or dwell is not within limits, replace contact points that are visibly burned or pitted and adjust the points to obtain the correct reading or spacing. This may be all that is required. Test the quality of the spark to determine if this is true.

(2) Test Battery to Coil Resistance. Since the output of the ignition secondary circuit is limited by the strength of the primary circuit, any extra resistance in the primary circuit will reduce the output of the coil. Test the resistance of the primary circuit (see "Primary Circuit Resistance," in this chapter) and make any corrections indicated. If the foregoing has not corrected the trouble, proceed as follows:

TEST COIL, CONDENSER, AND CONTACT POINTS. The order of procedure to follow in testing the coil, condenser, and contact points is as follows:

(1) Coil and Condenser. Remove the high-tension wire from the coil and install a 12 in. long jumper wire in the high-tension terminal of the coil. Turn the ignition switch on. Hold the end of this jumper wire $\frac{1}{4}$ in. from the cylinder head while the engine is being cranked. If the spark jumps this gap regularly both the coil and condenser are satisfactory.

If the spark fails to jump a $\frac{1}{4}$ in. gap replace the condenser with one known to be good. If the spark is now satisfactory the trouble has been corrected. If the spark still fails to jump this gap, remove and test the ignition coil output (see "Coil Output" in this chapter). If this test reveals the coil to be unsatisfactory, replace the coil and again test the spark from the end of each spark plug wire.

If the coil has been replaced with a new one or if the original coil and con-

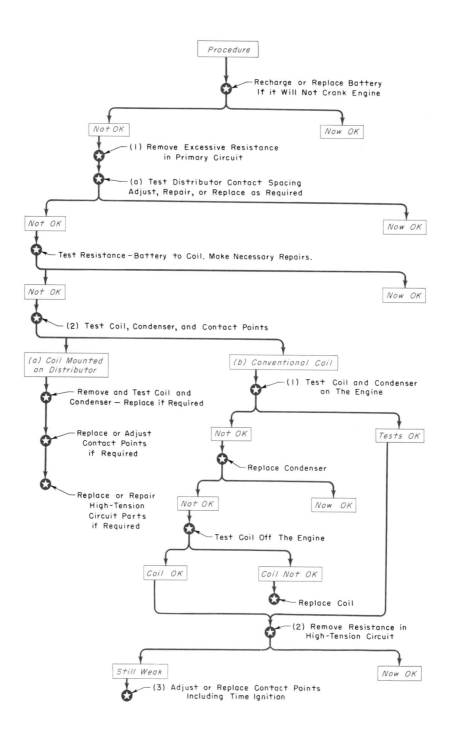

Fig. 4-13. Weak spark at all wires.

denser functioned satisfactorily, proceed as follows:

(2) High-Tension Circuit. Clean the distributor cap and rotor. Replace these parts if any carbon tracks are visible or if the electrodes have eroded to the extent that the rotor gap has been increased. Replace the rotor if there is any indication that it shorts through to the distributor shaft under load. Replace the rotor contact brush if it is broken or worn. Make sure all high-tension wire terminals are in good contact with the wires, and that their terminal sockets are free from corrosion.

(3) Contact Points. Replace the distributor contact points if they are burned or misaligned. Establish the correct spacing, dwell, or cam angle and reset the ignition timing.

SERVICING IGNITION SYSTEMS

Most engine trouble shooting procedures start with tests designed either to establish the ignition system as the seat of the fault or to permit the ignition system to be dropped from consideration. The ignition system usually is the least understood and, at the same time, the seat of more troubles than any other unit or system.

SPARK STRENGTH

A test of the strength of the spark from the end of each spark plug wire is the first test made in most engine trouble shooting procedures.

Run the engine at idle speed. Remove the wire from No. 1 spark plug and hold the wire terminal $1/4$ in. from the cylinder head and observe if the spark jumps the gap regularly without missing. Make this test at each spark plug wire.

If a satisfactory spark is not obtained at one or more cylinders, refer to the appropriate symptom in the first four sections of this chapter.

If a satisfactory spark from all wires is obtained, the ignition system in most instances can be dropped from further consideration as the seat of the trouble. This test is conclusive proof that (1) distributor contacts are in good condition (otherwise the spark would be irregular) and (2) the coil and the condenser are satisfactory. Occasionally, however, you will encounter a coil or condenser that performs perfectly when cold but will miss when hot. (3) The rotor and distributor cap are not shorted. Occasionally, these parts will perform perfectly when dry, but will leak through surface dust when wet or damp. (4) The rotor gap is not too great. (5) All of the spark plug wires are satisfactory, and are properly seated in the distributor cap.

SPARK PLUGS

While in most procedures the cleaning, adjusting, and testing of the spark plugs might be presented in a manner that makes the operation appear to be merely an incidental part of the compression test, this is not true. You should never test compression without doing whatever work is necessary on the spark plugs, nor should you ever remove the plugs for servicing without testing the compression. The various operations on the spark plugs presented here are (1) testing, in and out of the engine; (2) cleaning; (3) gap spacing; (4) analyzing suitability; and (5) installation.

(2) TESTING IN THE ENGINE. The best method of testing a spark plug is in its cylinder. The oscilloscope is the easiest and only sure way of testing spark plugs under operating conditions. If no scope is available proceed to check out the engine.

Scope testing of spark plugs is explained by the various scope manufacturers. With some practice it can be relatively easy to detect ignition troubles. See Figs. 4-14 and 4-15. These are merely examples to show how the scope pattern can be useful.

(2) TESTING OUT OF THE ENGINE. Several methods of testing spark plugs off the engine are in common use. One method measures the resistance of the spark plug electrically under approximately 5,000 volts. A second method and by far the more popular is a comparison between the plugs to be tested and a new spark plug. Both spark plugs are subjected to a specified air pressure, and a high-tension current is sent through first one plug and then the other. A window and mirror arrangement permits the operator to see the spark jumping the gap.

In either of these methods, it is important that the spark plug be properly cleaned and the gap set before the test is made. Otherwise, you may condemn good spark plugs.

CLEANING. Spark plugs, particularly if they are too cold for the operating conditions under which the engine is being used, will either foul and so add to the resistance of the gap that the plug will not fire, or the parallel path through these deposits will short out the plug.

The only truly satisfactory method of cleaning spark plugs is with a sandblast type spark plug cleaner. Sand-blast cleaners clean the plug by bombarding it with sharp particles of sand traveling at high velocity in a stream of air. Continue the operation only as long as necessary to thoroughly clean the plug. Prolonged or repeated blasting will seriously erode the porcelain.

File the electrodes before setting the gap. The gap always must be adjusted after cleaning. Be sure to remove any sand that may have become wedged between the porcelain and the outer case. Oily plugs must be dried before sand blasting.

Always be sure to clean the upper

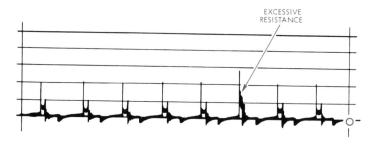

Fig. 4-14. Oscilloscope pattern of a fouled plug.

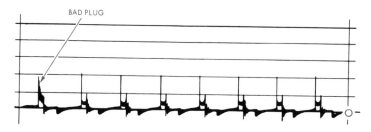

Fig. 4-15. Oscilloscope pattern showing excessive resistance in a cylinder.

portion of the ceramic insulator as deposits of dust or other matter on the outside may hold moisture and cause the plug to short during damp weather or when the vehicle is washed. It is not unusual for spark plugs to foul at relatively low mileage. Some high-performance engines require new spark plugs at very low mileage. The average spark plug should be replaced at yearly intervals or at 10,000-12,000 miles. Fuel additives and emission systems are factors which contribute to plug trouble. Often cleaning will not suffice at all. New spark plugs can make a great difference in overall ignition performance.

SPACING. Spark plug gaps usually increase at a rate of 0.0005 to 0.0015 in. for each 1,000 miles of operation, depending on the type of operation. Spark plug electrode erosion is accelerated at high temperatures. Engines operated at full load or high speeds usually will require more frequent attention.

Always adjust the spark plug gap by bending the outer electrode. Most spark plug manufacturers furnish bending tools gratis to persons in the service industry. These bending tools are specially designed for this job, permit accurate control of the gap, and reduce the possibility of breaking the ceramic insulator. Most car manufacturers specify the use of a wire gage rather than a blade for setting spark plug gaps.

Since spark plug gaps always increase in service, it generally is advisable to set the gap to the minimum limit rather than to the maximum, thereby providing longer life for the adjustment. The only exception to this is in engines that fail to idle properly with the smaller gap.

INSPECTING. All tune-up procedures and most trouble shooting procedures require the removal of the spark plugs. *NOTE. Removing the spark plug wires is the first step. The insulating boot of* *the wire often sticks to the spark plug. To remove, twist the insulating boot of the wire and pull on the boot only. Pulling on the wire could and probably would break it off or break it internally. Use great care when removing spark plug wires.*

When the plugs are first removed, a careful examination of them may provide some clues as to other troubles in the engine. Likewise, the color and condition of the spark plug itself is an important factor in your analysis. Carefully examine the spark plugs as removed and look for:

(1) Wetness. If the ceramic insulator is wet with oil, water, or gasoline, the plug has not been firing.

(2) Breakage. If the spark plug insulator is broken or cracked, replace the spark plug.

(3) Chippage. If the porcelain is chipped near the center electrode, it usually indicates someone has been careless in adjusting the gap. Replace the spark plug.

(4) Erosion. If the spark plug electrodes are badly eroded, the plug should be replaced.

(5) Color. Observe the color of the firing end of the ceramic insulation of the spark plugs as they are removed.

(a) Light Brown. If the color is light brown, the plug is of the right heat value and has been functioning properly.

(b) Dead White. If the color is a dead white, the plug is too hot (see Table 4-1) or the engine is running too hot.

(c) Black. If the plug has a black deposit on the firing end of the ceramic insulation, the plug is too cold (see Table 4-1) for the engine as it has been operated or as it is in its present mechanical condition. In some cases, an extremely rich idle mixture can account for this black deposit.

INSTALLATION. It usually is advisable to install new gaskets when the spark

TABLE 4-1. SPARK PLUG HEAT RANGE[1,2] COMPARISONS

←———————————————— H O T T E R ————————————

AC SPARK PLUG DIVISION OF GMC

14 mm 3/8" Reach	C49	48		46S* 46 R46 R46S*	R45 45S* 45 R45S*
14 mm 7/16" Reach		47L			45L 45LS* LM45L
14 mm 1/2" Reach		47FF	46FF 46FFX* R46FF	45FFS*	45FF 45F 45FD
14 mm 3/4" Reach		47XL	46XL 46N R46N	45N	45XL R45XL R45XLS* 45XLS*
18 mm 60° Seat			86T 86TS*		85T R85T 85TS* R85TS*

CHAMPION

14 mm 3/8" Reach	UJ-12†	J-11 XJ-20Y*	J-8 UJ-18Y† UJ-8†	J-14Y
14 mm 7/16" Reach	H-12	H-11 H-18Y*	H-10 H-14Y*	
14 mm 1/2" Reach				
14 mm 3/4" Reach	N-21		N-8 N-16Y*	
18 mm 60° Seat		870 UF-14Y*†		

AUTOLITE

14 mm 3/8" Reach	A11	AR10 AT10	A9 AZ9†	AR80	A82* AR82* AT8	A7
14 mm 7/16" Reach	AL11		AL9	ARL8 ATL8	ARL82* AL82*	AL7 AT6
14 mm 1/2" Reach				AE82*		AE6 AER6 AE62*
14 mm 3/4" Reach			4GS125		4GS-150 AGR82* AG82*	AG7 AGZ7†
18 mm 60° Seat			BF92*		BRF8 BF82* BRF82*	BF7

*Plugs with extended tip design
†Plugs with internal auxiliary gaps

TABLE 4-1. SPARK PLUG HEAT RANGE COMPARISONS (CONT'D)

⎯⎯ C O L D E R ⎯⎯⎯⎯⎯⎯⟶

AC SPARK PLUG DIVISION OF GMC

				Reach
44 R44	R44S* 44S*	43 R43	42 42S	14 mm 3/8" Reach
		43L		14 mm 7/16" Reach
44FF 44F			42FF	14 mm 1/2" Reach
44N R44N	R44XLS* R44XL	43N R43N	C42N	14 mm 3/4" Reach
	84T 84TS* R84TS*	C83T		18 mm 60° Seat

CHAMPION

						Reach
J-13Y	UJ-12Y*† XJ-12Y*	J-7	J-6 UJ-6†	UJ-10Y*†	J-4 J-9Y*	14 mm 3/8" Reach
		H-8				14 mm 7/16" Reach
	UL-15Y*†		UL-12Y*†			14 mm 1/2" Reach
N-6 N-14Y* XN-14Y*	N-5 UN-12Y* XN-12Y*	N-11Y*		N-10Y*	N-3 N-9Y*	14 mm 3/4" Reach
	860 UF-11Y*†	UF-9Y*†		F-10		18 mm 60° Seat

AUTOLITE

						Reach
AR51 A5	A52* AR52*	AR41 AT4	A42* AR42* AT42*	A3 AR32* A32*	AT3 AR31	14 mm 3/8" Reach
AL5 ARL5	AL52*	ATL4		ATL3		14 mm 7/16" Reach
AE52*		AE4 AE42* AER4	AE3	AE22*		14 mm 1/2" Reach
AGR51 AG5	AGR52* AG52*	AG42* AGR41 AGR42* AG4		AGR32* AGR31 AG3 AG32*		14 mm 3/4" Reach
BTF6 BRF6		BRF42* BF42*		BRF3 BTF3 BF32* BTF31		18 mm 60° Seat

[1] Do not use chart to convert from one manufacturer's lines to another; see *Spark Plug* listings for individual car models.

[2] Spark plugs with extended tip design usually cover a wider heat range than do conventional plugs; ranges for these plugs may overlap ranges of two or more conventional-design plugs.

(Ethyl Corp.—from "Brief Passenger Car Data")

plugs are installed in the engine. Spark plug gaskets are inexpensive and, when first installed, provide a tight seal that cannot be duplicated if gaskets are reused after having been given their original "set."

Open-end wrenches may slip off the plug and break the ceramic insulator. Box wrenches without the correct offset will not go on the spark plug squarely. Any wrench that is not square with the plug may distort its shell. Most wrench manufacturers have available deep socket wrenches for the removal and installation of spark plugs. A socket wrench is the only wrench which will avoid distortion of the plug and protect the ceramic insulator against damage or breakage.

A torque wrench should be used in conjunction with a deep socket when installing and tightening the spark plugs. The actual procedure to follow is: (1) Clean and space the spark plugs. (2) Clean the spark plug thread with a wire brush. (3) Run a tap in the spark plug hole just far enough to clean the threads. (4) Screw the spark plugs (with new gaskets) in place with the fingers. If plug does not start easily, look for and remove burrs from the spark plug threads. If the plug cannot be turned in at least two turns with the fingers, look carefully to make sure it is not cross threaded. (5) How tightly spark plug is tightened depends on whether the cylinder head is cast iron or aluminum, and the size of the spark plug. Using a deep socket and a torque wrench, tighten the spark plugs in place according to the manufacturer's specifications.

It is good practice to remove and install spark plugs from an aluminum head only when the head is cool. Expansion due to heat will allow removal but installation will be extremely difficult in the cooled down head. To avoid problems allow the engine to cool down before removing parts such as spark plugs.

NOTE: Often a ring of carbon forms in the spark plug hole at the bottom of the spark plug. If this ring is not removed when you install the spark plug, it may be stopped by the carbon, creating the impression that the plug is seated.

TIMING

Engines are provided with timing marks on a rotating member and a stationary pointer or index mark. Clean the area around the timing mark on the flywheel (Fig. 4-16) or vibration damper (Fig. 4-17). Mark this area with chalk so the timing mark will be distinct. If the chalk obscures the timing mark, a pencil line will bring it out.

The first step in timing ignition is to adjust and align the distributor contacts. If you are working on an engine equipped with a vacuum advance distributor, disconnect and plug the vacuum line running to the distributor.

Engine Not Running. If the engine is not running turn the engine until the pointer is exactly on the timing mark (Figs. 4-16 and 4-17). This can be accom-

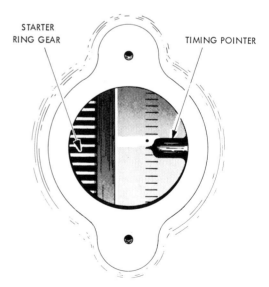

Fig. 4-16. Timing mark on the flywheel.

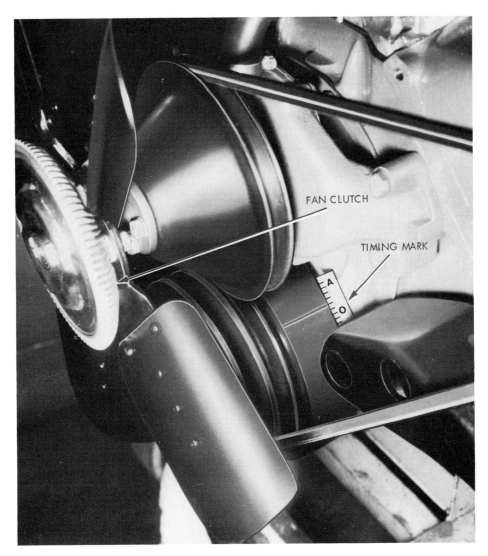

Fig. 4-17. Timing mark on the vibration damper. Chevrolet Motor Div., General Motors Corp.

plished by means of the belt (driven by the crankshaft pulley), or by putting the transmission in high gear and turning one rear wheel. It will be easier to turn the crankshaft and to stop it exactly where you want it if the spark plugs are removed first.

When the pointer is exactly on the timing mark, the distributor contacts should be just starting to open.

The opening of the distributor contact points can be accurately determined in any of three ways.

(1) Use of Test Light. Install a test light or voltmeter in series with the battery and the ignition contact points. Use a twelve-volt bulb and connect it directly to the battery and the distributor terminal of the coil. Leave the ignition switch off. While the contact points are closed

the light will be on or the voltmeter will read 12 volts. The light will go out when the contact points open. Fig. 4-18 shows this type of static timing check.

(2) Use of Ignition Timing Light. Connect an ignition timing light to No. 1 spark plug wire and position it so that you can see it flash when the distributor contacts open. A typical timing light is shown in Fig. 4-19.

(3) Use of Spark Plug Wire. Position No. 1 spark plug wire so its terminal is about $\frac{1}{8}$ in. from the cylinder head or other good ground.

Loosen the clamp holding the distributor. Rotate the distributor body in the direction of distributor rotation to retard the spark. Then slowly turn the distributor against the direction of rotation to the point where (1) the test light goes out, (2) the timing light flashes, or (3) a spark jumps the $\frac{1}{8}$ in. gap. Tighten the clamp to hold the distributor at this position.

ENGINE RUNNING. With the timing marks clean, the contacts correctly spaced

and aligned, the distributor vacuum line disconnected, the timing light properly connected, and the engine at normal operating temperature, set the engine speed according to specifications. Point the timing light at the timing mark and the

Fig. 4-19. Timing light being used to check timing specifications.

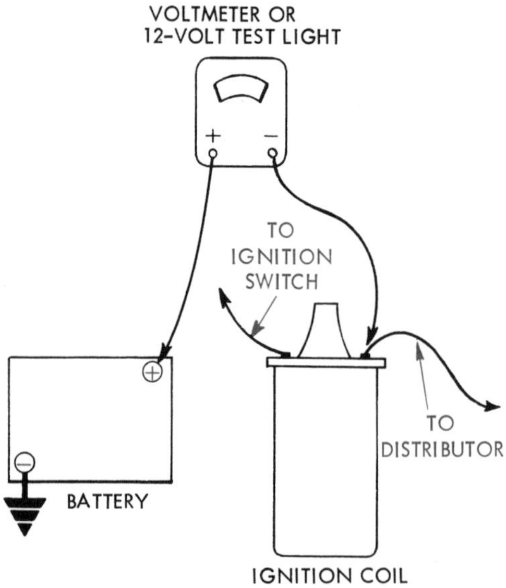

pointer (Fig. 4-19). The timing light will flash each time No. 1 spark plug fires and will give the timing mark the appearance of standing still. If the timing mark is not directly at the pointer, loosen the distributor base clamp and rotate the distributor in the required direction until the pointer is exactly on the timing mark. Lock the distributor in the position where the pointer is exactly on the mark.

SPARK ADVANCE

It is possible for the initial timing of the distributor to be correct, but for the timing at other speeds to be incorrect. The spark advance characteristics must be varied to suit both the speed and the load of the engine. Most of these characteristics, of course, are built into the dis-

VOLTMETER OR
12-VOLT TEST LIGHT

TO
IGNITION
SWITCH

TO
DISTRIBUTOR

BATTERY

IGNITION COIL

Fig. 4-18. A timing check with voltmeter or test light.

tributor, and a motor-driven test bench is required to determine whether or not they have changed. When a spark advance is exactly right at all speeds, the distributor is said to be "on its advance curve." If at one or several points the spark advances too far or is retarded, the distributor is said to be "off its advance curve." The spark advance at all points and at all vacuums can be checked, of course, only on a suitable test bench.

In some engines, marks are provided on the flywheel, crankshaft pulley, or damper, to indicate maximum spark advance. In such engines, the actual maximum advance (but not the curve) may be checked with a timing light as follows to determine whether the spark advances the full amount or not:

ON THE ENGINE. Clean the timing marks and the pointer. Connect the timing light. With the engine running at idle, point it directly toward the timing pointer to determine if the initial timing is correct, then increase the speed of the engine to the point where maximum advance is to be reached and observe whether or not the pointer points to the maximum advance mark (Fig. 4-20).

Some timing lights are designed to indicate ignition advance with a special adjustment knob. The knob is turned to cause the timing marks to indicate TDC. The actual total advance at that speed can be read off the advance meter.

ON THE TEST BENCH. Modern test benches are provided with means of checking not only the maximum spark advance but the degree of advance at any speed, or at any vacuum as well. These machines permit the spacing of contacts electrically, and show any variation in timing between cylinders as occurs with a bent shaft, inaccurate cam, or worn

Fig. 4-20. Timing light being used to check maximum spark advance. Plymouth Div., Chrysler Corp.

Fig. 4-21. Checking the distributor spark advance.

bearings. Test benches provide a means of timing the second set of contacts in relation to the first set on dual point distributors (commonly referred to as synchronizing the distributor). Each make of test bench comes with complete detailed instructions covering how the tests are made. (Fig. 4-21.)

COIL OUTPUT

Ignition coils rarely fail in service, and the various tests of coil output are defined not so much as a test of the coil itself but as a test of the entire ignition system. Low battery voltage and excessive resistance in the primary circuit at any point, including the distributor contacts, will reduce the coil output.

You will occasionally encounter an ignition coil that tests perfectly when cold, but will not be satisfactory when heated. For this reason, it is a good plan to warm the coil before you pass judgment on it.

Several different types of coil testing devices are in common use, and coils may be tested either on the engine or off the engine as follows:

ON THE ENGINE. Where the trouble shooting or tune up procedure calls for a

test of the ignition coil, the engine either may or may not be running.

(1) NOT RUNNING. If the engine is not running, but can be turned over with the starting motor, turn the ignition switch on. Make sure that battery current is being delivered to the coil and that the distributor contacts are opening properly.

Remove the coil-to-distributor high-tension wire from the distributor cap. Either connect the other end of the high-tension wire to a suitable spark gap or hold the end of the wire approximately $\frac{1}{4}$ in. away from the cylinder head while the engine is being cranked.

If a good quality spark is delivered regularly as the engine cranks, the coil probably is satisfactory and the cause of the engine not running lies elsewhere.

If a satisfactory spark is not delivered, replace the condenser and repeat the above test. If a satisfactory spark still is not delivered, replace the coil. If the new coil produces a satisfactory spark, the original coil is defective. If the new coil likewise fails to produce a good spark, the trouble lies elsewhere. Reinstall the first coil and correct the trouble in other portions of the circuit.

(2) RUNNING. If the engine is running, test the strength of the spark from the end of one spark plug wire. If a satisfactory spark is obtained, both the coil and the condenser are satisfactory. If the spark from this wire is not satisfactory, repeat the test at the other spark plug wires until either a satisfactory spark is obtained from one of the wires or all of the wires have been tested without a satisfactory spark. If a satisfactory spark is obtained from any one wire, the coil and the condenser both are satisfactory.

If a satisfactory spark is not obtained from any of the wires, either the coil, condenser, coil-to-distributor high-tension wire, the rotor, contacts, or primary circuit are at fault. If a test bench is not available, replace the coil with a new one. If the new coil tests the same, the trouble lies elsewhere. Reinstall the original coil. If a test bench is available, remove the coil and test it off the engine.

OFF THE ENGINE. Coil testers fall into two general classifications—those that duplicate the ignition circuit of the engine, and those that measure the resistance and continuity of the primary and secondary windings.

Testers that duplicate the ignition circuit of the engine permit the same tests that were described in the foregoing under "Running," plus high-speed tests. Some testers check the output voltage while others check the milliampere value of the spark as well. Milliampere specifications for coil output are arbitrary since the instantaneous values are not readable on the meter.

Testers that test the continuity and resistance of the coil primary and secondary circuits provide a comparison against the manufacturer's specifications.

HIGH-TENSION INSULATION

A test of spark strength is a check for insulation breakdown of the entire ignition high-tension circuit. In some instances where breakdown is indicated, the trouble may exist in one or more of several parts. To find the part at fault, individual parts such as rotors and distributor caps are best tested by subjecting them to a continuous high-tension current so any leakage can be observed. Always clean the part with carbon tetrachloride first to remove surface dirt which could "short" the part.

Any coil tester that duplicates the ignition system on the engine may be used to test insulation breakdown. Install a coil in the machine as though to test it. Interpose the part to be tested between the coil ground and the coil secondary output wire.

CAUTION: Don't drag the test spark over the insulation surface or you may burn a path that will short the part.

IGNITION CONTACT POINTS

The testing, alignment, and adjustment of ignition contact points divides itself into four separate steps or operations: inspection, replacement, alignment, and adjustment.

The ignition contacts in the distributor are about the hardest working parts of the automotive engine. This is generally recognized, and practically all manufacturers use precious metals in the contacts to prolong their life. Nevertheless, ignition contacts require periodic attention.

A number of faults in the contacts can exist, some as a result of normal wear or deterioration, and others as handicaps that cannot be considered as normal. Before getting into the discussion of the four separate operations involving ignition contact points, it is well to understand some of the factors that must be taken into account.

(1) Breaker Arm Spring Tension. Fig. 4-22 illustrates how breaker arm spring

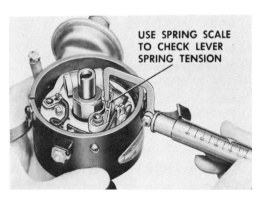

Fig. 4-22. Checking the breaker arm tension.

tension is measured. It is important that the measurement be taken as near the contacts as practical, otherwise a true reading will not be obtained. Breaker arm spring tension is important since, if the tension is too great, rapid wear of the rubbing block and cam will result. Moreover, at high speed the contacts will close so violently that they will bounce, in effect reducing the coil saturation period. If the breaker arm spring tension is too little, the rubbing block will not follow the contour of the cam at high speeds. This will reduce the coil saturation period.

(2) Breaker Arm Pivot Friction. Breaker arm pivot friction may be excessive and reduce the saturation period of the coil and, in some instances, may hold the contacts open, preventing starting.

Some breaker arm bearings are made of fiber which under some atmospheric conditions will swell and tighten.

(3) Contact Surfaces. The condition of the contact surfaces is an important consideration. The formation of oxides on the contact surfaces increases their resistance. Oil, even in minute quantities, on the contact surfaces will cause them to burn prematurely. Even slight pitting will cause an occasional miss. Contacts burned or pitted on one edge are the result of contact misalignment.

Contact points are comparatively inexpensive and should not be dressed (filed or honed) except in an emergency or as a temporary measure where new contacts are not available. The inadvisability of dressing points can be appreciated when it is pointed out that the precious metal surface is only a few thousandths of an inch thick.

(4) Contact Alignment. Alignment of the contacts is an important consideration (see Fig. 4-23) since misalignment

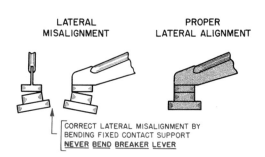

LATERAL MISALIGNMENT   PROPER LATERAL ALIGNMENT

CORRECT LATERAL MISALIGNMENT BY BENDING FIXED CONTACT SUPPORT <u>NEVER BEND BREAKER LEVER</u>

Fig. 4-23. The correct alignment of breaker points.

can account for reduced contact area and premature burning. As contacts pound in, their alignment is improved. This pounding in results in a change of the spacing (cam angle or dwell). However, it usually is advisable to accept a slight compromise in spacing rather than to destroy perfect alignment.

(5) Contact Resistance. Resistance of contacts can be a factor in the coil output. In most cases the cause of the excessive resistance will also promote rapid burning.

New contact sets are usually made up of one flat contact and one spherical contact (one- to two-inch radius). Because of this, slightly misaligned contacts will still make a center contact. This contact area may be small when new contacts are first installed, and their resistance will be slightly higher than the resistance of clean, old contacts that have pounded into each other, have corrected their misalignment, and have increased their area of contact.

(6) Spacing (Dwell or Cam Angle). The contact point spacing determines the period of saturation of the coil. Spacing decreases as the breaker-arm rubbing block wears. This causes increased dwell and at the same time retards the timing of the spark. Spacing increases as the contacts pound down, decreasing the dwell and advancing the spark timing.

In all instances, contacts must have

clean, smooth surfaces and be correctly aligned and spaced before timing the ignition.

INSPECTION. A visual inspection of ignition contacts should precede any attempt to adjust them. The need for adjustment can be established either by measuring the dwell or cam angle and the resistance of the contacts electrically or by a visual inspection.

(1) Visual. Hold the contacts open and inspect both surfaces. In some distributors a dental mirror (the instrument the dentist uses to inspect your teeth) can be used to advantage. Dental mirrors can be purchased for a nominal sum. If the contacts are deeply pitted or have built up, they should be replaced. If the contacts have been touching on only one side or edge, they should be aligned. Whether the contacts are being replaced or not, the color should be noted.

The color of the ignition contacts often will serve as a clue to the cause of their failure or their high resistance. The ideal color generally is gray, and this color usually indicates that the contacts are operating under normal conditions. This is not a hundred percent true, however. The tungsten employed in some contacts will form brown, light blue, or dark blue oxides during use. These differences in color are attributable to the differences in structure of the tungsten itself.

This light blue or dark blue oxide should not be confused with a blue oxide that probably is more clearly described as a gunmetal color. This color is caused by excessive peak amperages. In general, instantaneous amperages of approximately 7.3 or more will cause the formation of this type of blue oxide and at the same time will cause the contacts to burn and pit.

These high amperages are generally caused by cold weather operation. Most battery ignition systems have a normal temperature resistance of approximately 1.4-1.5 ohms which at 15.5 volts would permit a peak or instantaneous current of 10 amperes. As the temperature drops, the resistance of the primary circuit reduces rapidly so that in the neighborhood of 20° F, the instantaneous current increases to around 12 amperes. This amperage is considered the danger point. Higher amperages will cause this gunmetal-appearing blue oxide to form, and burning and pitting to occur. It should be noted that the amperages referred to are instantaneous values which cannot be read on the conventional ammeter since, with the ignition running, the amperage reading will represent the average current rather than the peak value.

Where subzero temperatures are commonly encountered, a temperature controlled resistance (Fig. 4-24) introduced into the ignition primary circuit has quite successfully solved this problem. This control is connected into a conventional ignition system. A ¾ ohm resistor is installed in series in the circuit. Two pairs of contact points are parallel to this resistance. A study of the drawing shows that the upper set of points is closed by a solenoid connected to the "cold" side of the starter switch. Every time the starter switch is closed, the added primary resistance is by-passed to facilitate starting.

The lower set of points mounted on a bimetal arm is temperature actuated. If the temperature is 20° F, or above, the points are closed, by-passing the resistance. In colder weather the points are open, and the ignition current must pass through the resistance (except when the starter switch is closed as explained above).

Black ignition contacts are a positive indication that oil is in some manner getting onto the contact points. This can be the result of over-lubrication of the distributor cam, in which case the excess

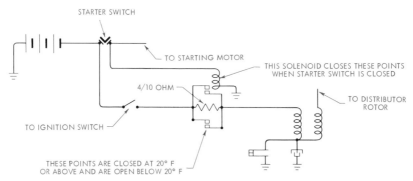

Fig. 4-24. Temperature controlled primary resistance.

lubricant slowly works its way out along the breaker arm and eventually gets onto the contact face. In some cases the oil can be the result of seepage or bleeding through the distributor shaft bushings onto the distributor cam from where it is thrown out onto the breaker arm. Occasionally you will encounter contacts with this black, burned look where there is no other evidence of oil. Nevertheless, you can be reasonably sure that some oil is reaching the contacts, and a permanent solution of the contact problem will not be reached until the source of this oil is uncovered and a correction made.

(2) Test Equipment. Much time can be saved by checking the dwell or cam angle electrically without removing the distributor cap or terminal plate. These machines measure the percentage of time during which the contacts are closed and the coil is being saturated. In addition, some of these machines provide a means of measuring the resistance of the contacts in fractions of an ohm.

When new ignition contacts have been installed, even though the electrical check shows the dwell or cam angle to be correct, confirm the spacing by means of a mechanical check. This is made necessary with new contacts since the new contact-point-arm rubbing block might have sharp corners that could result in a false

reading. This precaution is necessary only when new contact arms are installed. After a few hundred miles, the sharp corners of the rubbing block will become rounded, at which time the electrical test will give a true reading.

REPLACEMENT. When contacts are burned or pitted they must be replaced. However, it is important that you determine the cause of the failure in order to prevent future failures. If there are signs of oil on the contacts or breaker arm, try to determine and correct its source. If contacts are burned, and no oil is apparent, check the condenser connections (including ground). If the connections are good, it may be advisable to check the condenser. If you do not have a means of checking the condenser, replace it with a new one (condensers are inexpensive).

The procedure to follow in replacing distributor contacts is usually obvious once you remove the distributor cap. When the new contacts are installed and the spacing approximately set, they usually must be aligned.

ALIGNMENT. Contact alignment is usually accomplished by bending the stationary contact support. Correct alignment exists when the two contact surfaces meet squarely, touching at the center (Fig. 4-23). Several types of bending tools are available that permit the contact support to be either bent toward or away from the breaker arm contact or to be twisted in either direction. Such a tool is shown in Fig. 4-24. This is a multipurpose tool, and in this instance it is being used to adjust the contact point spacing. The portion of the tool used to bend the stationary point in order to achieve alignment is clearly shown.

ADJUSTMENT. Contact spacing is accomplished by moving the stationary contact toward or away from the breaker-arm contact. In some designs the stationary contact is on the end of a screw. In most designs the stationary contact is moved by means of an eccentric that can be turned with a screw driver or a similar blade (Fig. 4-25).

Regardless of the methods used to check or adjust the contact points, always lock the adjustment and recheck it after it is locked (sometimes the tightening of the lock will change the setting). Make sure, also, that the contacts are still in alignment.

Fig. 4-26 shows a distributor on which the contact point dwell can be adjusted from the outside with the engine running. A dwell meter is practically necessary for this type distributor although a feeler gage can be used in an emergency.

Distributor contact points must be absolutely clean when you are finished with whatever work you are doing on them. Even touching the contact surface with your fingers will leave a film of oil on the contacts. Thickness gage blades also will leave oil on the contacts. As a last operation, always clean the contacts. Chloroform is probably the best cleaning agent since, if properly used, it will leave no residue. Brush the contact surfaces with a stiff bristled brush dipped in chloroform to loosen any oil or grease that may be present, then spray the surface with

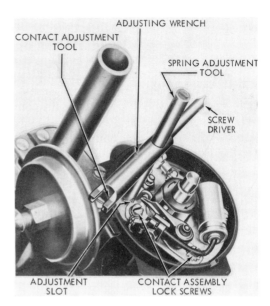

Fig. 4-25. A multipurpose tool for adjusting the distributor. Ford Motor Co.

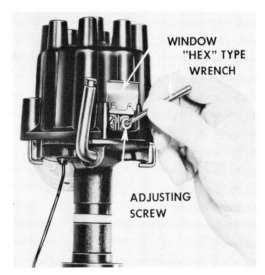

Fig. 4-26. Dwell is easily adjusted with this type of distributor.

chloroform from an atomizer to flush the contacts clean.

NOTE: Chloroform used in the open in this way is no more toxic than most cleaning agents and is entirely safe to use as described.

Distributor contacts can be adjusted electrically or to mechanical standards as follows:

(1) Mechanical Standards. Two methods of mechanically measuring ignition contact point gap or spacing are in common use. One method is to use an indicator, the other is with a feeler gage.

(a) Feeler Gage. Adjust the contacts to the specified gap as measured with a feeler gage (Fig. 4-27 top). Make sure the rubbing block is on the high point of the cam. A delicate sense of feel is required, otherwise the feeler gage will lift the rubbing block off the cam and will not represent the true spacing.

(b) Indicator. An indicator such as a dial indicator or any type of indicator

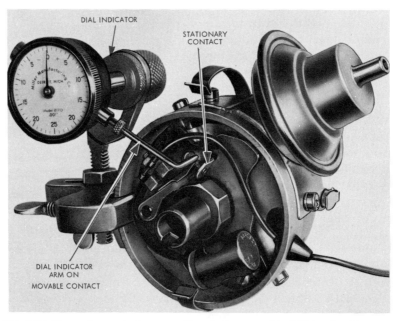

Fig. 4-27. Measuring contact space with a feeler gage. Ford Motor Co. Measuring the contact space with a dial indicator. Plymouth Div., Chrysler Corp.

that greatly amplifies the reading can be used to measure ignition contact spacing or gap (Fig. 4-27 bottom). The indicator should be set up so it indicates the total movement of the contact arm measured at the back of the contact as shown. With the indicator thus set up, rotate the distributor shaft and observe the total movement. Make sure that one contact has not "built up." If so, the reading might be deceptive.

(2) Electrical Standards. Various electrical test machines provide a reading of contact spacing in degrees of cam angle (Fig. 4-28) or percentage of dwell. This permits the distributor to be running while the contacts are adjusted. Some of these machines measure cam angle or dwell only on a distributor that is removed and installed in the machine. Other machines provide for making this measurement and adjustment right on the engine.

CAUTION: Sometimes when new breaker arms are installed, the correct electrical setting will result in the gap being too small. This is caused by sharp corners on the rubbing block causing the contacts to open early and close late. Contact arm rubbing blocks should have a small radius on the corners. Always confirm the electrical setting by checking with a thickness gage or indicator if the contacts are new. A gap that is too small will cause the contacts to burn prematurely.

Some variation exists among the various makes of electronic cam angle or dwell testers, and each has some exclusive features. Nevertheless, if you understand how one works in general, you will understand how all of them work. Such an electronic test circuit is illustrated in Fig. 4-29.

The purpose of the dwell circuit is to measure percent dwell of the distributor points while the engine is operating. Dwell is measured on a meter with a scale reading from 0 to 100 percent.

The fundamental theory of operation may be understood from the following explanation by referring to the circuit shown in Fig. 4-29. This circuit consists of a meter, a resistance, a rectifier, a battery, and two leads which are connected across the distributor points. When the distributor points are closed, it is the same as if leads *A* and *B* were connected directly together. This completes the circuit which allows current to flow. The meter is adjusted to read full scale by means of the rheostat. When the points open, the circuit is broken and the meter returns to zero. When the engine is running, these points are opening and closing many times a minute, at which time the meter alternately tries to read zero and full scale. However, since action is so swift, the meter never gets the chance to read either zero or full scale. Rather, it assumes a position on the scale which is an average reading. The extent of the deflection of the meter toward full scale will depend upon the percentage of time the points are closed (or open). The meter is graduated from 0 to 100 percent and,

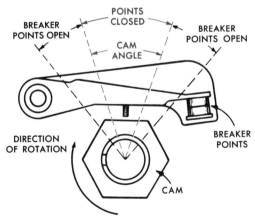

Fig. 4-28. Cam angle is degree that cam turns without opening the points.

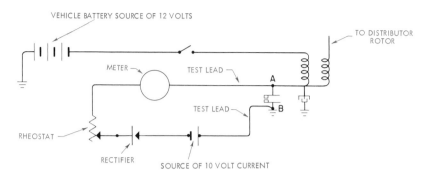

Fig. 4-29. Circuit designed to measure percent dwell of ignition points.

therefore, reads the percentage of time the points are closed.

As previously mentioned, when the distributor points are closed, current flows through the dwell circuit. At this time current also is flowing through the ignition primary circuit. When the points are closed, each of these circuits is complete in itself and does not affect the other. However, when the distributor points are open, the current in the ignition primary circuit attempts to flow through the dwell circuit, and the current in the dwell circuit attempts to flow through the ignition primary circuit. At this time, the two circuits are bucking each other.

The voltage of the ignition circuit is greater than that of the dwell circuit and in the opposite direction. It attempts, therefore, to force current from point *A* (Fig. 4-29) through the meter, rheostat, and rectifier to point *B*. The rectifier, however, allows current to flow only in the other direction and, therefore, stops this reverse flow of current. At this point the meter attempts to return to zero, and we have the same action as discussed earlier.

So far in this discussion we have assumed that when the breaker points are closed, there is no potential across the points. However, in operation there is always some contact resistance across the points so that when current is flowing in the primary ignition circuit, there is a small amount of voltage drop across the points. This small voltage opposes the voltage of the dwell circuit, and causes the reading of the meter to be slightly less than 100 percent when the ignition switch is turned on and before the engine is started. Therefore, before starting the engine to read percent dwell, always readjust the meter to 100 percent after the ignition switch has been turned on and with the points closed.

PRIMARY CIRCUIT RESISTANCE

Any excessive resistance at any point in the primary circuit will reduce the output of the coil. Each of the various dwell testers discussed in the preceding section provides a means of accurately measuring distributor contact resistance. In each case, the circuit in these testers is completed through the test leads, and the rheostat is adjusted to read 100 percent. The contact points are then introduced into the circuit, at which time the reading will drop to some point slightly below the 100 percent value, due to the added resistance of the points. This lowered reading reflects the additional resistance that has been introduced into the test circuit. An ohm scale on the meter indicates the resistance of the contact points in hundredths of an ohm. The scale is a reversed scale with the values decreasing toward the right-hand side.

To check primary circuit resistance a voltage drop check can be made from the battery to the battery terminal of the coil with the switch on and points closed. The voltage drop should generally not exceed 8 volts.

CONDENSER

Various devices are available for testing condensers. Generally such testers give three separate readings—capacity in microfarads, leakage, and series resist-

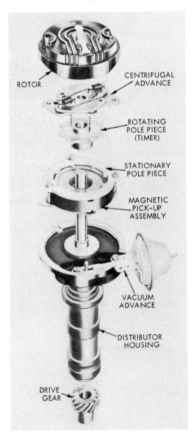

Fig. 4-30. A magnetic distributor. This has no breaker points.

ROTOR

CENTRIFUGAL ADVANCE

ROTATING POLE PIECE (TIMER)

STATIONARY POLE PIECE

MAGNETIC PICK-UP ASSEMBLY

VACUUM ADVANCE

DISTRIBUTOR HOUSING

DRIVE GEAR

ance. In most cases detailed instructions are provided with each machine.

Since condensers are very inexpensive, it is usually cheaper to replace them than to pay for the labor of testing them on a test bench. For the same reason, condensers are replaced each time a new set is installed.

A faulty condenser will cause a build-up of metal on the contact points. To check the condenser, visually inspect the contact points for a build-up of metal on one of the contact points. No build-up indicates that the condenser is operating at the correct capacity.

A condenser that is operating at over capacity will cause a build-up of metal on the negative side of the breaker points and under capacity will cause a build-up on the positive side.

In a negatively grounded system, the stationary breaker is the negative side and the movable breaker contact is the positive side. The reverse is true for a system that has a positive ground.

TRANSISTORIZED IGNITION SYSTEMS

CONTACT TYPE. If the transistorized system uses contact points the same general diagnosis procedure as used with conventional ignition systems can be followed. If all components test OK the amplifier can be considered as the defective unit.

The major difference in this system is the special coil and the transistor unit. The manufacturer's specifications should be followed when testing for voltage drops in the primary circuit. Check for poor grounds and other loose connections.

BREAKERLESS TYPE. This system, in addition to the transistor control unit, also uses a special type of distributor as shown in Fig. 4-30. The other system components are standard ignition units and are checked as you would conventional systems. The magnetic distributor can be checked on the vehicle with an ohmmeter. The procedure is outlined in detail in the manufacturer's shop manual. Since these systems are not very widely used the detailed procedures are not discussed.

TRADE COMPETENCY TEST

1. What kind of ignition systems do most automotive engines use?

2. What is the most common cause of no spark at any of the spark plug wires?

3. Give a definition of a satisfactory spark from the end of a spark plug wire.

4. What does an unsatisfactory spark at some but not all of the spark plug wires indicate?

5. Which part of the ignition circuit is given first consideration when the spark delivered at the end of the spark plug wire is satisfactory but intermittent?

6. What is the first step in the procedure for weak spark at all of the spark plug wires?

7. In testing the strength of the spark from the spark plug end of the spark plug wires, how far from the cylinder head should the wire terminal be held?

8. What is the most satisfactory method of cleaning spark plugs?

9. How is the spark plug gap adjusted?

10. Why is it advisable to set the gap to the minimum limit rather than to the maximum?

11. What is a popular method of testing spark plugs off the engine?

12. What are five things to look for when examining spark plugs just removed from an engine?

13. If the color of the spark plug is light brown, what does this indicate? If it is dead white? If it is black?

14. Why should new gaskets be used when installing spark plugs?

15. What is the first step in timing the ignition?

16. What term is used to describe the spark advance as being exactly right at all speeds?

17. What factors can reduce the coil output?

18. What are two types of testers for testing coil output off the engine?

19. What is the best way to check the individual parts of the ignition high-tension circuit for leakage?

20. What will happen to the distributor-contact-arm rubbing block and cam if the breaker arm spring tension is too great?

21. Why is correct alignment of the contacts important?

22. What is always the last operation when working on contacts?

23. What is the method for determining the primary circuit resistance?

CHAPTER 5

FUEL SYSTEMS

Fuel system troubles are indicated when *flooding, black exhaust smoke,* or *poor mileage* occurs. It is very important to remember that the fuel system is the least troublesome of all systems on the automobile. Many times fuel system complaints will be made, but very often the engine itself or the ignition system is the true source of trouble. These other systems should be checked first unless there is an obvious fuel problem. This chapter will present the usual type of fuel complaints which can lead to the location of other types of troubles in addition to the fuel malfunctions that could occur. Today's emission controlled engines do not allow for any major types of adjustments as were possible in the past.

Fuel system troubles will come to you as one of the symptoms described in this chapter, or as engine troubles as covered in Chapter 3. In most engine trouble shooting procedures, the strength of the spark from the end of the spark plug wires and the compression of the engine are measured, followed by cleaning and gapping of the spark plugs. The *ignition system* and the mechanical condition of *the engine* are either found to be the seat of the trouble or are eliminated from fur-

ther consideration. When the seat of the trouble is not uncovered by this operation, it is likely to be in the fuel system.

FUEL STARVATION

When the engine starts but fails to keep running, or if running normally it suddenly stops, nine times out of ten the trouble is that fuel is not being delivered to the carburetor. However, it is possible for the fuel to be suddenly shut off, or when it is apparently being delivered satisfactorily, to appear to have been suddenly shut off. Several conditions that can account for this should be understood before getting to the procedure (Fig. 5-1) to follow.

(1) Vacuum Leak. The fuel pump pushes fuel to the carburetor. Atmospheric pressure exerted on the surface of the fuel in the fuel tank pushes the fuel up to the pump. Leakage, at any point that will permit air to enter the suction side of the pump or fuel line, breaks the vacuum and no more fuel will be pushed up to the pump. This can occur at any time. The most common point of failure is the flexible fuel hose, usually located at the point where the fuel line leaves the frame or dash and connects to the pump.

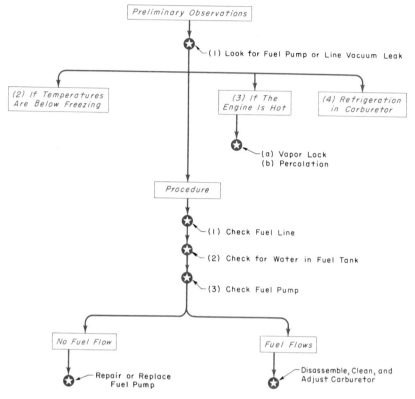

Fig. 5-1. Fuel starvation.

Other points (Fig. 5-2) of possible leakage are: loose fuel pump drain plug; any loose (or cross-threaded) connection anywhere in the fuel line; broken or weak fuel pump diaphragm or linkage springs; and a damaged sediment bowl gasket.

(2) Freezing Temperatures. At freezing temperatures water in the fuel pump can freeze and prevent the fuel from pumping or water anywhere in the line or in the gas tank can freeze and thus shut off the fuel. The fuel in the carburetor float bowl, still there from the previous running, will permit the engine to start, but since no more fuel is flowing to the carburetor, the engine will stop as soon as the fuel is used up. Since the engine will run only a few minutes, usually not enough heat is developed to melt the ice and the engine will not start again.

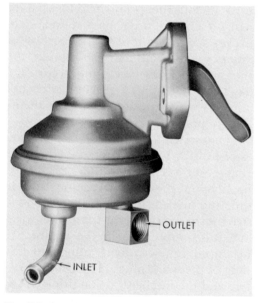

Fig. 5-2. A typical fuel pump. Chevrolet Div., General Motors Corp.

(3) High Temperatures. During hot weather, or when the engine is hot, two different kinds of trouble are common. They are, vapor lock, which shuts off the fuel, and fuel percolation, which floods the engine.

(a) Vapor Lock. When the engine is stopped while it is hot, heat from the engine may vaporize the fuel in the lines or fuel pump. This is commonly known as vapor lock and can also occur on the road under maximum load in hot weather. Restarting usually is easy when the vapor lock did not exist prior to stopping since the fuel in the carburetor is still liquid. However, as soon as this fuel is used up, no more fuel will flow to the carburetor until the vapor lock is relieved. Allowing the engine to sit for awhile or pouring cold water over the fuel pump and lines often will permit starting.

(b) Percolation. If the carburetor is insufficiently insulated from the heat of the engine, the carburetor becomes heated when the engine is stopped and the circulation of air around it is cut off. When the carburetor is hot, vaporized bubbles form in the fuel discharge tubes and passages. These bubbles rise in the tubes, pushing the liquid fuel above them into the carburetor throat in the same manner as the bubbles in a coffee percolator raise the liquid water in the percolator tube.

In updraft carburetors, this liquid fuel merely runs out, and the chief result is a lowered supply of fuel in the float bowl. In down-draft carburetors, the liquid fuel spills into the manifold or cylinders, and the engine is flooded. Of course the hot engine will usually vaporize this liquid fuel before the engine cools, but in the meantime the engine is flooded and may not restart.

If the engine will not start and perco-lation is suspected, hold the throttle wide open, using care to guard against over-manipulation of the accelerator pump, and crank the engine to exhaust the rich mixture in the cylinders.

To determine if, in a downdraft car-buretor, percolation exists with the engine hot, stop the engine, remove the air cleaner, and look into the carburetor throat. If the carburetor is percolating, the fuel discharge tubes will spit raw fuel into the carburetor throat as the bubbles rise in them.

(4) Refrigeration. As air passes through the carburetor venturi and past the throttle, it reaches peak velocity. After passing this restriction, the speed of the air continues, due to inertia. However, the pressure in the cylinders is low (high vacuum) which permits the air to expand rapidly. As air expands, it gets colder. This is the principle on which refrigerators work. If the atmospheric temperature is just barely above freezing and the humidity is high (such as in a heavy fog), this drop in temperature inside the carburetor can cause the moisture in the air to form ice which may shut off the air-fuel mixture.

Usually, if the engine is allowed to sit for five minutes, the heat from the engine will melt the ice and the engine can be started.

TROUBLE SHOOTING PROCEDURE

Make sure that there is fuel in the tank and that the fuel tank vent is operating. Aside from the above observations, the procedure to follow when fuel is not reaching the carburetor consists of three steps (see Fig. 5-1).

CHECK FUEL LINE. Remove the flexible line from the fuel pump and replace it if it leaks air or if the passage is obstructed (at times the lining of this hose comes loose and obstructs the passage under suction). Also, some replacement lines are not reinforced, and collapse under suction. Remove the fuel tank filler cap and blow out the fuel line.

CHECK FUEL TANK. Remove the drain plug and drain any accumulation of water or sediment from the tank. In freezing weather, water in the fuel tank will freeze and may shut off fuel from the fuel line. Allow the tank to reach room temperature before draining. If it is impractical to drain the tank, add alcohol to the fuel in the tank.

CHECK FUEL PUMP. Remove the fuel line between the fuel pump and the carburetor and blow through the line to make sure it is not clogged. With the ignition switch off, crank the engine with the starter. If a free flow of fuel is not evident, it indicates the fuel pump is faulty and must be repaired or replaced. If the fuel pump and the fuel line are found satisfactory, an obstruction exists in the carburetor. Remove the carburetor, and clean and inspect the carburetor float valve mechanism.

CHECK GAS FILTERS. Fuel filters are located in many places. Locate and clean, if possible, or replace these filters. Some fuel pumps contain a replaceable filter. Other cars place a filter in the pump to carburetor line. Still other vehicles have a fuel filter in the carburetor inlet. Some will have more than one filter.

A rather unusual fuel supply complaint can be attributed to a defective fuel tank filter. Normally this filter never requires service, but occasionally a poor fuel supply can be traced by a process of elimination to the tank. The filter is usually attached to the fuel gage sending unit.

CHECK ELECTRIC PUMPS. Some cars will have an electric pump installed in the fuel tank. The pump should deliver fuel to the carburetor when the ignition switch is turned on. If the pump fails to operate, check for proper electrical grounds and connections.

CHECK FUEL PUMP VAPOR RETURN LINE. Fuel pump vapors are often routed back to the fuel tank to eliminate vapor emission to the surrounding atmosphere. This line should be free of any sharp bends and be connected properly.

FLOODING

In addition to uneven running of the engine, a strong odor of gasoline usually is present when the carburetor is flooding. If the carburetor flooding is due to overchoking or fuel percolation open the throttle wide and crank the engine to exhaust the rich gases.

TROUBLE SHOOTING PROCEDURE

Constant carburetor flooding is usually the result of faulty choke action, high fuel pump pressure, high float level, or a leaking float valve in the carburetor. The following operations are presented in order of ease of performance. The procedure is illustrated in Fig. 5-3.

CHECK CHOKE ACTION. Remove the air cleaner, operate the choke, and observe if the carburetor choke valve opens freely. If the choke action is faulty, make necessary corrections.

CHECK FUEL PUMP PRESSURE. Test the fuel pump pressure with the engine running at idle speed (see "Fuel Pump Tests," this chapter). If the pressure is found to be higher than normal, test the push rod stroke and the rocker arm free play, and make the necessary repairs or replacements.

DISASSEMBLE AND CLEAN CARBURETOR. Remove and disassemble the carburetor. Clean all parts. Examine the float for a leak and note the condition of the float needle valve and seat. Make repairs

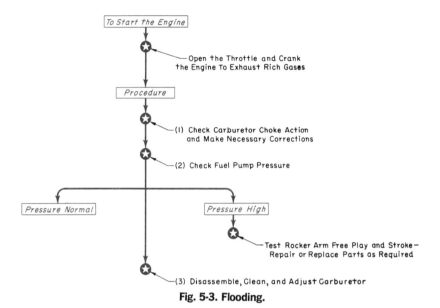

Fig. 5-3. Flooding.

as required, and set the float level. Reinstall the carburetor on the engine.

MIXTURE TOO LEAN

Obviously, if the fuel mixture to the cylinders is too lean, the carburetor should be adjusted. In most carburetors, however, the fuel mixture is adjustable only at idle and a lean mixture can exist at other than idle speeds.

Some of the conditions which might cause fuel to be shut off completely can also cause a reduction in the amount of fuel without shutting it off completely.

TROUBLE SHOOTING PROCEDURE

If, as a result of a test, such as a combination analysis, or from observations, it is determined that the fuel mixture is too lean, proceed as follows until the trouble is corrected (see Fig. 5-4).

ADJUST CARBURETOR. Adjust the carburetor idle fuel supply and speed if this has not already been done (see "Carburetor Tests and Adjustments," this chapter).

TEST FUEL TANK AND LINES. Make sure the fuel pump drain plug is seated firmly and not leaking, and that the fuel tank vent is open and unrestricted. Remove the flexible line at the intake side of the fuel pump and replace if there is any indication of leakage. Remove the fuel tank cap, then blow compressed air back through the fuel line to remove any obstructions.

TEST FUEL PUMP. Check the fuel pump pressure. If the pressure is not normal, remove the fuel pump and make the necessary repairs or replacements. Also check the fuel pump push rod stroke and the rocker arm free play.

DISASSEMBLE AND CLEAN CARBURETOR. Remove, disassemble, clean, and adjust the carburetor. Adjust the accelerator pump stroke for the prevailing temperature. Make sure the accelerator linkage provides a full throttle opening.

TEST ENGINE VACUUM. Tighten the intake manifold screws or nuts. Connect a vacuum gage to the intake manifold, and observe the reading as the engine

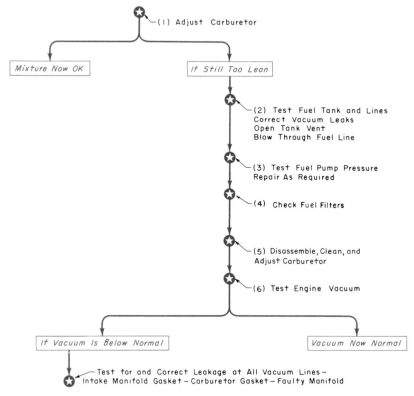

(1) Adjust Carburetor

Mixture Now OK

If Still Too Lean

(2) Test Fuel Tank and Lines
Correct Vacuum Leaks
Open Tank Vent
Blow Through Fuel Line

(3) Test Fuel Pump Pressure
Repair As Required

(4) Check Fuel Filters

(5) Disassemble, Clean, and
Adjust Carburetor

(6) Test Engine Vacuum

If Vacuum Is Below Normal

Vacuum Now Normal

Test for and Correct Leakage at All Vacuum Lines —
Intake Manifold Gasket — Carburetor Gasket — Faulty Manifold

Fig. 5-4. Mixture too lean.

idles. If the vacuum is lower than normal, it is probably due to leakage.

Points at which the manifold vacuum may leak are any vacuum line (distributor, two-speed axle shift, power brake, etc.), intake manifold gasket, carburetor gasket, or faulty intake manifold (porous, warped, or cracked). Once the leakage is corrected, readjust the carburetor.

MIXTURE TOO RICH

If the mixture is too rich at speeds at which the carburetor is adjustable, adjust the carburetor. In many instances, however, the too-rich mixture will be caused by something not influenced by adjustments. Before starting this procedure you should know the things, other than normal adjustments, that can account for the fuel mixture's being too rich.

When too rich a fuel mixture is encountered, generally the cause of the trouble will be that the fuel level in the carburetor float bowl is too high, or something is mechanically wrong within the carburetor.

High fuel level can be the result of an improperly adjusted float, a faulty float valve seat, or high fuel pressure. If the carburetor float is designed to maintain the correct fuel level at a specific pressure, a pressure several pounds greater than this amount would result in a high float level and a consequently richer fuel mixture.

Larger than standard carburetor jets in the carburetor would result in a richer mixture. Leaking power jets or valves would permit extra fuel to be discharged into the carburetor throat when the engine is not under full load.

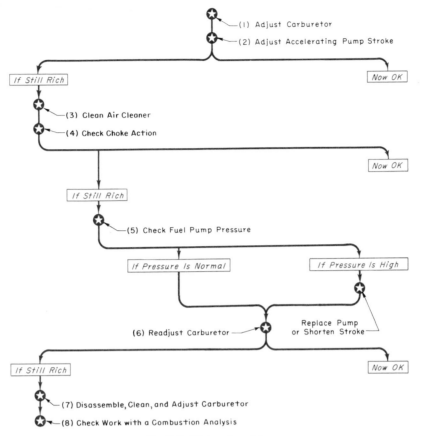

(1) Adjust Carburetor
(2) Adjust Accelerating Pump Stroke

If Still Rich

Now OK

(3) Clean Air Cleaner
(4) Check Choke Action

Now OK

If Still Rich

(5) Check Fuel Pump Pressure

If Pressure Is Normal

If Pressure Is High

(6) Readjust Carburetor

Replace Pump
or Shorten Stroke

If Still Rich

Now OK

(7) Disassemble, Clean, and Adjust Carburetor
(8) Check Work with a Combustion Analysis

Fig. 5-5. Mixture too rich.

Faulty choke operation would restrict the incoming air, and a rich mixture would result.

Any restriction to the incoming air, as caused by a dirty screen or air cleaner, would cause a rich fuel mixture. A felt silencer pad is sometimes employed in air cleaners. If wetted, this pad will sag, restricting the incoming air.

An improperly adjusted accelerating pump stroke will cause too much fuel to be pumped into the carburetor throat each time the accelerator pedal is depressed.

Any vacuum leak not corrected when the carburetor is adjusted at idle will cause the mixture to be too rich at speeds above idle up to the point where the main jets supply the full fuel requirements.

Carburetors designed to operate at sea level will produce a rich fuel mixture at high elevations such as Denver or Mexico City. The reverse is also true. Carburetors designed to operate at high elevations will produce a lean mixture at lower elevations.

The procedure to follow, when too rich a fuel mixture is encountered, is illustrated in Fig. 5-5.

TROUBLE SHOOTING
PROCEDURE

A too-rich fuel mixture is usually detected by a combustion analysis or as a result of attempting to reduce fuel consumption. The correction often involves only one fault, and the isolation and correction of the trouble can involve anywhere from five minutes to an hour or more. For this reason, the things that can be checked with the least amount of work are presented first. This arrangement does not necessarily follow the order of likelihood.

ADJUST CARBURETOR. Adjust the carburetor idle speed and idle fuel supply if this has not already been done.

CHECK ACCELERATING PUMP LINKAGE. Make sure the accelerating pump stroke setting is correct for the prevailing temperature.

CHECK AIR CLEANER. Remove the carburetor air cleaner and make sure that no restriction to incoming air exists. Clean the air cleaner. If the air cleaner is of the oil bath type, make sure that the correct quantity of oil is in the cleaner—leave the air cleaner off.

CHECK CHOKE ACTION. While the air cleaner is off, make sure the choke valve opens fully.

CHECK FUEL PUMP PRESSURE. Check the fuel pump pressure. If the pressure is too high, it will be necessary either to shorten the fuel pump stroke or replace the pump.

READJUST CARBURETOR. If any corrections have been made in the preceding steps, set the air cleaner in place, and again adjust the carburetor idle speed and idle fuel supply (see "Carburetor Tests and Adjustments" this chapter). Stop any vacuum leaks, and check for leaky power valve or dirt accumulation in the throttle body throat.

If the carburetor provides a means of checking the fuel level in the float bowl without disassembling the carburetor, check the float level at this time.

DISASSEMBLE AND CLEAN CARBURETOR. If the procedure, so far, has not corrected the trouble, or if the float adjustment is known to be wrong or, if the design of the carburetor requires disassembly to check the float level, the carburetor must be disassembled and cleaned. Adjust the float level, looking particularly for a leaking float or float valve. Replace any jets or power valves that have the wrong size orifice or where the size of the orifice has been enlarged by an attempt at cleaning it by running a wire through it. Replace vacuum-operated power valves if they leak.

COMBUSTION. Make a combustion (exhaust) analysis (see "Combustion," Chapter 3) to check your work.

POOR MILEAGE

The procedure to follow to check poor gas mileage takes into account all of the things that usually are encountered when this trouble is experienced. However, excessive fuel consumption can be the result of several things not included in this procedure. These are presented under the heading, "Other Causes."

Owners will often complain of high fuel consumption which is due to things over which you have no control. These things are presented here first. An understanding of the points made will help you to intelligently discuss fuel consumption.

In general, if the gross weight is high, it takes more fuel to move it. At high speeds, more fuel is used in overcoming wind resistance. Extremely low speeds likewise are not economical.

In passenger car operation, the greatest factor in fuel consumption is how the operator drives. Rapid acceleration is costly. Every time the vehicle is stopped, the fuel used to bring it up to speed again is lost. All that the car or truck manufacturer can do is to design and build a vehicle which, when operated at a constant speed, and without stops, will deliver a certain number of miles per gallon at given speeds. They cannot anticipate how the individual will drive, nor can they do anything about hills, heavy traffic, or head winds.

As a service man you can only hope to bring a vehicle to normal. Once this has been established, the rest is up to the operator and to other factors over which you have no control.

TROUBLE SHOOTING PROCEDURE

The only way to establish the facts in a complaint of excessive fuel consumption is to make a mileage test. Since the mileage test is costly, it is advisable before recommending a mileage test to check and, if necessary, correct several units that might account for the trouble. The

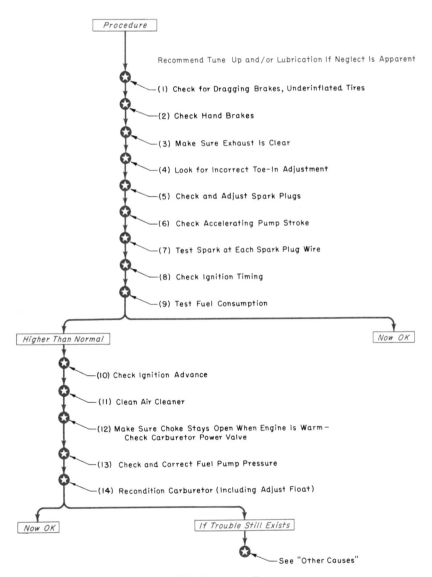

Fig. 5-6. Poor gas mileage.

procedure to follow is illustrated in Fig. 5-6.

NOTE: Some variation in fuel consumption is to be expected at higher elevations. Atmospheric conditions likewise are factors, and the results will be affected by air temperature and pressure.

So many factors can result in excessive fuel consumption that, where the vehicle obviously has been neglected, it may often be advisable to recommend lubrication and/or an engine tune-up which will eliminate much of the following procedure or, in most cases, will correct the trouble.

(1) Brakes and Tires. Make sure the brakes are not dragging and that the tires are inflated to the specified pressure. Make sure that the brake pedal has necessary free travel and that the brake master cylinder vent is not obstructed.

(2) Hand Brake. Owner may not have been releasing hand brake fully, or, due to friction in the linkage (cables binding in their conduit), the hand brake may be dragging.

(3) Exhaust. Make sure the exhaust tail pipe has not been bent or plugged with mud so as to cause restriction of the exhaust. Engines equipped with a thermostatic exhaust control valve which has become inoperative and sticks in closed position will have excessive fuel consumption. The exhaust control valve, in such a case, must be repaired or replaced. If it is suspected that there is excessive exhaust back pressure, make the fuel consumption test with the exhaust disconnected. On engines with positive crankcase ventilation, clean the system if it is clogged.

(4) Wheel Alignment. Observe the type of wear on the front tires to determine if the toe-in adjustment is correct. Adjust the toe-in if it is incorrect.

(5) Spark Plugs. Test spark plugs to make sure that they are spaced correctly and are of the correct heat range. Replace any faulty plugs.

(6) Accelerating Pump. Make sure the accelerating pump stroke is adjusted correctly for the season.

(7) Ignition. Run the engine at idle speed. Remove the wire from No. 1 spark plug and hold it $1/4$ in. from the cylinder head and observe if the spark jumps the $1/4$ in. gap regularly without missing. Make this test at each of the spark plug wires. If an unsatisfactory spark is delivered from any of the wires determine the source of trouble (see whichever symptom that applies in Chapter 4).

(8) Ignition Timing. Except on engines which provide neither a timing pin nor flywheel mark, check the timing of the ignition.

(9) Fuel Consumption. If the preceding procedure has revealed nothing that could account for excessive fuel consumption, a mileage test may be made at this time (see "Fuel Consumption Test," in this chapter).

(10) Ignition Advance. If, as a result of the mileage test, the fuel consumption is found to be higher than normal, accelerate the engine with the brakes partially applied. If a ping is not heard, it indicates the ignition timing may be late. Check any vacuum lines running to the distributor for air leaks or for a clogged condition. Usually, if a slight ping cannot be obtained, either the basic ignition timing or the spark advance characteristics are wrong and must be corrected.

If the procedure so far has not corrected the higher-than-normal fuel consumption, proceed as follows, omitting those operations that have already been performed.

(11) Air Cleaner. Clean the filter element of the air cleaner. Replace the dampening pad in the cover of the filter

if it is sagged and restricting the air flow. If the vehicle is equipped with an oil bath cleaner, clean it thoroughly, and refill it to the specified level with the same grade of oil as used in the engine.

(12) Fuel Mixture. With the air cleaner removed, make sure the choke valve opens fully each time the choke is operated. If the engine is equipped with an automatic choke, make sure it opens when the engine is warm. Make whatever adjustments are required. If the engine is equipped with a vacuum-operated power jet or an economizer valve, run the engine at idle speed and turn the idle fuel adjusting screws completely closed. If the engine continues to run, if only for a short period, it indicates that either the economizer valve is leaking and must be replaced, or that deposits on the wall of the throttle body are preventing the throttle valve from operating in the normal position.

(13) Fuel Pump Pressure. Measure the fuel pump pressure with the engine running at idle speed. If the pressure is not normal, remove the fuel pump, and check the fuel pump push rod stroke and the rocker arm free travel. Make the necessary repairs or replacements.

(14) Carburetor. Remove and disassemble the carburetor. Clean all parts, and examine the float for leakage. Examine the condition of the float valve and seat. Check the size of the main metering jets. Make repairs as required and set the float level. Test the power valve for leakage on carburetors so equipped. If found leaking, it will be necessary to either install a new gasket or replace the valve.

NOTE: It should be noted that in the foregoing procedure, the carburetor is considered last. Contrary to common belief, the carburetor is not the most likely cause of excessive fuel consumption.

OTHER CAUSES

The foregoing procedure will correct excessive fuel consumption in nearly every case. However, several other unlikely conditions are possible, and, if the trouble still is not corrected, one of the following may be the cause:

(1) Camshaft Out of Time. If either timing gear has been replaced, major repairs have just been made, or if the main bearings have been replaced, the crankshaft may have been dropped low enough to get the gear out of time. Remove the gear cover and make an inspection.

(2) Valve Clearance Inadequate. Too little valve lash results in valves not completely closing when hot (does not apply with hydraulic lifters). Remove the valve chamber cover and check valve clearance.

(3) Valve Clearance Excessive. Too much valve lash results in valves opening late and closing early (does not apply with hydraulic lifters). Remove valve chamber cover and inspect valve clearance.

(4) Recent Engine Repairs. Wrong sized parts may have been installed. A good example is piston rings which have been installed without sufficient gap.

(5) Valves Sticking. It is possible for the valve action to be sluggish during operation and not show up as noisy during engine idle.

SERVICING FUEL SYSTEMS

The two major units of gasoline fuel systems are the fuel pump and the carburetor. The fuel pump delivers fuel to the carburetor, which mixes the fuel with air and delivers it to the engine.

FUEL PUMP TESTS

The type of fuel pump test that can be made depends upon whether or not the engine is running and the kind of equipment available. Five different kinds of fuel pump tests are covered here.

PRIMING. Probably nothing is more exasperating to an owner than when he runs out of fuel and, after adding a gallon to the tank, finds that the engine will not start because of the fuel pump's failure to prime. A priming test can be made either on the engine or off the engine.

(1) On the Engine. If the engine can be cranked, a good fuel pump should prime itself with twenty seconds of engine cranking.

If the engine cannot be cranked, the fuel pump mounting screws should be removed without disconnecting the fuel intake line. Pull the pump away from its mounting surface and work the pump operating lever. In most vehicles, the pump should prime itself and start pumping fuel in thirty full strokes or less.

If the pump fails to do this, the pump is defective. Possibly the pump valves are not seating.

(2) Off the Engine. A priming test of the fuel pump off the engine is made by working the fuel pump operating lever. Install a thirty-inch long intake line to the intake opening of the pump. Place the other end of this line in a container of kerosene. Hold the fuel pump approximately thirty inches above the container and operate the fuel pump lever by hand. A pump in good condition will prime itself and start pumping the kerosene in thirty strokes or less.

FUEL DELIVERY. Three methods of determining whether or not fuel is being delivered to the carburetor are possible. The one to be used on a particular engine is controlled by the design and accessibility. Select whichever of these appears to be best suited to the particular engine or vehicle being worked on.

(1) Accelerating Pump Discharge. Remove the carburetor air cleaner. While looking down the throat of a downdraft carburetor (with the aid of a flashlight if required), manipulate the accelerating pump. With each stroke of the pump a small stream of fuel should be squirted into the carburetor throat which indicates that the carburetor float bowl contains fuel.

If no fuel is noted, either the float bowl is empty because fuel is not being delivered to the carburetor or the accelerating pump is not functioning.

(2) Float Bowl Drain Plug. If the carburetor is provided with a drain plug, loosen but don't remove it. If fuel runs out, the float bowl contains fuel. If fuel does not run out, fuel is not being delivered to the carburetor.

(3) Carburetor Fuel Line. By disconnecting the fuel-pump-to-carburetor fuel line at the carburetor and cranking the engine, it is easy to determine if fuel is being delivered to the carburetor. If fuel is not being delivered from this line as the engine is cranked, fuel is not being delivered to the carburetor.

VACUUM. A fuel pump in good condition with valves that are seating properly will develop a vacuum of from six to ten inches. A vacuum test is recommended when the pump fails to prime, and in general checking operations intended to uncover sources of possible trouble.

Disconnect the intake line from the fuel pump and connect a vacuum gage to the pump at this point. Start the engine and observe the vacuum gage. The reading should climb to from six to ten inches in a few revolutions. When the reading stops advancing, stop the engine and note how long it takes the vacuum reading to drop to or almost to zero. The reading on a pump in good condition should not return to zero in less than one minute. If the vacuum test indicates that the pump is good, reconnect the fuel line and run the engine long enough to refill the carburetor bowl before proceeding with the next test.

PRESSURE. The float mechanism in

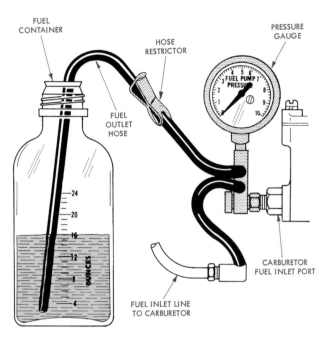

Fig. 5-7. Testing fuel pump delivery with a gage. Ford Motor Co.

most carburetors is designed to shut off the fuel at a given height for a given pressure. If the fuel is being delivered at a lower pressure, the carburetor fuel level will be low. If the fuel is being delivered at a higher pressure, the carburetor fuel level will be high. Low fuel pressures increase any tendency toward vapor lock in the fuel-pump-to-carburetor fuel line. Higher fuel pump pressures reduce the tendency toward vapor lock.

Disconnect the pump-to-carburetor line at the fuel pump and connect a pressure gage to the fuel pump outlet (see Fig. 5-7). Start the engine and observe the fuel pressure. The pressure will build up to its maximum in a few revolutions. Most carburetor float mechanisms are designed for from three to five pounds pressure. A tolerance of from one to one-and-one-half pounds either higher or lower is usually acceptable.

STROKE. Wear of the eccentric or fuel pump push rod will shorten the fuel pump stroke. This may reduce the pump output to the point where, under maximum load or speed, sufficient fuel is not supplied to the carburetor. The fuel pump pressure test will usually indicate this deficiency. As fuel pumps wear, the clearances increase at each of the pivot points from the pump-operating or rocker arm to the diaphragm, thus reducing the diaphragm stroke. This condition also can account for loss of power or top speed if the amount of free play materially reduces the pump output.

CARBURETOR TESTS AND ADJUSTMENTS

Carburetor float level is an important performance consideration. High or low fuel level in the carburetor can be caused by high or low fuel pump pressure. For this reason, a fuel pump pressure test should precede any measure of the fuel level in the carburetor.

Two different types of specifications

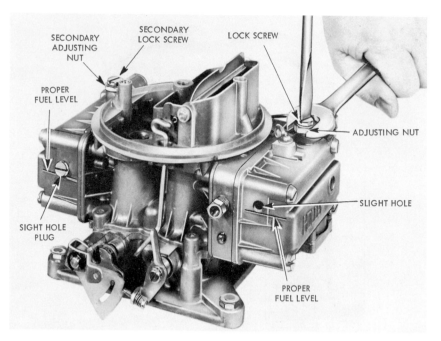

Fig. 5-8. Fuel level sight plug.

are used for establishing the correct fuel level in the various carburetors. One type of specification is for a measurement from the float bowl cover to the surface of the fuel. In other cases, based on the assumption that in a given make and model of carburetor, all floats are of a uniform weight and displace the same amount of fuel, the measurement is from the float bowl cover to the bottom or top of the float or to the float seam. In carburetors having divided floats, the measurement must be made to each half.

FUEL LEVEL. Some carburetors are provided with a tapped hole and a plug to permit checking the fuel level. Fig. 5-8. On these carburetors, with the vehicle level, merely remove the plug. If fuel runs out of the hole, the fuel level is too high. Reset the float. The fuel level plug provides a means of determining fuel level with the engine running.

Some carburetors have the float mounted in the float bowl while others

have the float mounted on the float bowl cover. If the float is mounted in the bowl instead of on the cover, the specification may be for fuel level. In these carburetors, run the engine for a few minutes, then remove the float bowl cover and measure from the top of the bowl to the surface of the fuel. Fig. 5-9. In most cases with these carburetors, the engine can be run with the float bowl cover removed.

A carburetor in which the float is mounted on the float bowl cover is checked by measuring the position of the float with regard to the float bowl cover. Fig. 5-10 illustrates a typical float level gage being used to measure the float position. Always measure both ends of the float. Both measurements should be equal.

FLOAT LEVEL. Regardless of whether the specification is for fuel level or for float level, the adjustment consists of changing the float position. Float position can be changed by bending the float arm

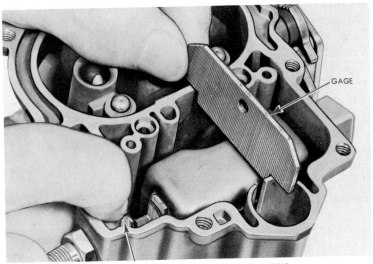

FLOAT LIP HELD AGAINST FUEL INLET NEEDLE

Fig. 5-9. Fuel level float adjustment.

or by moving the float valve seat.

(1) Moving Float Valve Seat. Movement of the float valve seat toward or away from the needle valve will change the height of the float. Some carburetors are built with shims that can be removed to raise the float, or shims may be added to lower the float.

(2) Bending Float Arm. On carburetors where no provision is made to move the location of the float valve, the portion of the float arm that contacts the needle valve should be bent. Care must be exercised not to bend any other portion of the float.

FLOAT DROP. It is necessary to check

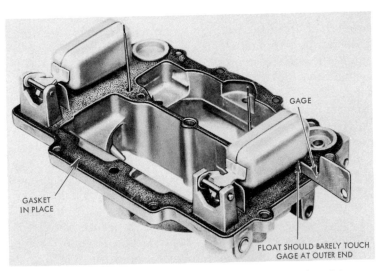

GASKET IN PLACE

FLOAT SHOULD BARELY TOUCH GAGE AT OUTER END

Fig. 5-10. Typical method of checking float alignment, level, and drop.

the amount the float is allowed to travel down to insure maximum fuel flow at high speeds. Float alignment should also be checked to be certain the float(s) operate freely within the fuel bowl.

ADJUSTMENTS. Carburetors are provided with three separate adjustments in addition to the float or fuel level adjustment. These three adjustments are: idle speed, idle fuel mixture, and accelerating pump stroke. In setting idle speed and in adjusting idle fuel supply, a tachometer can be used to advantage. In all cases when adjusting the idle speed and the idle fuel mixture, the engine should be running at normal operating temperature.

The adjustment of the carburetor generally is the last operation performed in a tune-up and the last consideration in most trouble shooting procedures. The elimination of ignition and other units from consideration permits adjustments to be made by sound or by using a vacuum gage, tachometer, or combustion analyzer, each of which reflects everything affecting performance.

The adjustments on various types of popular carburetors are shown in Fig. 5-11.

(1) Idle Speed. Before attempting to adjust the carburetor, run the engine until normal operating temperature is reached. Tighten the intake manifold nuts or screws and any intake manifold vacuum connections.

Idle speed is established by adjusting the throttle valve stopscrew. If possible, use a tachometer for greater accuracy when setting the idle speed. The idle speed adjustment usually has to be made at least twice each time the carburetor is adjusted—before the idle fuel adjustment is made, and as a final operation after the idle fuel adjustment is made. When making this final idle speed adjustment, on a vehicle equipped with a fluid drive or

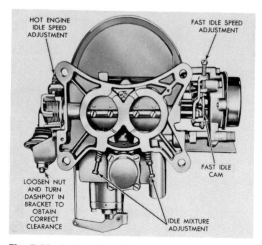

Fig. 5-11. Carburetor adjustments. Ford Motor Co.

torque converter, be careful to follow the manufacturer's recommendations for idle speed. Otherwise, the idle adjustment may cause the vehicle to "creep," a condition which an owner will find especially annoying at stoplights.

On vehicles where a specification to the contrary is not given, set the idle speed between 500 and 600 rpm. Some carburetors are equipped with a fast or cold idle adjustment which gives high rpm on initial start to prevent stalling and a hot idle adjustment which provides for idle speed control after the engine is warmed up. Follow manufacturer's specifications for these types of carburetors.

Idle or stop solenoids are often used to help emission controlled engines to be shut off. The idle speed is set at the solenoid. When the engine ignition switch is turned off, the solenoid will be turned off, and this will allow the throttle to close more and enable the engine to stop. Higher idle speeds are required to reduce emissions. Many engines, especially when warmed up, will not stop when the ignition is turned off because of the high idle speed. This is often referred to as dieseling or after-run. Fig. 5-12 shows a typical idle or stop solenoid.

Fig. 5-12. Carburetor with a solenoid throttle positioner. Ford Motor Co.

(2) Idle Mixture. The idle fuel adjustment may be made either at normal idle speed or at a higher speed and then confirmed at the normal speed. In some carburetors a better adjustment is possible if the idle fuel adjustment is made at from 700 to 900 rpm, then reset to normal idle speed. In most cases, if the carburetor is adjusted so the engine runs smoothly at the higher rpm, it should run smoothly at the low speed.

Lacking specific recommendations to the contrary, make the idle fuel adjustment at about 800 rpm. If the engine no longer runs smoothly with this adjustment when the speed is reduced to normal idle speed (450 to 500 rpm), it may be an indication that a manifold vacuum or power jet leak exists. Idling represents only a small portion of the engine's operation. Part-throttle operation in traffic is the more important consideration. By making the idle fuel adjustment at about 800 rpm, the best over-all economy is obtained.

A sensitive tachometer is the best device for making the fuel adjustment, not only because it automatically gives you the idle speed, but because it does not have the drawbacks inherent in a vacuum reading, an exhaust reading, or adjustment by ear.

A vacuum gage reflects faulty ignition or valve action even if only slightly off, but a combustion analysis or exhaust gas reading does not immediately reflect an adjustment. Moreover, when working on a dual carburetor you are adjusting two separate carburetors even though only one float may be used. One of these carburetors could be rich and the other lean, and the exhaust gas, which is the product of the two carburetors, could show a perfect mixture.

Emission controlled engines have carburetors with lean idle mixtures. The amount of adjustment is limited by special plastic covers on the mixture screws, or by the internal design of the carburetor with special restrictions.

The idle specifications for low emission engines vary with the manufacturer. The procedure will not always provide the highest vacuum for speed at idle. As an example, one carburetor is adjusted so that after maximum idle speed is obtained the screws are turned out to cause a 20 rpm drop in idle speed. This is known as "lean roll." To properly adjust low emission carburetors, the exact procedure of the manufacturer must be followed.

With any given throttle position, the fuel adjustment that causes the engine to run the fastest is the most efficient adjustment. With a vacuum gage, the higher speed results in higher vacuum.

Set the throttle valve stop screw to obtain the speed desired during the adjustment. Using the sound of the engine, the intake manifold vacuum, the engine speed shown on a tachometer, or the air-fuel ratio as a guide, adjust the idle fuel supply to obtain the best setting.

If the adjustment is made at fast idle (800 rpm), readjust the idle speed to normal idle speed (as specified, or 500 to 600 rpm) after obtaining the best fuel adjustment at the higher speed.

The engine should run smoothly without "rolling." If it is necessary to make a compromise on the adjustment, adjust toward rich rather than lean.

If the idle fuel adjustment is set all the way lean, yet the mixture is too rich, the float level is too high, the throttle body is dirty, or the power jet is leaking. If the idle fuel adjustment has to be turned considerably richer at normal idle speed than at fast idle, it is an almost positive indication of a vacuum leak. Connect a vacuum gage to the intake manifold.

Where other vacuum leaks are suspected, stop the engine and set the throttle valve stop screw so that the throttle is closed tightly. Crank the engine and observe the vacuum developed. If a vacuum of fifteen in. is obtained at cranking speed, you can be reasonably sure no vacuum leak exists.

(3) Accelerating Pump Stroke. Most carburetors employing an accelerating pump provide a means of adjusting the length of the pump stroke. The longer the stroke, the more fuel that is injected into the throat of the carburetor. The shorter the stroke, the less fuel.

Accelerating pump stroke adjustment is made to suit either the current season or in anticipation of the approaching season. In cold weather, more fuel is required and the stroke should be longer. In hot weather, less fuel is required and the stroke should be shorter.

AUTOMATIC CHOKE

If difficulty in starting is only when the engine is cold, the automatic choke should be checked.

Chokes employ a thermostatic spring which reacts to temperature changes. This spring should close the choke when

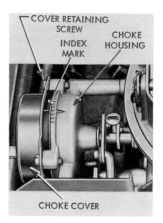

Fig. 5-13. Accelerating pump, stroke and idle speed adjustments. Ford Motor Co.

the engine and spring are cold. (See Figs. 5-13 and 5-14.) To help open the choke, the spring is heated by exhaust warmed air. There is also provision for engine vacuum to kick or pull the choke open.

All vacuum passages, the thermostatic coil, and heat supply tubes should be inspected. When the choke is on, the carburetor idle speed is controlled by the fast idle cam and linkage. Typical fast idle speed is 1600 rpm, with engine warm, for automatic transmission equipped cars. Fast idle speed is set by placing the cam in its cold start position, with the engine warmed up, and turning a fast idle speed screw.

FUEL CONSUMPTION TEST

Use a mileage tester having a $\frac{1}{10}$ gallon measure, and multiply the speedometer readings by 10 to obtain the miles per gallon. The test must be made on a straight and level road at a constant speed, and must be taken both with and against the wind to arrive at the average miles per gallon. If possible, have the owner along during the test. Make one test while driving the vehicle. If the fuel consumption is normal for the particular make of car, run a second test with the owner driving.

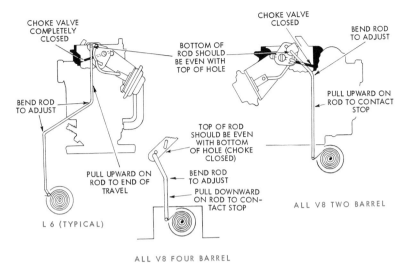

Fig. 5-14. Automatic choke thermostatic spring adjustment. Chevrolet Div., General Motors Corp.

While the owner is driving, observe his driving habits and tactfully point out to him any practices that may account for the excessive fuel consumption. Let him see how quickly 1/10 gallon of fuel is used up during acceleration. This will help to counteract any tendency on the part of the driver to make excessive use of the throttle and accelerating pump.

TRADE COMPETENCY TEST

1. What is the usual cause when the engine starts but fails to keep running?

2. What is the effect of leakage in the suction side of the fuel pump or line?

3. What is percolation?

4. What is the usual indication that a carburetor is flooding?

5. Aside from excessive use of the accelerating pump and percolation, what are the common causes of carburetor flooding?

6. How is a fuel mixture that is too rich usually detected?

7. Aside from the efficiency of the engine involved, what factors control the rate of fuel consumption?

8. Is the exhaust system a factor in fuel consumption?

9. Is a fault in the carburetor the most likely cause of excessive fuel consumption?

10. How long should it take to prime a fuel pump when the engine is cranked?

11. What three methods are used to determine whether fuel is being delivered to the carburetor?

12. Can the length of the fuel pump stroke become shortened as a result of wear?

13. What two types of specifications are used for establishing the correct fuel level in various carburetors?

14. What two methods are used to adjust float position?

15. What means are provided for adjusting idle speed?

16. Why is it sometimes desirable to make the idle fuel adjustment at approximately 800 rpm?

CHAPTER 6

EMISSION CONTROLS

Today's vehicles are being equipped with many types of accessories and modifications to reduce their emission levels. This chapter will explain what has been done as of this writing to accomplish lower emissions. Most of these controls can result in poor vehicle operation if they are not serviced and maintained exactly as required.

Emission controls are not difficult to understand or maintain. As you read through this chapter your ability to understand and service vehicles equipped with emission controls will be improved greatly. Because many of the emission controls are also a part of the fuel and ignition systems it is wise to keep those systems in mind when working toward improvement of emission levels.

AIR POLLUTION

Early in the 1960's the State of Cali-

TABLE 6-1. PROGRESS OF AUTOMOTIVE EMISSION CONTROLS

CHART BELOW SHOWS REDUCTIONS IN EMISSIONS FROM 1961 THROUGH 1971 (PERCENTAGE CHANGE COMPARED WITH VEHICLES WITHOUT EMISSION CONTROLS)			
CALIFORNIA FEDERAL	1961 1963	1966 1968	1970 1971
HYDROCARBONS	−21%	−62%	−83%
CARBON MONOXIDE	NO CHANGE	−54%	−70%
CONTROL METHOD	CRANKCASE	+EXHAUST	+EVAPORATION

SOURCE: U.S. DEPT. OF HEALTH, EDUCATION AND WELFARE, MARCH, 1970.

CHART BELOW SHOWS GOALS FOR REDUCTIONS OF EMISSION THROUGH 1980				
CALIFORNIA FEDERAL	1972 1973@	1974 (CAL. ONLY)	1975@	1980@
HYDROCARBONS	−88% Cal. −83% Fed.	−88%	−95%	−97%
CARBON MONOXIDE	−70%	−70%	−86%	−94%
NITROGEN OXIDES	−44%*	−76%	−83%	−93%
EXHAUST PARTICLES	NO CHANGE	NO CHANGE	−67%	−90%

* −26% CALIFORNIA IN 1971.

@ BASED ON HEW PROPOSED STANDARDS.

NOTE: ALL CARS MUST MEET THE SAME EMISSION WEIGHT STANDARDS FOR A GIVEN YEAR REGARDLESS OF CAR OR ENGINE SIZE-- STARTING WITH 1970 MODELS. DATA COMPILED BY AUTOMOTIVE EMISSIONS OFFICE, FORD MOTOR CO.

fornia required that all registered motor vehicles must have a pollution control device to reduce engine emissions to the atmosphere. This action has now led to federal government regulation of all motor vehicles with regard to engine and vehicle emissions. Table 6-1.

The emissions that were of particular concern were hydrocarbons, carbon monoxide, and nitrous oxides.

Much research and engineering effort have been directed toward reducing these pollutants to our atmosphere. Studies have provided information that these undesirable gases were being discharged by the engine crankcase and out the exhaust system. In addition, significant amounts of hydrocarbons were found to have come from the carburetor and fuel tank through evaporation.

Today, the automobile manufacturers are striving to meet changing federal standards. In order to meet these regulations, the vehicle, in particular the engine and its systems, has been modified in various ways. These changes will be discussed in this chapter. Crankcase controls, air injection systems, engine modifications, and evaporative emission controls are the major areas. Table 6-2.

TABLE 6-2. EXHAUST EMISSION REQUIREMENTS

GRAMS PER MILE[1]

POLLUTANT	1972	1973	1974
HYDROCARBONS (HC)	3.2* 3.4	2.8* 3.0	2.8* 3.0
CARBON MONOXIDE (CO)	34	28	28
NITRIC OXIDES (NO$_x$)	3.2*	3.1	3.1

* CALIFORNIA ONLY

1 FORMERLY GOVERNMNET REGULATIONS ALLOWED MEASUREMENTS TO BE IN PARTS PER MILLION OR PPM. GRAMS PER MILE IS NOW USED FOR MEASURING POLLUTANTS.

CRANKCASE CONTROLS

The engine crankcase ventilation system can produce a large amount of emissions through the gases which we refer to as "blow-by." (Blow-by are gases that pass the piston rings and into the crankcase.) Originally, engines were equipped with a road draft tube to draw these gases out as the vehicle was moving down the road. Air was drawn in by the oil filler cap and out through the road draft tube. Fig. 6-1 shows a typical open crankcase system. The first change in this system was to positive crankcase ventilation (PCV). This has since been further improved to what can be called a 'closed' PCV system. Figs. 5-2 and 5-3 illustrate these two systems. Positive crankcase ventilation involves the induction of crankcase gases into the intake manifold of the engine. These gases are burned more completely as they pass through the engine. The open PCV system draws in outside air through the oil filler cap in most cases. The closed PCV system uses air that has been first filtered by the carburetor air cleaner. The PCV valve is the heart of the system. It is designed to vent the crankcase during all engine operating conditions through a spring and special valve and orifice. PCV valves should be checked by shaking them with the engine off. Also the entire system can be quickly checked by noting if a slight vacuum exists at the oil filler cap when the engine is idling.

If the PCV system is plugged, the engine will not idle properly. It will be too rich, because of loss of crankcase air into the intake manifold.

If the system is plugged badly, oil will be forced to leak at virtually every point it can. This is due to excessive pressure being built up in the crankcase.

Proper oil change intervals and periodic checks are the major service require-

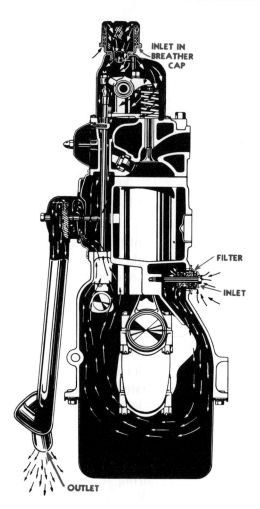

Fig. 6-1. Open crankcase ventilating system.

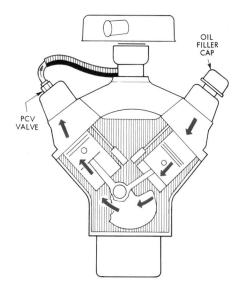

Fig. 6-2. Open PCV system draws air for crankcase through oil filler cap.

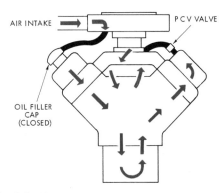

Fig. 6-3. Closed PCV system draws air for crankcase through air cleaner.

ments. It is very likely that the vacuum hoses or other passages could be plugged or restricted in addition to the PCV valve being inoperative. Most manufacturers suggest replacing the PCV valve at least once a year and checking it every 6 months or 6,000 miles.

Often closed PCV systems will have a screen or filter that should be cleaned or replaced if required. Usually it will be located in the air cleaner.

AIR INJECTION

The control of tailpipe or exhaust emissions has introduced some changes which we can readily see and other changes which cannot be visually identified.

The air injection method of reducing tailpipe emissions is a system which is quite easy to identify. The main components are the air pump, anti-backfire valve, manifold tubes, and the connecting hoses. Fig. 6-4 shows a typical air injection system. The operation of this system is very simple. The air pump supplies air through the check valve into the mani-

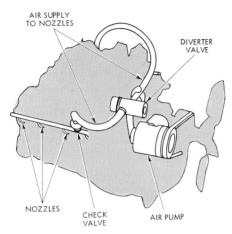

Fig. 6-4. Air injection system includes pump, nozzles, and valves.

folds where the air is injected into the exhaust stream (Fig. 6-5). The addition of this air causes the exhaust gases to burn longer and more completely. The anti-backfire valve is designed to divert the air flow to the manifold during deceleration. If air were allowed under

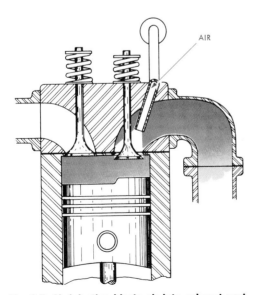

Fig. 6-5. Air injection blasts air into exhaust port.

deceleration the richer mixture in the exhaust manifold might burn too rapidly causing a popping or backfiring in the exhaust system. The check valve located just ahead of the manifold is needed to prevent exhaust gases or backfires from reaching the air pump. The anti-backfire valve is designed to either divert pump air to the air cleaner, to the atmosphere, or into the intake manifold. To determine the type you may be working with check the shop manual.

The air system is used along with ignition timing changes and leaner calibrated carburetors. The air cleaner is changed so it is delivering heated air to the carburetor at all times. This helps the lean carburetor by providing a more constant air intake temperature. These units will be discussed in the following sections which deal with engine modifications.

Troubles with the air system include noisy pump, backfiring, and high emissions when checked with a combustion tester.

Backfiring in most cases is due to the anti-backfire valve. It cannot be serviced and must be replaced if defective.

The air pump is somewhat noisy by its design. If the noise is objectionable, the pump air filter, which is a plastic piece attached to the shaft, and pulley could be producing the noise. A pump could become defective but this is not a frequent problem. The pump drive belt should be properly tightened to insure adequate air flow.

ENGINE MODIFICATIONS

If the vehicle does not have the air pump but is equipped to control tail pipe emissions, the engine will have modifications which are not readily apparent.

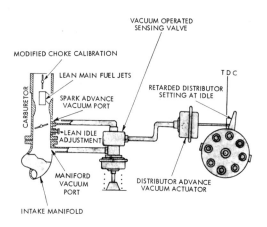

Fig. 6-6. Chrysler clean air system.

Basically these changes include changes in camshaft design, lower compression ratio, lean calibrated carburetor, higher temperature thermostat, and more precisely calibrated distributor advance and retard curve. (Fig. 6-6.)

A common change is the thermostatically controlled air cleaner which is designed to keep the carburetor inlet air temperature at a more constant value thereby enabling the engine to operate with the lean air-fuel ratios. (Fig. 6-7.)

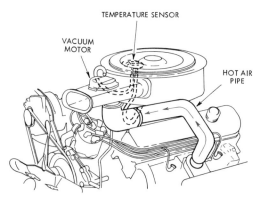

Fig. 6-7. Another type of clean air system. Chrysler Corp.

A visual inspection to be certain the air cleaner is correctly installed is part of the air cleaner service. Any vacuum connections and crankcase vent tubing must be firmly in position. A check of the vacuum operated air cleaner is performed by noting if the air diverter door will move as vacuum is applied.

The service and trouble shooting of engines with these modifications has not changed from earlier procedures. The door should be checked to see that it can move to its open or closed position with no binding or sticking. To test the thermostat, a pan of water heated to 135°F or more should cause the valve to operate. The air cleaner is now a part of the fuel system rather than simply a filter and silencer as in the past. It controls air flow into the engine and crankcase. It also filters the engine and the crankcase air supply. The air cleaner regulates the temperature of this incoming air to insure proper operation with the leaner carburetion.

An air cleaner is an essential part of the emission control system. After servicing the engine, the final adjustments, especially of idle speed, should be checked with the air cleaner installed.

The strict adherence to the specifications of the manufacturer is an absolute necessity. Slight timing variations are not permissible and idle speeds must be adjusted accurately.

Carburetor mixture adjustments are limited to a rather narrow range and usually will make little change in engine operation. (Figs. 6-8 and 6-9.)

Because the range of possible adjustment is so limited it is imperative that the engine compression be within acceptable limits. If poor compression exists, the engine will not operate well at all, and the proper emission level will be difficult to maintain.

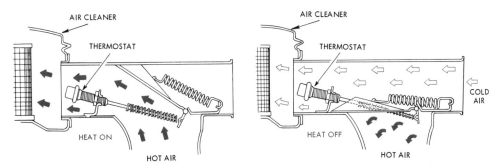

Fig. 6-8. The Ford clean air system.

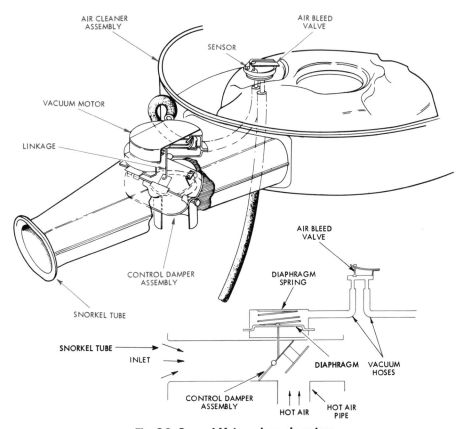

Fig. 6-9. General Motors clean air system.

The low emission engine should be serviced exactly as other engines. It is very important to set idle speed and ignition timing properly. A final check with an exhaust analyzer will help determine if the tailpipe emission level is within specifications at idle. If the air-fuel ratio seems too rich, a re-check should be made of all ignition and carburetor adjustments. If the level is too high or too low, the engine or the carburetor could be at fault. If the engine has proper compression in all cylinders, the carburetor should be thoroughly cleaned and re-adjusted. Most of these vehicles will have a decal in the engine compartment which specifies the tune-up requirements. (Fig. 6-10.)

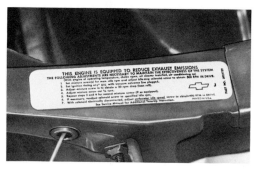

Fig. 6-10. Tune-up decal. Chevrolet Motor Div., General Motors Corp.

EVAPORATIVE LOSS CONTROL

In 1970, California required that all new vehicles sold be equipped with a system that would reduce evaporation losses from the carburetor and the fuel tank. These systems will be used in all vehicles shortly. (Fig. 6-11.)

Two methods of absorbing these vapors are presently employed. One vents the vapors into the engine crankcase while the more common method is to send the vapors into a can filled with charcoal granules. Both systems are able to burn these trapped fumes as the engine is being driven. The PCV system carries the crankcase vapors to the intake manifold while the canister vapors usually are drawn into the carburetor air cleaner when the vehicle is operating.

The carbon canister may need to be replaced or a filter replaced at yearly intervals, while the other components merely need to be inspected for proper and secure connections.

SPECIAL DEVICES

As emission controls are being developed, often other devices are incorporated to meet government standards.

At this writing, many vehicles are equipped with devices which shut off

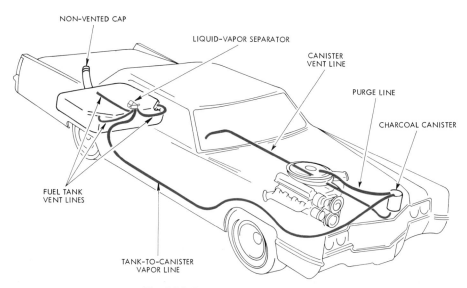

Fig. 6-11. Evaporative loss control system.

distributor spark advance at low speeds. One company controls this system with a speed sensor (Fig. 6-12) and another uses a switch mounted on the transmission. (Fig. 6-13.) These units, if not operating properly, will cause poor low speed operation, and generally poor mileage. These units are engineered to be inoperative when the ambient temperature is below about 60° F.

Trouble shooting these units is merely determining that vacuum to the distributor is or is not available under certain speeds and temperature conditions. Use the shop manual for the vehicle being checked.

These systems of spark control have been appropriately named by the manufacturers. The speed sensor system modulates or controls vacuum according to vehicle speed and is called distributor modulator or Disto-Vac. The transmission controlled vacuum advance is called TCS (transmission controlled spark). The

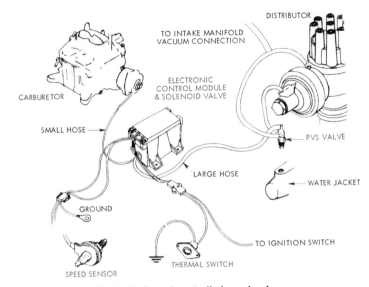

Fig. 6-12. Speed controlled spark advance.

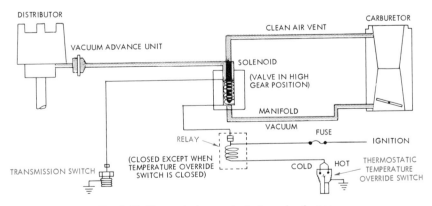

Fig. 6-13. Transmission controlled spark advance.

TABLE 6-3. EMISSION SYSTEM TERMS

CAP	CLEANER AIR PACKAGE (CHRYSLER)
CAS	CLEAN AIR SYSTEM (CHRYSLER)
AIR	AIR INJECTION REACTION (GM)
CCS	CONTROLLED COMBUSTION SYSTEM (GM)
TCS	TRANSMISSION CONTROLLED SPARK (GM)
TRS	TRANSMISSION REGULATED SPARK (GM)
ECS	ELECTRONICALLY CONTROLLED SPARK (DISTO-VAC) (FORD)
CEC	SOLENOID COMBINATION EMISSION CONTROL (GM)
PCV	POSITIVE CRANKCASE VENTILATION (ALL CARS)
PVS	PORTED VACUUM SWITCH (ALL CARS)
IMCO	IMPROVED COMBUSTION SYSTEM (FORD)
AIR GUARD	AIR INJECTION SYSTEM (AMERICAN MOTORS)
VAPOR SAVER	EVAPORATION CONTROL SYSTEM (CHRYSLER)
THERMACTOR	AIR INJECTION SYSTEM (FORD)

electrically operated distributor is called the solenoid retard system. Table 6-3.

To help reduce emissions during deceleration, engines will often utilize a dashpot which will close the throttle slowly when the driver releases the accelerator pedal. (Tampering with emission control systems is illegal in some states.) The system should be serviced as prescribed by the manufacturer.

A device known as an idle stop solenoid is also used to maintain the proper idle speed (Fig. 6-14). This device is controlled by the ignition switch. When the ignition switch is turned on, the solenoid is energized. This will establish the proper idle speed.

When the engine is turned off, the solenoid is de-energized. This allows the throttle valve of the carburetor to close more than when the engine was idling. This cuts down the idle speed enough to enable the engine to stop. (Typically, with the solenoid "on," idle speed would be 700 rpm; with the solenoid "off," the idle speed is 400 rpm.)

Fig. 6-14. Adjusting the idle solenoid.

EGR-EXHAUST GAS RECIRCULATION

Most of the changes mentioned before have been to reduce hydrocarbon and carbon monoxide levels with only a slight lowering of nitrous oxides.

The control of the nitrous oxides (NO_x) is a serious problem. EGR is the common one being proposed to reduce these levels at this time. In combination with camshaft overlap increases, the EGR system seems to be successful. To reduce NO_x levels, the basic idea is to lower the temperature of the combustion gases. To accomplish this, the EGR system allows exhaust gases to be recirculated back into the intake manifold. This dilution by the exhaust stream lowers NO_x levels. A valve controls the flow of gases to be recirculated. The valve controls the exhaust gas flow like the throttle valve of the carburetor and allows more recirculation as the engine speed increases.

LATEST DEVELOPMENTS

The latest move to reduce emissions of vehicles is the availability of non-leaded gasoline. Non-leaded fuel burns more rapidly, thereby improving emission levels. The availability of non-leaded fuel will allow vehicle manufacturers to incorporate catalytic and thermal converters as part of the total emission control system. These converters were not feasible with leaded fuel.

Other changes will be made to allow vehicles to use non-leaded fuel. Some of the modifications include lower compression ratios and richer fuel-air ratios. Prior to this time the air-fuel ratios were being made leaner. Use of non-leaded fuels, lower compression ratios, and richer air-fuel ratios will lead to somewhat poorer performance and lower gasoline mileage. Converters will require special service when they are available. These facts, however, are apparently inescapable and well worth the slight extra operating costs to insure that atmospheric pollution by automobiles is kept at the very lowest level.

Testing equipment to determine the levels of auto emissions is available and helps in making the correct adjustments. These testers are used before and after

Fig. 6-15. Equipment for testing engine emissions. Sun Electric Co.

adjusting the engine and are very effective in showing the improvement. Fig. 6-15 and Fig. 6-16.

Until the piston engine is replaced by some other power source, these changes will adequately reduce vehicle emissions.

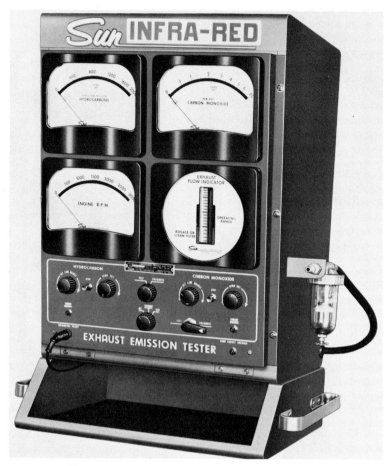

Fig. 6-16. Tester for engine emissions. Sun Electric Co.

Fuel injection systems may become more popular in the future also. The manufacturers are presently working with a variety of electronic fuel injection systems.

TRADE COMPETENCY TEST

1. What types of emissions are being regulated today?
2. What are the major areas to be controlled?
3. How does a closed PCV system operate?
4. What are indications of crankcase ventilation problems?
5. Explain what AIR means. How does it work?
6. What would be the likely cause of backfire with the air injection system?
7. What kinds of changes are provided to reduce emissions within the engine?
8. Describe how you would check the heated air type air cleaner for proper operation.
9. What type instrument is necessary to check emissions?
10. What kind of service should be performed on the evaporation control system?
11. What is meant by TCS? What is its purpose?
12. Why is the idle solenoid used? How does it operate?
13. What is the reason for using non-leaded fuel?
14. Describe what the EGR system accomplishes.

CHAPTER 7

COOLING SYSTEMS

Until the driver of a vehicle experiences difficulty with the cooling system of his vehicle, he is not likely to realize how important it really is. Typically, anti-freeze solutions are maintained and if a leak develops it is repaired. The average cooling system requires very little service or maintenance. It is very important, however, for the services to be performed as prescribed, or serious problems will result. To prevent complaints of *hot light on* or *adding water,* an adequate cooling system check should be performed. Many times overheating can be traced to excessive loads on the system, such as pulling steep grades with air conditioning on and with high outside temperatures. In cases such as this the cooling system is not able to handle the heat load imposed. When this happens troubles begin. The cooling system that runs too cool is just as troublesome as the one that operates too hot. This chapter will give the service technician the help he needs to locate and correct cooling system complaints.

Cooling system troubles have to do with the engine overheating, running too cold, or the loss of coolant.

Engines are designed to operate at a definite temperature, generally between 180° and 212° F. Usually each manu-facturer indicates a "normal" range on the temperature gage. Lower than normal temperatures result in loss of efficiency and crankcase dilution. Higher than normal operating temperatures can cause thinning of the oil, extra wear, extra oil consumption, and in some cases, pre-ignition.

If the temperature reaches the boiling point of the coolant, rapid loss of the coolant occurs with still further overheating.

ENGINE OVERHEATS

The various factors that control the cooling of the engine provide a liberal margin of safety. In most cases, correction or adjustment of these controls will re-establish adequate cooling.

On trucks, the fan shrouds assure that the air will be drawn through the radiator. If the shroud has been removed, it should be installed before any tests are made. Likewise, any air baffles that were provided originally should be in place to prevent recirculation of the warm air from the engine compartment back through the radiator.

SHROUD: In most fan and radiator arrangements, a modified funnel gathers air behind the radiator cooling fins and

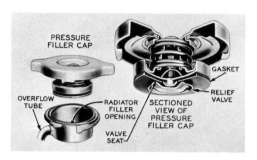

Fig. 7-1. Pressure radiator cap.

directs it into the fan. This funnel is referred to as a shroud. Without this shroud, eddy currents of air would reduce the efficiency of the fan.

Sometimes heavy-duty or desert operation requires additional cooling equipment such as a heavy-duty fan which increases the volume of air through the radiator. Most automobile cooling systems employ a pressure cap (see Fig. 7-1) on the radiator to raise the pressure within the system, allowing for higher operating temperatures. Pressure caps raise the boiling point of the coolant to as high at 250° F. depending on how much pressure the cap is designed to hold. Pressure caps have a vacuum valve which opens when the engine is stopped, allowing outside air to enter the system. Without this valve, a pressure difference would exist between the outside air and the sealed system after the system cooled. The radiator would be subjected to great strain if this occurred and could even collapse.

Heavy-duty operation on north and south runs in winter requires the use of ethylene glycol or some other permanent

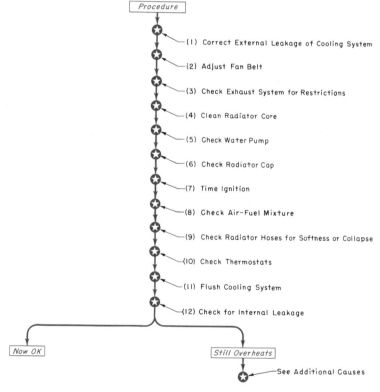

Procedure

(1) Correct External Leakage of Cooling System

(2) Adjust Fan Belt

(3) Check Exhaust System for Restrictions

(4) Clean Radiator Core

(5) Check Water Pump

(6) Check Radiator Cap

(7) Time Ignition

(8) Check Air-Fuel Mixture

(9) Check Radiator Hoses for Softness or Collapse

(10) Check Thermostats

(11) Flush Cooling System

(12) Check for Internal Leakage

Now OK

Still Overheats

See Additional Causes

Fig. 7-2. Engine overheats.

type of organic antifreeze in preference to alcohol. Use of a permanent type antifreeze raises the boiling point of the coolant from 160° to 212°F. and eliminates overheating arising from the loss of coolant due to evaporation of the alcohol.

TROUBLE SHOOTING PROCEDURE

Overheating will be corrected by the following procedure. Follow each step in turn until the trouble is corrected. This procedure in abbreviated form is shown in Fig. 7-2. The possible areas of trouble in a cooling system are shown in Fig. 7-3.

REPAIR EXTERNAL LEAKAGE. Fill the cooling system and idle the engine. Inspect for leakage at all hoses and hose connections. Tighten connections or replace hose as required. Inspect the radiator cap for tightness and note the condition of the gasket. If leakage is observed at the cylinder head gaskets, replace the gaskets. (This operation should include the removal of any carbon.) Inspect the radiator for leakage, and repair or replace if defective. Rust spots or wet spots on the radiator core are an indication of radiator leakage even though there is no dripping.

ADJUST THE FAN BELT. Adjust the fan belt or replace if worn. (See "Servicing Cooling Systems" this chapter.)

CHECK EXHAUST SYSTEM. Inspect the exhaust pipes, muffler, and tail pipe for evidence of dents, kinks, collapse, or re-

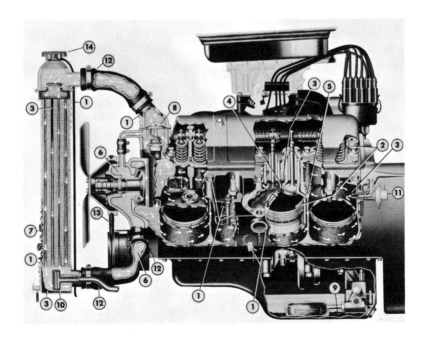

Fig. 7-3. Water cooled engine, cutaway view.

strictions of any kind. Make any necessary corrections.

If the exhaust includes an exhaust thermostat, move the counterweight on the exhaust thermostat valve through the entire range of action. If the counterweight arm sticks or is loose, the passage of exhaust gases may be restricted. Remove the exhaust thermostate valve, and free the action or, if defective, replace the unit.

CLEAN RADIATOR CORE. If the air flow through the radiator is restricted (insects, leaves, grease, dirt, etc.), clean the fins and air passages. Blowing through the back of the radiator fins with an air hose is an effective means of removing obstructions.

CHECK WATER PUMP. Inspect the water pump for leakage around the pump shaft and for looseness of the shaft in its bearings. If it shows any indication of leakage or wear, it should be removed for further inspection and repair.

CHECK RADIATOR CAP. Check the radiator cap to see that it holds the pressure specified for the system. Cap testers are simple devices which use a hand operated pump to build up pressure against the cap and have a gage which shows the point at which the cap releases the pressure.

A cap which does not hold the specified pressure will cause overheating. If it holds little or no pressure, there will be a loss of coolant through the overflow vent from the surging forward of the liquid when the brakes are applied.

TIME IGNITION. Check the spark advance and time the ignition. (See "Timing" Chapter 4.)

CHECK AIR-FUEL MIXTURE. A lean air-fuel mixture can cause engine overheating. Adjust the carburetor, looking particularly for low float level and plugged or undersized main and power jets. (See "Mixture Too Lean" Chapter 5.)

CHECK RADIATOR HOSE. Inspect the radiator hoses and replace any hose that has become soft or has collapsed. Sometimes hoses collapse at high speeds as the increased flow of coolant creates a venturi effect and lowers the internal pressure of the hose.

CHECK THERMOSTAT. Remove the thermostat and test it. (See "Thermostats" in this chapter.)

FLUSH COOLING SYSTEM. Flush the cooling system with a good cleaner according to the directions on the cleaner container.

REPAIR INTERNAL LEAKAGE. Drain the oil from the engine oil pan and observe if there is water in the oil. (Water, being heavier than the oil, will go to the bottom of a container. In moderate quantities, it will look like a bubble at the bottom of the oil.) If an abnormal amount of water is found in the oil, remove the spark plugs and observe if water is present at the plug holes. With the engine cold, fill the radiator to the top. Remove the fan belt so that the water pump (or pumps) will not operate. Run the engine at fast idle for 60 seconds. If water runs out of the radiator filler pipe or overflow, or if bubbles come to the surface of the water in the radiator, leakage exists between one or more of the cylinders and the cooling system. If leakage is evident from any of these inspections, check the cylinder head bolts, using a torque wrench. If the bolts do not show signs of looseness, remove the cylinder head and inspect for a faulty gasket.

Examine the cylinder block and head for cracks, paying particular attention in the vicinity of the valve ports. Replace the cylinder head gasket or make necessary corrections in case of a cracked block or head. When installing the head, tighten the head bolts according to the manufacturer's specifications.

CHECK WATER FLOW. If the foregoing

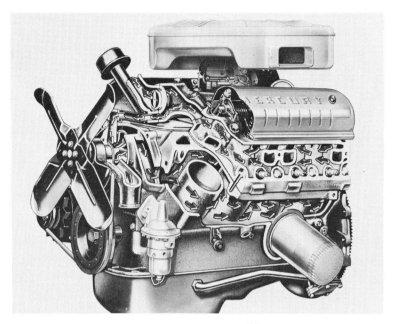

Fig. 7-4. Water cooled engine. V-8 type.

procedure has been followed carefully without correcting the overheating, the radiator tubes may be plugged. Usually this results in excessive quantities of water being forced out of the overflow pipe. If there is no indication of this, remove the cylinder heads and inspect the water openings in the cylinder heads and cylinder block for excessive lime deposits. If excessive lime deposits are present, the cylinder block and heads must be cleaned with an acid type cleaner or replaced, as ordinary flushing will not remove these deposits. Fig. 7-4 shows typical water passages in a cylinder block and cylinder head.

NOTE: Excessive deposits of lime are the result of using "hard" water having a high mineral content in the cooling system. Recommend the use of "soft" or rain water.

SPECIAL FANS

Vehicles may overheat under extremely hot operating conditions if the fluid fan drive unit does not operate properly. Fig. 7-5. These fan drive units may be thermostatically controlled or just a straight fluid coupling. In either case the coupling should drive the fan for better cooling at lower engine speeds. It should be free running when the engine is not overheated.

Fig. 7-6 shows two types of these fan

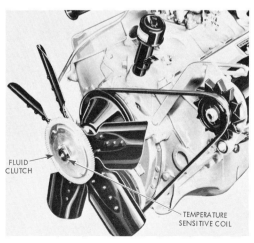

Fig. 7-5. A fan clutch.

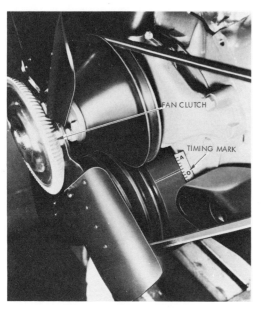

Fig. 7-6. A fluid fan clutch.

drives. The unit cannot be serviced and if defective should be replaced. In cold weather the fluid will drive the fan until the coupling warms up. This is a normal situation. To check the fan operation the engine must be overheated by running it with the radiator covered. When the engine is hot and turned off, the fan should require a reasonable amount of effort to force it to slip within the coupling.

Fig. 7-7 shows a fan with flexible blades. At higher speeds the blades straighten out and the fan in effect does less work. An inspection of this fan, to be certain all the blades are intact, is the only possible check.

ENGINE FAILS TO WARM UP

Start the engine and allow it to idle. Cover the front of the radiator core until the engine temperature is at least normal. If the gage still reads "Cold," the gage is at fault and should be replaced.

If, by the preceding operation, it is determined that the gage is not at fault, the thermostat probably is not closing. Remove and test it. (See "Thermostats" in this chapter.)

If the engine still fails to warm up, check the exhaust thermostat (if there is one) as outlined previously.

COOLANT LOSS

Loss of coolant results in overheating. The correction of the trouble is achieved by following the procedure given there. However, for engines that are definitely losing the coolant, the following discussion may be helpful to you.

A leaking head gasket can permit leakage of the coolant into the cylinders. Likewise air or exhaust gases can be blown past the leaking gasket into the cooling system. This gas will increase the pressure in the system until the pressure cap will be forced off its seat, allowing coolant to be blown out of the overflow.

A cracked cylinder block will permit coolant to enter the crankcase. In this case, the coolant contaminates the oil, usually with more serious results than the mere loss of coolant. Often these cracks

Fig. 7-7. Flexible fan blades.

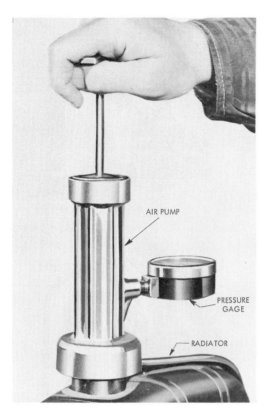

Fig. 7-8. The cooling system pressure check.

the second one that has occurred in the engine.

About the only effective test for cooling system cracks is to subject the water jackets to pressure.

Fig. 7-8 illustrates a typical cooling system pressure tester. Using this tool the cooling system can be checked for leaks at various points and with the engine running or turned off. The tester manufacturer instructions should be followed in all cases.

It is important that this type test never use a pressure greater than the rated radiator cap pressure. Damage to the water pump, radiator, and hoses can result from excessive test pressure.

SERVICING COOLING SYSTEMS

THERMOSTATS

A typical cooling system thermostat is shown in Fig. 7-9. These thermostats are designed to start opening at a particular temperature and to be fully opened at another (higher) temperature. To test a thermostat, it is necessary to have an accurate thermometer that will read tempera-

are watertight when the block is cold, but open up under normal or slightly higher than normal operating temperatures. This, of course, makes it difficult to locate the cracks. In nearly every case, sealing compounds placed in the cooling system will not seal the cracks.

The most common location of these cracks is at one or several of the exhaust valve seats. The crack can run radially in any direction, often running to the cylinder bore.

Sometimes a crack will be so located that the coolant will spray the valve springs. This nearly always will cause the valve springs to break prematurely. It might be well to consider the possibility of a cracked block in any case where valve spring breakage is encountered. This is particularly true if the spring failure is

Fig. 7-9. Replacing a thermostat.

tures up to 212° F. Fig. 7-10 shows the operation of the typical pellet type thermostat.

Heat a pan of water to 10° colder than the temperature at which the thermostat should start to open. This temperature is marked on many thermostats. Place the thermostat in the water. The thermostat should remain closed. If it starts to open, the thermostat is faulty—discard it.

If the thermostat remains closed in the above test, raise the temperature of the water to 25° hotter than the temperature at which it should start to open. The thermostat should now open fully. If not, it is faulty—discard it.

Usually thermostats are designed to start opening at 177° F. to 183° F. Some variation from this will be encountered where a higher wide-open point is used to increase the efficiency of hot-water heaters and improve emissions.

Thermostats intended for use with permanent antifreeze solutions (ethylene glycol) are designed to begin operating at around 177-180° F. and to be wide open at 194° F.

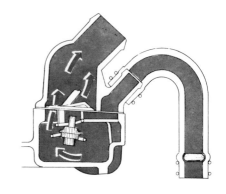

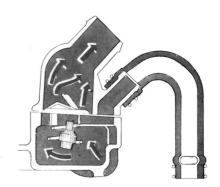

Fig. 7-11. Thermostat installation. Top is incorrect, bottom is correct.

In all cases, check the operation of the thermostat against the manufacturer's specifications.

Thermostats require that the thermal element be directed to the engine. Some vehicles also must have the thermostat positioned for proper coolant flow as shown in Fig. 7-11.

FAN AND WATER PUMP BELTS

A number of different belt arrangements are in common use. In each, a different means is provided to take up the loose play of the belt or belts. In all designs, the means of making the adjustment are usually apparent. The amount of free play or lash is checked at a point midway between two pulleys.

Grasp the belt with the thumb and finger and push it away from you at right

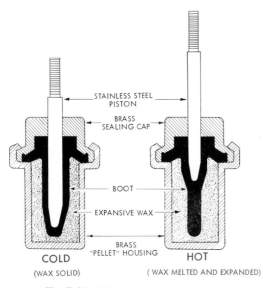

Fig. 7-10. Pellet type of thermostat.

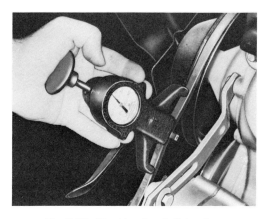

Fig. 7-12. Checking fan belt tension.

angles to the belt, and then pull it toward you. The total amount of this movement is used to determine whether or not the belt requires adjustment.

Usually belt tension is considered to be a critical adjustment. In all cases, follow manufacturer's recommendations very carefully.

Belt tension can be checked with a special tool as shown in Fig. 7-12. This type of check insures that the belt is adjusted properly.

FLUSHING

Sometimes overheating in an engine can be caused by the coolant not circulating freely throughout the cooling system. Scale, rust, and other accumulations can cause the water passages to become restricted. The coolant then is unable to reach some of the parts of the engine in the volume required to cool it.

In some instances, the unrestricted flow of water through the system will remove the loose material, correcting the trouble. Often, however, the rust, scale, and other deposits must be loosened or dissolved by a chemical process.

After cleaning the water passages by whichever method used, blow out (from the back of the radiator core) the insects and other foreign material from the cooling fins and air passages, using a compressed air hose.

Sometimes after flushing, radiators develop small leaks from pin holes (caused by electrolytic action) in the core. These holes can be soldered shut, or a radiator sealing compound can be added to the coolant to stop the leaks.

Most manufacturers recommend that rust inhibitor be added to the coolant. The inhibitor helps to prevent electrolytic action and retards the formation of scale and rust. Normally permanent type anti-freeze will have all necessary inhibitors. In addition these newer brands also contain leak-stop additives. Changes of coolant are recommended once a year to maintain the strength of these additives. Anti-freeze is commonly referred to as summer coolant.

SOLVENT FLUSHING. To clean the cooling system with a cleaner that dissolves rust, scale, and grease or oil, put the cleaning agent into the radiator and add water so the radiator is filled to about three inches below the overflow pipe. Bring the engine temperature up to normal operating temperature, and continue to run the engine at a moderate speed until the cleaning solution has circulated for some time throughout the cooling system. Usually the amount of time needed for the solvent to loosen the rust and scale, is stated in the manufacturer's instructions. After the engine has been stopped, drain the cooling system and flush with clear water.

PRESSURE FLUSHING. In pressure flushing, air pressure is used to both agitate and circulate the water through the cooling system.

Some manufacturers recommend that the cylinder block be pressure flushed in the direction of flow, while others recommend reverse flushing. However, on some engines the water pump design does not permit flushing. Always follow the manufacturer's recommendation for the

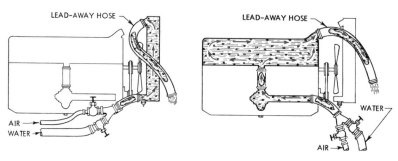

REVERSE FLUSHING OF RADIATOR   FLUSHING MOTOR WATER JACKET

Fig. 7-13. Reverse flushing of cooling system.

particular engine being worked on.

(1) Straight Flushing. Connect the lead-away hose to the water outlet connection on the engine (Fig. 7-13). Insert the flushing gun in the hose attached to the water pump inlet connection. Turn on the water until the water passages are filled, and then release the air in short

blasts, allowing the water to fill the engine after each blast. Repeat this operation until the water running from the lead-away hose is clear.

(2) Reverse Flushing. Always remove the thermostat before reverse flushing.

(a) Radiator. Disconnect the upper radiator hose from the engine and attach

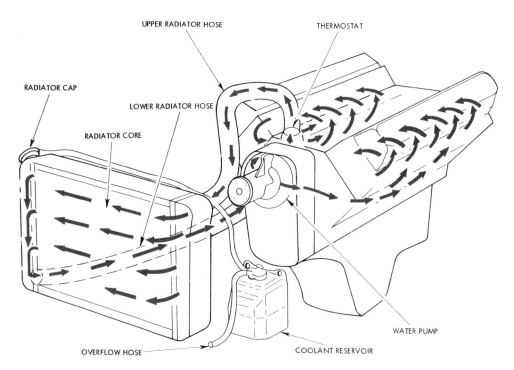

Fig. 7-14. Closed cooling system.

a lead-away hose to the radiator. Disconnect the lower radiator connection from the water pump and insert the flushing gun into the lower radiator hose. (Fig. 7-13). Connect the water and air hoses to the gun. Turn on the water and fill the radiator to the top. Release the air in short blasts, and allow the water to fill the radiator between each blast.

NOTE: Most radiators will be damaged if the pressure exceeds 20 lbs. Since most air lines carry 100 to 125 lbs pressure, caution must be exercised to avoid building up excessive pressure.

Continue the operation until the water from the lead-away hose is clear.

(b) Engine. To reverse flush the engine, the lead-away hose is connected to the water pump inlet connection and the flushing gun is connected to the water outlet connection on the cylinder head. Follow the same procedure as outlined for the radiator and continue until the water from the lead-away hose runs clear.

Install the thermostat, connect the radiator hoses, and refill the cooling system with coolant.

CLOSED COOLING SYSTEM

Some vehicles employ a sealed type cooling system (Fig. 7-14). The major difference between this system and the standard cooling system is the coolant reservoir. This is an extra container which will help keep the system full at all times. Expansion of the coolant will tend to raise the reservoir level and during cool-down the reservoir will be able to supply the radiator with needed coolant. Service to this system is no different than the standard cooling system discussed earlier in this chapter. Coolant is added at the reservoir. The radiator cap need not be removed except when draining or if the reservoir level is below the "add" mark.

TRADE COMPETENCY-TEST

1. What temperature is considered normal for most automotive engines?

2. What is the function of the shroud on a radiator?

3. What effect does a lean air-fuel mixture have on engine temperature?

4. If a cracked cylinder block is suspected as the cause for loss of coolant, where is the first place to look for the cracks?

5. What is the most effective test for locating cooling system cracks?

6. Where is the free play or lash checked on fan or water pump belts?

7. What is the best rule to follow when adjusting the fan or water pump belt?

8. What causes the water passages in the cooling system to become restricted?

9. What are two methods of cleaning the cooling system?

10. What is the purpose of adding a rust inhibitor to the coolant?

11. How is pressure provided when pressure-flushing the cooling system?

CHAPTER 8

INSTRUMENTS

Instruments and gages on today's cars do not give a great deal of trouble. Occasionally you will encounter a warning light or indicating gage which is not operating properly. If you do not know the trouble-shooting steps to take the problem will become even more troublesome. In this chapter you will find examples of various types of instruments and gages with simple procedures to follow to track down and locate the trouble with little difficulty.

Maintenance of these devices is not really possible so most of the chapter will detail troubles and how to locate them.

OPERATING PRINCIPLES

Trouble shooting procedures for the many types of instruments used on automotive vehicles must be varied to suit the basic design of the instrument. Obviously, different methods are used in testing electrical instruments than are used to test nonelectrical instruments. Even within these two broad classifications, a variety of basically different types are used.

In general, the instruments with which automotive vehicles are equipped are not to be considered as accurate measuring devices but rather merely as "indicators" that are entirely adequate for their intended purpose.

ELECTRICAL INSTRUMENTS

To understand an electrical instrument, it is necessary to know the entire circuit of the particular instrument being considered. Moreover, several basically different types of electrical instruments are commonly used to do the same job in different makes of vehicles.

The generator-battery circuit represents the source of current for all of the electrical requirements of the vehicle, and at least a part of this circuit is a part of each of the other circuits as well. Electrical instrument circuits are energized from the battery-generator circuit. An understanding of how they operate must be based on an appreciation not only of how the instrument works but its relationship to these other circuits.

Most instruments are connected into the ignition circuit. The instrument circuits are connected to the cold side of the ignition switch so that when the ignition switch is turned off, the instruments are likewise off. An exception to this is the ammeter, which is in series in the generator to battery circuit.

Both a properly operating generator and a fully charged battery are necessary for continued vehicle operation. The indicator light and the ammeter perform an important function in keeping the driver constantly informed about the performance of the generator and battery circuit.

AMMETERS. The ammeter indicates the direction of flow of current. Ammeters offer practically no resistance to the flow of current and are always connected in series. When the battery is being charged by the generator, the ammeter hand will indicate on the positive (+) side of the instrument the strength of current flowing into the battery. When the current is used for lights, engine, or other electrical accessories, the amount used is subtracted from the amount of current flowing into the battery. If the battery is being discharged under such conditions, the ammeter will indicate on the negative (−) side of the instrument, the strength of current flowing out of the battery. The ammeter will show little or no charging rate when the battery is fully charged. A typical ammeter circuit is shown in Fig. 8-1.

Ammeters commonly used in automotive vehicles are the moving vane type or loop type.

(1) Moving Vane Type. The moving vane type ammeter (Fig. 8-2 top) has two terminals and consists of a frame to which is attached a permanent magnet. The magnet holds the armature on which the pointer is mounted so that it points to zero when no current is flowing through the instrument. As current passes through the ammeter in either direction, a magnetic field is built up around the armature. This overcomes the effect of the permanent magnet, thus giving a reading proportional to the strength of the current passing through the instrument.

(2) Loop Type. The loop type ammeter (Fig. 8-2, lower) consists of a magnet and pointer assembly. No terminals are used on this type. When current flows

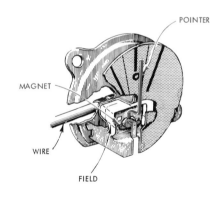

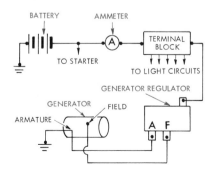

Fig. 8-1. Wiring circuit for a typical ammeter.

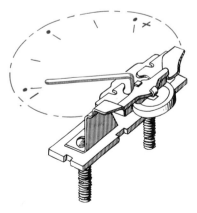

Fig. 8-2. Construction details of ammeters.

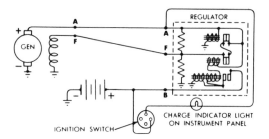

Fig. 8-3. Generator charging circuit with an indicator lamp.

tery is discharging and the generator is not supplying current. The indicator lamp is connected between the armature terminal of the generator regulator and the IGN. terminal of the ignition switch. This places the lamp in parallel with the regulator cut-out contacts, and it will flash on and off as the contacts open and close, but not in conjunction with them. If the ignition switch is on (engine not running), the cut-out contacts are open and the charge indicator lamp will light up, indicating that the generator is not charging the battery. The circuit for the lamp is from the battery, through the lamp, and through the generator armature to ground as shown in Fig. 8-3. As soon as the generator output equals that of the battery, the lamp no longer grounds at the armature, thus the circuit is broken and the lamp goes out. At approximately the same time the cut-out

through the wire assembled through a loop in the back of the instrument, a magnetic field is created around the wire. This causes the pointer assembly to move in proportion to the strength of the magnetic field.

INDICATOR LIGHT. A red generator charge indicator lamp is used on most cars, instead of an ammeter with a dial and pointer. This lamp lights if the bat-

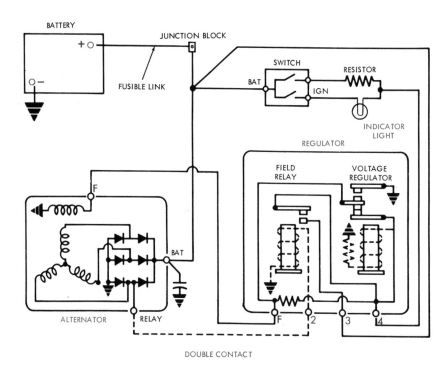

Fig. 8-4. Alternator charging circuit with indicator lamp.

contacts close, and the generator output will flow to the battery. Fig. 8-4 shows the circuitry for an alternator equipped vehicle.

FUEL LEVEL GAGES. On present-day automobiles, the fuel gage usually consists of two units. The "sending" unit is installed in the fuel tank, and the "receiving" unit is mounted on the instrument panel. The sending unit is operated by the fuel level in the tank. Operation of the sending unit is transmitted to the receiving unit electrically.

INSTRUMENT VOLTAGE REGULATOR (IVR)

Some vehicles use a voltage regulator to provide the instruments with a constant regulated voltage supply. The voltage to the instruments is kept to a value of 5 volts. This protects the instruments from voltage variations within the vehicle electrical system. It is important to know if the vehicle you are to be trouble shooting has an instrument voltage regulator or not. Fig. 8-5 shows the IVR circuit for a fuel gage.

Some IVR units are built into an instrument while others are separate units.

Fig. 8-6. They are located at the rear of the instrument panel.

Fig. 8-7 shows a typical circuit arrangement with an IVR included. Note that the IVR is common to all of the gage circuits. If all gages read incorrectly, or not at all, the voltage regulator can be the trouble. A poor ground connection at the instrument panel also will affect all the gages. If the voltage regulator is defective, it must be replaced.

If difficulty with a single gage is the complaint, then that circuit only needs to be checked.

Instruments are easily checked at the sending unit.

Gages which use the voltage regulator are usually the thermal type. These operate because electric current passes through a heating coil. As the heating coil is warmed, it also heats a bimetal strip which is connected through linkage to the gage pointer. As more current passes through the coil, the bimetal strip bends more, causing the gage to deflect, or indicate a higher reading. The sending unit is a variable resistance which determines how much current is allowed to go to ground from the instrument panel gage. See Fig. 8-7.

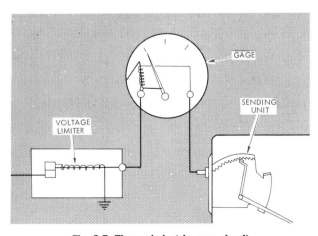

Fig. 8-5. Thermal-electric gage circuit.

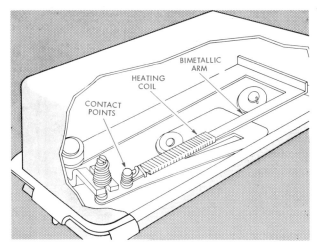

Fig. 8-6. Instrument voltage regulator. (IVR)

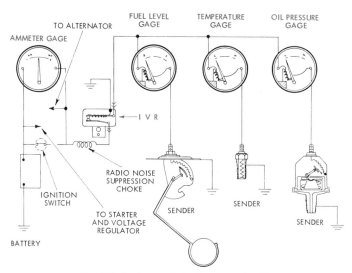

Fig. 8-7. Instrument cluster gage circuits.

BALANCING COIL GAGES

Balancing coil gages are used on some vehicles also. These usually do not use a voltage regulator. Often the gage needle is damped so that the gage seems to not turn off. This is a design feature to slow down needle movement. Without this dampening, this type of gage registered any slight movement of the sending unit.

(Particularly the fuel tank sender.) Fig. 8-8.

In the balanced coil type gage, the sending unit mounted in the tank and the receiving unit mounted on the instrument panel are connected by a single wire (Fig. 8-8). Each unit is grounded through the car frame to complete the electrical circuit.

The sending unit is actually a rheo-

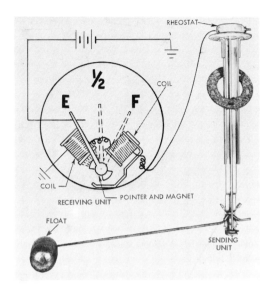

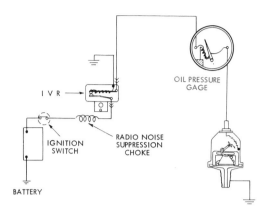

Fig. 8-9. Oil pressure gage with circuit.

Fig. 8-8. Balanced coil fuel gage. Rheostat lowers the resistance at higher fuel level causing an increase in the current to the right side coil and the pointer moves to the right.

stat (or variable resistance unit) with a brush which contacts the resistance unit. The brush is operated by the float arm. Variations in resistance are produced by movement of the contacting brush as fuel height changes in the tank. This variation changes the value of the current in the two receiving unit coils. These are spaced 90 degrees apart with an armature and pointer at the intersection of the coil axis. As the current in the receiving unit coils changes, the pointer moves, indicating the quantity of fuel in the tank.

OIL PRESSURE INDICATORS. Oil pressure indicators are of two types, those which give a reading of the oil pressure, and warning lights which light up when the oil pressure is low. Figs. 8-9 and 8-10.

(1) Warning Lights. Most cars are equipped with a red indicator lamp which lights when the oil pressure is below a safe value. The lamp should light when the ignition switch is first turned on, and it should go out when the engine starts. The lamp is connected between the oil pressure switch (sending unit) and the IGN terminal of the ignition switch.

When the engine is not operating, the oil pressure sending unit switch is closed. Thus, with no oil pressure, current flows from IGN terminal of the ignition switch through the lamp, and through the oil pressure sending unit to ground.

When the engine starts, the oil pressure increases. After the pressure has risen to a safe value, the pressure operated switch opens up, allowing the light to go out. As long as the oil pressure is maintained, the indicator lamp will remain out. If at any time the oil pressure in the system drops below about seven pounds, the switch closes and the lamp lights.

(2) Gages. As full-pressure engine lubricating systems became more commonly used, it was found desirable to know that oil was being supplied to the various engine bearings. Excessive leakage or failure of the oil pump to function will cause loss of oil pressure and oil circulation. The oil pressure gage, therefore, is an important instrument on automobiles and trucks because without proper oil circulation, bearings and other internal engine parts would not receive adequate lubrication.

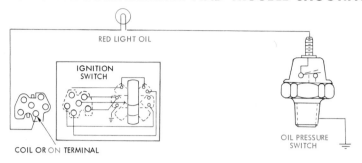

Fig. 8-10. Oil pressure circuit with warning light.

NOTE: The oil pressure gage indicates engine oil pressure in pounds per square inch (psi); it does not indicate the amount of oil in the engine.

Two units comprise the electrical type oil pressure gage. The sending unit is installed in the engine cylinder block at the main oil line gallery. The receiving unit is mounted on the instrument panel. The two units are connected by a single wire, and the circuit is completed through the battery and ignition switch.

The sending unit of an electrical type oil pressure gage contains a diaphragm which is deflected in proportion to the pressure of oil in the line. When the diaphragm is deflected, current flows through a resistance unit which changes the strength of current in the receiving unit coils. The change in resistance in the sending unit changes the strength of the indicating unit coils and causes the pointer to register the oil pressure.

In bimetal type oil pressure gages a bimetal arm wound with a heater wire is used to open and close a set of contacts in the two units in much the same manner as in the bimetal fuel gage (Fig. 8-10). As the wire becomes heated in the sending unit, the bimetal arm distorts, causing a similar action in the receiving unit. By linking the receiving unit bimetal arm to the gage pointer, the amount of

distortion measures the amount of oil pressure.

TEMPERATURE GAGES. Two types of gages described under the electric fuel gage circuits are also used as engine temperature gages. The sending unit for these two types differs mechanically from the sending unit in the corresponding fuel gage circuit. In both of these temperature gage circuits, the sending unit is actuated by temperature. Fig. 8-11. Fig. 8-12 shows the arrangement of a hot and cold light circuit. When the coolant is at operating temperature no ground is available for either bulb. If the bulbs are not burned out the temperature switch should be replaced. As usual check the circuit for grounds and loose connections as well as wiring continuity. Fig. 8-13 shows a tem-

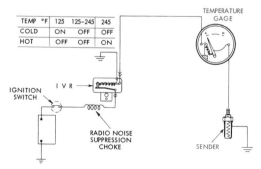

TEMP °F	125	125-245	245
COLD	ON	OFF	OFF
HOT	OFF	OFF	ON

Fig. 8-11. Engine temperature gage and circuit.

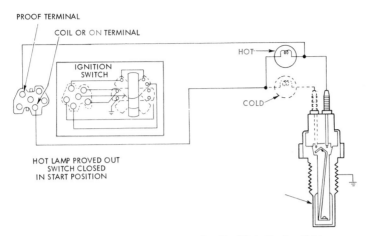

Fig. 8-12. Engine temperature circuit with indicator lights.

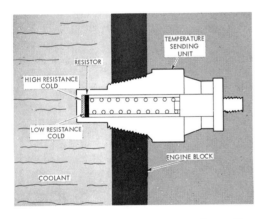

Fig. 8-13. Engine temperature sending unit.

perature sending unit used with a thermal type gage.

ELECTRIC SPEEDOMETERS. Electric speedometers, so far as trouble shooting is concerned, are just like mechanical speedometers except that the sending unit generates an electric current which is carried to the speedometer head through wires. Since this circuit generates its own current, the circuit is entirely independent of the battery-generator circuit.

Electric speedometers (or tachometers) generally are used on vehicles only where it would be impractical to connect the speedometer drive gear directly to the head through a mechanical drive cable. A bus, in which the engine is mounted at the rear, is a good example of the kind of vehicle that uses an electric speedometer.

NONELECTRICAL INSTRUMENTS

In addition to the electrical instruments discussed in the preceding section, some vehicles use some nonelectrical or mechanical instruments. The various nonelectrical instruments used measure pressure, temperature, and speed. Electrical instruments have mechanical parts that convert a mechanical pressure or a temperature to an electrical value that is read in terms of pressure or temperature at the receiving unit.

In general, the nonelectrical instruments are completely nonelectrical. An exception to this is the mechanical speedometer that, while mechanical in construction, uses a magnetic field in the head unit to reflect the speed. Mechanical speedometers are mechanical in the sense that they are driven mechanically. In the speedometer head a permanent magnet rotates with the drive cable. It is this rotating magnet that causes the speedometer pointer to deflect in proportion to speed. Thus, we see that the mechanical speedometer is actually magnetic.

Pressures can be measured with a bourdon tube or a diaphragm. Both are used as dash instruments and each of these is briefly discussed here.

Bourdon tube gages are used primarily to indicate engine oil pressure. The instrument is connected directly to an engine oil line through tubing.

A diaphragm exposed to pressure on one side and having mechanism to resist movement on the other side can be used to measure pressures directly or as a part of a sending unit in electrical instrument circuits.

Mechanical temperature gages are known as the *vapor pressure* type. In this type of instrument, temperature is indicated by means of pressure. The principles of operation that apply to pressure measurements are presented in the following paragraphs.

PRESSURE MEASUREMENTS. Pressures are measured in pounds per square inch (psi). A pressure of one hundred pounds per square inch means a total pressure of one hundred multiplied by the number of square inches on which it is working. Thus, this one hundred pound pressure working against a diaphragm or piston of five square inches in area would exert a lifting force of five hundred pounds. Or, if working against an area of one-half square inch, it would exert a lifting force of fifty pounds.

The atmosphere around the earth has a pressure of approximately 14.7 psi at sea level. Pressures less than atmospheric are referred to as vacuums. The value of the vacuum is the difference between the atmospheric pressure and the pressure within the vessel under vacuum.

The unit of measurement for the vacuum is inches of mercury. This unit of measurement is based on the ability of

the pressure differential to lift mercury in a tube. The common forms of pressure gages are bourdon tubes, and diaphragms.

(1) Bourdon Tube. A bourdon tube gage consists essentially of a curved, slightly elastic tube, oval in section. One end of this tube is open to the pressure to be measured. The other end of the tube is closed and is connected to a movable hand or pointer that indicates the pressure on a dial. See Fig. 8-14.

An increase in pressure in the tube causes the curve to straighten in proportion to the pressure.

Bourdon tube gages are used to measure either liquid or gas pressures. The instrument generally is connected directly to the source of pressure through tubing.

In maintenance work, bourdon tube gages are commonly used to measure intake manifold vacuum (range 0 to 30 ins. of mercury), fuel pump vacuum (range 0 to 30 ins. of mercury), fuel pump pressure (range 0 to 10 lbs), engine compression (range 0 to 200 lbs), and engine oil pressure (range 0 to 100 lbs).

Bourdon tube gages are used also to measure the hydraulic pressures used to actuate automatic transmission gear shifts and the hydraulic pressures in tractor hydraulic systems used to lift or control the implements.

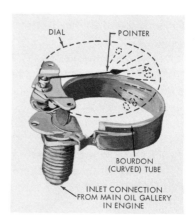

Fig. 8-14. Pressure expansion (Bourdon tube) oil pressure gage.

(2) Diaphragm. A diaphragm exposed to pressure on one side and having a mechanism to resist movement on the other, can be used to measure pressures directly. This type of pressure gage has been used on some distributor test benches. The more common use of the diaphragm, however, is as a part of a sending unit in electrical instrument circuits.

AMMETERS

The only troubles encountered with an ammeter are that it fails to register, reads incorrectly, or reads backward.

FAILS TO REGISTER. If the ammeter fails to register, the following procedure will merely confirm this fact: Turn off all lights and electrical accessories, start the engine in neutral and run it at a speed equivalent to a car speed of about 20 mph. If the ammeter pointer fails to indicate "charge" for at least the time required to restore the current used in starting, either the generating system or the ammeter is at fault.

Stop the engine and turn on the head lights. The pointer should move to the discharge side of the dial. If the pointer will not indicate on either side of the dial, the instrument should be replaced.

If the ammeter pointer or dial is distorted, or if the instrument itself is faulty, it is not practical to attempt repairs. A new instrument should be installed.
NOTE: If the mounting nuts on the back of the ammeter are tightened too much, short circuits or distortion of the mechanism within the instrument may occur.

INCORRECT READING

If it is reported or suspected that the ammeter reads incorrectly, connect an accurate test ammeter in series with the ammeter on the vehicle and test to compare the readings of the two instruments.

NOTE: Most ammeters used in passenger or commercial vehicles only indicate the flow of current. They seldom show accurately how much current is flowing. Consequently, the dials of these ammeters are not calibrated to show actual amperes; on some instruments only the words "charge" or "discharge" are used.

REVERSED READING

If the ammeter reads backward, it is connected wrong. If the wires connected to the binding posts on the back of the "hot wire" type ammeter are reversed, the ammeter indication will be reversed. Likewise, if the wire running through the loop of a "loop" type ammeter passes through the loop in the wrong direction, the ammeter will read backward. Disconnect one end of this wire, remove it from the loop, and thread it through in the opposite direction.

FUEL LEVEL GAGES

This section contains trouble shooting procedures for electrical and nonelectrical type fuel gages.

These procedures do not take into consideration the possibility that the instrument pointer might be stuck or bent, or that the float arm of the tank unit (sending unit) might be bent, causing an inaccurate reading. If there is doubt about these possible conditions, the old unit can be checked against a new one known to be good.

FAILS TO REGISTER

If the gage fails to register, it is necessary to determine whether the sending unit, the receiving unit, or the wiring which connects the two units is at fault. The tests necessary to locate the cause of the trouble may be performed in two ways. The first method requires the use of a spare sending unit known to be in good condition. The second method involves "shorting" the sending unit.

TESTING. A fuel gage sending unit can also be used as a testing device for electrically operated oil pressure gages, or temperature gages, as explained later in this chapter.

(1) With Spare Sending Unit. Select a fuel gage sending unit known to be satisfactory for testing purposes.

NOTE: If there is any doubt about the satisfactory operation of the sending unit selected, connect it in series with a receiving unit known to be satisfactory and a battery. Operate the sending unit float arm by hand. If the receiving unit reads "zero" with the float in its bottom position and "full" with the float in its top position, the spare sending unit can be considered as a satisfactory testing device.

Disconnect the sending unit being tested. In its place connect the sending unit selected for a tester. Use two ten-foot lengths of insulated wire equipped with clip terminals at each end to make this connection so that the test can be made sitting in the driver's seat where the operation of the receiving unit can be observed.

Turn on the ignition switch. With the float of the spare tank unit being used as a tester at the bottom position, the receiving unit should register at the bottom mark on the dial. By moving the float of the tester toward its top position, the receiving unit pointer should gradually move to the top mark on the dial. It is necessary to allow about one minute for the receiving unit to heat up.

If the receiving unit operates satisfactorily, inspect the sending unit on the vehicle to be sure that it is properly grounded. If the vehicle is equipped with a radio, a condenser is usually installed at the sending unit. If the condenser is shorted, the receiving unit will over-read.

If the sending unit is properly grounded and the receiving unit registers properly, install a new sending unit.

If the receiving unit does not operate or fails to indicate correctly, inspect the wiring between the two units for open circuits or grounds. If the wiring is satisfactory, install a new receiving unit.

A special gage tester which will substitute three sizes of resistance is available. Fig. 8-15 shows how this tester is used. Caution should be exercised to be certain that the sending unit wire not be grounded as this could cause excessive current to flow in the gage. This will likely ruin the gage. All gage circuits operate similarly, and the testing of these units involves a determination that the wiring, ground, and sending unit are intact and operating. If the gage does not register correctly, it should then be replaced. Because most gages are rather difficult to get to in the dash panel, all other possibilities for trouble should be eliminated before checking the gage itself.

(2) By Shorting Out Sending Unit. Use a "jumper" for this (a wire with clip terminals on each end). Attach one end of the jumper to the terminal screw of the

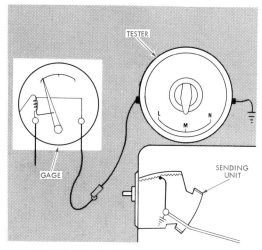

Fig. 8-15. Gage tester connected into circuit.

sending unit and the other end to a good ground on the engine or frame. Turn on the ignition switch. If the receiving unit registers, install a new sending unit.

CAUTION: When making this test, turn off the ignition switch as soon as the pointer of the receiving unit moves about half the distance across the dial. When the ignition switch is turned on, the gage unit is subjected to a full twelve volts and will burn out if the jumper is connected for too long a period of time.

If the receiving unit fails to register when the sending unit is shorted out and the ignition switch is on, inspect the wiring and connections between the two units for open circuits or grounds. If the wiring is satisfactory, install a new receiving unit and repeat the test.

OIL PRESSURE INDICATORS

Trouble shooting procedures in this section pertain to the three types of oil pressure indicators commonly used. Two are operated electrically and the other is a pressure-expansion type.

ELECTRICAL GAGE

An electric oil pressure gage (Fig. 8-16) operates on the same principle as the electrical fuel level gage described previously.

Since the unit is the same in principle as the electric fuel level gage, the same tests may be used to locate trouble.

PRESSURE-EXPANSION GAGE

When the engine is idling, the oil pressure gage should show a small amount of pressure. As the engine is speeded up, the gage should register a higher pressure. On most vehicles, an engine speed equivalent to a car speed of 30 mph will cause the gage to show its maximum pressure. A typical, pressure-expansion type, oil pressure gage is illustrated in Fig. 8-14.

NOTE: When an engine has seen much service, clearance in the main and connecting rod bearings and in the camshaft bearings will cause a drop in oil pressure readings, particularly at idling speeds. If the oil pressure gage shows no pressure at idling speed but indicates pressure as soon as the engine is speeded up, the gage is not faulty.

If the gage fails to register or if the pointer sticks, is jumpy, or uneven, replace the gage as it is not practical to attempt repairs.

INDICATOR LAMP

The other type of oil pressure indicator is a warning light rather than a

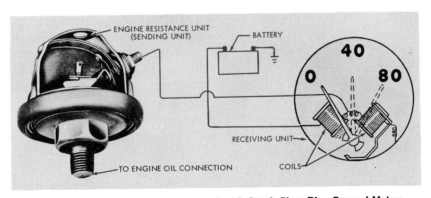

Fig. 8-16. Oil pressure gage and circuit. AC Spark Plug. Div., General Motors.

gage. To test the indicator lamp turn on ignition switch. Do not start the engine. The lamp should light. If it does not, replace the lamp. Check the circuit if the new lamp does not light. Start the engine. The lamp should go out, indicating that oil pressure has built up to a safe value. If the lamp does not go out, check the engine oil pressure using a pressure type tester. If pressure is normal replace the indicator lamp switch.

TEMPERATURE GAGES

The trouble shooting procedures in this section pertain to the two types of temperature gages commonly used. One type is operated electrically by a sending unit mounted on the engine.

Another type of temperature indicator is the vapor-pressure type (Fig. 8-17).

ELECTRICAL TYPE

This type of gage should read "cold" with the ignition switch off. When the

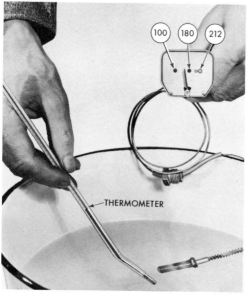

Fig. 8-17. Testing a temperature gage with a thermometer. AC Spark Plug Div., General Motors.

ignition switch is on, the pointer should move to indicate the current engine temperature. If the gage does not operate in this manner, there is a short or open circuit in the wiring, or the sending units or the instrument itself is at fault.

If the wiring is grounded, the gage will read in the "hot" position with the ignition switch on, regardless of the temperature. If there is an open circuit in the wiring, the instrument will read "cold" with the ignition switch on, regardless of the engine temperature.

To determine if trouble exists in the wiring, or if the sending units or instrument is at fault: (1) Turn on the ignition switch and leave it on during the test. (2) Ground the terminal of the sending unit which is farthest from the instrument. (3) If the pointer failed to move to the "hot" position, but now moves to "hot" when the terminals are shorted, the sending unit is at fault. (4) If the pointer stays at the "cold" position when the sending unit terminal is shorted, an "open" exists between the sending unit and the instrument. (5) To determine where the "open" is, short out in turn each terminal between the sending unit and the instrument until a reading is obtained. The wire or unit between the point where a reading is obtained, and the last point where a reading was not obtained, is at fault.

The electrical temperature gage with a single sending unit operates on the same principle as an electrical fuel level gage.

The same tests used to locate trouble in the electric fuel gage may be used for this type gage. These tests are made with a fuel gage spare tank sending unit.

VAPOR-PRESSURE TYPE

The normal operating temperature of most liquid cooled internal-combustion engines is from 180 to 220° F. In localities where atmospheric temperatures rise higher than 100° F. or in pressure cap sealed systems, the gage may register engine temperatures of 240° or higher.

If the gage fails to register after the engine has reached normal operating temperature, or continues to register high temperatures when the engine is cold, drain the engine cooling system and remove the gage bulb from the cylinder head.

Heat a pan of water and immerse the bulb of the gage in the water. To check the gage, also immerse a thermometer which registers up to 212° F. (Fig. 8-17) or higher. Compare the reading on the thermometer with that on the gage. If the gage is inaccurate or will not register, it cannot be repaired. The entire unit must be replaced.

SPEEDOMETERS

MECHANICAL

The troubles experienced with mechanically operated speedometers are that they (1) fail to show both speed and mileage, or that the pointers fluctuate; (2) fail to show either speed or mileage, or the pointers will not return to zero; or that they give an inaccurate reading.

CABLE. Fluctuation of the speedometer pointer, or failure to indicate speed and mileage, is usually caused by a kinked or broken drive cable or casing. Remove and inspect the speedometer cable; if broken or kinked, install a new assembly. When the speedometer cable is installed, it should be positioned so that there are no sharp kinks or bends in the cable housing. A typical speedometer drive cable and casing is shown in Fig. 8-18.

To test for a kink in the cable, hold the two ends of the cable in the hands with the cable looped down (Fig. 8-19). Turn the cable slowly. If kinked, the looped end of the cable will "flop."
NOTE: Breakage of the speedometer cable sometimes results from the use of a cable assembly which is too long. When a cable is replaced, be sure the new cable has exactly the same over-all length.

If the drive cable is satisfactory, test the speedometer head for binding (Fig. 8-19). This can be done by using a short piece of speedometer cable (about 3 or 4 in. long) with a tip to fit the speedometer on which the test is being made. With the speedometer drive cable disconnected, insert the tip end of the short piece of cable

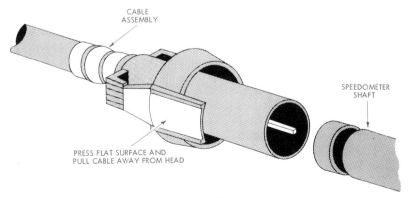

CABLE ASSEMBLY

SPEEDOMETER SHAFT

PRESS FLAT SURFACE AND PULL CABLE AWAY FROM HEAD

Fig. 8-18. Speedometer cable to head connection.

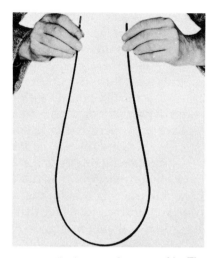

Fig. 8-19. Testing speedometer cable. The cable will flop if it is kinked. Check the head for binding.

in the speedometer socket. Spin the cable between the thumb and forefinger in the proper direction to cause the pointer to indicate speed on the speedometer dial. If there is any tendency for the speedometer to bind, remove the head for the necessary repairs. If the test indicates that there is no binding when the cable is spun, the speedometer head may be considered to be in satisfactory condition.

HEAD. If the speedometer pointer fails to return to zero or fails to indicate either speed or mileage, the trouble is within the speedometer head itself. Remove and replace the head or make the necessary repairs.

AXLE RATIO AND TIRES. If the reading is inaccurate, inspect the tires on the vehicle to see that they are the correct size. The number of teeth in the speedometer drive gears in the transmission (or transfer case used on four-wheel-drive vehicles) depends on the size of the tires and the gear ratio of the rear axle with which the vehicle was originally equipped. Any change in tire size or axle ratio will cause the speedometer to register either too slow or too fast. If the tire size is correct (same size as original equipment tires) remove the speedometer head for the necessary repairs. The cable may be binding or the head may be defective.

TRADE COMPETENCY TEST

1. At what point are most electrical instruments connected?

2. What two types of inexpensive ammeters are commonly used?

3. What is the instrument voltage regulator?

4. What are the three types of electrical fuel level gages in common use?

5. Which two basic types of instruments are used to indicate engine oil pressure?

6. In what types of installations are electric speedometers (rather than mechanical drive) used?

7. What is indicated when an ammeter reads backward?

8. What two different types of tests are possible when testing an electric fuel level gage?

9. How is a vapor-pressure type temperature gage tested?

10. How is a speedometer drive cable tested for being kinked?

CHAPTER 9

STEERING CONTROL AND TIRES

This is a large chapter. In it are included the steering control systems, both manual and power, and also the alignment and balancing of the wheels of the vehicle.

Usually steering control troubles will be rather obvious except possibly for the power systems. With a logical approach and an understanding of the steering complaint, most problems will be easily corrected.

The maintenance of adequate steering control and proper tire wear today is most important. Periodic motor vehicle inspection (PMVI) laws in some states require that a certified inspection station check the vehicle for correct steering and proper tire tread. The purpose of PMVI is to eliminate steering and tires as causes of accidents. This chapter will provide you with the procedures necessary to inspect, service, and correct steering control and tire wear complaints.

TIRE WEAR

Normal tread wear varies in relation to the type of road surface, the number of hills and curves, the amount of traffic, the temperature, and the driving habits of the driver. Abnormal wear in varying degrees can be accounted for by such conditions as incorrect air pressure, faulty wheel alignment, faulty brake adjustment, and overloading.

Tire wear is the result of the tire rubbing on the road surface when it should be stationary in relation to the road. All tire wear is either fore-and-aft wear or cross wear, and only those things that can cause the tire tread to move in either one or both of these directions can cause tire wear. The causes of tire wear and the direction of the wear are listed in Table 9-1. Any tire wear (exclusive of cutting that occurs on sharp road surfaces such as cinders, crushed stone, and shell) that you encounter will be the result of one of the factors or conditions listed.

Do not attribute tire wear to any condition not shown in the table. A bent tie road would cause toe-out; nevertheless the condition that causes the wear is the toe-out.

Tire wear is divided into two general classifications: fore-and-aft wear, and cross wear.

Fig. 9-1 shows the tread wear indicators that are built into the tire to identify a tire that has a worn tread.

TABLE 9-1. CAUSES OF TIRE WEAR

Condition	Fore-and-Aft Wear	Cross Wear
Underinflation or overloading.............................	yes	yes
Toe-in or toe-out...	...	yes
Wheel spin..	yes	...
Resist rotation (brakes, tight bearings, etc.).................	yes	...
Camber...	yes	yes
Overinflation...	...	localizes
Inadequate grooves in tread.............................	yes	yes
Nonskid knobs...	yes	...
Toe-out on turns...	...	yes

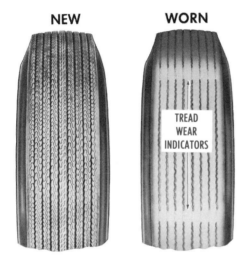

Fig. 9-1. Tread wear indicators are built into some styles of tires. Cadillac Motor Div., General Motors Corp.

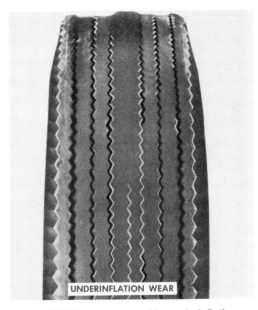

Fig. 9-2. Tire wear caused by underinflation.

FORE-AND-AFT WEAR

The tire illustrated in Fig. 9-2 is an example of lengthwise or fore-and-aft wear of the tire shoulder. In this case (underinflation) the rolling radius of the tire was reduced, with the result that the excessive rubber was forced to pile up ahead of the wheel. When the excess rubber reached the limit of its distortion, it then passed under the wheel in a lump, and just as it left the road, the rubber snapped back to its original shape, scraping on the road surface as it did so. This accounts for cupping shown in the photograph.

Wear around the tire (rather than across the tire), sometimes called "heel and toe wear," is due to the following causes: (1) The wheel always resists rotation, even when everything is correct. Fore-and-aft wear around the tire is accelerated by anything that increases the tendency to either spin or resist rotation, as, for example, dragging brakes, excessive use of the brakes, tight wheel bearings, or spinning the wheels during rapid acceleration. (2) Due to camber, the wheel has several diameters. (3) Nonskids, or knobs on the tread, are distorted as they contact the road and a fore-and-aft wear of that portion of each knob that is still in contact with the road occurs as the knob resumes its normal shape and position. Likewise, the first edge of the tread that grips the road when the brakes are applied wears off.

CROSS WEAR

Fig. 9-3 is a photograph of a tire having severe cross wear on one shoulder. This is a front tire since rear tires seldom feather-edge. The wheel on which this tire was mounted had toe-out which caused the wear to occur from the center line of the tire out.

The most common condition to look for would be a bent tie rod since most cases of toe-out are a result of the tie rod having struck some object in the road.

Fig. 9-4 illustrates a case of severe cross wear. Wear confined to the center of the tire indicates that the tire has been kept overinflated. Underinflation causes tires to wear on the two shoulders, whereas overinflation causes the tires to wear in the center.

The condition of this tire also indicates excessive toe-in, since the feather-edge is on the side of the ribs toward the center of the car. The wear on this tire would have been several times as great

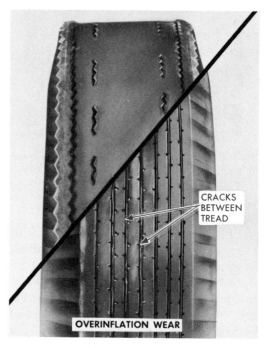

CRACKS BETWEEN TREAD

OVERINFLATION WEAR

Fig. 9-4. Overinflation is a source of tire wear.

Fig. 9-3. Toe-out of tires.

if the tire pressure had been permitted to get low. Fig. 9-5 shows a method for checking cross wear on a tire not so severely worn as those in Fig. 9-4.

Sometimes all side wear is referred to

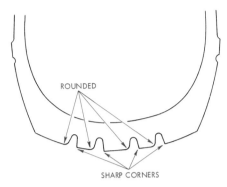

Fig. 9-5. Crosswear can be detected by running the hand across the tread. One edge will be sharp and the opposite edge round.

as "camber wear." However, the use of this term is not advisable since other factors can cause side wear. Camber wear can be a combination of both cross wear and fore-and-aft wear. Side wear is due to the following causes.

TOE-IN. If the front wheels toe in when the vehicle is in forward motion, the two front wheels are father apart when they leave the road than when they contact it. This means that the tread of the tire must move away from the center line of the car. The road, of course, resists this movement. Normally, the tire flexes enough to absorb the movement until just before contact with the road is broken. The tendency of the tread is to resume its normal position at the time when, just before it leaves the road, the resistance of the road lessens. This movement of the tread causes cross wear .

Occasionally a tire subjected to severe wear will develop a featheredge as a result of too much toe-in or toe-out. Cross wear usually is not severe enough for this to happen, and the edge of the rib merely becomes sharp, as shown in Fig. 9-5.

Maximum tread contact area and traction with minimum tire wear are present when the tire is properly inflated and the recommended load intensity is evenly distributed over the tread contact area. Underinflation destroys this balance and per-

mits a greater movement between the tread and the road. This further increases cross wear if excessive toe-in exists. Overinflation by reducing the contact area decreases traction and localizes cross wear at the center ribs of the tire.

A slight amount of toe-in usually is necessary because of lash or looseness in the steering connections. This amount of toe-in does not cause tire wear. When the car is in operation on the road, the wheels are pushed back and the backlash is absorbed. If the toe-in were just enough so that with all lash removed the front wheels were exactly parallel, no wear would result from toe-in.

Toe-in in excess of the amount required to absorb the lash in the steering connections always results in cross wear of the tire since the wheels are farther apart at the point where they leave the road than they are at the point where they contact the road.

CAMBER. If the front wheel has positive camber, the bottom of the wheel is nearer to the center line of the car than the top of the wheel. When camber is excessive or when the grooves in the tire are unable to absorb the distortion that occurs as between A and B, Fig. 9-6, cross wear occurs between A and B. Toe-out on turns, if not correct, may also contribute slightly to cross wear of the tires.

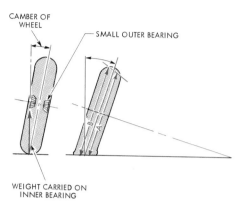

Fig. 9-6. Correct camber, left. Excessive camber, right, causes tire wear when the tread cannot absorb the distortion between A and B.

STEERING CONTROL

In those rare cases where the causes of steering trouble are not apparent, you can be reasonably sure that one of the following is true: (1) The trouble may not actually exist: make a road test. (2) The trouble occurred under some condition of loading that was not in effect when you made your tests and measurements. (3) The accuracy of your equipment may have changed. Check your equipment. This change in equipment is more likely with equipment used on built-up ramps, since the ramp may have been thrown out of alignment by being bumped by a vehicle.

Remember that all a wheel can possibly do is to: (1) go straight ahead, (2) go backward, (3) turn in, (4) turn out, (5) go upward, or (6) go downward.

Study the conditions found, and interpret the directional tendency created by each factor. Likewise, study the condition of each factor to see if any of the stabilizing influences have been lessened. The various directional tendencies and stabilizing influences are separated into types in Table 9-2. This table separates the factors according to the direction of the tendency created. Columns (1), (2), and (3) indicate the conditions that im-

part directional tendencies. Columns (4), (5), and (6) indicate the effect on stability.

It should be noted that during the universal checking procedure, certain corrective operations are indicated before proceeding with the remainder of the check. The reason for this is that unless these corrections are made at that time, readings obtained in subsequent checks, in most cases, may not reflect the true condition.

Where it is possible to make the corrections of looseness, tightness, etc., during the checking procedure, many of the factors will automatically be removed from further consideration. This greatly simplifies the diagnosis. What remains after these preliminary corrections is shown in Table 9-3.

There are no so-called short cuts or cure-alls in wheel alignment: every conclusion must be based on facts. Likewise, without all of the facts, no one can consistently come up with the right answer.

DIRECTIONAL TENDENCIES

If, from what the owner has told you or from your own observation during the road test, the trouble is directional (vehicle pulls to either side), disregard those factors that cannot account for a tendency to pull in one direction. Remember that each directional tendency should be balanced by a like but directly opposite tendency at the opposite wheel. Compare the readings obtained at the two wheels and disregard those that are equal. If what is left creates a definite tendency in one direction, several choices are available: (1) restore all factors to manufacturer's specifications, (2) reduce the value of the factor involved, (3) increase the value of the same factor at the opposite wheel, (4) create a counter or opposite influence by changing some other factor either at the same or the opposite wheel, or (5) in in-

TABLE 9-2. FACTORS WHICH AFFECT STEERING CONTROL

FACTORS	DIRECTIONAL TENDENCIES			STABILITY EFFECTS		
	(1) Backwards	(2) Turn In	(3) Turn Out	(4) Upwards	(5) Downwards	(6) Straight Ahead
Underinflation, one front wheel			yes		yes	
Underinflation, one rear wheel		yes			yes	
Loose wheel bearings		yes				no
Tight wheel bearings			yes		yes	
Loose kingpins or bushings		yes &	yes			no
Tight kingpins or bushings						no
Loose steering connections		yes &	yes			
Loose steering gear mounting		yes &	yes			
Loose U bolts, clips, or spring tie bolt				yes &	yes	
Loose radius rod		yes &	yes			no
Radial run-out				yes &	yes	
Wheel wobble		yes &	yes			
Wheel balance		yes &	yes	yes &	yes	
Camber			yes			
Negative camber		yes				
Caster		yes				yes
Negative caster			yes			no
Shock absorbers too tight				no	no	
Shock absorbers too loose				yes &	yes	
Steering gear off midposition		yes or	yes			
Steering gear mesh loose		yes &	yes			
Steering gear mesh too tight or distortion and binding in steering column						no
Toe-in		yes &	yes			
Zero toe-in						yes
Toe-out		yes &	yes			
Rear wheel toe-in (one wheel)			yes			no
Rear wheel toe-out (one wheel)		yes				no
Wheel base short on one side			yes			no
Wheel base long on one side		yes				no
Toe-out on turn too great						
Toe-out on turn too little						
Brake drag	yes					
Uneven brake adjustment	yes					
Out-of-round brake drum	yes					

NO indicates strength normal tendency is reduced.   YES & YES indicates both tendencies are created.
YES indicates the tendency is created.   YES OR YES indicates one but not both tendencies are created.

TABLE 9-3. STEERING CONTROL FACTORS AND INFLUENCES REMAINING AFTER PRELIMINARY CORRECTIONS

FACTORS	DIRECTIONAL TENDENCIES			STABILITY EFFECTS		
	(1) Backwards	(2) Turn In	(3) Turn Out	(4) Upwards	(5) Downwards	(6) Straight Ahead
Wheel balance		yes &	yes	yes &	yes	
Camber			yes			
Negative camber		yes				
Caster		yes				yes
Negative caster			yes			no
Toe-in		yes &	yes			
Zero toe-in						yes
Toe-out		yes &	yes			
Rear wheel toe-in (one wheel)			yes			no
Rear wheel toe-out (one wheel)		yes				no
Wheel base short on one side			yes			no
Wheel base long on one side		yes				no
Toe-out on turn too great						
Toe-out on turn too little						

Note: NO indicates strength normal tendency is reduced.
YES indicates the tendency is created.
YES & YES indicates both tendencies are created.

stances where it is possible, reduce a slight directional tendency by increasing the influence of some stabilizing factor.

LACK OF STABILITY

If the fault is lack of stability, and if corrections of all faults of looseness or tightness in the steering gear or steering connections were made during the checking procedure without correcting the fault, consider the various angles that are factors. Remember that positive directional tendencies balanced against directly opposite tendencies of equal strength are usually more desirable than indefinite tendencies that can change their direction, causing hunting. When a tendency is positive in one direction, it can be restrained without lash or can be canceled out by a positive but opposite tendency.

COMPLETE DIAGNOSIS

A complete analysis of steering control and tire wear trouble and their causes is given in Table 9-4. In this table each fault appears at the top of the table. Since each fault provides clues to the causes, they are referred to as symptoms. Each is identified by a number. This same number is used to identify the paragraph in which the particular symptom is discussed on the following pages.

In this same table, the more common causes of trouble are designated as factors and are listed along the side. The factors that can contribute to the greatest number of symptoms are listed first. Under each symptom, the particular factor that can account for the symptom is indicated by a number. The value of the particular number indicates the approximate order of probability.

The various symptoms of steering control and tire wear troubles are:

(1) Tire Wear. While tire wear is discussed elsewhere in this chapter, it cannot be completely separated from the considerations of steering control since it is a major symptom of steering control troubles.

(2) Wander. Wander is the tendency for a vehicle to turn slightly first to one side and then to the other when the driver is trying to go straight ahead.

(3) Pull to One Side. The tendency of a vehicle to pull continually to one side is often caused by a maladjustment on the opposite side. Pulling can be one of the most difficult troubles to remedy.

(4) Wheel Tramp. Wheel tramp is an oscillating motion in the front wheels at high speeds resulting in uncontrollable motion of the front of the vehicle, usually both up-and-down and sidewise. The disagreeable motion is the least at a point over the rear axle. Much of this disagreeable motion is transmitted to the steering wheel. Wheel tramp not only can result in premature failure of affected parts, but renders the vehicle unsafe as well.

Where wheel tramp is reported, yet a check of wheel balance off the vehicle indicates the wheels are in balance, check the wheels on the spindle where the reaction of the complete assembly can be observed. This is the only method that takes all of the units (hub, brake drum, wheel nuts, hub cap, wheel, tire, and tube) into account.

(5) Cupped Tires. Cupping is a form of tire wear usually caused by underinflation. This condition may be a strong clue to factors that also impair steering control.

(6) Road Sway—Darting. Road sway is a rocking motion of the vehicle similar to the rolling of a ship. Darting is a tendency to change direction suddenly without the steering wheel having been turned. Vehicles susceptible to crosswinds fit in this category.

(7) Jerky Steering—Road Shock. When small depressions or obstacles in the road surface are felt in the steering wheel, the condition is usually referred to as road shock or jerky steering.

In addition to the faults, listed in Table 9-4, wear in the steering gear increases the lash and may cause road shock. Look for wear in the sector and roller shaft bushings or needle bearings. On worm and roller types of steering gears, look for wear in the roller bushing or shaft or needle bearings. End play or lash of either the steering worm or cross shaft likewise can result in road shock.

(8) Shimmy. Shimmy is an oscillating motion in the front wheels at low speeds, sometimes resulting in a violent, uncontrollable motion of the steering wheel.

(9) Loose Steering. Loose steering will result if the steering gear is not properly adjusted. Loose steering is one of the more dangerous of the faults listed.

(10) Hard Steering. Steering that is harder than normal may be caused by lack of lubrication or any one of several other faults.

(11) Hard Turning When Stationary. Hard turning when stationary is the major symptom of underinflation.

(12) Erratic Steering When Braking. Erratic steering only when braking is an indication of faulty brakes on one side of the vehicle.

(13) Tire Squeal on Turns. Tire squeal at any time is an indication of movement of the tire while in contact with the road surface. A tendency for the rear tires to slip is created during rapid acceleration. A tendency to slide exists when brakes are applied. A tendency for the wheels to slip sidewise is created on turns. The strength of this tendency is controlled by the speed and the sharpness of the turn. Some tire squeal must be con-

TABLE 9-4. CAUSES OF TROUBLE AND ORDER OF PROBABILITY

SYMPTOM

FACTORS	(1) TIRE WEAR	(2) WANDER	(3) PULL TO ONE SIDE	(4) WHEEL TRAMP	(5) CUPPED TIRES	(6) ROAD SWAY	(7) JERKY STEERING	(8) SHIMMY	(9) LOOSE STEERING	(10) HARD STEERING	(11) HARD TURNING WHEN STATIONARY	(12) ERRATIC STEERING WHEN BRAKING	(13) TIRE SQUEAL ON TURNS
1. Tire pressure incorrect	1	1	2	11	1	1	9	1		1	1		1
2. Loose Ball Joints	6	2			4	2		2	1				
3. Loose tie rod ends	14	10		6	3			4	3				
4. Loose drag link ends	15	9	6	5	2			3	2				
5. Loose spring U bolts	13	13		8	5	8		6	5				
6. Broken spring tie bolts	13	11		9	6	9		7	6			6	
7. Tire overload	5	18			8	5				4	7	5	
8. Broken spring	11	12	8	10	7	10		8	7			4	
9. Loose steering gear mountings		14		7		7		5	4				
10. Wheel balance	8			1	9	6	4						
11. Steering gear bind		3								2	2		
12. Caster lower than standard		3					10						
13. Bent spindle		16	14	12			8			5			5
14. Camber plus side inclination unequal			9		13								4
15. Radius rod loose		15		14			11	9	8				
16. Toe-in too great	2	8					5						3
17. Radial run-out				2	10		6						
18. Lateral run-out				3	11								

TABLE 9-4. CAUSES OF TROUBLE AND ORDER OF PROBABILITY (CONT.)

Cause	1	2	3	4	5	6	7	8	9	10	11
19. Unequal brake adjustment	10									2	2
20. Bent spindle arm	17	13									6
21. Camber low	7										
22. Caster high								3	3		
23. Caster uneven	4										
24. Camber plus side inclination high	5								4		
25. Camber plus side inclination low	6								5		
26. Steering gear off center		10				1					
27. Spring sag	12				11						7
28. Loose or worn shock absorber			4		4						
29. Cupped tires			13			3					
30. Oversize tires							10		6		
31. Unequal tire diameter	7	4									
32. Bent rear axle housing	16	11									
33. Bent frame	20	12									
34. Dragging brakes	3	15									2
35. Camber high	4										
36. Camber uneven		7									
37. Tight wheel bearings		5									
38. Loose wheel bearings										3	
39. Toe-in too little	19										
40. Incorrect drag link adjustment						2					
41. Loose or worn stabilizer					3						
42. Not tracking	9	16									
43. Rear axle toe-in	17										
44. Rear axle toe-out	18										
45. Rear axle camber	19										
46. Out-of-round brake drum				12							1
47. Bent Pitman arm						7					

sidered as normal. The so-called low-pressure tires will squeal more readily on turns than high-pressure tires.

ROAD TESTS

As a wheel alignment specialist you will often receive complaints of noise. In many cases the complaint of noise will be in addition to a steering control or tire wear complaint. Noise nearly always is associated with looseness. The checking and correction procedure discussed under wheel alignment in this chapter covers most of the usual sources of looseness and noise. However, there are several trials that can be made during a road test to make it possible to locate the source of the undesirable noise more readily. These trials are all in the order of the direction of movement of the wheel or suspension, and the road test can include several steps to reveal the source of the noise.

If the noise occurs during acceleration, then the noise is occurring in the parts that deliver the torque to the rear axles or the parts that accept the torque from the rear axle. The universal joints, drive line, etc., are delivering torque to the rear axle and the springs and their hangers accept the torque of the rear axle.

If the noise occurs during stopping, it must be remembered that when the brakes are applied they endeavor to hold the wheel from turning, and in so doing, they themselves try to rotate with the wheel. This means, then, that everything to which the wheels are secured tries to rotate with the wheels. If the noise occurs during brake application, a clue has been provided as to where the source of the noise might be.

If the noise occurs when driving diagonally across street car or railroad tracks, remember that the wheels during this time are trying to oscillate sidewise and that only those things that create noise during such sidewise or back-and-forth movement of the wheels can account for that noise. This would include the ball joints, the steering linkage, and the steering gear itself.

In making a road test, it is well to have a definite route and procedure. The ideal route is one that permits speeds of at least 60 miles per hour on a straight, level road. A choice of directions is desirable so as to permit checking the behavior of the car in a cross wind. The passing of a long tractor trailer combination usually brings about the same tendencies as a sudden exposure to a severe crosswind.

Before starting the road test, to make sure the vehicle is reasonably safe to drive, perform the following three steps.

(1) Brakes. Check the brake pedal reserve. If insufficient, adjust the brakes before making the road test.

(2) Looseness. Check the free play of the steering linkage. This should not exceed 1½ in. movement at the rim of the steering wheel. If excessive looseness exists, correct it before attempting high-speed driving. Likewise, if the wheels turn hard, the car may be dangerous to drive.

(3) Tires. Inflate the tires to the recommended pressure and at the same time look for anything that may render the vehicle unsafe.

In many instances you will be making the road test to determine only if a specific trouble exists. In other instances you will be making the road test to determine if any steering control fault exists. In this case, however, it is assumed you will want to perform all of the tests.

TEST PROCEDURE

The following arrangement does not necessarily represent the order in which the test should be made. The procedure can be varied to suit the test route. However, be sure to make all of the tests.

Each of the following tests is headed by the name of the trouble which the test is designed to reveal. In those instances where you are checking for a specific fault, merely follow the procedure that applies.

ROAD SHOCK. Drive the car straight ahead to check steering gear midposition and note the position of the steering wheel when the vehicle is going straight ahead. If you experience road shock during this test, the position of the steering wheel while driving straight ahead in most cars and trucks provides the needed clue to the cause of the trouble or eliminates several possible causes of the trouble from further consideration.

Grip the spokes of the steering wheel tightly while you drive from 15 to 20 miles per hour and feel for hammerlike blows being transmitted to your hands as first one wheel and then the other runs over slight bumps in the pavement.

SHIMMY. Cross streetcar or railroad tracks on a slight angle with the vehicle traveling between 15 to 20 miles per hour, and observe any tendency to shimmy.

TRAMP — WANDER. Drive the car at high speed, watching for any tendency of the front wheels to shimmy or tramp. While driving at high speed, allow the hands merely to lie on the steering wheel spokes. If the owner's complaint is wander, but no wander is noted, grip the wheel tightly and slightly stiffen your arms. If a tendency to wander is now noted, it is a good indication that the complaint of wander is, at least in part, the result of "oversteering" due to the owner's tenseness. However, a reduction of steering lash and an increase in one of the stability factors, such as caster, will reduce the tendency of a tense driver to oversteer.

PULL TO ONE SIDE. At a moderate speed, span the crown of the road and release (but keep your hands near) the steering wheel. If during this test the vehicle travels straight for 0.2 miles, you can discount any complaints of pulling to one side. However, if in your community the roads have high crowns, complaints of pulling to the right may be due to high camber created at the right wheel by the road crown. In this case, four courses for the correction of this trouble are open. These are: (1) reduce camber of right wheel, (2) increase camber of left wheel, (3) increase caster of right wheel, or (4) reduce caster of left wheel.

NOTE: Before starting this check, determine if there were any passengers in the car at the time of pulling, and where they were seated.

DARTING — SUSCEPTIBILITY TO CROSSWINDS. Select a road running at right angles to the direction of the wind. Grip the steering wheel loosely and at speeds in the neighborhood of 40 miles per hour, look for darting as the vehicle goes into or comes out of stretches of the road where the wind is obstructed by buildings, trees, or other vehicles. If no tendency to dart is noted, repeat the test, holding the wheel tightly and with the arms stiffened. A tendency to dart can now, at least in part, be attributed to oversteering by and tenseness of the driver.

HARD STEERING—RETURN TO STRAIGHT AHEAD. If traffic conditions permit, at 30 miles per hour, weave the vehicle rapidly from one side of the road to the other, noting any difficulty of either turning or recovery.

Make several turns at different speeds, again noting any difficulty in turning. As the vehicle comes out of the turn, release the wheel and observe whether or not the various factors that cause the wheel to go straight ahead are strong enough to straighten the course of the vehicle.

BRAKES — EFFECT ON STEERING. Stop the vehicle from several speeds to observe any tendency for it to swerve due to un-equalized or faulty brakes. "Axle roll" or "spring wrap" (tendency for spring to become distorted, permitting axle roll) during the stop might also account for undesirable effect on steering due to the reduction of caster on actual movement of the steering connections.

Obviously, the road test cannot duplicate all conditions. The owner's account of the trouble and a description of the conditions when it was experienced may provide a clue, however, which will enable you to improvise a test.

Some peculiarity of loading or distribution of the load may have to be taken into account. This makes a very definite difference in the case of trucks, busses, and commercial vehicles. Occasionally, loading will make a difference on passenger cars. For example, a salesman has 500 lbs of samples in the trunk of a sedan (behind the rear axle). Without the samples (or an equal weight), the condition complained of could not be duplicated on a road test. Likewise, an analysis of the factors measured at curb weight would provide no clue to the cause of the trouble. If you cannot account for the reported trouble, particularly when working on trucks, repeat the checking procedure with the vehicle under normal load distributed in the same manner as when the trouble was experienced.

WHEEL ALIGNMENT

Regardless of whether the car or truck is experiencing unusual tire wear or faulty steering control as discussed in the preceding pages, both the determination of the cause of the trouble and its correction must take into account all of the factors of wheel alignment. These factors of wheel alignment, along with the

troubles they commonly cause, are listed in Table 9-4. Correction of wheel alignment takes these factors into consideration in the same order as their measurement. Both the checking and correcting of wheel alignment, therefore, are presented here as a single procedure.

Regardless of the particular equipment being used, it is recommended that each operation be performed in exactly the order presented here.

Forms which provide a means of recording the various readings involved usually are available from the manufacturers of the equipment, vehicle manufacturers, and other sources. In the checking procedure, it is assumed that the wheel alignment specialist will record his findings. It is usually advisable to check all of the factors before attempting the diagnosis. Typical equipment used in checking alignment is shown in Fig. 9-7.

Checking without authority to correct is the most popular type of wheel alignment service. It permits the shop to advertise "Free Wheel Alignment Checks" or wheel alignment or safety inspection at some nominal fee. This is a good way

Fig. 9-7. A portable wheel alignment tester. Bear Mfg. Co.

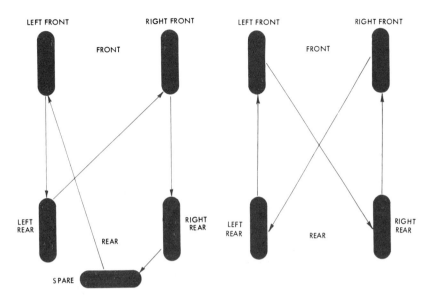

Fig. 9-8. Effects of tire wear can be equalized by tire rotation as shown.

to build business since the vehicle owner or operator can have all or any portion of the corrections made at his option. As a wheel alignment specialist you will have to do both types of jobs.

The preliminary steps of wheel alignment have to do with the establishment of the correct tire inflation and the determination of the steering wheel position when the front wheels are traveling straight ahead. Both of these things are important since they have a direct influence on subsequent tests and adjustments.

(1) Inflate Tires. Inflate the tires to the recommended pressure. If the front tires are "cupped" or have been wearing unevenly, they should be changed to difference locations as shown in Fig. 9-8. If a spare tire is involved, the pattern shown in the left-hand diagram should be followed. If no spare is involved, follow the pattern shown in the right-hand illustration.

(2) Mark Straight Ahead Position. While driving the car in the straight ahead position, place a pencil mark on the steering wheel hub and steering column jacket (Fig. 9-9) to establish the straight ahead position of the steering gear for later reference during the checking procedure.

NOTE: A "china crayon" pencil is ideal for this purpose since it will not mar the paint and can be wiped off easily.

LOOSENESS

Excessive looseness in the steering linkage, suspension, or spring mountings will prevent the establishment of good steering control and will make the correction of the causes of tire wear difficult if not impossible. The checking and correcting of looseness is as follows:

WHEEL BEARINGS. Raise the front wheels off the floor. Rotate one front wheel slowly and note any tendency for binding. Grasp the wheel at the top and bottom and push in and pull out. Repeat this procedure for the opposite wheel. If any free play (or binding) is noticed, adjust the wheel bearings.

ALIGNMENT MARKS

Fig. 9-9. Alignment marks are used on some steering wheels.

To adjust front wheel bearings, remove the cotter pin and tighten the nut to 12 lbs torque. Rotate the wheel to insure that none of the bearing rollers are cocked or misaligned. Back off the nut one castellation slot, then turn back to the nearest cotter pin hole. If the wheel bearing is the type with a special cover to lock the spindle nut, the nut must be adjusted with a torque wrench. Install a new cotter pin. The two types of front wheel bearings in common use are shown in Figs. 9-10 and 9-11. End play of most wheels with bearings properly adjusted should be .001 to .008 inch.

BALL JOINTS AND SUSPENSION ARM BUSHINGS. Some vehicle manufacturers produce cars where the ball joints are "unloaded" when the wheel is off the ground. When servicing these cars, be sure the ball joints are lubricated. Elimi-

nate any looseness detected in either upper or lower suspension arm bushings.

When prescribing corrections for looseness or noise at any point, don't lose sight of the fact that in many instances some looseness is desirable and intended by the manufacturer (such as with ball joints). Certain minimum clearances must be maintained for all moving parts, and corrections that reduce clearance below these minimums can result in such troubles as wander and hard steering.

TIE ROD AND DRAG LINK ENDS. Grasp the front of the front wheels (Fig. 9-12), push them away from each other, and then pull them toward each other, observing the tie rod and drag link ends for looseness. Replace loose tie rod and drag link ends, and replace or straighten bent tie rods or drag link.

NOTE: In the previous steps, the front

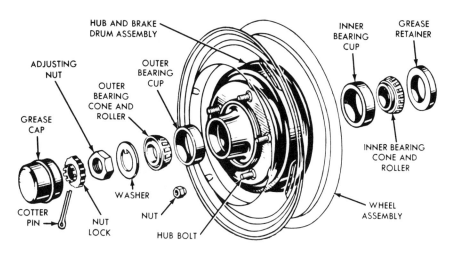

Fig. 9-10. The front end wheel assembly.

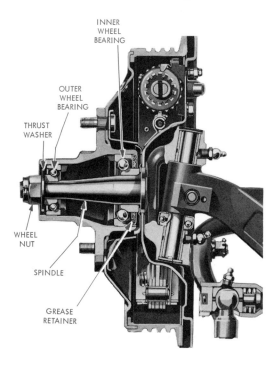

Fig. 9-11. Front wheel ball bearings. With the wheel off the ground push and pull the tire at the top and bottom to check for slack in the bearing. General Motors Corp.

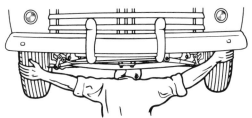

Fig. 9-12. Checking looseness in tie rod and drag link ends. Worn ends must be replaced but tie rods and drag links can be straightened if bent.

wheels of the vehicle are off the floor. In these steps and throughout the following procedures at any time when the wheels are lowered to the floor, make sure the full weight of the car or truck is on the wheels and not partially on the jack.

STEERING GEAR MOUNTING. Check the steering gear mounting bolts and tighten them if required. If the vehicle is equipped with a rubber mounting pad for the steering gear, make sure it is in good condition and in the proper position before tightening the mounting bolts.

SHOCK ABSORBERS. Check the shock absorbers for leakage. Tighten the shock absorber mountings if loose.

Most faulty shock absorbers are detected by jouncing the vehicle at each corner. As you push down on the car bumper, resistance to the movement will be noted.

As you raise up on the bumper, more resistance should be noted. Repeat this up-and-down movement several times, increasing the length of the stroke each time and releasing the bumper at the bottom of a down stroke. If when released the up-and-down motion stops quickly, the shock absorbers are probably functioning as intended. If, however, the vehicle continues its up-and-down motion for two or more cycles, the spring action is not being dampened. Make sure the shock absorbers (if refillable) have sufficient fluid and repeat the test after refilling if the fluid level was low. If the resistance is still low, adjust the shock absorbers if means of adjustment is provided. If no adjustment is provided, or, if after the adjustment the resistance is still low, the shock absorbers should be replaced.

RADIUS ROD. If the vehicle is equipped with a front axle radius rod, check the radius rod ball joint for looseness, and tighten or replace the ball joint parts, whichever is required. If the vehicle has a torque tube drive rear axle provided with radius rods, make sure they are not loose or bent.

STEERING GEAR

Five separate steps are involved in checking the steering gear. You will find usually that when one fault is uncovered, it is advisable to make a complete adjustment of the steering gear. Most of the separate adjustments of the steering gear each have some influence on the other adjustments. For this reason, the complete steering gear adjustment is recommended when any one of the separate adjustments is required.

The five separate steps of the checking and adjusting procedure are as follows:

MIDPOSITION. Align the pencil marks on the steering wheel and steering column (Fig. 9-9). This will put the front wheels in the same position they were when the vehicle was traveling straight ahead. Determine if the steering gear is in its midposition while the wheels are straight ahead, as follows:

In most steering systems, the midposition of the steering gear is indicated when the steering wheel spokes are in a certain position. With two-spoke steering wheels, the spokes should be in a horizontal position. On such vehicles, if the spokes are not in the correct position, adjust the steering gear or linkage to bring the spokes to the correct position while the front wheels are straight ahead.

With steering gears that do not have the midposition indicated by either some marking or by a steering wheel spoke position, remove the Pitman, turn the steering wheel all the way to the right and then all the way to the left, counting the turns. Half the total turns is the midposition. If the steering gear is not at this midposition while the front wheels are straight ahead, adjust the steering gear or linkage to establish this correct relationship.

BINDING. With the wheels off the floor, turn the steering wheel through the entire range of travel in both directions to check for bind in the mechanism. If bind is noticed, disconnect the steering linkage from the pitman, and check again. If bind still exists, adjust the steering gear, including all steering gear adjustments. If a satisfactory adjustment cannot be made, overhaul the steering gear.

If no bind is present when turning the steering wheel with the linkage disconnected, the bind is in the steering linkage. Check all pivot points in the steering linkage.

WHEEL LASH. With the front wheels on the floor and straight ahead, lightly grasp the steering wheel between thumb and forefinger at the rim and move the wheel back and forth to determine the amount of play. Manufacturers' specifications vary with respect to steering gear mesh adjustment. However, if there is any steering wheel play, the steering gear mesh requires adjustment.

CROSS SHAFT END PLAY. Grasp the steering gear pitman and push and pull on the sector shaft. If end play exists, adjust the steering gear, including the sector shaft.

ADJUSTMENTS. Four adjustments are involved in all steering gear adjustment procedures: worm end play, sector shaft play, gear mesh or lash, and centralization of tooth contact or midposition adjustment. In some steering gears, this last adjustment is made within the steering gear proper. In other steering gears, this is an external adjustment. Centralization

of tooth contact is a definite part of steering gear adjustment even though a means of making the adjustment within the steering gear proper is not always provided.

Adjustments generally are made to take up normal wear in the steering gear. Correct adjustment results in a definite drag or preload, but must not cause binding in the steering gear at any point of the turn.

In all steering gears, a means of taking up wear is provided at all points where wear occurs. Wear is taken up by means of shims, thrust screws or nuts, or eccentric bushings. Disconnect the steering linkage from the lower end of the pitman when making steering gear adjustments.

(1) WORM END PLAY. If, in the preceding tests, worm end play is indicated, it is removed by tightening the worm bear-

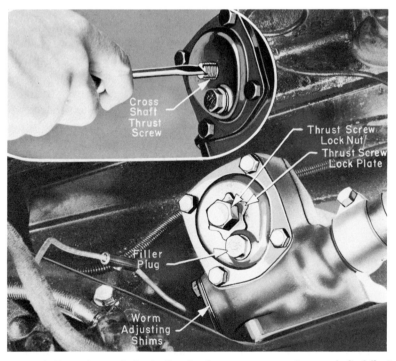

Fig. 9-13. Removing end play in the steering gear worm and cross shaft. Adjust worm gear by removing shims. The cross shaft has a screw adjustment. Chrysler Div., Chrysler Corp.

ings. This is accomplished in some steering gears by an adjusting nut or screw or by means of shims as follows:

(a) SHIMS. If the shim pack is located at the top (column end of worm), loosen the column jacket clamp, loosen the housing cover cap screws, and slide the cover up along the column to gain access to the shims.

If the shim pack is located at the lower end of the worm (Fig. 9-13), loosen the screws and move the plate about ⅜ in. away from the housing to expose the shims.

NOTE: Do not remove the plate, or the lubricant will run out.

Carefully separate one shim, using a jackknife or other suitable blade. Slit the shim at one side and remove it from the gear. Tighten the plate, or the cover and jacket clamp. Test the adjustment, and remove additional shims if necessary. Always remove one shim at a time to avoid binding.

(b) Adjusting Nut or Screw. A typical steering gear thrust nut or screw, used to maintain the desired preload on worm bearings, is illustrated in Fig. 9-14. To make the adjustment, loosen the lock nut and tighten the worm bearing adjuster as required.

(2) Cross Shaft End Play. All makes

of steering gears are equipped with a cross shaft thrust screw. On many vehicles still in use where movement of the cross shaft in one direction is prevented by a thrust shoulder in the steering gear housing, this thrust screw is used to adjust cross shaft end play only. Fig. 9-13.

In some worm and roller types and in all recirculating ball steering gears, end play is maintained by the head of the thrust screw which fits into a slot. Fig. 9-15. In such steering gears, end play of the cross shaft cannot be adjusted except by replacing the worn parts. The thrust screw in this instance is used to adjust gear mesh only.

End play, as such, is not adjustable in cam and lever steering gears. The thrust screw is used to establish proper mesh of the studs of the cam.

On steering gears where end play is adjustable, loosen the lock nut and turn the thrust screw in until all end play is removed from the cross shaft. Excessive tightening causes binding. Grasp the pitman and push the cross shaft in and out to feel the amount of end play.

(3) Gear Mesh or Lash. Wear is always greatest at the straight ahead position. With the steering gear in midposition (point of least lash), the gears should mesh as closely as possible without binding. Each type of steering gear is provided with one of three different means of adjusting the mesh; thrust screw, shims, or an eccentric. In all types, the procedure moves worm and sector closer together.

(a) Thrust Screw. In steering gears having no external adjustment for cross shaft end play, gear lash is adjusted by moving the sector device closer to the worm with the thrust screw provided. An adjustment of this nature on a worm and roller steering gear is shown in Fig. 9-13. Recirculating ball steering gears, Fig. 9-15, and cam and lever steering gears are adjusted in this manner for gear lash.

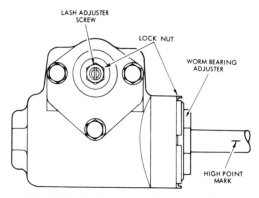

Fig. 9-14. Steering gear adjustment points.

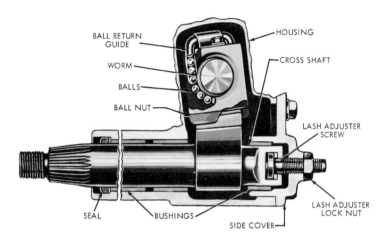

Fig. 9-15. Steering gear with no adjustment for end play. The end screw is used to adjust gear mesh.

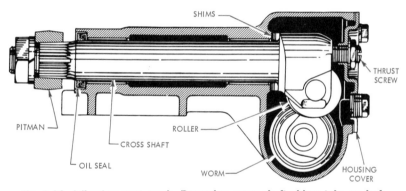

Fig. 9-16. Adjusting gear mesh. Removing cross shaft shims take up lash.

(b) Shims. On steering gears having a cross shaft end play external adjustment, but no eccentric for adjusting mesh, mesh adjustment is accomplished by removing cross shaft shims to reduce gear lash. (Fig. 9-16)

Remove the Pitman and the housing cover without disturbing the thrust screw. Push out the cross shaft and take out one shim. Reassemble the gear and check the lash. If necessary, remove additional shims and reassemble, rechecking after each is removed. (When finished, don't forget to replenish the lubricant.)

NOTE: Most of today's automobiles use the recirculating ball type steering gear.

(4) Centralization of Tooth Contact. Centralization of tooth contact adjustment of the steering gear consists of whatever adjustment is required to establish the steering gear on the midposition, high point, or point of least lash when the vehicle is traveling straight ahead. Steering gear midposition is established by one of two methods: by changing the angle or position of the Pitman on the steering gear cross shaft, or by shortening one tie

rod and lengthening the other tie rod on vehicles using two tie rods.

The steering wheel spoke position in most vehicles is related to the steering gear midposition adjustment. When this adjustment has been made you will find that the spokes on these vehicles are in the correct position. An exception to this would be when one or several of the parts involved are bent or twisted.

(a) Adjustable Pitman Position. Some axle suspensions having a nonadjustable drag link are provided with an adjustable pitman that permits a centralization of tooth contact adjustment.

Set the front wheels in the straight ahead position. Disconnect the drag link. Set the steering gear in midposition. Remove the pitman, and reposition it so that the drag link is just the right length without turning either the front wheels or the steering wheel.

(b) Adjustable Tie Rods. In vehicles using two separate adjustable tie rods, the steering gear is put on the high point by shortening one tie rod and lengthening the other exactly the same amount. Always check, and, if necessary, adjust toe-in after making adjustments of the tie rods. *NOTE: After establishing steering gear midposition and placing the steering wheel spokes in the correct straight ahead position, rub out the marks previously made and make new ones (Fig. 9-9) on the steering wheel and steering column to permit turning back to midposition in later tests.*

WHEELS

The wheels and tires are an important part of wheel alignment. The steps to be performed are:

RUN-OUT. Raise the front wheels off the floor. Spin the wheels by hand and observe the radial run-out at the top or front of the wheel. If the run-out is in excess of $\frac{1}{16}$ in., make sure the tire is seated properly on the wheel rim. If the tire is installed properly but runs out excessively, it may be advisable to install the wheel on the rear axle.

NOTE: If the equipment to be used requires establishment of the true plane of the wheel by scribed line, time will be saved if the line is scribed at this time.

WHEEL WOBBLE. Observe the amount of wheel wobble. If the wheel wobble is more than $\frac{1}{8}$ in., it may be necessary to replace the wheel. In some instances the wheel will perform satisfactorily on the rear. If the equipment to be used requires establishment of the true plane of the wheel, hub, or side of the tire, establish the true plane at this time.

WHEEL BALANCE. Using a wheel spinner (Fig. 9-17), spin each front wheel in turn. A wheel that is out of balance will cause the front of the vehicle to shake. Balance the wheels if required. The use of a wheel spinner permits you to check wheel balance more quickly by a method that the vehicle owner will readily appreciate.

If a wheel spinner is not available, the wheel can be removed, checked, and corrected on any conventional wheel balancer, but the front wheels can be checked and corrected more easily if a wheel spinner is used. Fig. 9-18.

Occasionally you will encounter a vehicle that tramps due to one or both rear wheels being out of balance. This is not difficult to check but the correction is more involved than the correction of a front wheel out of balance.

Fortunately, rear wheel balance is rarely a factor and generally is only checked when road tramp is experienced that cannot be accounted for in any other way. Before performing this check, be certain that the vehicle does not have a

Fig. 9-17. Tire balancing on a car saves time and work. Bear Mfg. Corp.

power directed differential. If rear wheel balance is to be checked, proceed as follows: Jack up one rear wheel and block the other three wheels. Start the engine and drive the raised wheel in high gear. Observe the end of the rear bumper for vibration. If the bumper does not vibrate, that wheel is balanced and will not cause road tramp at that speed. If the bumper does vibrate, the wheel or the parts that revolve with it are out of balance. True speed will be double the speedometer reading. If the speedometer reads 35 mph the rear wheel is running at 70 mph.

NOTE: A greatly amplified indication will be obtained if a door is opened wide. Observe the vibration of the door rather than the bumper.

ANGLES AND TOE-IN

CAMBER. Use the marks previously placed on the steering wheel, to set the front wheels straight ahead. (Fig. 9-9) If the equipment being used measures camber from the side of the wheel, tire, or

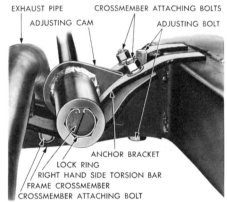

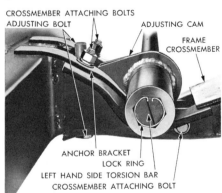

Fig. 9-18. Torsion bar adjustment. The adjusting bolt turns the adjusting cam and changes the torsion of the bar. Chrysler Corp.

hub, jack up the front wheels and position them with the true plane of both wheels vertical. Fig. 9-18. Lower the wheels. Always make sure the full weight is on the wheels. It is a good plan to move the back of the car up and down a few times to allow the springs to settle. This is particularly true for cars equipped with coil springs. If riding height is specified, the car should be pulled down to that point before checking. Fig. 9-19.

Measure and record the camber of the wheels.

On independent suspensions camber is adjusted by changing the spindle sidewise inclination. Incorrect camber setting does not have the same significance as it does on solid axles. If the camber on vehicles with independent suspensions is either correct or incorrect and there is no indication of bent parts, or if there is no directional tendency that can be attributed to incorrectly positioned point of intersection, it usually is reasonably safe to omit the checking. Merely adjust the camber to the recommended setting.

STEERING AXIS INCLINATION (Spindle Pivot Center Line). The only reason for ever checking sidewise inclination of the steering axis is to determine if the knuckle is bent. With axle suspensions, camber is adjusted by changing the king-pin inclination. In independent suspensions where a means of adjusting camber is provided, the camber is also changed by changing steering axis inclination, usually by changing the position of the upper control arm.

Regardless of how the steering axis angle is changed on any suspension, the relationship between the center line of the axis and the center of the contact area of the tire remains the same. This relationship changes only when the knuckle is bent. A severe collision is about the only way that a knuckle can be bent.

On independent suspensions, if there is no indication of a collision, this operation can safely be omitted from the procedure. On axle suspensions, if the camber is correct, there is little reason to check kingpin inclination and this operation can safely be omitted from the procedure.

If the need for checking axis inclination exists, such as a strong directional tendency that cannot be accounted for in any other way, proceed as follows:

The sidewise inclination of the steer-

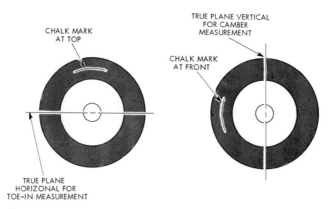

Fig. 9-19. Positioning the true plane of the tire for toe-in (left) and camber (right) measurement.

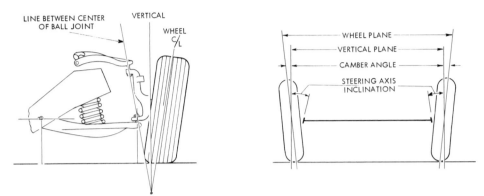

Fig. 9-20. Relation of camber and steering axis inclination. Ball joint system is typical.

ing axis is determined and this angle is added to the camber reading previously obtained. Fig. 9-20. Of course if a negative camber reading was obtained, the amount of negative camber is subtracted from the angle. If the camber plus steering axis angle is not correct, the knuckle is at fault. This will change the location of the point of intersection.

If the combined angle is too great, the point of intersection will be raised. This will create a tendency for the wheel to turn in or reduce the tendency to turn out. If the combined angle is too small, the point of intersection will be lowered. This will increase the tendency of the wheel to turn out.

Any change in the combined angle from the original combined angle means that the bushings are worn or the knuckle has become bent and that these parts will have to be replaced. Since these combined angles locate the point of intersection and since the point of intersection creates a definite tendency, the combined angle should be equal at both wheels. Otherwise, a difference in the strength of the tendency at each wheel will result.

In the measurement of sidewise inclination knowledge of how the inclination is determined is important in order to appreciate the various steps of the proce-

dure. Make sure of the accuracy of your readings before replacing the knuckle or bending the support. Several considerations affecting the accuracy of your readings are as follows:

On any suspension in which the camber changes at different spring heights, it is important that a constant spring height be maintained not only during the steering axis inclination test but during the camber check as well. Constant spring height can best be maintained by compressing the springs to a point that can be maintained.

This is an important consideration since in these cars the camber may change if a door is left open or will vary depending on which door the driver left the car.

Raising the car with a jack between the time the camber is checked and the time the final steering axis inclination reading is taken, will change the inclination reading unless a constant spring height is maintained.

Where the springs are compressed to a definite height, the camber must be checked again at this height. This camber measurement is not necessarily the normal camber of the vehicle, but it is the camber measurement that must be added to the steering axis inclination reading to determine the combined angle. The combined camber and axis angle is, of course, what you are interested in.

If a horizontal line were drawn on the end of the front spindle of a vehicle with the wheel in one position, this line would not remain horizontal when the steering knuckle is turned. This is because the steering axis is tipped sidewise (side inclination). The more the axis is tipped, the greater this change from horizontal will be. This is the principle on which the measurement of side inclination is based in all wheel alignment equipment.

As the spindle is turned away from the straight ahead position, the end will travel through a plane that must parallel the ground. However, due to the inclination of the spindle pivot center line, the end of the spindle has a tendency to turn downward. The wheel remains unchanged, hence the front end of the vehicle is raised. This fact utilizes the effects of gravity in returning the spindle to the straight ahead position, thus giving inherent stability.

The measurement of the horizontal line and its relationship to true horizontal, when the steering knuckle has been turned, is the measurement of an angle. This change is the result of sidewise inclination of the steering axis. By measuring this change, the angle is determined. *NOTE: Steering axis inclination, ball joint inclination, and kingpin inclination are terms used to describe the same angle. The kingpin is found only on vehicles with solid front axles.*

(1) The Degree of Turn. In the above just how far the steering knuckle is turned was not emphasized since we were merely trying to demonstrate that a line parallel to the floor or table does not remain parallel during a turn. Most equipment manufacturers calibrate their equipment to measure this change during turn of a specific number of degrees. Accuracy in measurement requires accuracy of the turn. Therefore, careful work and an accurate means of establishing the specific degree turn is required (20 degrees out, then 20 degrees in is the most popular range of measurement).

(a) From the Tire. When measuring side inclination a high percentage of the equipment either secures to or measures from the wheel or the tire. When working with equipment that locates from the wheel, tire, or hub, it is necessary to lock the wheel to prevent its turning. Any turning of the wheel will result in an error in the reading. The usual method of locking the wheel from turning is either to tighten the brakes by means of the brake shoe adjustment, or to apply the brakes by means of a pedal jack. The pedal jack should be spring-loaded if it is to be used on hydraulic brake systems.

(b) From the Spindle. As previously mentioned, with wheel alignment equipment that is secured to the spindle rather than to the wheel, tire, or hub, it is not necessary to lock the wheel during the check, although it is necessary to make sure that the device is fastened to the spindle securely so that it cannot turn as the steering knuckle turns.

CASTER. A wheel mounting is said to have positive caster when an imaginary pivot centerline strikes the ground ahead of the wheel point of contact (Fig. 9-21). Positive caster creates a tendency for the wheel to turn in. If the caster is unequal, this tendency will be unequal and must be corrected. If the caster is too great, it will be difficult to turn the wheels. If the caster is too little, straight ahead stability may be lessened and the wheels might not have the tendency to come back to straight ahead when coming out of a turn. A number of mistakes are possible if you do not thoroughly understand just how caster is measured.

(1) Measuring Caster. With most wheel alignment equipment, caster is de-

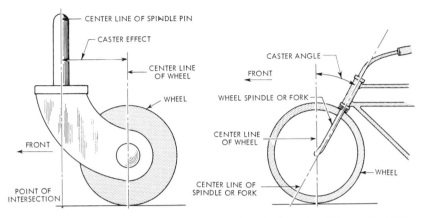

Fig. 9-21. Caster effect. Since the centerline of the wheel is behind the pivot center-line the wheel will track behind the pivots.

termined by measuring the change of camber which occurs during a 40 degree turn as a result of caster.

Since the wheel is secured to the spindle, any change in the angle of the spindle results in a similar change in the camber angle. This change is the result of caster. By measuring the amount of the change either at the spindle or any part of the wheel, the caster can be determined.

Equipment secured directly to the spindle (Fig. 9-22) interprets the change of the spindle's relationship to the floor (horizontal) in degrees of caster.

Other equipment works from the wheel, hub, or tire. Since the wheel runs on the spindle, it is at right angles to it. Therefore the amount of change from vertical is interpreted in degrees of caster.

Since the change varies with the degree of turn, it is important during this measurement of caster that the amount of turn be rigidly controlled. With most equipment, accuracy is based on a turn of 40 degrees (20 degrees out, then 20 degrees in). Errors in turning the wheels the correct amount will result in errors in the reading.

If it is to be changed, correct the caster angle at this time. After making the

Fig. 9-22. Equipment for measuring caster by the spindle's relation to the floor. Bear Mfg. Co.

correction, recheck camber. If camber has changed during the caster change, re-establish the desired camber.

(2) Correcting Caster. The method of changing caster varies with the type of suspension. The various methods for the three more common types are presented separately.

(a) Axle with Two Springs. If the caster on both sides is unequal, the spring pads on the axle are not parallel due to the axle having been twisted or because

unequal wedges are employed on both sides, causing the axle to twist. If the caster is the same on both sides, it can be changed by adding to or increasing the size of the shims between the spring pads and the springs.

These recommendations, of course, assume the springs to be in good condition. If the springs are obviously sagged, they should be replaced. This may be all that is required to correct the caster.

(b) Axle with Transverse Spring. The up-and-down movement of this axle pivots from a radius rod ball joint to the rear of the axle. A sagged spring will result in higher caster. A spring with too much arch will result in low caster. Unequal caster indicates that the axle beam is twisted or the radius rod is bent. The remedy, of course, is to straighten or untwist the part or parts at fault.

(c) Wishbone Type Independent Suspensions. Caster is changed in wishbone type independent front suspensions by means of eccentric bushings, eccentric pivot pins, threaded bushings, shims, or adjusting bolts and lock nuts. A close examination of the particular suspension being worked on will reveal which method is employed. Remember that to increase caster you want to either move the top of the spindle pivot backward or the bottom of the spindle pivot forward. To decrease caster move the top of the spindle pivot forward or the bottom of the spindle pivot backward.

(d) Collision Damage. You will occasionally encounter jobs in which you cannot establish the desired caster by the usual means. These instances may be the result of a collision or other unusual circumstance in which something was changed from its original position. Whether the changed part is the frame, the individual parts of the suspension, etc., remember that at one time the vehicle was normal. By replacing or restoring the part at fault, the normal range of adjustment will be re-established.

It may help you to locate the part at fault or to establish a means of correction if you remember that anything that tilts the top of the spindle pivot backward in relation to the rest of the car will increase caster. Anything that tilts it forward will decrease caster. Select the simplest method of correction consistent with the condition of the vehicle.

CAMBER. Camber adjustment in all types of suspensions is accomplished by changing the sidewise inclination of the kingpin or spindle pivot.

In axle suspensions camber is changed by bending the axle beam. Most independent suspensions provide a method of adjustment, usually by means of an eccentric bushing, eccentric pin, or shims. In some suspensions, a single, threaded eccentric bushing or pin is used for both caster and camber adjustments. The procedure with these suspensions is to obtain the desired caster first, then by means of a partial turn of the eccentric, to adjust the camber.

Other suspensions provide a separate adjustment for camber. In either case, the full range of the camber adjustment is obtained with one half turn of the eccentric.

Regardless of the means of adjustment encountered, remember that you are moving one end of the spindle pivot sideways. Moving the top of the spindle pivot inward or the bottom outward will decrease positive camber or increase the amount of negative camber. Moving the top of the spindle pivot outward or the bottom inward will increase positive camber or decrease the amount of negative camber.

TOE-IN. Toe-in is generally a linear measurement. However, in some instances a protractor at each wheel is used to establish whether or not the front wheels are parallel and, if not, the amount they are out of parallel in degrees. In some instances, the protractor is provided with a toe-in scale that converts the angle to a linear measurement of toe-in or toe-out. With most equipment, however, toe-in is actually a linear measurement, or a comparison of the distance between the front of the front wheels and the distance between the back of the front wheels.

Remember when checking or correcting the toe-in of the front wheels, the predominant tendencies, as the vehicle is being propelled along the road, tend to make the wheels toe-out. The ideal toe-in is that amount which, when the vehicle is in motion, will result in the wheels being exactly parallel. This means that with the vehicle stationary and none of the forces in effect that normally turn the wheels out, a slight toe-in generally is required.

It is usually necessary to pull the vehicle forward or to push the front of the wheels away from the center of the vehicle to get the wheels into their on-the-road position, when toe-in is being measured.

Specifications recommended by some manufacturers may appear to contradict these basic principles. It should be remembered, however, that toe-in specifications are for checking the vehicle at curb weight.

Such specifications do not mean that the vehicle has or should have unusual toe-in or toe-out under normal operating conditions. Under normal load the alignment in these vehicles changes to zero or a slight toe-in.

(1) Toe-In Adjustment. Toe-in is adjusted by changing the length of the tie rods by turning the rods on the end fittings. Fig. 9-23.

(a) One Tie Rod. Loosen the tie rod end clamps and turn the tie rod or clamp in the desired direction. Recheck the

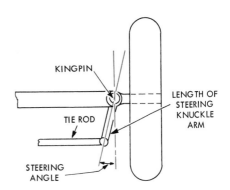

Fig. 9-23. Toe-out on turns is accomplished by having the ends of the steering knuckle arms closer together than the steering axis. Adjustment is by changing the angle of the steering arms.

toe-in measurement, repeating the adjustment if necessary. Tighten the tie rod end clamps.

(b) Two Tie Rods. If only one tie rod is adjustable, establish toe-in by adjusting the length of the one tie rod. If both tie rods are adjustable, make sure the steering gear is in the straight-ahead position when the wheels are straight ahead before attempting to adjust toe-in. Once this is established, adjust toe-in by lengthening or shortening both tie rods by the same amount.

Recheck toe-in and readjust if necessary. Tighten the clamps.

FINAL OPERATIONS

To assure completeness of the wheel alignment check, several additional factors of alignment must be checked. The checking of these factors is discussed in the following paragraphs. While wheel alignment faults attributable to these factors are not common, the following conditions are encountered often enough to warrant making these checks on every job.

REAR WHEEL TOE-IN AND CAMBER. If the rear tires show unusual wear, check the rear wheels for toe-in (or toe-out) and camber in the same manner as for checking toe-in and camber of the front wheels. If the rear wheels have a toe-in or camber reading, a distorted axle or bent radius rods is usually indicated. Repair or replace the parts involved, whichever is required.

WHEEL BASE. Wheel base, of course, is a linear measurement and is generally made with trammels. It is also measured with equipment that is provided with calibrated scales (usually on the side of the runways).

With either type of measuring instrument, place the front wheels in the straight ahead position. Measure the distance between the center of the rear axle shaft and the center of the front wheel spindle. Check the opposite side of the vehicle and compare the readings. If the readings on the two sides are equal, it usually is safe to assume that the relationship of the rear axle to the center line of the frame is satisfactory. If unequal readings are obtained on the two sides, one end of either the rear axle or the front suspension has moved forward or backward, or the axle housing is bent. The readings obtained are the wheel base of the vehicle and even when equal readings are obtained, they should be within $3/8$ in. of the specified wheel base.

Correction of errors in wheel base usually represents a major operation, some of which are in the realm of collision work rather than wheel alignment. If establishing the specified relationship between axle and spring is ineffective in correcting wheel alignment on vehicles having longitudinal springing, satisfactory adjustment sometimes can be made by relocating spring hangers or by establishing a new tie bolt hole in the spring main leaf.

TOE-OUT ON TURNS. Toe-out on turns is controlled by the steering knuckle arm angle and its length (if one steering knuckle arm is bent, it might be shorter than the other). Steering knuckle arm angle and length should be the same at both wheels. If no equipment for measuring this factor is available, measure the distance between the arm and the brake plate. While usually effective, measurement of the angle of the steering arm is not an actual measurement of toe-out on turns, but is a measurement of the thing that causes toe-out on turns.

The usual means of checking toe-out on turns is to turn the one wheel in 20 degrees and measure the degree of turn "out" of the opposite wheel. If the toe-out on turns is incorrect, replace or bend the steering arm to obtain the correct angle.

If the toe-out of the right-hand wheel is incorrect during a right turn, the correction must be made at the right-hand steering knuckle arm. If the toe-out of the left-hand wheel is incorrect during a left turn, the correction must be made at the left-hand steering knuckle arm. No adjustment is generally provided. The knuckle will have to be replaced if toe-out on turns is incorrect.

BRAKES. Make a sudden stop on a dry surface from a speed of from 15 to 20 miles per hour. In many shops this test can be made without leaving the shop. Note any tendency of the vehicle to swerve. This can be felt during the stop or observed by a study of the tire marks on the floor. If the brakes are uneven or the vehicle swerves, the brakes will have to be adjusted.

POWER STEERING

The constantly increasing number of women driving cars has forced car manufacturers, by means of gears and levers, to provide more and more mechanical advantage to the driver through the steering mechanisms. A practical limit, however, exists as to the steering ratio. The more mechanical advantage desired, the more the steering wheel must be turned to turn the front wheels a given number of degrees. The obvious answer to this problem is to provide mechanical assistance rather than mechanical advantage to the driver. This has been accomplished by the power steering systems now available in most cars as optional equipment. A source of power easily tapped exists in the automotive electrical system, and it would be an easy matter to design an all electric power steering system. However, the automotive electrical system is already overloaded, so manufacturers have almost universally adopted hydraulically operated power steering systems.

OPERATIONAL FEATURES

Power in abundance exists in the modern automobile engine, and this power can be put to work to turn the wheels quite simply. Several things are desirable and have been provided in all types of power steering. First of all a sense of "feel" must be retained. To retain this sense of "feel" all power steering systems have been designed so that some manual effort on the part of the driver is required before the power mechanism takes over. This generally amounts to from one to four pounds of pull at the steering wheel rim before power assistance is provided. Without this resistance the driver would have a feeling of insecurity. A shift of position by the driver, such as when reaching to turn the headlights on, might cause him to slightly turn the steering wheel without wanting to. This hazard has been eliminated in all power steering systems by having a resistance that must be overcome before the power takes over.

All power steering systems require the engine to be running in order to supply the power. This means that if the car is being towed or pushed with the transmission in neutral, or the clutch disengaged, no power is available to assist the steering. All designs provide for manual steering under this condition, or whenever the power steering system fails. If the power steering mechanism drive belt should break, or if some other failure should occur, the car can still be steered.

All power steering systems reduce the tendency of the front wheels to make unwanted turns. With manual steering, when one front wheel suddenly hits a bump or puddle of water, or when a front tire blows out, there is often a tendency for the steering wheel to be violently jerked out of the driver's hand. In all types of power steering systems this is reduced to a moderate tendency of the steering wheel to turn that is easy to control. This is an important safety factor.

MECHANICAL FEATURES

The most common type of power steering system employs a belt driven hydraulic pump that runs all the time the engine is running. Fig. 9-24. This pump may be either the vane or rotor type. The hydraulic fluid from this pump flows to a valve which directs the fluid as controlled by the movement or lack of movement of the steering wheel. In the straight ahead position this valve sends the fluid back to the pump and it continues to circulate without doing any work and consequently uses very little power. In either a right-hand or left-hand turn the flow of fluid back to the pump is shut off and the fluid pressure builds up. This built-up pressure is then used to turn the front wheels.

Many hydraulic power steering systems employ a rotor type hydraulic pump. These pumps are similar to rotor type engine oil pumps and the repair procedures are similar. However, the valving

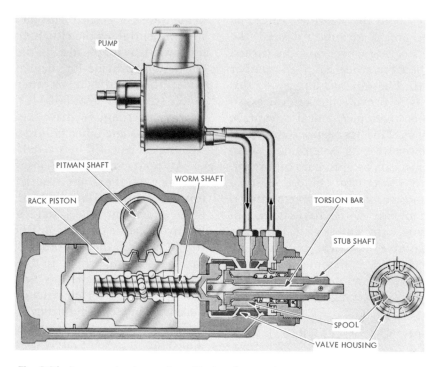

Fig. 9-24. A power steering system. Moving the steering wheel causes pressure to increase on one side of the rack piston and decrease on the other. This gives a pressure boost to the movement of the rack piston. Cadillac Motor Div., General Motors Corp.

and passages generally are more complex. Fig. 9-25 is a disassembled view of an armature shaft-driven rotor type hydraulic pump used in a power steering system. In this illustration, the parts are arranged in the order of assembly or disassembly. Many cars use a vane type power steering hydraulic pump. Fig. 9-26 shows vane type hydraulic pumps. Note the direction arrows on the cam ring. Be sure to assemble the ring with these arrows in the correct position as shown.

All designs provide a pressure-limiter valve that prevents the fluid pressure from exceeding a predetermined high. Without this feature, if a front wheel was tight against a high curb so it couldn't turn, the pressure might build up to a point where the steering linkage or hydraulic system would break.

INTEGRAL SYSTEMS. An integral type of power system is one in which the power operating unit is part of the steering gear.

Recirculating Ball. A cutaway view (Fig. 9-27) shows the construction of the recirculating ball type power steering gear. This type of power steering gear is basically the standard gear with a built-in power or hydraulic piston constructed about the ball nut. It also incorporates some type of valve and a valve-operating mechanism. The typical unit uses a torsion bar operated valve as shown in Fig. 9-28. The operation of this valve is controlled through the twisting effort placed on the torsion bar by the driver of the vehicle. This torque, transmitted through the torsion bar, causes the valve spool to uncover one port and close another thus permitting oil under pressure to one side

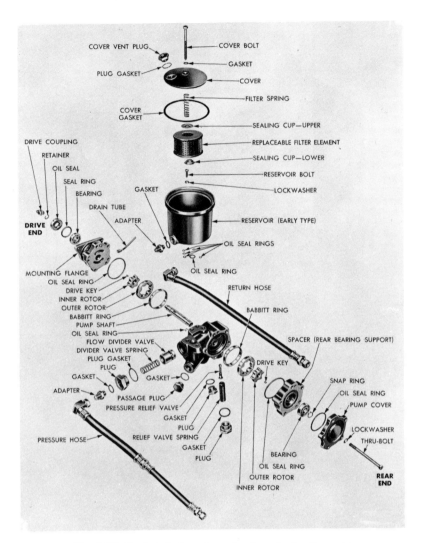

Fig. 9-25. Exploded view of a rotor type hydraulic pump for a power steering system. Chrysler Corp.

or the other of the power piston. A careful examination of Fig. 9-28 should indicate the flow through the valve assembly. If the torsion bar should break a mechanical connection is provided to the worm shaft. This insures that steering will be possible if a valve failure or hydraulic pressure loss occurs.

LINKAGE SYSTEMS. The linkage types of power steering differ from the other hydraulic power steering systems in that

no differences exist in the steering gear proper, instead, the power cylinder and control valve are a part of the steering linkage. The conventional manual steering gear itself is unchanged. In one design, a control valve assembly is incorporated in the pitman-arm to the idler-arm rod. Fig. 9-29. A power cylinder piston rod is secured to the frame, and the piston is attached to the steering idler-arm rod. The control valve assembly and the

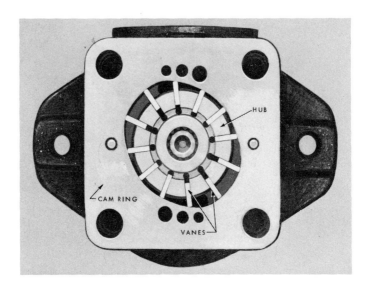

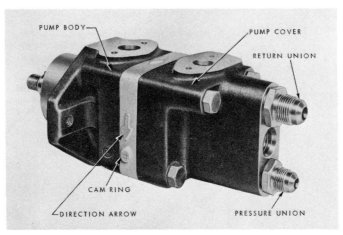

Fig. 9-26. Vane type hydraulic pump showing interior and the assembled pump. Be sure to follow manufacturer's directions when positioning cam ring during reassembly. Arrows (bottom view) aid in positioning the ring. Chevrolet Div., General Motors Corp.

power cylinder assembly in this design are, of course, connected by flexible hoses. The power link shown in Fig. 9-30 has the control valve and power cylinder forming a single unit with internal valve to cylinder passages. The control valve assembly, in all cases, is connected to the hydraulic pump with two flexible hoses. Fig. 9-29 illustrates the installation of a linkage type hydraulic power steering unit on a popular car.

The steering-gear pitman-arm ball joint actuates a spool valve in the control valve. This valve is held in a neutral position by spring pressure when the steering wheel is not turned. Initial movement of the steering wheel against spring pressure moves this valve spool. This shuts off the flow of fluid under pressure to one side of the power cylinder piston, and directs fluid pressure to the other side. The side shut off is not only shut off to

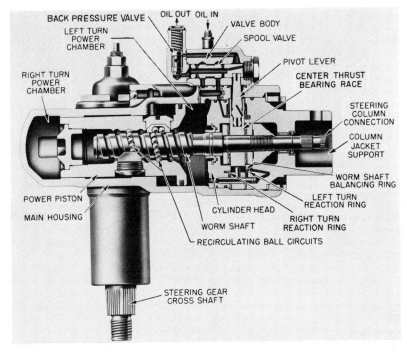

BACK PRESSURE VALVE — OIL OUT OIL IN — VALVE BODY
LEFT TURN POWER CHAMBER — SPOOL VALVE
RIGHT TURN POWER CHAMBER
PIVOT LEVER
CENTER THRUST BEARING RACE
STEERING COLUMN CONNECTION
COLUMN JACKET SUPPORT
WORM SHAFT BALANCING RING
POWER PISTON
LEFT TURN REACTION RING
MAIN HOUSING
CYLINDER HEAD
RIGHT TURN REACTION RING
WORM SHAFT
RECIRCULATING BALL CIRCUITS
STEERING GEAR CROSS SHAFT

Fig. 9-27. Recirculating ball nut type power steering. Chrysler Corp.

pressure but is opened to permit return of the fluid, already on that side of the piston, back to the pump. Fig. 9-31 illustrates the position of the control valve and the flow of the hydraulic fluid for right and left turns, as well as for neutral (straight ahead) position.

ADJUSTMENTS

The types of adjustment made on a power steering installation depends upon whether it is a linkage system or an integral system.

INTEGRAL SYSTEMS. There are two basic adjustments to the integral type power steering system. These are: (1) thrust bearing pre-load adjustment and (2) high point or mid-position adjustment.
NOTE: All steering gear adjustments are checked with the pitman arm disconnected from the steering linkage.
(1) Thrust Bearing Pre-Load Adjust-

ment. Thrust bearing pre-load may be checked by turning the steering wheel to its lock position and in the lash range of the steering gear. The spring scale pull as measured at the rim of the steering wheel should be approximately one-half pound. If the spring scale registers less than one-half pound of pull, the steering gear must be adjusted. Usually, the steering gear will have to be removed from the vehicle. However, some units may be adjusted while the unit is mounted on the vehicle.

(2) High Point or Mid-Position Adjustment. The high point adjustment for power steering is the same type of adjustment as manual steering gear adjustment. First remove the linkage from the steering gear. Then, using a spring scale, pull the steering wheel through its high point noting the amount of pull that this requires. A pull of one pound more than that of the thrust bearing load is consid-

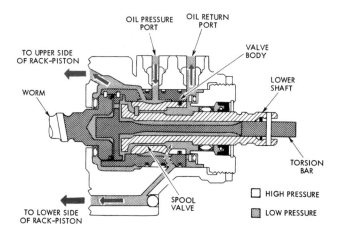

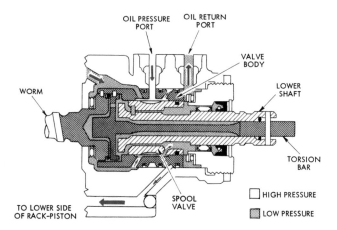

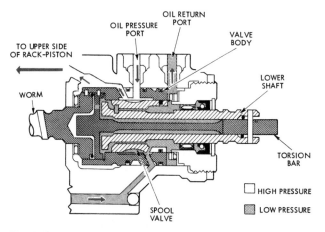

Fig. 9-28. Recirculating ball power steering hydraulic circuits for a left turn. The return action of the valve plunger makes it possible to hold the wheels at any position. Chevrolet Div., General Motors Corp.

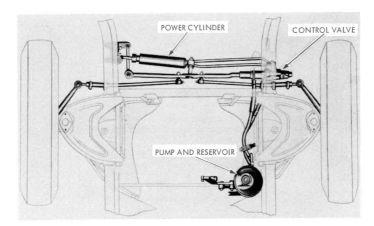

Fig. 9-29. Linkage type power steering. Spool type valve regulates pressure to the power cylinder. Chevrolet Div., General Motors Corp.

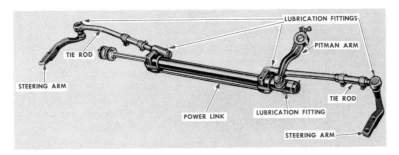

Fig. 9-30. Linkage type power steering unit connected to two tie rod design linkage. Shaft from the power link goes to a control valve assembly (not shown).

ered adequate. The engine does not have to be running to adjust integral power steering gear except on the Chrysler power steering system.

In the Chrysler type power steering, the thrust bearing load is determined for all other systems, but to make the high point or over-center adjustment the engine must be running to provide hydraulic pressure for the steering gear. The high point adjustment screw located in the steering gear housing is turned into the housing until a very slight movement of the steering wheel will cause the front wheels to move. When all excess steering wheel play has been removed, turn the high point adjusting screw inward an additional one-half turn. This additional one-half turn will adjust a bind or high point into the steering gear. If all excess play is not removed from the steering gear after a few turns of the adjusting screw, the thrust bearings or the worm and ball nut are excessively worn, therefore necessitating the removal of the steering gear for overhaul.

It is good practice to secure the manufacturer's adjustment specifications as not

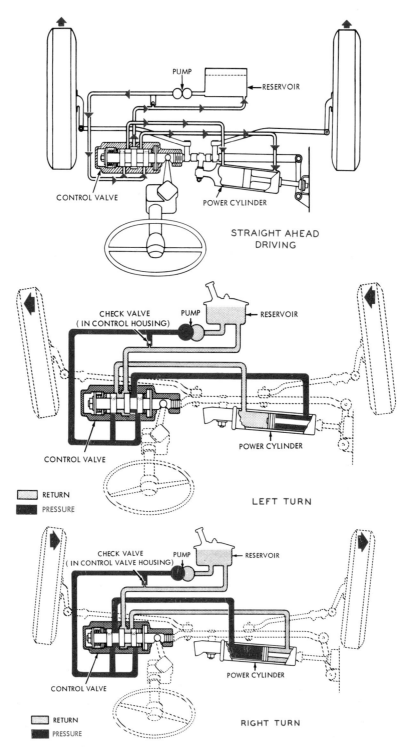

Fig. 9-31. Linkage type power steering hydraulic circuits. Power steering is really a power boost to driver's efforts. The car can still be steered manually. Ford Motor Co.

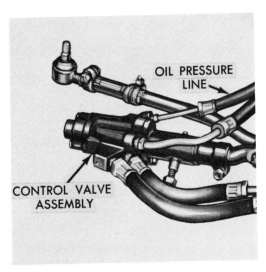

Fig. 9-32. Adjusting linkage type control valve to the center or balanced position. Chevrolet Motor Div., General Motors Corp.

all will agree with the above general procedure.

A pressure gage and valve attachment should be used when checking all power steering gear systems. The pressure gage and valve are mounted between the hydraulic pump and the high pressure hose leading to the steering gear. If the power steering unit fails to give hydraulic assistance, the trouble may be due to either a faulty pump or a faulty steering gear. By using the gage, the faulty unit may be detected and repaired, thereby eliminating the possibility of testing both units. Turn the front wheels to their maximum position either left or right. The hydraulic fluid pressure within the system should be approximately 1,000 pounds. If the gage reads 500 pounds, the system is failing. By closing the valve mounted between the gage and the steering gear, the pump must produce maximum pressure. If it does not, the low reading, 500 psi

pressure, is due to a faulty power steering pump.

LINKAGE SYSTEMS. The linkage type of power steering system consists of hydraulically controlled linkage used in conjunction with a conventional manual steering gear. Such steering gears are adjusted in the same manner as any other manually operated steering gear. The hydraulic part of the steering system has one adjustment. To make this adjustment, just remove the small cover at the end of the control valve which screws into the end of the relay rod. Under this cover is either a small self-locking nut or cotter keyed nut as shown in Fig. 9-32. This nut must be tightened firmly and then backed off a quarter of a turn or, if using a torque wrench, until the torque reading is 25 pounds. Later model vehicles using this type power steering employ a different method of adjusting the nut. Support the car on a hoist and disconnect the hydraulic ram from the frame of the vehicle. Start the engine, then turn the control valve nut in one direction until the cylinder or piston rod moves. Then turn the nut in the opposite direction until the cylinder or piston rod again moves. Notice the total turns made by the nut and turn the nut halfway between position where cylinder or push rod moved. If this adjustment is not made properly, the vehicle will pull or steer itself to one side of the road. Should the control valve leak hydraulic fluid, the valve may be removed and the hydraulic seals replaced. The seal in the hydraulic cylinder is also replaceable and should the cylinder leak fluid around the piston rod the seal should be replaced. The piston and piston rings within the cylinder cannot be serviced and, therefore, if either fails the unit must be replaced.

TRADE COMPETENCY TEST

1. What are the two general classifications of tire wear?

2. What causes feather edging?

3. Describe what is meant by the term "wander."

4. Does wheel tramp occur at low or high speeds?

5. What is road shock?

6. What effect does shimmy sometimes have on the steering wheel?

7. Is tire squeal always a symptom of tire trouble?

8. What are the three things to check before starting a steering control road test?

9. Why is it advisable during a driving test to mark the position of the steering wheel when the vehicle is going straight ahead?

CHAPTER 10

BRAKES

This chapter is related to Chapter nine because brakes can influence steering control and even tire wear. The condition of tires also influences steering and braking response of the vehicle. It is the purpose of this chapter to describe the newest braking systems, including disc brakes, and to inform the service technician of the types of complaints he will encounter. Both manual and power systems are described along with drum and disc type brakes.

In particular, you should study the safety features incorporated in the new brake systems. The dual master cylinder and the brake warning light are two safety features which are included. Other special valves are also described which are used on some cars.

The troubles common to automotive brakes and several maintenance and adjustment procedures for drum and disc brakes are treated as well as the power unit and dual braking systems. Figs. 10-1 and 10-2 show typical disc brakes. Figs. 10-3, 10-4, and 10-5 show common disc brake arrangements. When checking brake complaints it is good practice to

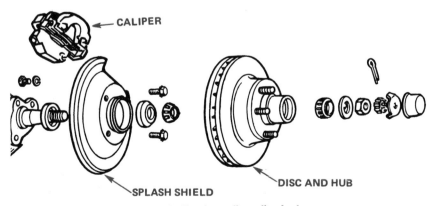

Fig. 10-1. Floating caliper disc brake.

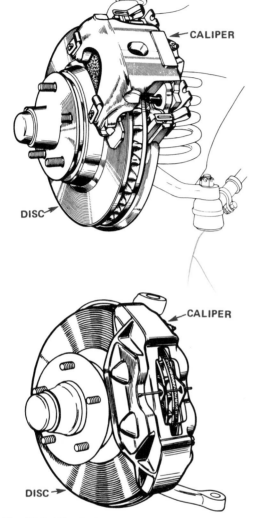

CALIPER

DISC

CALIPER ASSEMBLY

ROTOR ASSEMBLY

Fig. 10-3. Disc brake showing caliper assembly, left; hub and rotor, right.

CALIPER

DISC

Fig. 10-2. Disc brakes, Budd design, left: floating caliper, right.

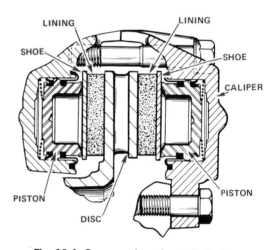

LINING

LINING

SHOE

SHOE

CALIPER

PISTON

PISTON

DISC

Fig. 10-4. Cross section of a typical caliper.

verify the complaint by a road test, if at all possible. The following topics describe typical braking complaints.

LOW PEDAL

During normal operation of any type brake, a little of the brake lining wears away each time the brakes are applied. On hydraulic brakes, the pedal reserve decreases as the wear increases. This wear is compensated for by a minor brake ad-justment which restores pedal reserve. On cars with self-adjusting brakes, the adjusting mechanism may be failing to operate. Fig. 10-6 shows two typical self-adjusters. Disc brakes are self-adjusting. Fig. 10-7. The amount of pedal reserve has become very small with power brakes and with the suspended type of brake pedal. This means that brakes must be kept properly adjusted at all times. Fig. 10-8.

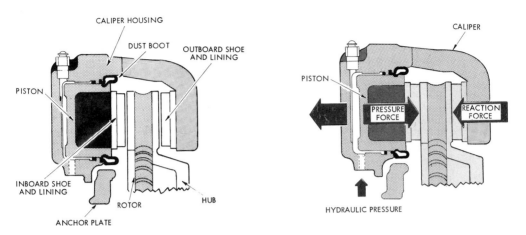

Fig. 10-5. Floating caliper assembly and operation.

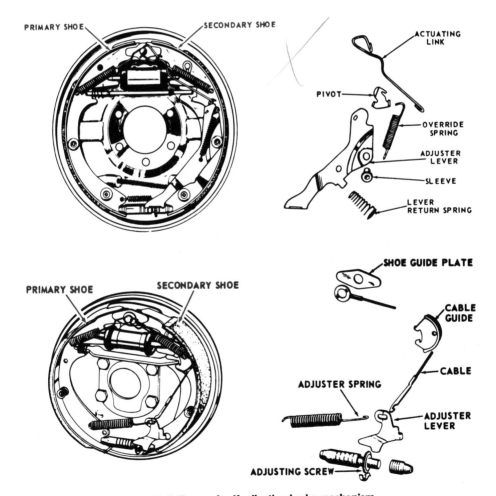

Fig. 10-6. Types of self-adjusting brake mechanism.

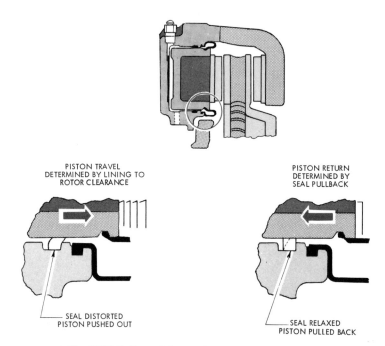

Fig. 10-7. Caliper piston seals control self-adjustment.

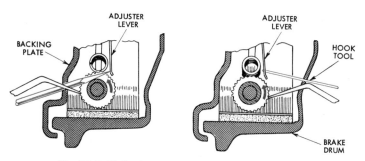

Fig. 10-8. Methods of releasing self-adjusting brakes.

PEDAL RESERVE

This term refers to the distance between the brake pedal and the toeboard when the brakes are fully applied. Less than two inches of reserve is considered dangerous. During severe application, the brake drums get hot and expand, thus further reducing the pedal reserve.

Disc brakes do not, however, reduce pedal reserve when brakes are hot. The disc is clamped and cannot expand as the brake drum would. (Fig. 10-5) It is also possible that low fluid level, or, with disc brakes, a loose wheel bearing could result in a low pedal complaint. The rotor, if not held securely, will kick the linings back into the caliper causing a low pedal.

NOISY OPERATION

Noisy brakes may be due to dirty or

worn brake linings, loose lining rivets, twisted or sprung brake shoes, distorted brake drums, incorrectly adjusted anchors, or broken brake shoe return springs. It will usually be necessary to remove all of the drums to determine the cause.

A discussion of noises that occur when the brakes are applied is presented in the wheel alignment road test in Chapter nine. This discussion points out those things not usually associated with the brakes that can be noisy during brake application.

HARD ACTION

Hard brake action and its remedy in hydraulic brake systems, with or without boosters, is discussed under this system.

HYDRAULIC BRAKES

Hard brake action or excessive brake pressure required to stop a vehicle with hydraulic brakes may be caused by normal wear of brake linings. Make a minor brake adjustment to compensate for lining wear. If this does not correct the trouble, repairs are required. (Usually new linings will be required to correct the problem.) Improper lining to drum contact is another cause of hard braking. Inspect the linings to determine if they are making full contact with the drum.

POWER BRAKES

If the power booster unit is not operating, braking will be hard. To check

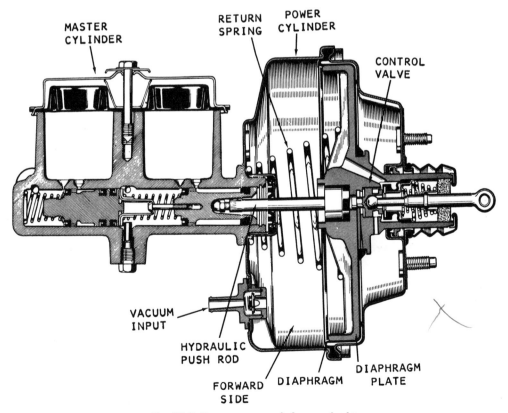

Fig. 10-9. Vacuum suspended power brake.

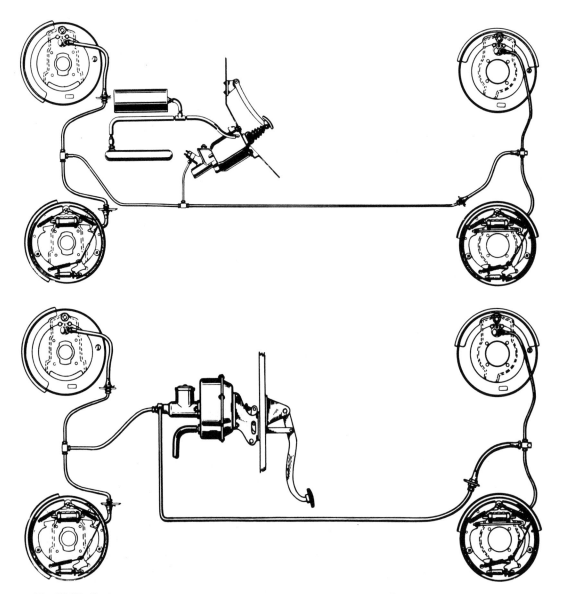

Fig. 10-10. Typical power brake systems, atmospheric suspended, top: vacuum suspended, bottom.

the booster, pump the brake pedal several times with the engine shut off to eliminate any reserve vacuum. Then, while holding the pedal down, start the engine. If the pedal falls away when the engine starts, the unit is operating. If the pedal doesn't fall away, check to be sure the vacuum hoses are connected properly, before replacing the power booster unit.

Normally repairs are not made on power booster units. Fig. 10-9 shows a dual system power unit. Fig. 10-10 is the older style single master cylinder power unit.

UNEVEN ACTION

On all types of brakes, if the brake action is uneven, adjust the brake shoes. If, after a minor adjustment, the brakes are still uneven, further checks need to be performed. With the drums off, check for corroded or bent brake mechanism

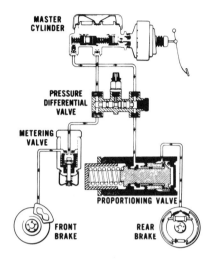

Fig. 10-11. Proportioning valve balances pressure between front disc and rear drum brakes.

and weak or broken brake shoe return springs. In addition, check the drums for an out-of-round condition and for deteriorated cups in wheel cylinders. Repair or replace parts as required.

Very often uneven braking is due to brake fluid or grease which has leaked onto the brake assembly upsetting the frictional characteristics of that brake. It is not unusual for a rear wheel to cause a pull to one side during braking. Usually the wheel that is creating the problem will be on the same side as the directional instability is noted. The proportioning valve used with disc brakes will, if malfunctioning, also cause uneven braking. This valve is designed to balance the hydraulic pressure between the front disc brakes and the rear drum brakes, especially during hard braking. The valve is not serviceable at all, it must be replaced. (Fig. 10-11.)

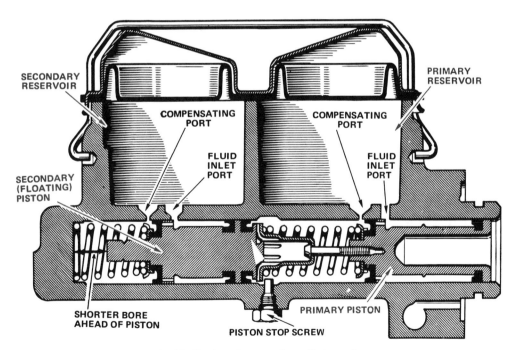

Fig. 10-12. Dual system master cylinder, primary-secondary design.

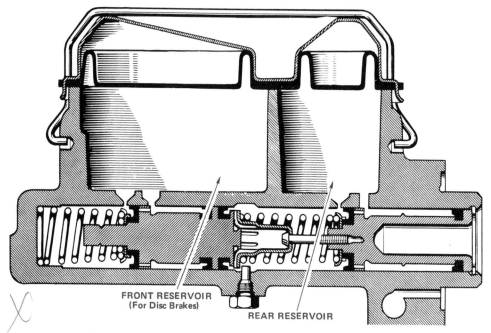

FRONT RESERVOIR
(For Disc Brakes)

REAR RESERVOIR

Fig. 10-13. Front-rear dual system master cylinder for disc brakes.

Always service brake systems as a unit. If one front wheel is to be repaired, the opposite wheel should also be serviced. It is preferable that all the wheels be serviced at one time, especially with the dual braking systems being used today. To insure operational reliability, it is wise to service the complete brake system. Fig. 10-12 and 10-13 show typical dual master cylinders.

SPONGY PEDAL

A spongy pedal on hydraulic brake systems may be due to excessive clearance between the shoes and drum, or air in the system. Adjust the brake shoes and bleed the brake system.

If this has not corrected the trouble, look for bent or otherwise distorted brake shoes. Brake linings that do not fit the drum make it necessary to bend the shoe in order to obtain full contact with the drum. This at times will also result in a

brake action which feels as if you were pushing against a spring instead of against something solid.

BRAKES LOCK DURING OPERATION

Locked brakes may be due to a restricted by-pass port in the master cylinder (Fig. 10-14), improperly adjusted

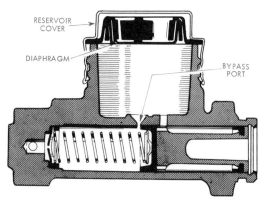

RESERVOIR COVER

DIAPHRAGM

BYPASS PORT

Fig. 10-14. Single system master cylinder.

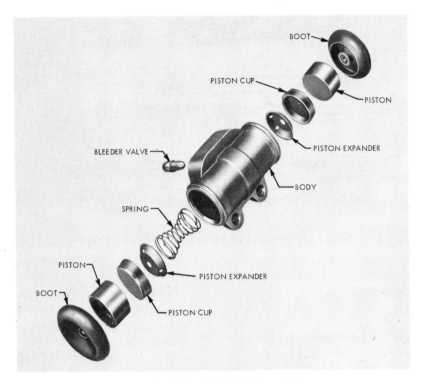

Fig. 10-15. Typical wheel brake cylinder.

linkage, a swollen master cylinder piston primary cup, or dirt in the brake fluid. *NOTE:* If the brakes are locked, preventing movement of vehicle, momentarily open the bleeder valve screw (Fig. 10-15) at any wheel cylinder. A few drops of fluid will come out, relieving the pressure, thus freeing the brakes. This is merely a temporary expedient and does not correct the cause of the trouble. Vehicles equipped with a dual braking system can be relieved of pressure by opening the bleeder screws or loosening the lines at the master cylinder.

BRAKES FAIL TO APPLY

With hydraulic brakes, the pedal should travel just far enough to develop the hydraulic pressure required to apply the brakes. If the pedal goes to the floor suddenly, it may be due to a leak in the hydraulic system, or the pedal linkage may be broken or disconnected. Check for broken or leaking lines or connections, especially in the flexible lines. (Fig. 10-16) Tighten connections or replace damaged parts. If air has entered the hydraulic system, the brake pedal will have a "spongy" feel when depressed, and may travel all the way to the floorboard without developing sufficient hydraulic pressure to stop the vehicle.

Air will enter the hydraulic system if the fluid in the master cylinder is too low or if there is excessive clearance between the brake linings and the drums, or if the pistons of the wheel cylinders are not held firmly in place when the tension of the brake shoe retracting springs are removed while servicing the brakes.

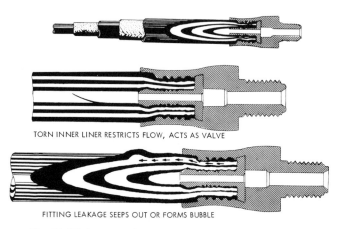

TORN INNER LINER RESTRICTS FLOW, ACTS AS VALVE

FITTING LEAKAGE SEEPS OUT OR FORMS BUBBLE

Fig. 10-16. Cross section and some possible hose defects.

SERVICING BRAKES

Normal servicing of brakes usually involves bleeding, adjustment, and occasionally, freeing the action of the pedal linkage. Major work can involve replacing the hydraulic system, new linings or shoes, and "turning" out of round drums. Disc brake rotors will often have to be replaced or refinished.

BLEEDING

The flushing of a hydraulic brake system either to clean it, replace the fluid, or to remove air from the system, is referred to as "bleeding." The procedure is essentially the same on all vehicles having hydraulic brakes. Vehicles equipped with a brake booster have additional bleed points which will be described later. Aside from this, the only variations in the procedure are those differences in the method of keeping the master cylinder full during the operation. It is suggested that master cylinders be bench bled before installation. Fig. 10-17. This type of bleeding should be performed before the brake lines are attached, if not performed on the bench.

In addition to the equipment used to keep the reservoir full, you will need a bleeder tube and a glass jar with which you may observe the air bubbles coming out of the system.

Regardless of the procedure followed, always remove all surface dirt from the area around the reservoir filler plug. Even one grain of sand in the brake fluid can cause serious damage to the hydraulic system. For the same reason, the container for brake fluid should be kept covered. Never use brake fluid that has been bled from a brake system. A diaphragm is used on master cylinders to keep dirt and air out of the system. (Fig. 10-14.)

If you do not have a filler, or if you have a gravity filler, the job is best performed by two people, one at the brake pedal and the other observing the discharge at each wheel in turn.

No Filler. If you do not have a filler, fill the master cylinder with brake fluid before beginning the bleeding operation. Keep the reservoir at least half full of fluid at all times. Loosen the bleeder valve at the wheel cylinder and install a bleeder tube. Submerge the bleeding end of tube in a glass container partially filled

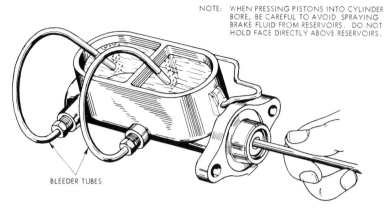

NOTE: WHEN PRESSING PISTONS INTO CYLINDER BORE, BE CAREFUL TO AVOID SPRAYING BRAKE FLUID FROM RESERVOIRS. DO NOT HOLD FACE DIRECTLY ABOVE RESERVOIRS.

BLEEDER TUBES

Fig. 10-17. Bleeding master cylinder with bleeder tubes.

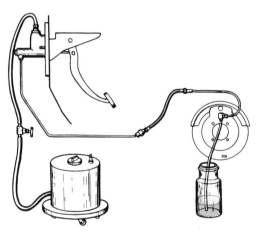

Fig. 10-18. Pressure bleeding brake system.

Fig. 10-19. Valve in filler automatically keeps brake fluid at proper level while bleeding. Chevrolet Motor Div., General Motors Corp.

with clean fluid. Fig. 10-18. Depress the foot pedal slowly by hand, allowing the return spring to bring the pedal back. This produces a pumping action which forces fluid through the tubing and out at the wheel cylinder, carrying with it any air that may be present.

Observe the flow of fluid from the hose. When air bubbles cease to appear in the fluid stream, the air has been removed in the lines to that point. Continue to pump the pedal until the fluid runs clear. Close the bleeder valve. Repeat the bleeding operation at each wheel

cylinder. Replenish the fluid in the master cylinder after each wheel cylinder is bled. When the bleeding operation is completed, refill the master cylinder.

GRAVITY FILLER. The gravity type filler shown in Fig. 10-19 is equipped with a valve that automatically keeps the fluid at the correct level at all times. Fill the bottle with clean fluid and insert the filler spout into the master cylinder filler hole as shown. Otherwise the procedure is exactly the same as outlined previously.

PRESSURE FILLER. A pressure filler makes brake bleeding a one-man operation. The pressure filler not only maintains the correct fluid level in the master cylinder reservoir, but eliminates the necessity for brake pedal manipulation as is required for other methods.

The pressure filler consists of a pressure tank partially filled with clean brake fluid. The tank is then sealed and compressed air at 30 psi is introduced into the tank through a tire valve.

The pressure tank is connected to the master cylinder with a pressure tight connection. (If the reservoir is completely empty, fill it before attaching the pressure filler line.) After the pressure filler line is tightly connected, the valve in the filler line is then opened. This places 30 psi on the entire hydraulic system.

Open the bleeder valves at each of the wheel cylinders in turn until the bubbles stop and the fluid runs clear (Fig. 10-18). When the bleeding is finished, close the valve in the filler line before disconnecting it from the master cylinder.

VACUUM BOOSTER. On vehicles equipped with a brake booster, the booster not only must be bled first, but the two bleeder valves must be bled in the right order. Bleeding is in the same order as the pressure is applied. The first point to bleed is at the control valve. The second point is where the fluid pressure leaves and goes into the lines to the wheel cylinders. The engine must not be running and there must be no vacuum in the system.

(1) Pressure Bleeding. With a pressure type brake fluid filler the bleeding procedure is just the same as for a conventional hydraulic system, except that the vacuum unit is bled before the wheel cylinders.

(2) Manual Bleeding. If the fluid is being forced through the hydraulic system by manipulation of the brake pedal, not only must the booster be bled first, but the brake pedal must not be allowed to return while either booster bleeder valve is open. With the first bleeder valve open, push the brake pedal down and hold it down until a second person closes the bleeder valve. Then allow the pedal to return. Again apply pressure to the pedal while your assistant again opens the bleeder valve. Repeat this cycle until the bleeding of the booster is complete, then bleed the wheel cylinders.

(3) Gravity Bleeding. Metering valves and design often cause the bleeding of disc brakes to be very difficult. In these cases gravity bleeding is recommended. The bleeder screw is opened fully and fluid is allowed to drain out by gravity. A very light pressure on the brake pedal can be used to speed up the gravity bleeding. Keep the master cylinder full during bleeding.

BRAKE WARNING LIGHT

Most vehicles with dual master cylinders will have a pressure differential switch located near the master cylinder. Fig. 10-11. During the bleeding operations just described, the switch, if it is not self-centering, will have to be centered in order to put out the brake warning light. To do this merely requires that pressure be relieved from the opposite side of the last bled section of the system. A quick, short release of pressure will allow the valve to center and turn off the light. This warning light procedure will not work on all cars. If you are in doubt, check the manufacturer's specifications. Newer vehicles will have a self-centering switch which doesn't require the special procedure discussed in this paragraph.

A special tool is available to hold the

switch in its centered position until bleeding is completed. This tool is screwed into the switch in place of the electrical contact assembly.

PROPORTIONING OR BALANCE VALVE

Cars equipped with disc brakes at the front wheels only will usually have a balance or proportioning valve. Fig. 10-11. This unit serves to reduce braking pressure to the rear brakes during severe braking. This valve, if it is not operating properly can cause poor vehicle control during severe stops. It can be checked by installing a pressure gage ahead of the valve and another gage past the valve. Check manufacturer's specifications as the valve is calibrated according to the vehicle on which it is installed. If the proportioning valve is defective it must be replaced. Do not attempt to adjust it.

METERING VALVES

A few vehicles with disc brakes use a metering valve for better control of the disc brakes. Fig. 10-11. This valve is also referred to as a "hold off" valve. It operates to prevent disc brake operation until a certain pressure is developed by the master cylinder. In effect, then, this metering valve causes the rear brakes to contribute to a greater portion of the total stopping effort, especially when light braking effort is necessary. These valves are not serviceable and if a pressure check indicates the valve is not operating at proper pressures it must be replaced.

BRAKE ADJUSTMENT

Very often you will encounter vehicles that come in for minor brake adjustment where, unknown to both you and the owner, the condition of the linings and the drums are such that the vehicle is unsafe. When a vehicle comes in for service, you have no way of knowing whether or not an adjustment will suffice unless you make an inspection. This inspection can, in most cases, be limited to an inspection of the linings and drums at one front wheel. For this reason, the removal of one front drum has been made a part of the adjustment presented here. If a vehicle is equipped with disc and drum brakes, both front and rear brake condition needs to be established.

PROCEDURE. Remove one front brake drum and look for the following conditions: brake drum scored, out of round, or bell-mouthed; lining oil soaked; lining worn to less than 1/32 in. from the rivet heads; and lining not making full contact with the drum. Check for signs of brake fluid leakage at the calipers or wheel cylinders.

In some cases the mechanic is legally responsible if the vehicle is allowed to be used with known defects.

Reinstall the brake drum that was removed, and raise all four wheels free of the floor. Adjust all shoes out to compensate for lining wear. A means of accomplishing this is provided with most types of brakes. Disc brakes automatically will be positioned correctly with firm pedal application. After completing the adjustment of the shoes, check the pedal reserve. If the pedal reserve is less than half the total distance to the toe-board, readjust the shoes more carefully. If this does not establish normal pedal reserve, an inspection of each of the wheels is required.

BRAKE FLUID

The fluid is one of the most important parts of the brake system. Federal laws require that brake fluid meet exacting specifications. Other brakes used what was called heavy-duty brake fluid. Today there are super heavy-duty and extra heavy-duty designations.

Regardless of what the name implies, be certain that the fluid is correct for the type braking system being serviced. Disc brakes, in particular, and power brakes require brake fluid with greater quality. The most important difference between the various brake fluids is the boiling point. The range is from 300° F. to 600° F.

Brake fluid has a very strong attraction (affinity) to water. Uncovered fluid can easily become water contaminated by exposure to the humidity of the air. It is good practice to flush brake systems of old fluid and renew with fresh brake fluid at least every two years.

BRAKE HOSES

Flexible brake hoses should be inspected carefully during a brake check. Look for cracks or bulging at connectors. Also check to be sure there will be no severe bends or contact with surrounding suspension components. Replace and relocate where necessary. Fig. 10-16.

To facilitate trouble shooting, Table 10-1 and Table 10-2 will quickly help determine the causes of typical brake complaints.

Table 10-1 shows detailed information for trouble shooting drum brake systems. Table 10-2 shows disc brake trouble shooting procedures.

TABLE 10-1 DRUM BRAKE TROUBLE SHOOTING

LOW PEDAL
(EXCESSIVE PEDAL TRAVEL TO APPLY BRAKES)

WHEEL BRAKE	HYDRAULIC SYSTEM	POWER BRAKE
1. SHOES AND LININGS SHOES IMPROPERLY ADJUSTED (TOO MUCH CLEARANCE) - ADJUST. LININGS WORN THIN - REPLACE WITH NEW LINED BRAKE SHOES. BRAKE SHOES BENT OR DISTORTED - REPLACE WITH NEW LINED BRAKE SHOES.	1. FLUID LOW - FILL TO PROPER LEVEL. AIR IN SYSTEM - BLEED AND REFILL WITH APPROVED FLUID. POOR QUALITY (LOW BOILING POINT) - REPLACE WITH APPROVED FLUID.	1. POWER UNIT PEDAL AND VALVE ROD LINKAGE IMPROPERLY ADJUSTED OR WORN - ADJUST OR REPLACE. HYDRAULIC PUSH ROD IMPROPERLY ADJUSTED - ADJUST.
2. DRUMS CRACKED; THIN (EXPANDING WHEN HOT CAUSING TOO MUCH CLEARANCE); OVERSIZE (BEYOND .060'' OF ORIGINAL SPECIFICATION) - REPLACE.	2. HOSES SOFT OR WEAK (EXPANDING UNDER PRESSURE) - REPLACE. 3. PEDAL PUSH ROD EXCESSIVE FREE PLAY - ADJUST.	
3. MECHANICAL PARTS AUTOMATIC ADJUSTER CORRODED, DISTORTED OR BROKEN - REPAIR AND LUBRICATE OR REPLACE.		

TABLE 10-1 DRUM BRAKE TROUBLE SHOOTING (CONT'D)

SPONGY PEDAL
(A SPRINGY SENSATION TO PEDAL UPON APPLICATION)

WHEEL BRAKE ASSEMBLY	HYDRAULIC SYSTEM	POWER BRAKE
1. SHOES AND LININGS SHOES WARPED - REPLACE WITH NEW LINED BRAKE SHOES. PARTIAL LINING TO DRUM CONTACT; SHOES NOT CENTERED IN DRUM - ADJUST ANCHORS. 2. DRUMS TAPERED; OUT OF ROUND; WORN THIN - REFINISH WITHIN .060'' OF ORIGINAL SPECIFICATION OR REPLACE.	1. FLUID LOW - FILL TO PROPER LEVEL. AIR IN SYSTEM - BLEED AND REFILL WITH APPROVED FLUID. POOR QUALITY (LOW BOILING POINT) - REPLACE WITH APPROVED FLUID. 2. HOSES SOFT OR WEAK (EXPANDING UNDER PRESSURE) - REPLACE. 3. MASTER CYLINDER CHECK VALVE FAULTY - REPLACE CHECK VALVE. 4. WHEEL CYLINDERS CUPS SOFT OR SWOLLEN - FLUSH HYDRAULIC SYSTEM WITH ALCOHOL TO REMOVE CONTAMINATED FLUID AND REPLACE ALL CUPS AND SEALS.	THIS CONDITION NOT CAUSED BY POWER BRAKE.

HARD PEDAL
(EXCESSIVE PEDAL PRESSURE NEEDED TO STOP VEHICLE)

WHEEL BRAKE ASSEMBLY	HYDRAULIC SYSTEM	POWER BRAKE
1. SHOES AND LININGS SHOES WORN, DISTORTED OR DAMAGED - REPLACE WITH NEW LINED BRAKE SHOES. INADEQUATE LINING TO DRUM CLEARANCE - ADJUST. LININGS WORN, GLAZED, POOR QUALITY OR SOILED - REPLACE WITH NEW LINED BRAKE SHOES. 2. ANCHORS OUT OF ADJUSTMENT - ADJUST. 3. MECHANICAL PARTS SHOE LEDGES RUSTED OR GROOVED - CLEAN AND SMOOTH LEDGES, AND LUBRICATE.	1. LINES, HOSES AND CONNECTIONS KINKED, COLLAPSED, DENTED OR CLOGGED - REPAIR OR REPLACE. 2. MASTER CYLINDER CUPS SWOLLEN - FLUSH HYDRAULIC SYSTEM WITH ALCOHOL TO REMOVE CONTAMINATED FLUID AND REPLACE ALL CUPS AND SEALS. BORE ROUGH OR CORRODED - REPAIR OR REPLACE MASTER CYLINDER. 3. WHEEL CYLINDERS CUPS SWOLLEN - FLUSH HYDRAULIC SYSTEM WITH ALCOHOL TO REMOVE CONTAMINATED FLUID AND REPLACE ALL CUPS AND SEALS. BORES ROUGH OR CORRODED - REPAIR OR REPLACE WHEEL CYLINDERS.	1. CHECK VALVE DEFECTIVE; STICKING - REPLACE. 2. VACUUM LINES LOOSE; BROKEN; COLLAPSED - TIGHTEN OR REPLACE. 3. AIR FILTER DIRTY; CLOGGED - CLEAN OR REPLACE. 4. ENGINE VACUUM LOW - CHECK OUT TO MANUFACTURERS' SPECIFICATIONS USING VACUUM GAUGE. 5. POWER UNIT CUPS IN HYDRAULIC SECTION SWOLLEN - FLUSH HYDRAULIC SYSTEM WITH ALCOHOL TO REMOVE CONTAMINATED FLUID AND REPLACE ALL CUPS AND SEALS. BORE IN HYDRAULIC SECTION ROUGH OR CORRODED - REPAIR OR REPLACE HYDRAULIC SECTION. CORROSION OR LACK OF LUBRICATION IN POWER CYLINDER - REPAIR OR LUBRICATE. CONTROL VALVE, POWER CYLINDER, PISTON OR DIAPHRAGM DEFECTIVE - REPLACE DEFECTIVE PART OR POWER UNIT.

TABLE 10-1 DRUM BRAKE TROUBLE SHOOTING (CONT'D)

GRABBING OR PULLING

(SEVERE REACTION TO PEDAL PRESSURE AND OUT OF LINE STOPS)

WHEEL BRAKE ASSEMBLY	HYDRAULIC SYSTEM	POWER BRAKE
1. SHOES AND LININGS SHOES IMPROPERLY ADJUSTED - ADJUST. SHOES DISTORTED OR IN-CORRECT; LININGS INCORRECT, LOOSE OR SOILED WITH GREASE OR BRAKE FLUID - REPLACE WITH NEW LINED BRAKE SHOES. 2. MECHANICAL PARTS ANCHORS NOT SET PROPERLY (CAUSING INCORRECT LINING TO DRUM CONTACT) - ADJUST. BACKING PLATE LOOSE, WORN OR DISTORTED - TIGHTEN OR REPLACE. SHOE RETURN SPRINGS WEAK, BROKEN, IMPROPERLY IN-STALLED - REPLACE OR IN-STALL CORRECTLY. AUTOMATIC ADJUSTER PARTS CORRODED, DISTORTED OR BROKEN - FREE UP AND LUBRICATE OR REPLACE. WHEEL BEARINGS LOOSE-ADJUST. 3. DRUMS THIN (EXPANDING WHEN HOT); OVERSIZE (BEYOND .060'' OF ORIGINAL SPEC-IFICATION) - REPLACE. SCORED, HARD SPOTTED OR OUT OF ROUND - REFINISH OR REPLACE.	1. LINES, HOSES AND CONNECTIONS. KINKED, COLLAPSED, DENTED OR CLOGGED - REPAIR OR REPLACED. 2. MASTER CYLINDER BORE ROUGH OR CORRODED - REPAIR OR REPLACE MASTER CYLINDER. 3. WHEEL CYLINDERS CUPS SWOLLEN - FLUSH HYDRAULIC SYSTEM WITH ALCOHOL TO REMOVE CON-TAMINATED FLUID AND RE-PLACE ALL CUPS AND SEALS. BORES ROUGH OR CORRODED - REPAIR OR REPLACE WHEEL CYLINDERS. STEP-BORE CYLINDER IN-STALLED BACKWARD - REMOVE AND INSTALL COR-RECTLY. CYLINDERS MISMATCHED - REPLACE WITH CORRECT CYLINDERS. 4. PEDAL LINKAGE BINDING - FREE UP AND LUBRICATE.	1. POWER UNIT CONTROL VALVE DEFECTIVE - REPAIR OR REPLACE. POWER PISTON BINDING AND SUDDENLY RELEASING - REPAIR AND LUBRICATE. VALVE ROD LINKAGE BINDING - FREE UP AND LUBRICATE.

DRAGGING BRAKES

(SLOW OR INCOMPLETE RELEASE OF BRAKES)

WHEEL BRAKE ASSEMBLY	HYDRAULIC SYSTEM	POWER BRAKE
1. SHOES AND LININGS SHOES IMPROPERLY ADJUSTED - ADJUST. SHOES DISTORTED OR IN-CORRECT - REPLACE WITH NEW LINED BRAKE SHOES. LININGS SOILED WITH GREASE OR BRAKE FLUID - REPLACE WITH NEW LINED BRAKE SHOES. 2. MECHANICAL PARTS RETURN SPRINGS INCORRECT OR WEAK - REPLACE. SHOE LEDGES GROOVED OR RUSTED - SMOOTH LEDGES AND LUBRICATE. BACKING PLATE LOOSE - TIGHTEN. 3. PARKING BRAKE IMPROPERLY ADJUSTED - ADJUST. CABLES AND LINKAGE STICK-ING, DIRTY OR CORRODED - FREE UP AND LUBRICATE. 4. WHEEL BEARINGS LOOSE ADJUSTMENT OR WORN - ADJUST OR REPLACE.	1. FLUID SLUGGISH - REPLACE WITH APPROVED FLUID. 2. LINES, HOSES AND CONNECTIONS KINKED, COLLAPSED, DENTED OR CLOGGED - REPAIR OR REPLACE. 3. MASTER CYLINDER COMPENSATING PORT RE-STRICTED BY SWOLLEN PRI-MARY CUP - FLUSH HYDRAULIC SYSTEM WITH ALCOHOL TO RE-MOVE CONTAMINATED FLUID AND REPLACE ALL CUPS AND SEALS. CHECK VALVE FAULTY - REPLACE. 4. WHEEL CYLINDERS CUPS SWOLLEN - FLUSH HY-DRAULIC SYSTEM WITH ALCOHOL TO REMOVE CONTAMINATED FLUID AND REPLACED ALL CUPS AND SEALS. BORES ROUGH OR CORRODED - REPAIR OR REPLACE WHEEL CYLINDERS. 5. PEDAL PUSH ROD AND LINKAGE OUT OF ADJUSTMENT; BINDING - ADJUST OR FREE UP AND LUBRICATE.	1. POWER UNIT CUPS IN HYDRAULIC SECTION SWOLLEN - FLUSH HYDRAULIC SYSTEM WITH ALCOHOL TO RE-MOVE CONTAMINATED FLUID AND REPLACE ALL CUPS AND SEALS. BORE IN HYDRAULIC SECTION ROUGH OR CORRODED - REPAIR OR REPLACE HYDRAULIC SEC-TION. CHECK VALVE IN HYDRAULIC SECTION FAULTY - REPLACE. CORROSION OR LACK OF LUB-RICATION IN POWER CYLINDER - REPAIR OR LUBRICATE. CONTROL VALVE OR POWER CYLINDER DEFECTIVE - REPLACE DEFECTIVE PART OR POWER UNIT. AIR TRAPPED IN HUB CAVITY OF MASTER CYLINDER (ON POWER UNITS THAT DO NOT REQUIRE MASTER CYLINDER HUB SEAL) - INSPECT AND, IF HUB SEAL IS PRESENT, RE-MOVE AND DISCARD. 2. VALVE ROD/PEDAL LINKAGE LINKAGE BINDING AND NOT ALLOWING UNIT TO RELEASE - FREE UP AND LUBRICATE.

TABLE 10-1 DRUM BRAKE TROUBLE SHOOTING (CONT'D)

NOISE AND CHATTER

(SQUEALING, CLICKING OR SCRAPING
NOISE UPON APPLICATION OF BRAKES)

WHEEL BRAKE ASSEMBLY	HYDRAULIC SYSTEM	POWER BRAKE
1. SHOES AND LININGS SHOES TWISTED, DISTORTED, INCORRECT, OR BROKEN; CRACKED WELDS – REPLACE WITH NEW LINED BRAKE SHOES. LININGS WORN OUT, GLAZED, INCORRECT, LOOSE OR SOILED WITH GREASE OR BRAKE FLUID; FOREIGN MATTER IMBEDDED IN LININGS; INCORRECT GRIND OR LINING POSITION – REPLACE WITH NEW LINED BRAKE SHOES. 2. MECHANICAL PARTS SHOE RETURN SPRINGS WEAK; ANCHOR PINS OR BACKING PLATES LOOSE OR DEFECTIVE; HOLD DOWN PARTS DEFECTIVE – TIGHTEN OR REPLACE AND LUBRICATE ALL POINTS OF WEAR. SHOE LEDGES ROUGH OR GROOVED – SMOOTH LEDGES AND LUBRICATE. 3. DRUMS THIN; CRACKED; LOOSE; SCORED; THREADED WITH LATHE MARKS – REFINISH WITHIN .060'' OF ORIGINAL SPECIFICATION OR REPLACE.	THIS CONDITION NOT CAUSED BY HYDRAULIC SYSTEM.	1. POWER UNIT VACUUM LEAK; CONTROL VALVE DEFECTIVE (CAUSING EXCESSIVE NOISE) – REPAIR OR REPLACE CONTROL VALVE. 2. CHECK VALVE BROKEN OR LEAKING – REPLACE.

FADING PEDAL

(A FALLING AWAY OF PEDAL UNDER STEADY FOOT PRESSURE)

WHEEL BRAKE ASSEMBLY	HYDRAULIC SYSTEM	POWER BRAKE
1. DRUMS CRACKED; THIN (EXPANDING WHEN HOT CAUSING TOO MUCH CLEARANCE) – REPLACE.	1. FLUID POOR QUALITY (LOW BOILING POINT) – REPLACE WITH APPROVED FLUID. 2. HOSES AND LINES LOOSE CONNECTIONS; RUPTURED; DAMAGED (CAUSING LEAKAGE) – TIGHTEN OR REPLACE. 3. MASTER CYLINDER PRIMARY CUP WORN OR DAMAGED; BORE WORN OR CORRODED (CAUSING LEAKAGE) – REPAIR OR REPLACE MASTER CYLINDER. 4. WHEEL CYLINDERS CUPS WORN OR DAMAGED; BORES WORN OR CORRODED (CAUSING LEAKAGE) – REPAIR OR REPLACE WHEEL CYLINDERS.	1. POWER UNIT INTERNAL HYDRAULIC LEAK – REPAIR OR REPLACE UNIT

TABLE 10-2 DISC BRAKE TROUBLE SHOOTING

SPONGY PEDAL
(A SPRINGY SENSATION TO PEDAL UPON APPLICATION)

DISC BRAKE ASSEMBLY	HYDRAULIC SYSTEM

THIS CONDITION NOT CAUSED BY DISC BRAKE ASSEMBLY.	1. FLUID
	   LOW - FILL TO PROPER LEVEL.
	
	   POOR QUALITY (LOW BOILING POINT) - REPLACE WITH HIGH TEMPERATURE FLUID.
	
	   AIR IN SYSTEM - BLEED AND REFILL WITH APPROVED FLUID.
	
	2. HOSES
	   SOFT OR WEAK (EXPANDING UNDER PRESSURE) - REPLACE.
	3. CALIPER PISTONS
	   SOFT OR SWOLLEN SEALS - FLUSH HYDRAULIC SYSTEMS WITH ALCOHOL TO REMOVE CONTAMINATED FLUID AND REPLACE ALL CUPS, SEALS AND "O" -RINGS IN HYDRAULIC SYSTEM.

HARD PEDAL
(EXCESSIVE PEDAL PRESSURE NEEDED TO STOP VEHICLE)

DISC BRAKE ASSEMBLY	HYDRAULIC SYSTEM

1. LININGS
   SOILED WITH BRAKE FLUID, OIL OR GREASE - REPLACE.
	1. LINES, HOSES AND CONNECTIONS
	   KINKED, COLLAPSED, DENTED OR CLOGGED - REPAIR OR REPLACE.
	2. MASTER CYLINDER
	   SWOLLEN CUPS - FLUSH HYDRAULIC SYSTEM WITH ALCOHOL TO REMOVE CONTAMINATED FLUID AND REPLACE ALL CUPS, SEALS AND "O" -RINGS IN HYDRAULIC SYSTEM.
	   CORRODED OR ROUGH BORE - REPAIR OR REPLACE MASTER CYLINDER.
	3. CALIPER PISTONS
	   FROZEN OR SEIZED - FREE UP AND REPLACE IF DAMAGED.
	4. CALIPER CYLINDER BORES
	   CORRODED OR ROUGH - REPAIR OR REPLACE CALIPER.
	5. PEDAL PUSH ROD AND LINKAGE
	   BINDING - FREE UP AND LUBRICATE
	6. PROPORTIONING VALVE
	   NOT WORKING PROPERLY - REPAIR OR REPLACE.

GRABBING OR PULLING
(SEVERE REACTION TO PEDAL PRESSURE AND OUT OF LINE STOPS)

DISC BRAKE ASSEMBLY	HYDRAULIC SYSTEM

1. LININGS
   SOILED WITH BRAKE FLUID, OIL OR GREASE - REPLACE
2. CALIPER
   NOT ALIGNED WITH DISC - ALIGN.
 	
   LOOSE - TIGHTEN CALIPER MOUNTING BOLTS TO SPECIFIED TORQUE.
	1. LINES, HOSES AND CONNECTIONS
	   KINKED, COLLAPSED, DENTED, OR CLOGGED - REPAIR OR REPLACE.
	2. MASTER CYLINDER
	   CORRODED OR ROUGH BORE - REPAIR OR REPLACE.
	3. CALIPER PISTONS
	   FROZEN OR SEIZED - FREE UP AND REPLACE IF DAMAGED.
	   SWOLLEN SEALS - FLUSH HYDRAULIC SYSTEM WITH ALCOHOL TO REMOVE CONTAMINATED FLUID AND REPLACE ALL CUPS, SEALS AND "O" -RINGS IN HYDRAULIC SYSTEM.
	4. CALIPER CYLINDER BORES
	   CORRODED OR ROUGH - REPAIR OR REPLACE CALIPER.
	5. PEDAL LINKAGE
	   BINDING - FREE UP AND LUBRICATE.
	6. PROPORTIONING VALVE
	   NOT WORKING PROPERLY - REPAIR OR REPLACE.

LOW PEDAL
(EXCESSIVE PEDAL TRAVEL TO APPLY BRAKES)

DISC BRAKE ASSEMBLY	HYDRAULIC SYSTEM

1. SHOES AND LININGS
   NORMAL SHOE AND LINING KNOCKBACK AFTER VIOLENT CORNERING - PUMP PEDAL TO RESTORE NORMAL PEDAL HEIGHT.
 	
   SHOE AND LINING KNOCKBACK CAUSED BY LOOSE OR WORN WHEEL BEARINGS OR STEERING PARTS - ADJUST OR REPLACE FAULTY PARTS.
	1. FLUID
	   LOW - FILL TO PROPER LEVEL.
	
	   POOR QUALITY (LOW BOILING POINT) - REPLACE WITH HIGH TEMPERATURE FLUID.
	
	   AIR IN SYSTEM - BLEED AND REFILL WITH APPROVED FLUID.
	
	2. HOSES
	   SOFT OR WEAK (EXPANDING UNDER PRESSURE) - REPLACE.
	
	3. PEDAL PUSH ROD
	   EXCESSIVE FREE PLAY - ADJUST.

TABLE 10-2 DISC BRAKE TROUBLE SHOOTING (CONT'D)
FADING PEDAL
(A FALLING AWAY UNDER STEADY FOOT PRESSURE)

DISC BRAKE ASSEMBLY	HYDRAULIC SYSTEM
THIS CONDITION NOT CAUSED BY DISC BRAKE ASSEMBLY.	1. FLUID POOR QUALITY (LOW BOILING POINT) - REPLACE WITH HIGH TEMPERATURE FLUID. 2. HOSES AND LINES LOOSE CONNECTIONS; RUPTURED OR DAMAGED (CAUSING LEAKAGE) - TIGHTEN OR REPLACE. 3. MASTER CYLINDER WORN OR DAMAGED PRIMARY CUP; WORN OR CORRODED BORE (CAUSING LEAKAGE) - REPAIR OR REPLACE MASTER CYLINDER. 4. CALIPER PISTONS WORN OR DAMAGED SEALS - REPLACE SEALS. 5. CALIPER CYLINDER BORES CORRODED, SCORED OR WORN - REPAIR OR REPLACE CALIPER.

NOISE AND CHATTER
(MAY BE ACCOMPANIED BY BRAKE ROUGHNESS AND PEDAL PUMPING)

DISC BRAKE ASSEMBLY	HYDRAULIC SYSTEM
1. DISC EXCESSIVE LATERAL RUNOUT OR EXCESSIVE THICKNESS VARIATIONS (OUT OF PARALLEL) - REPLACE OR REFINISH DISC AS RECOMMENDED BY VEHICLE MANUFACTURER. 2. SHOE AND LINING MISSING OR MISALIGNED ANTI-RATTLE SPRING - INSTALL SPRING CORRECTLY. GROAN DURING BRAKE APPLICATION - INCREASE OR DECREASE PEDAL EFFORT SLIGHTLY.	THIS CONDITION NOT CAUSED BY HYDRAULIC SYSTEM.

DRAGGING BRAKES
(SLOW OR INCOMPLETE RELEASE OF BRAKES)

DISC BRAKE ASSEMBLY	HYDRAULIC SYSTEM
THIS CONDITION NOT CAUSED BY DISC BRAKE ASSEMBLY.	1. LINES, HOSES AND CONNECTIONS KINKED, COLLAPSED, DENTED OR CLOGGED - REPAIR OR REPLACE. 2. MASTER CYLINDER COMPENSATING PORT RESTRICTED BY SWOLLEN PRIMARY CUP - FLUSH HYDRAULIC SYSTEM WITH ALCOHOL TO REMOVE CONTAMINATED FLUID AND REPLACE ALL CUPS, SEALS AND "O" -RINGS IN HYDRAULIC SYSTEM. RESIDUAL PRESSURE CHECK VALVE IN LINE TO FRONT WHEELS - REMOVE CHECK VALVE AND INSTALL LINES CORRECTLY. 3. CALIPER PISTONS FROZEN OR SEIZED - FREE UP AND REPLACE IF DAMAGED. SWOLLEN SEALS - FLUSH HYDRAULIC SYSTEM WITH ALCOHOL TO REMOVE CONTAMINATED FLUID AND REPLACE ALL CUPS, SEALS AND "O" -RINGS IN HYDRAULIC SYSTEM. 4. CALIPER CYLINDER BORES CORRODED OR ROUGH - REPAIR OR REPLACE CALIPER. 5. PEDAL PUSH ROD AND LINKAGE OUT OF ADJUSTMENT OR BINDING (CAUSING PRIMARY CUP TO RESTRICT MASTER CYLINDER COMPENSATING PORT) - ADJUST OR FREE UP AND LUBRICATE.

TRADE COMPETENCY TEST

1. As linings wear, a low pedal might result. How can this be remedied?

2. What is pedal reserve?

3. How can the cause of noisy brakes be determined?

4. If excessive pressure is needed to stop the vehicle what is likely to be the trouble?

5. How do you check a power brake unit?

6. What is most likely to be the cause of uneven brake action?

7. What can cause a spongy pedal?

8. Why would a brake pedal go all the way to the floor?

9. Why is bleeding of brakes necessary?

10. What are several methods of bleeding brakes?

11. How can you tell that all air has been removed from a brake line?

12. Why is it good practice to inspect brake linings before an adjustment?

13. What is necessary if the brake warning light stays on?

14. Why is it important to keep brake fluid covered?

CHAPTER 11

HEATING AND AIR CONDITIONING

Heating and air conditioning are comfort accessories which are now built into the vehicle and are truly a part of the car. Indeed, when the heater or air conditioner does not operate normally, the operator and his passengers are in an uncomfortable situation. This chapter will assist you, the service technician, in locating and correcting difficulties with automotive heaters and air conditioners.

The rapid acceptance of air conditioning for vehicles requires that the competent service technician be able to diagnose and service these units to provide complete service. With some practical experience and the information supplied in this chapter you will be the up-to-date diagnostician that is so widely needed.

First, make sure the heater is installed according to the manufacturer's instructions for that particular vehicle. Some cases of trouble can be eliminated by correcting an improper installation. In addition, regardless of the trouble being encountered, make sure the control knobs or switches are operating satisfactorily.

In the various trouble shooting procedures presented in this chapter, most of the repairs that can be effective are pre-sented as a part of trouble shooting procedure. Heaters, aside from the complexities that exist in the controls, are generally quite simple, and, where the seat of the trouble is located, the method of making the correction or repair is generally obvious.

DESCRIPTION

Hot water heaters are equipped with a radiator or core through which water from the engine cooling system is circulated. Engine cooling systems are equipped with thermostats which prevent circulation of the water through the entire cooling system until the water reaches a predetermined temperature. The water pump, of course, is running all the time the engine is running, so circulation to the heater core starts as soon as the engine is started.

Some hot water heaters are equipped with an adjustable, thermostatically controlled valve which shuts off circulation to the heater core when a predetermined temperature is reached. The adjustment is dash controlled and permits the operator to limit the temperature at whatever

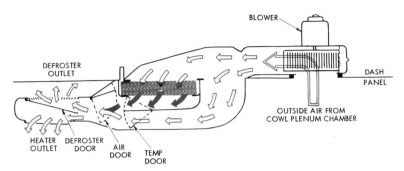

Fig. 11-1. Heater air flow.

point is desired. The same control permits complete shutoff of the circulation through the heater and no other adjustment is required for summer operation.

Many systems do not shut off water to the heater core. These heaters use an air-blend system to regulate the temperature of the heated air. Figs. 11-1 and 11-2 show this type.

Other adjustable, thermostatically controlled heater valves are indirect acting. In these heaters, the thermostat merely opens or closes a vacuum valve, and engine vacuum provides the power needed to open or close the water valve. This arrangement permits the control thermostat to be located away from the heater lines or radiator where it will respond to the temperature of the air in the car without being influenced by the temperature of the water or heater parts. Hot water heaters not equipped with an adjustable, thermostatically controlled valve are sometimes provided with a shutoff valve in one of the coolant lines running to the heater.

Some heater installations are designed only for recirculation of the air in the vehicle through the heater radiator. These heaters always use a blower to move the air. Other hot water heaters are provided with air ducts through which air from the outside is either forced in by the forward motion of the vehicle or drawn in by means of a blower. These ducts may be closed at the driver's option, and the blower can be used to recirculate the air already in the vehicle (Figs. 11-1 and 11-2).

It must be appreciated that when outside air is being forced into the vehicle, the vehicle interior will become pressurized unless a window or ventilator is opened to permit an equal amount of air to leave. When the body or cab is pressurized, the amount of air coming in is reduced almost to the vanishing point (depending on how "tight" or well sealed the body is), and the effectiveness of the heater is reduced. It is a good plan to explain this point to your customers. This condition, of course, is not true for recirculator heaters (heaters that recirculate the air already within the vehicle).

Most heaters are equipped with defrosters to remove fog from the inside of the windshield and to melt ice or snow on the outside. Defrosters consist of flexible tubes which carry air from the heater up to narrow openings just below the inside lower edge of the windshield. These tubes are equipped with manually operated valves which permit the closing off of air through the tubes. Circulation to the defrosters can be either by means of the blower or by making use of the air being forced through the air ducts from the outside.

The temperature of the engine cool-

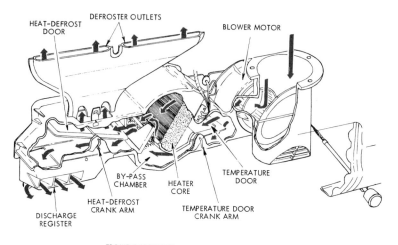

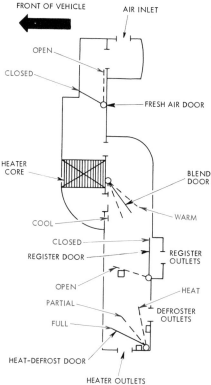

Fig. 11-2. Modulated heater air flow.

ant (water), of course, establishes the maximum heat that can be expected from the heater. The temperature of the engine coolant is generally controlled by a cooling system thermostat.

A typical hot water heater and venti-lating system is shown in Fig. 11-3. This installation embodies a heater radiator, a blower, fresh air ducts, defrosters, manu-ally controlled temperature valve, and the necessary controls.

Fig. 11-4 shows a disassembled instal-

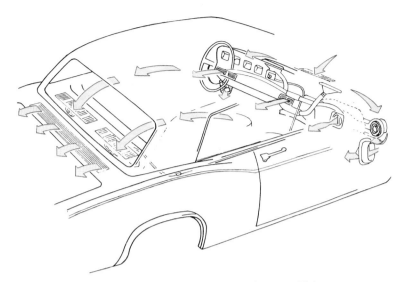

Fig. 11-3. Body ventilation system of some vehicles.

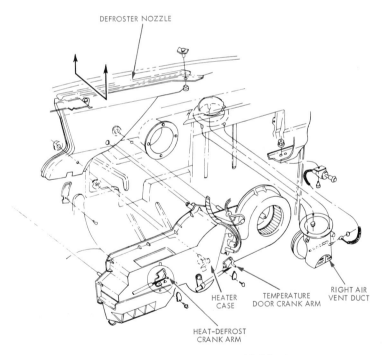

Fig. 11-4. View of a disassembled heater.

lation as viewed from the inside of the vehicle.

The size, shape, and location of the various components (parts) and the design and arrangement of the controls will vary, of course, in the different makes and models of vehicles. Nevertheless, a great degree of similarity exists among heaters of this type.

INSUFFICIENT HEAT

If the hot water heater lines are equipped with a shutoff valve, make sure it is open. A lack of heat from the heater can be caused by a restricted water flow through the heater core, by an inoperative blower motor, or by a "cool-running" engine. Check the supply hoses to determine if they are kinked or collapsed. If the hoses are several years old, the rubber may have swelled inside the hose, restricting the water supply. Make sure the heater itself is not at fault (improper core construction, such as no baffle in the core tank). The lack of a baffle can be detected by touching the heater core. One side of the core will be cool as compared to the other if there is no baffle to distribute the flow of water evenly.

If the heater is equipped with a thermostatic control valve, check the action of the valve when the control knob or lever is moved from the hot to the cold position. If the controls are correctly installed, they will move the valve mechanism through its full travel.

If the trouble has not already been found, inspect the heater blower motor circuit for a burned out fuse or loose wires. Make sure the connections that complete the motor circuit to chassis ground are in good condition and tight.

If the heater is apparently in good operating condition, run the engine until it reaches normal operating temperature. Check the temperature of the coolant in the radiator with a 200°F thermometer. If it is much below 180°F, check the action of the thermostat to make sure it is operating correctly. It may be necessary to use an extra high temperature thermostat in cold climates.

Air leaks in the ventilation system should next be checked if the complaint still exists. Make sure the ventilation control valve does not leak air directly into the passenger compartment when it is in the position to direct the flow of outside air through the heater. Look for grommets missing in the dash panel or a missing felt pad around the accelerator rod. Check for body air leaks caused by poor seals around the doors or windows.

INSUFFICIENT DEFROSTING

If the heater is supplying heat and the blower is operating, the only possible causes of an inoperative defroster are obstructions in the defroster hose lines or a closed defroster door. Many people have the habit of laying a pencil on the windshield molding. In some installations, it is possible for the pencil to drop out of sight into the defroster slot, effectively blocking it. This occurs often enough to justify looking into these slots before doing any other work. Make sure the defroster hoses are properly connected at both ends and that the nozzles are attached to the windshield molding slots. Check the action of the defroster door when the control lever is moved through its range. It should open completely when the lever is moved to the defrost position. Be sure the slots in the windshield molding are not obstructed and that nothing is blocking the hoses.

INSUFFICIENT VENTILATION

The symptom "insufficient or no ventilation" applies, of course, to installations where a combination heating and ventilating system is used and to air duct type ventilating systems which are independent of a heater installation. Insufficient ventilation is generally caused by clogged air ducts.

In the ventilated heater system, check the operation of the air valves to see that they operate properly through correct control cable adjustment. Make sure the air valve damper is tight on its control shaft, and check for obstructions in the air ducts or at the intake screen.

Some provision is usually made to shut off the supply of water to the heater core when the vehicle is operated under summer conditions. A shutoff valve (which may be part of the thermostatic control valve) is usually provided for this purpose. Be sure it is closed completely.

AIR CONDITIONERS

Some heater-ventilator combinations have been referred to as air conditioners, but the air conditioners discussed here actually extract heat from the air in the car. Air conditioning units in automobiles all use the mechanical power from the automobile engine to drive the compressor needed to obtain refrigeration. Since the automobile engine is required to run at an infinite variety of speeds, this imposes an additional complication to the cooling of the vehicle passenger compartment.

As shown in Fig. 11-5, in most types the compressor pump is mounted on, and driven from the engine. A condenser is placed in the windstream generally just forward of the engine cooling system ra-

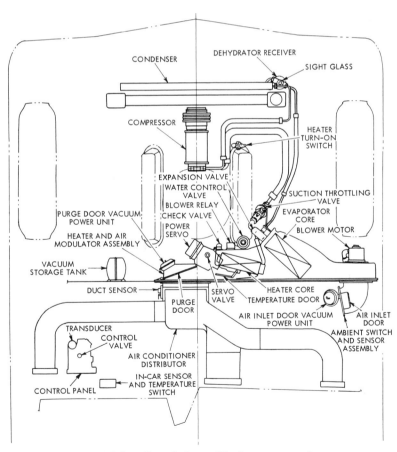

Fig. 11-5. Location of air conditioning components.

diator to take advantage of the large volume of air available at this point. This air passing over the fins of the condenser removes the heat from the refrigerant. Most installations provide a means of drawing air from outside the car into the system. Louvers are generally provided at some point in the car to admit this additional air. The cooled air enters the passenger compartment from the front of the instrument panel at several points.

Automobile air conditioning systems generally use a refrigerant known as Freon-12, which changes from a liquid to a gas at atmospheric pressure (14.7 lbs.) and a temperature of $-21.7°F$. Under sufficient pressure a gas can be converted to a liquid at almost any temperature. Air conditioning units take advantage of this fact. The liquid Freon-12 (under pressure) is forced through a restriction and upon entering a low pressure evaporator is able to absorb a large amount of heat. Air is blown past the fins of this evaporator and loses its heat to the refrigerant (gas) in the evaporator. This

refrigerant (still in the gaseous state) then flows to a compressor which pumps it under pressure to a condenser located in the windstream of the car. It is still in the gaseous state as it enters the condenser but with its excess heat removed by the air stream, it converts to a liquid in the condenser. From the condenser, it flows to a receiver tank, and then flows through a dehydrator back to the evaporator, thus completing the cycle.

As shown in Fig. 11-6, every automotive air conditioner consists of the following units:

(1) A compressor, driven by the engine which compresses the refrigerant, thereby raising its temperature.

(2) A condenser, which receives this compressed refrigerant and passes heat from the refrigerant into the atmosphere. This lowering of its temperature permits the refrigerant, still under pressure, to return to liquid form.

(3) A receiver-drier which receives the liquid refrigerant from the condenser. The refrigerant is still under pressure

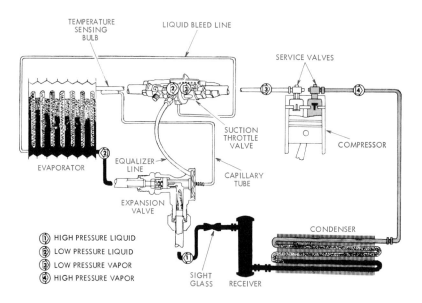

Fig. 11-6. Refrigeration circuit diagram.

and has had excess heat removed. Any small amounts of moisture are held by a dessicant or drying chemical.

(4) An expansion valve, which controls the flow of liquid refrigerant, under pressure, into the low pressure evaporator thus permitting the refrigerant to expand.

(5) The evaporator filled with refrigerant, which has just been changed from a liquid under pressure to a gas under low pressure.

(6) A low pressure valve, through which refrigerant flows to the compressor from the evaporator. This is often called a suction throttling valve or P.O.A. valve. It has the task of preventing the evaporator from freezing due to extremely low evaporator pressure or compressor suction.

NOTE: Many systems will not have this type of valve. These will have a thermostatic switch which will cycle (turn on and off) the compressor clutch to prevent icing of the evaporator.

Blowers are provided to draw air either from the interior of the car or from the exterior, at the driver's option, and to blow it through the cold evaporator core into the car interior. In passing through the evaporator core, the heat from the air passes into the evaporator and is readily accepted by the refrigerant.

Automatic control of the temperature is accomplished by the expansion valve which contains a heat sensitive material which adjusts the size of the restriction according to the temperature of the refrigerant at the evaporator outlet. Temperature control from the driver's seat is made possible through a variety of devices.

AIR CONDITIONER DIAGNOSIS

The initial procedure is to verify the complaint. Check to be sure the system is being properly operated. During this time it is convenient to note the volume of air being discharged at various speeds and control positions. Very often a loose compressor belt or blown fuse in the blower circuits is the only difficulty.

If poor cooling still is present, then the following quick checks can be performed. When preparing for these checks, a visual inspection should be made for signs of oil loss from the compressor, broken or kinked lines, condition of drive belt, and cleanliness of the condenser.

1. Refrigeration. A check should be made first to determine if proper refrigerant is in the system.

2. Performance. The system should then be given a performance check. To make this check, a gage set is necessary. Also two thermometers will be needed. Fig. 11-7 shows a gage set. The installation of the gage set is dependent on the type of service valves the system is equipped with.

3. If the first two steps have not located the source of trouble, a check then should be made to be certain that the air distribution through the system is correct.

The refrigerant check will establish whether or not there is a proper charge of refrigerant in the system. The amount of charge as a possibility of trouble can then be eliminated.

To make this check, start the engine and run at fast idle with all controls at maximum cold and blower on high. Observe the sight glass. Fig. 11-8. If bubbles are present, the system is low in charge. The reason for the loss of refrigerant should be found and corrected. If no bubbles appear in the sight glass the system is either empty or properly filled. Feel the high and low pressure lines of the system. If there is little temperature difference felt, the system is empty or nearly empty. Shut off the engine so as not to damage the compressor. Partial

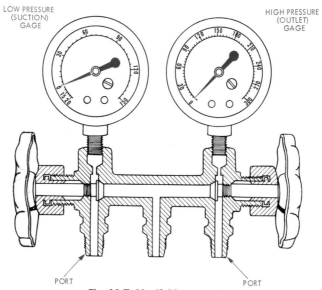

Fig. 11-7. Manifold gage set.

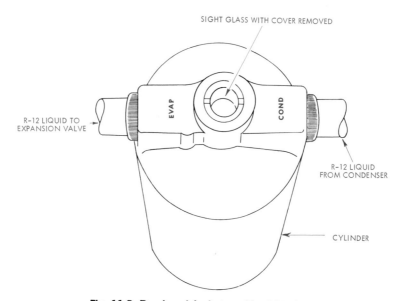

Fig. 11-8. Receiver-dehydrator with sight glass.

charge the system and locate the leak. If there is a good temperature difference felt at the compressor, it indicates the system is probably full, however, it may be overcharged. To determine if there is an over-charge, disconnect the compressor clutch lead while system is still running and look into the sight glass. If foam and bubbles appear in less than one minute it indicates the system is properly charged.

If the system still does not operate properly a performance test should be made.

PERFORMANCE TEST:

If it has been established that a proper charge is in the system, the performance test will help pin-point sources of trouble or show the air conditioning unit to be operating satisfactorily.

A gage set (Fig. 11-9) must be attached to indicate low and high side pressures. A thermometer should be placed in front of the condenser and at an inside air dis-

charge opening, usually on the right side of the interior. The air conditioner should be operating at maximum cooling and high blower speed. After running ten minutes at 1500 to 2000 rpm note the low and high pressures. Also record the two temperatures. Consult a performance chart provided by the manufacturer or use the chart shown in Fig. 11-10 as a general guide.

NOTE: Safety goggles should be worn whenever a gage set is being used or refrigerant is handled in any manner. Liquid R-12 will freeze any surface it touches. Vapors of R-12 are not danger-

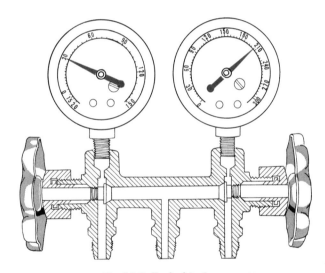

Fig. 11-9. Typical test pressures.

TEMPERATURE OF AIR ENTERING CONDENSER	70°	80°	90°	100°	110°	120°
ENGINE RPM			2000			
COMPRESSOR HEAD PRESSURE	130 140	150 160	175 185	205 215	245 255	280 290
EVAPORATOR PRESSURE			28.5-29.5 PSI			
DISCHARGE AIR TEMP. RIGHT HAND OUTLET	37-40	38-41	38-42	40-43	42-45	43-46

Fig. 11-10. Performance test specifications for air conditioned vehicles.

ous if there is adequate ventilation. Be careful to avoid heating cans of refrigerant such as by setting them on a hot engine or in the sun.

If pressures are within specifications, the system is OK to this point. If pressures are not satisfactory, further checks will be necessary to determine which component of the system is malfunctioning. The expansion valve, thermostatic switch, suction throttling valve, and compressor are the most likely units to present problems.

By touching various points in the circuit, the temperatures felt will often indicate the location of a defective component. Review the refrigeration cycle to refresh yourself with the low pressure (cool) and high pressure (warm) sections of the system when operating properly.

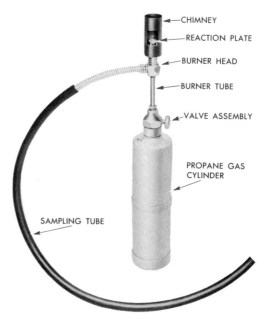

CHIMNEY
REACTION PLATE
BURNER HEAD
BURNER TUBE
VALVE ASSEMBLY
PROPANE GAS CYLINDER
SAMPLING TUBE

Fig. 11-11. Leak detector.

AIR DISTRIBUTION:

This requires a systematic check to be certain that the various door and valves operate correctly. Your sense of sound and temperature are all that is necessary.

Operate the unit through several modes such as heat, defrost, recirculate, and outside air. Note that the air volume is satisfactory and is coming from the proper outlets.

By operating the controls it should be apparent which functions are being performed properly. As an example, if no defrosting air flow is felt, the location of this difficulty can be localized quite easily to a defrost door not operating or the nozzles being disconnected.

LEAK TESTING

After any refrigerant system has been serviced it should be checked to be certain no leaks exist. A flame-type leak de-

tector is a common device for this. Fig. 11-11. There are more expensive electronic leak detectors available also.

With the flame-type detector, the sampling tube is placed near a suspected leak. If the flame changes color (to a green) in the reaction area, a leak exists.

Caution: Freon-12 or R-12 refrigerant forms deadly phosgene gas when it is burned. Do not breathe these gases. There must be no leaks in the system. If the flame-type detector indicates a leak the leak should be corrected. It will not locate very small leaks readily.

NOTE: It is possible for a system to lose up to a pound of refrigerant in a year even if no leaks are detected. Some small loss of refrigerant is normal over an extended period of time.

CHECKING OIL

Oil is carried through the system by the refrigerant. It is not recommended that the oil be checked as a matter of course. Generally, compressor oil level should be checked only where there is evidence of a major loss of system oil such as might be caused by a broken refrigerant hose, a leak in the hose fitting, a badly leaking compressor seal, or collision damage to the system components. If an oil check is necessary, consult the manufacturer's specifications for the procedure. Also use only the special refrigerant oils recommended.

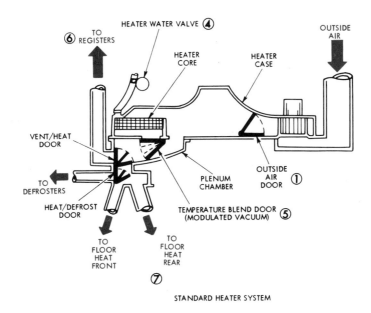

STANDARD HEATER SYSTEM

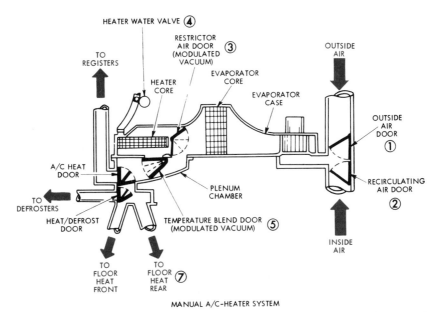

MANUAL A/C-HEATER SYSTEM

Fig. 11-12. Standard manual heater system at top. Lower shows air conditioner-heater system.

AUTOMATIC UNITS

The type of air conditioning and heating systems discussed in this chapter require that certain manual operations be performed. Fig. 11-12. The driver has to select a mode such as heat, defrost, vent, or cool.

An automatic temperature controlled system is designed to electronically sense several temperatures and when turned on and set to a desired temperature will automatically operate to maintain that preset temperature. These systems are basically the same as a combination heater and air conditioner. Fig. 11-13.

The major change is the addition of an electronic control which performs all of the operations as needed. The outside or ambient air, inside air, and engine coolant temperatures are delivered to the control unit. These temperatures are then interpreted electrically to various vacuum components which control heat, defrost, or air conditioning.

Trouble shooting these systems involves determining what functions are not being performed properly. The air conditioner itself is unchanged. Difficulty with the system should be systematically checked with the help of the manufacturer's manual. A special tester is often required to check the various electrical and vacuum devices. Fig. 11-14.

Quick checks as presented in the air conditioning section will be very helpful to prove the refrigeration system functional.

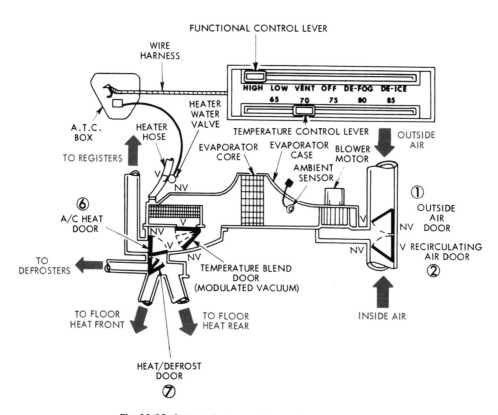

Fig. 11-13. Automatic air conditioner-heater system.

Fig. 11-14. Air conditioner tester. Sun Electric Co.

TRADE COMPETENCY TEST

1. What are the steps to follow when insufficient heat is the problem?

2. If insufficient defrosting is reported, what can be the cause?

3. Describe how you would proceed if a complaint of poor ventilation is encountered?

4. What are the main components of an air conditioning system?

5. What will determine if an air conditioner is low on charge?

6. How can an overcharge of refrigerant be detected?

7. Explain how to make the air conditioner performance test.

8. How can air conditioning leaks be detected?

9. When is it necessary to check oil level in the air conditioner?

10. Can the automatic temperature control system be given quick checks as a standard air conditioner?

CHAPTER 12

POWER OPERATED ACCESSORIES

Today's vehicles are equipped with an ever-increasing and ever-changing number of optional accessories. This chapter presents the most common accessories and describes the kinds of trouble they might present. Vacuum and electrically operated devices are included.

Most accessories do their job very well. When they stop operating or do not function properly it is your job to do the trouble shooting and make the proper correction. In this chapter you will find the procedures necessary to do just that.

POWER-OPERATED ACCESSORIES

Automobiles today use a great variety of accessories, which are designed to improve driver and passenger comfort and safety. Many of these units are electrically powered. Others use vacuum as a power source. In this chapter only the accessories which are commonly found will be discussed. Maintenance and trouble shooting procedures will be presented to assist in locating the source of difficulty as quickly as possible.

GENERAL TROUBLE SHOOTING

Accessories, whether vacuum or electrically operated, can be diagnosed with similar techniques.

As an example, an electrical circuit must have a source of power. Vacuum units must have a power source, usually the engine. In either type, vacuum or electric, there must also be a unit which uses the power. A power window is simply the addition of an electric motor to operate the window cranking mechanism. Instead of an electric solenoid, a vacuum motor can be used to pull a door lock lever.

The control of these motors or solenoids is provided by relays or simple switches. Of course there must be a path (wiring) for the electrons to follow to allow electrical units to operate. Vacuum devices require hoses or tubes to carry the vacuum from the source to the control switch and finally to the actual vacuum motor.

Consider, again, that when diagnosing troubles, there must be a power source, a control, and a unit to use the power.

If this concept is kept in mind and understood fully, troubles can be located much faster and with a minimum of lost time and wasted effort.

The first step in trouble shooting is to verify the complaint and determine exactly what does take place and what does not occur. Usually, this approach will locate the trouble such as no power at all, power for only part of the operation, or erratic operation. The procedure then should be a logical step-by-step process to eliminate by tests all circuit components that could be causing the trouble. If no operation at all is the problem, a check for power at the source would be a first step. Partial operation would indicate a defective switch or power unit. Erratic or slow operation could be due to loose or corroded connections, or defective controls as well.

The complaint of the driver is that his radio stopped operating after his car hit a severe bump in the road. Several service people when asked to look at this problem refused. They would not even check to see if the complaint was legitimate. Finally, a technician was found who listened to the customer's complaint, verified it, and looked under the dash to examine the radio and its fuse. The source of trouble was immediately located. The feed wire to the radio had been jarred off its terminal (slip-on type). It was replaced securely and the problem was solved. The point here is that anyone could have found this loose wire if he only would have given it a try. Most problems have fairly simple causes and solutions. It is necessary now to state that with some electrical circuits, such as speed controls, the previous statements may tend to be an over-simplification of the situation. Some circuits are quite a bit more complex and can't be readily placed in a simple procedure.

WINDSHIELD WIPERS

Wipers on most cars are electrical with a choice of one or two wiping speeds. An electric motor is connected to the wiper mechanism by a unit which is called the transmission. Fig. 12-1, 12-2.

Wiper arms can be adjusted by moving their position on the pivot to assure

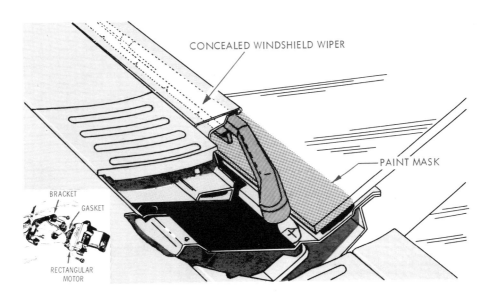

Fig. 12-1. Windshield wiper assembly. Depressed type is in lower view. Ford Motor Co.

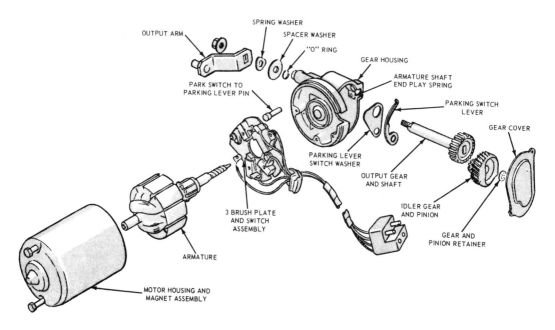

Fig. 12-2. Typical windshield wiper motor.

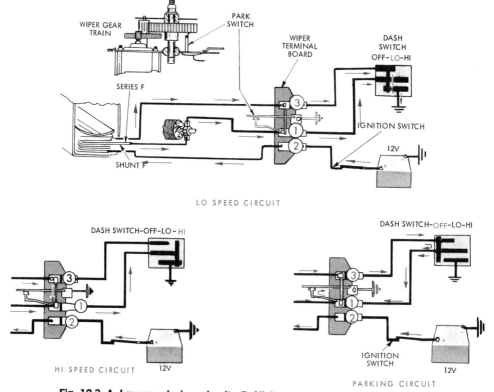

Fig. 12-3. A. Low speed wiper circuit, B. High speed circuit, C. Parking circuit.

proper sweep of the blades while wiping. This is the only adjustment possible to the windshield wiper.

Electrically, the wiper circuit consists of the motor, control switch, and a park switch which turns off the wipers when the arms are in the off or parked position. Fig. 12-3.

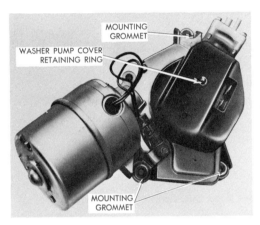

Fig. 12-4. Depressed park two speed wiper motor. Chevrolet Motor Div., General Motors Corp.

Fig. 12-5. Non-depressed park wiper. Chevrolet Motor Div., General Motors Corp.

Many vehicles have the arms in a depressed park position to conceal the wipers when they are not being used. Conventional wipers are called the non-depressed type. Figs. 12-4 and 12-5.

WIPERS DO NOT OPERATE

When a wiper problem is encountered it is first necessary to inspect carefully for proper connections and tight mountings. Also, if a fuse is used, it should be checked. With the ignition switch on there should be a 12 volt supply to the motor. If there is no supply voltage to the motor, check for a defective feed wire or fuse.

If the wipers do not operate now, disconnect the connector at wiper motor and determine if the motor will operate with the use of jumper wires as indicated by Figs. 12-6 and 12-7. If the wiper will operate normally the control switch and wiring should be checked and repaired or replaced as necessary.

If the motor will not operate it is probably defective. Remove the motor for repair or replacement. With the motor disconnected, the arms and blades can be manually moved to be certain the linkage is free.

WIPER SPEEDS

A wiper can, because of its internal wiring, operate too fast, only at low speed, or only on high speed. Operate the motor with jumpers and if normal operation is possible, the switch should be checked and replaced if defective. (Fig. 12-3)

WIPERS WILL NOT SHUT OFF

Usually the park switch contacts are not operating to open the motor circuit in these cases. In some cases the park switch will need adjustment. In others, the failure to shut off is an indication of

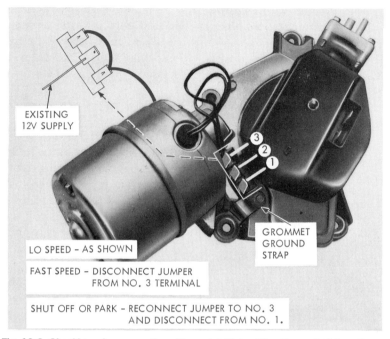

EXISTING
12V SUPPLY

3
2
1

GROMMET
GROUND
STRAP

LO SPEED – AS SHOWN

FAST SPEED – DISCONNECT JUMPER
FROM NO. 3 TERMINAL

SHUT OFF OR PARK – RECONNECT JUMPER TO NO. 3
AND DISCONNECT FROM NO. 1.

Fig. 12-6. Checking wiper operation. Chevrolet Motor Div., General Motors Corp.

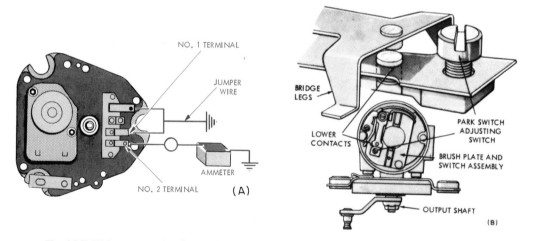

NO. 1 TERMINAL

JUMPER
WIRE

AMMETER

NO. 2 TERMINAL   (A)

BRIDGE
LEGS

LOWER
CONTACTS

PARK SWITCH
ADJUSTING
SWITCH

BRUSH PLATE AND
SWITCH ASSEMBLY

OUTPUT SHAFT

(B)

Fig. 12-7. Wiring connection for windshield wiper; park switch adjustment of windshield wiper.

a ground lead or even a defective switch. Figs. 12-6 and 12-7 indicate how some wipers are checked with a jumper wire or wires. (Fig. 12-7A shows a park switch test.)

WASHERS

Washers are usually connected into the wiper circuit so that when washers are turned on wipers will also operate.

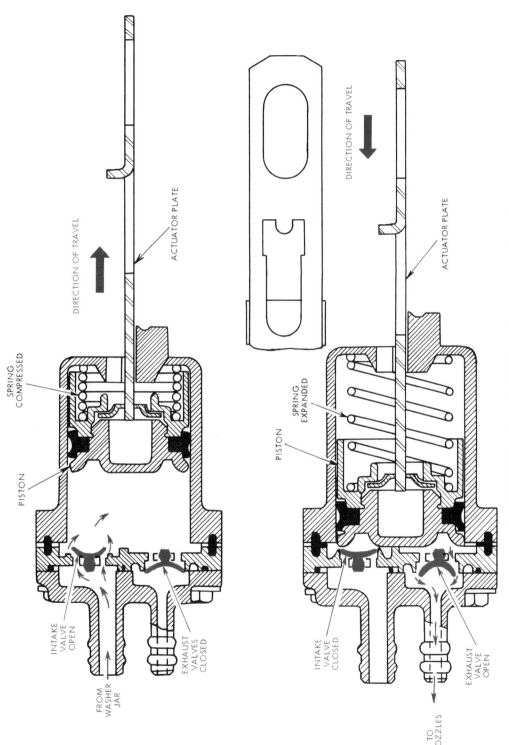

Fig. 12-8. Piston type windshield washer pump showing action.

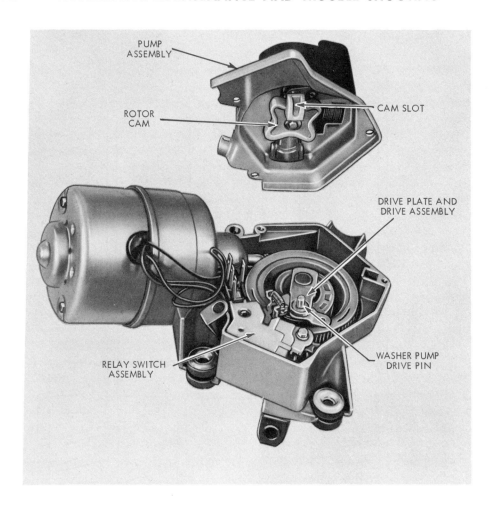

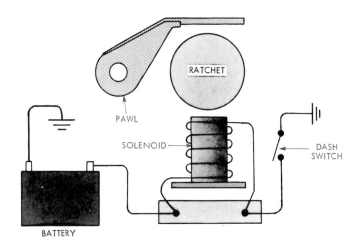

Fig. 12-9. Windshield washer pump assembly and wiring circuit. Chevrolet Motor Div., General Motors Corp.

Some washers use a piston type pump with an electric drive mechanism. Figs. 12-8 and 12-9. Others use an impeller type pump in the washer circuit. Manually operated washers utilize a pressure bulb which forces fluid to the washer nozzles. Fig. 12-10.

Washers which do not operate should be checked first for presence of solution in the reservoir. Also the hoses to the nozzles can be cleaned with light air pressure. The nozzles can be reverse flushed with compressed air also.

If washer will not operate check the electrical connections to be sure a wire has not become disconnected. Test for presence of power at the washer terminal when the switch is turned on. If there is power and adequate liquid, the pump should operate. Be certain that the pump intake area is not clogged. The washer pump on some models can be serviced and on others it must be replaced if it will not operate.

INTERMITTENT WIPERS

This is a special feature which controls wiper operation during conditions of very light rain or drizzle. It is a unit which is either transistorized or vacuum and electrically operated. It is connected into the low speed system of the wipers. The frequency of wiping is controlled by a driver control. The intermittent operation is by-passed during heavy acceleration such as passing. If wiper operation is normal without intermittent control, then it can be assumed the unit is defective. Before replacement, check to be certain that the connections are complete and properly made. Fig. 12-11.

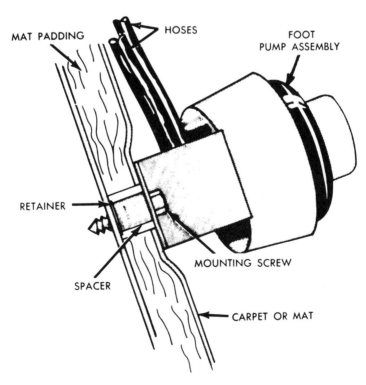

Fig. 12-10. Windshield washer foot pump.

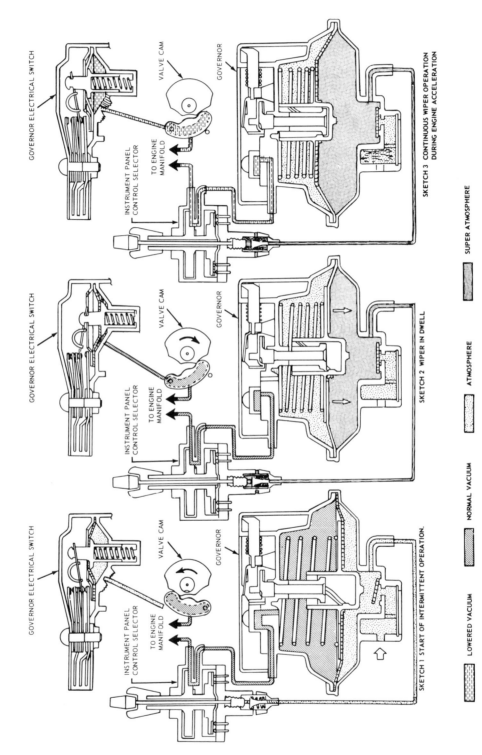

Fig. 12-11. Operation of intermittent windshield wiper.

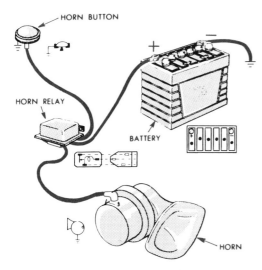

Fig. 12-12. Horn circuit.

HORNS

Horns usually will develop complaints such as, only one of two operate, no horn action, or horn sounds continually. Intermittent unwanted horn operation is also a typical complaint.

Understanding the horn circuit is a valuable help to trouble shooting. Fig. 12-12. Horns are usually operated by a relay which is controlled by a switch on the steering wheel. When the steering wheel switch is closed, this completes the horn relay ground circuit. The relay points close which sends battery power to the horns. Some cars do not use a horn relay and complete the horn circuit at the

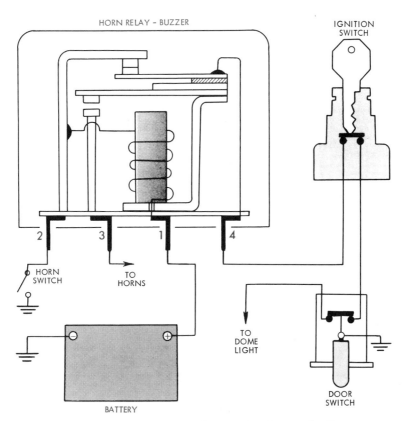

Fig. 12-13. Wiring diagram for open door buzzer circuit.

steering wheel horn switch. In addition, vehicles also incorporate a theft deterrent buzzer circuit which operates from a special type of horn relay. Fig. 12-13. With these various circuits understood, trouble shooting includes locating the component in the circuit that is malfunctioning and replacing it or repairing it if possible.

ONE HORN ONLY SOUNDS

Two horns are used to deliver a pleasant sound. Some vehicles use only one horn. Check to see that two horns are used. While looking, see that all wires are attached. Use a jumper wire at the inoperative horn. If it will not operate, it should be replaced. A current draw test can be performed to be sure the horn is defective. Fig. 12-14. No current is an indication of an open circuit. If current flow is high but not sounding the horn, it is

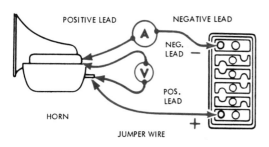

Fig. 12-14. Horn circuit current draw test.

either shorted or grounded internally. Some horns can be adjusted. The adjustment will vary the current flow and thus alter the tone also. Most horns are subjected to road splash and are susceptible to rust. The adjustment will not usually help the operation of a rusted horn.

NO HORN

Check all connections first. Operate the horn button. If a click is heard, this

indicates the relay is operating and the trouble is with the horns. If the relay does not click it indicates a relay or switch problem. Connect a test light into the switch wire at the relay. If the light operates when the button is operated, the relay is defective. Replace the relay. If the light did not light in this test, the horn switch is where the trouble lies or in the wiring to the switch.

HORNS OPERATE CONTINUOUSLY

The relay is stuck closed or the switch or its wire is grounded. Usually the horn switch is the source of trouble. Continuous horn operation can discharge the battery quickly in addition to the unpleasant sound. Disconnect the battery ground cable or the horn wires to stop horn operation.

INTERMITTENT UNWANTED OPERATION

Usually this trouble occurs due to loose or worn parts in the steering wheel switch. Disconnect the switch to determine if it is the source of trouble. Repair as required.

RADIO PROBLEMS

Good trouble shooting procedure for radios involves checking the complaint to be sure that a problem does exist.

NO RECEPTION

A check should be made to determine if voltage is being supplied and that the fuse is good. Also the radio should be securely grounded. The speaker wires and the antenna lead should be checked also. A majority of complaints will be corrected with these checks.

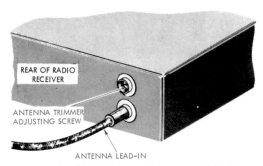

ANTENNA TRIMMER
ADJUSTING SCREW

ANTENNA LEAD-IN

Fig. 12-15. Antenna trimmer and lead.

POOR RECEPTION

Check the antenna lead and the antenna ground. Most radios have a trimmer adjustment at the rear of the receiver. The procedure for this adjustment involves raising the antenna fully, selecting a near station in the 1400 KHz (KC) range. Turn the trimmer screw to achieve the greatest volume from the radio. Fig. 12-15.

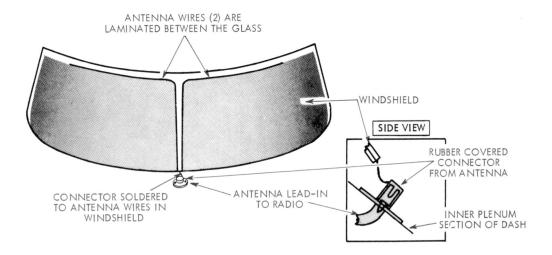

ANTENNA WIRES (2) ARE
LAMINATED BETWEEN THE GLASS

WINDSHIELD

SIDE VIEW

RUBBER COVERED
CONNECTOR
FROM ANTENNA

CONNECTOR SOLDERED
TO ANTENNA WIRES IN
WINDSHIELD

ANTENNA LEAD-IN
TO RADIO

INNER PLENUM
SECTION OF DASH

IMPORTANT:

FOR MAXIMUM EFFICIENCY, THE ANTENNA TRIMMER MUST BE ADJUSTED TO EXACT PEAK (LOUDEST SIGNAL) WITH RADIO TUNED TO A WEAK STATION NEAR 1400 KC (140) AND VOLUMN ON FULL.
TO TEST ANTENNA FOR SHORT CIRCUIT
1. REMOVE ANTENNA LEAD-IN FROM RADIO.
2. CONNECT 12 VOLT TEST LIGHT TO 12 VOLT SOURCE AND TO ANTENNA LEAD-IN CENTER TERMINAL.
   A. IF TEST LIGHT IS "OFF," ANTENNA IS NOT SHORTED.
   B. IF TEST LIGHT IS "ON," DISCONNECT ANTENNA FROM LEAD-IN SOCKET AT BASE OF WINDSHIELD. IF TEST LIGHT TURNS OFF, SHORT CIRCUIT WAS IN SHORT WIRE TO WINDSHIELD. TAPE IT AND POSITION IT TO PREVENT SHORT CIRCUIT FROM OCCURRING. IF TEST LIGHT STAYS ON, REMOVE LEAD-IN AND REPAIR OR REPLACE AS REQUIRED.

A WHIP ANTENNA CAN BE ADJUSTED TO 25-30 INCHES AND TEMPORARILY CONNECTED TO THE RADIO TO DETERMINE IF ANTENNA OR LEAD-IN IS AT FAULT. IF THERE IS CONSIDERABLE IMPROVEMENT IN RECEPTION, THE CONNECTOR AT THE BASE OF THE WINDSHIELD SHOULD BE INSPECTED FOR CORROSION AND LOOSE CONNECTIONS. THE ANTENNA WIRES CAN BE VISUALLY INSPECTED FOR BREAKS. A CRACK IN THE GLASS ACROSS ONE OF THE WIRES WOULD PROBABLY BREAK THE WIRE. IF THE PROBLEM IS IN THE ANTENNA WIRES OR WIRE TO THE CONNECTOR AND CANNOT BE REPAIRED, A WHIP ANTENNA CAN BE INSTALLED OR THE WINDSHIELD REPLACED.

Fig. 12-16. Radio antenna, windshield type.

WINDSHIELD ANTENNA

Recently, the radio antenna has been imbedded in the windshield glass. Fig. 12-16. This type of installation is becoming very popular. If this antenna is suspected of being a source of trouble, a conventional whip antenna can be plugged into the receiver as a substitute. If the antenna is defective the windshield must be replaced or a whip type antenna installed.

RADIO TESTER

If these simple checks do not solve radio problems, a radio tester can be used to determine the source of trouble. If a tester is not available, a radio technician should be consulted.

POWER WINDOWS

Electrically operated window mechanisms are simply electric motors which are connected to the window regulator mechanism. Fig. 12-17. These motors are able to operate in two rotations. One for the window up movement and the reverse for window down operation. Each window has its own switch and the driver has a set of switches to control all the windows. A relay, which is energized by the ignition switch is incorporated into the main circuit. A circuit breaker is used for overload protection.

Power window troubles are found in three categories. One window will not operate from either switch, a window will not operate from one switch, or all windows will not operate.

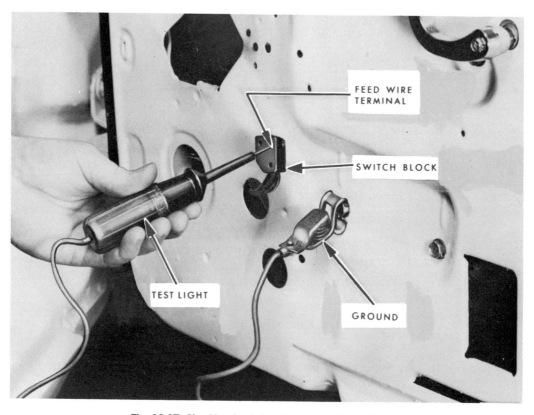

Fig. 12-17. Checking feed circuit. General Motors Corp.

WINDOW WILL NOT OPERATE FROM EITHER SWITCH

This is an indication that the motor is defective or the window mechanism is jammed, thereby locking the window so it cannot be moved up or down.

WINDOW WILL NOT OPERATE FROM ONE SWITCH

This normally is a defective switch. However, check wiring and connections also at the suspected switch. Figs. 12-17 and 12-18.

ALL WINDOWS DO NOT OPERATE

This trouble normally is in the relay, circuit breaker, and the associated wiring. Test the circuit breaker for continuity, then check for power to the relay. If there is power to the relay it should click when the ignition switch is turned on. If it does not click, the relay is no good.

POWER TAILGATE WINDOW

The circuit for this window is somewhat different when compared to a power side window. Fig. 12-19. The motor is required to develop a great deal of torque. A permanent magnet motor is not sufficient. A series motor is used with two field windings wound in opposite directions. This allows an up and down circuit for the tailgate window. Figs. 12-20 and 12-21.

As with power windows, a safety relay is used but only for the dash panel switch. The lock switch is fed directly and can be operated with the key. The relay prevents accidental operation of the tailgate window if the ignition switch is off.

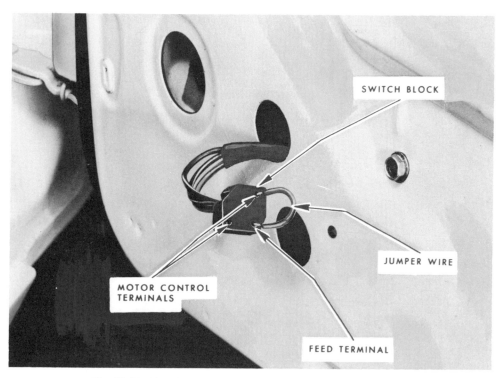

Fig. 12-18. Checking window control switch. General Motors Corp.

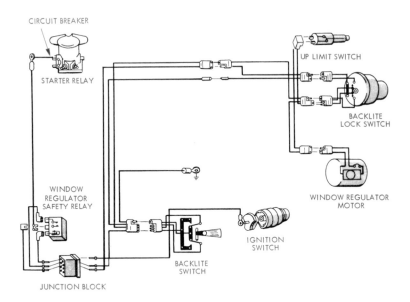

Fig. 12-19. Typical tailgate window circuit.

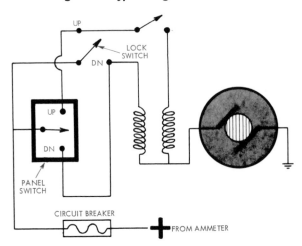

Fig. 12-20. Tailgate window circuit.

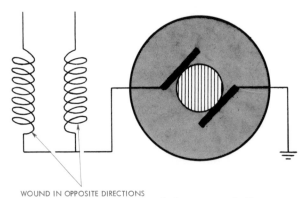

Fig. 12-21. Tailgate window motor windings.

A limit switch is used to prevent the window from being operated with the tailgate down.

The diagnosis of troubles is very much the same as for power windows: window will not operate, or operates only from one switch.

If the window will not operate, start at the power source and follow, by testing for power, the circuit until the defect has been located.

When window operates only from one switch, the procedure is to trace the power source to the switch and through the switch. If the dash switch does not operate the window, the relay or switch itself is defective.

POWER SEATS

Seats can be electrically powered to provide horizontal, vertical, or tilting action to a single bucket seat or a bench type seat. Up to six motions can be provided.

Two, four, and six-way power seats are used. These all use an electric motor which, through solenoids placing a transmission into the proper position, move the seat as required. Fig. 12-22 shows a typical four-way power seat transmission. Fig. 12-23 shows the adjuster mechanism that is operated by the transmission. Often cables are used to connect transmission to adjuster mechanisms.

Problems with power seats are: motor

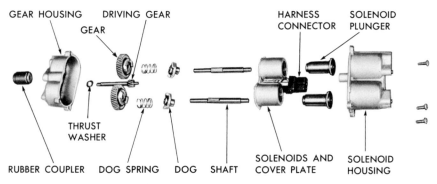

Fig. 12-22. Four way seat adjuster transmission. Buick Motor Div., General Motors Corp.

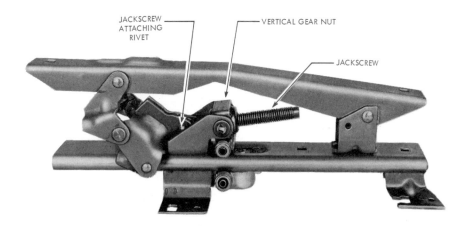

Fig. 12-23. Four way seat adjuster mechanism. Buick Motor Div., General Motors Corp.

does not operate; motor runs, seat doesn't move; and seat moves in all but one direction.

MOTOR DOES NOT OPERATE

Start with a check at the power source and follow this power to the switch, relays, and motor. The ignition switch should be on. Look for obvious defects such as connections pulled apart or loose connections. Listen for sounds, such as motors, relay, and solenoids clicking. These sounds often can tell you much about where the trouble is located. Repair or replace as necessary.

MOTORS OPERATE, NO SEAT MOVEMENT

This indicates that the transmission or adjusters are not operating. Inspect connections and observe if the transmission is operating while the motor is turned on and running. Repair as required.

SEAT OPERATES PARTIALLY

Determine exactly what the seat is not doing. This will give clues as to which parts are malfunctioning. Check, then, the relays, solenoids, and connections to determine where the exact trouble is. Start with a power source test with a test light and trace until the defect is located. Fig. 12-24 shows a typical six-way power seat circuit.

SPEED CONTROL UNITS

A fairly recent addition to accessories for vehicles is the automatic speed con-

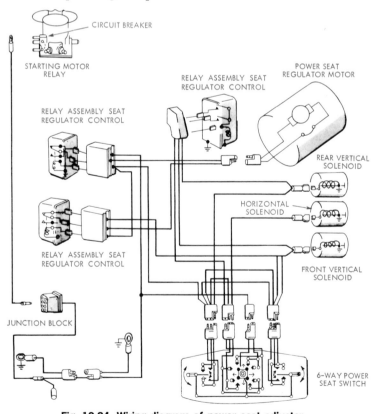

Fig. 12-24. Wiring diagram of power seat adjuster.

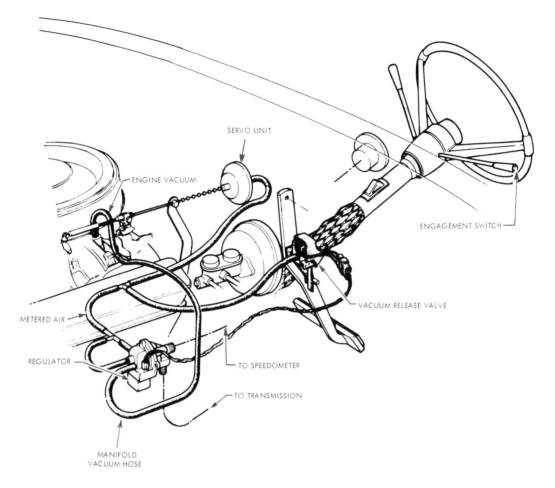

Fig. 12-25. Cruise master speed control system.

trol. These units will maintain a selected speed with the driver's foot off the accelerator pedal. The basic components used are a regulator or transducer, a vacuum servo, and an engaging switch located in the vehicle at the turn signal lever or in the steering wheel.

A brake release or disengaging switch is also used to allow the driver complete control at all times. Fig. 12-25 shows a typical layout for a speed control system. Note that the vehicle speed, through the speedometer cable, is sensed by the regulator. The regulator converts this speed signal (acting as a transducer) to a vacuum

valve which supplies the servo unit. The servo holds the throttle open for the set speed.

Other systems are similar to this unit. Improper operation is best diagnosed with the help of a diagnostic guide as shown in Fig. 12-26. Because each system is slightly different refer to a shop manual for specific information on trouble shooting.

Generally, follow a procedure as mentioned in earlier parts of this chapter. Look for obvious improper connections, and check for vacuum and electrical power.

CRUISE MASTER SYSTEM CHECKS

PROBLEM	CAUSE	CORRECTION
WILL NOT ENGAGE—SYSTEM INOPERATIVE	BRAKE SWITCH CIRCUIT OPEN CLUTCH SWITCH CIRCUIT OPEN	CHECK CONNECTIONS—ADJUST OR REPLACE SWITCH. REFER TO ELECTRICAL CHECK OUT.
	FUSE BLOWN	REPLACE FUSE—IF IT BLOWS AGAIN, CHECK FOR: 1. ENGAGE SWITCH STUCK IN THE CENTER OF TRAVEL—REFER TO ELECTRICAL CHECK OUT. 2. INCORRECT WIRING—REFER TO ELECTRICAL CHECK OUT. 3. SHORT TO GROUND—REFER TO ELECTRICAL CHECK OUT. MAKE NECESSARY CORRECTIONS.
	DEFECTIVE ENGAGE SWITCH	REPLACE AS NEEDED—REFER TO ELECTRICAL CHECK OUT.
	VACUUM LEAK IN SERVO AND/OR BRAKE CONNECTING LINES. VACUUM HOSE NOT CONNECTED TO VACUUM SWITCH	VACUUM TEST AND REPAIR OR REPLACE AS NEEDED. REFER TO SERVO AND VACUUM SYSTEM CHECK OUT.
	VACUUM RELEASE SWITCH MISADJUSTED (ALWAYS OPEN)	READJUST SWITCH.
	CROSSED HOSE AT REGULATOR	REROUTE HOSES.
	OPEN IN WIRING HARNESS	REPAIR OR REPLACE AS NEEDED.
	PINCHED OR PLUGGED HOSE THAT IS CONNECTED TO THE SERVO	FREE OR REPLACE HOSE.
	DEFECTIVE REGULATOR	REPLACE REGULATOR.
DOES NOT CRUISE AT ENGAGEMENT SPEED	ORIFICE TUBE MISADJUSTED	ADJUST AS REQUIRED.
	BEAD CHAIN LOOSE	TIGHTEN BEAD CHAIN.
SYSTEM HUNTS, PULSES, OR SURGES	KINKED OR DETERIORATED HOSES (AIR LEAK)	REPAIR OR REPLACE.
	DEFECTIVE AND/OR IMPROPERLY POSITIONED DRIVE CABLES AND/OR CASING ASSEMBLIES	REPAIR OR REPLACE AS NEEDED.
	DEFECTIVE REGULATOR	REPLACE REGULATOR.
SYSTEM DOES NOT DISENGAGE—WITH BRAKE PEDAL	BRAKE AND/OR VACUUM SWITCH—MISADJUSTED OR DEFECTIVE	ADJUST OR REPLACE AS REQUIRED. REFER TO SERVO AND VACUUM SYSTEM CHECK OUT AND ELECTRICAL CHECK OUT.
	RED WIRES (WHICH SHOULD BE CONNECTED TO THE PEDAL SWITCH(ES) CONNECTED TO THE FUSE BLOCK	REROUTE WIRES TO STOPLIGHT SWITCH.
SYSTEM STEADILY ACCELERATES OR APPLIES FULL THROTTLE WHEN ENGAGED	MANIFOLD VACUUM CONNECTED DIRECTLY TO SERVO	REROUTE HOSE.
	DEFECTIVE REGULATOR	REPLACE REGULATOR.
CANNOT ADJUST SPEED DOWNWARD WITH ENGAGE BUTTON	DEFECTIVE ENGAGEMENT SWITCH OR WIRING	REPLACE AS NEEDED. REFER TO ELECTRICAL CHECK OUT.
DOES NOT ENGAGE OR ENGAGES LOWER THAN LIMITS REFERRED TO IN "DRIVER OPERATION"	DEFECTIVE REGULATOR	REPLACE REGULATOR.
SLOW THROTTLE RETURN TO IDLE AFTER BRAKE IS DEPRESSED	PINCHED AIR HOSE AT VACUUM RELEASE SWITCH	FREE OR REPLACE HOSE.
SYSTEM OPERATES CORRECTLY, BUT CONSTANT VACUUM BLEED WHEN SYSTEM IS DISENGAGED	CROSSED VACUUM HOSES AT REGULATOR	REROUTE HOSES.
HIGH ENGINE IDLE SPEED—INDEPENDENT OF CARBURETOR ADJUSTMENTS. CONSTANT AIR BLEED THROUGH SYSTEM	TIGHT SERVO CHAIN	LOOSEN CHAIN ADJUSTMENT.
CONSTANT DRAIN ON BATTERY	POWER LEAD CONNECTED TO "FUSED BATTERY" TERMINAL OF FUSE BLOCK	REROUTE TO "FUSED IGN" TERMINAL.
SYSTEM CAN BE ENGAGED AT IDLE BY DEPRESSING SWITCH, BUT WILL DROP OUT WHEN SWITCH IS RELEASED. SOLENOID CAN BE HEARD WHEN SWITCH IS DEPRESSED WHEN THE VEHICLE IS STANDING STILL	WIRES REVERSED AT REGULATOR	REVERSE WIRES.

Fig. 12-26. Cruise master speed control trouble chart.

HEADLIGHTS

A typical headlight circuit is not always fully understood. Study the circuit diagrams shown in Fig. 12-27 and Fig. 12-28 for the two and four headlight systems. Note that the foot dimmer switch is the source of power to the headlights. Lights which burn out frequently indi-

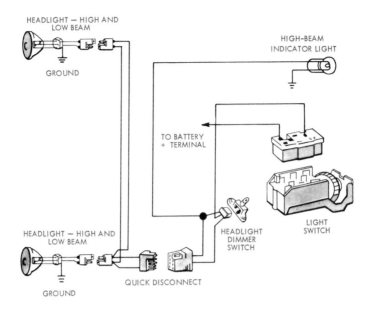

Fig. 12-27. Headlight circuit wiring diagram, two lamp system.

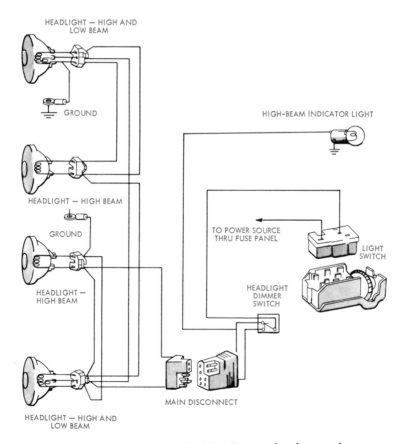

Fig. 12-28. Headlight circuit wiring diagram, four lamp system.

cate that loose connections exist in the circuit or a high charging voltage is causing early failure.

Troubles with lights are: one light inoperative, all lights out, blinking or flickering, lights are dim, either at idle only or all the time.

ONE LIGHT OUT

Usually this is simply a burned out bulb. Occasionally a defective socket or wire will be found also. Check for power to the bulb connector with the lights on to determine the trouble. Repair as necessary.

ALL LIGHTS OUT (High or low beam only)

Usually the foot dimmer switch is the source of trouble in this case. Check for power at the switch and at the high and low beam feed wires as the switch is operated.

This is a sign that no power is reaching the lights. Check for power at the light switch. If there is power, the dimmer switch should also receive power. If the dimmer switch does not receive power the light switch is probably defective and will have to be replaced.

Fig. 12-29 shows the retainer which must be depressed in order to remove the knob shaft before replacing the switch.

DIM LIGHTS

A low battery or poor connections which cause high resistance is usually the reason for dim lights. Check the battery first. Also, check the light ground connectors.

ADJUSTMENT OF HEADLIGHTS

Headlights should be checked frequently to be certain they are properly aimed. Horizontal and vertical adjustments can be made easily. Fig. 12-30. An aiming screen or headlight aiming device can be used. Figs. 12-31, 12-32. Follow manufacturer's instructions with the aiming unit. The aiming of lights should be done with the vehicle normally loaded. If adjustments are made, keep in mind that the suspension height of the vehicle and the level of the vehicle influence the light placed ahead of the car. A heavily loaded car will have lights aimed too high if they are adjusted with no load in the vehicle.

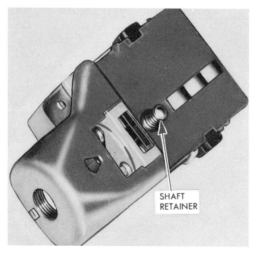

Fig. 12-29. Shaft retainer. Chevrolet Motor Div., General Motors Corp.

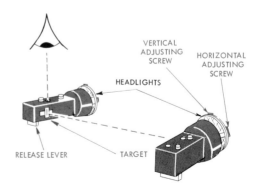

Fig. 12-30. Headlight adjustment points. Plymouth Div., Chrysler Corp.

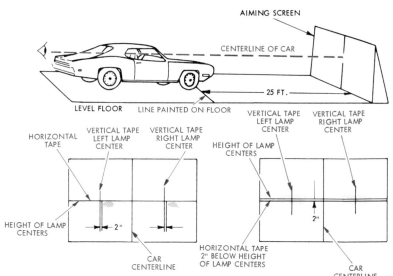

Fig. 12-31. Checking and aiming headlights.

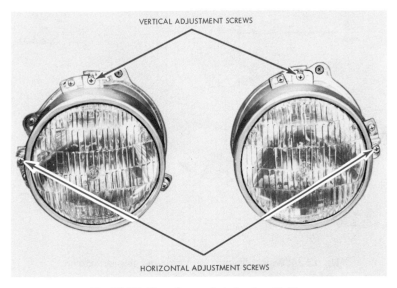

Fig. 12-32. Mounting and aiming headlights.

TURN SIGNALS — HAZARD WARNING LIGHTS

A typical turn signal circuit is shown in Figs. 12-33 and 12-34. The hazard warning system uses all of the turn signal lamps but uses a separate flasher which is designed to operate with a doubled electrical load. The turn signal flasher is a separate unit. Since the signals are interconnected, problems with turn signals

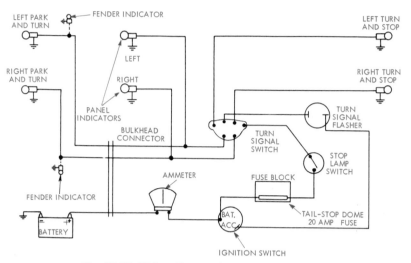

Fig. 12-33. Wiring diagram for turn signals circuit.

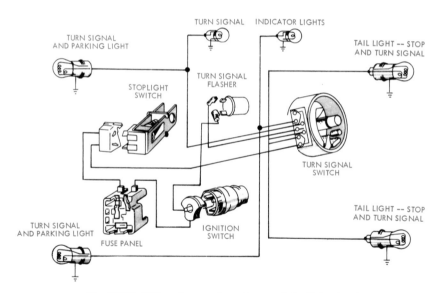

Fig. 12-34. Wiring diagram for a turn and stoplight circuit.

will often become hazard circuit problems. Troubles that usually develop in the turn signals are:

SYSTEM DOES NOT FLASH

If no flashing takes place for either right or left turn position this usually indicates a defective flasher. If flashing occurs on one side and not the other, the flasher is not the trouble. Most frequently, turn signal troubles are due to a burned out bulb or a corroded or rusty socket. Observation of the system with the parking lights on will give valuable clues to the cause of trouble. If all parking lights operate and the stop lights are also functioning the wiring and grounds are probably good. If a light is out or is dim, it is very likely the source of turn signal trouble. Replace the bulb, socket, or clean up the connections as required.

NO OPERATION

If nothing is operating, check the fuse and the flasher.

FAILS TO CANCEL

Usually the switch is defective. If the signals operate correctly but will not cancel or turn off with steering wheel movement it indicates a broken or loose switch in the steering wheel.

If the system operates correctly but

the dash indicator light does not, it is an indication that the indicator bulb is burned out or has become dislodged.

HAZARD WARNING LIGHTS

If the circuit fails to operate and the turn signals are operating, no power is reaching the flasher or the flasher is defective. Also the switch could be defective. Check for power first, then the flasher. The switch is the least likely source of trouble.

On many cars, the hazard flasher is very difficult to locate. Be sure you do not confuse the two flashers.

SIDE MARKER LIGHTS

Many circuits now include a side marker light in the turn signal system.

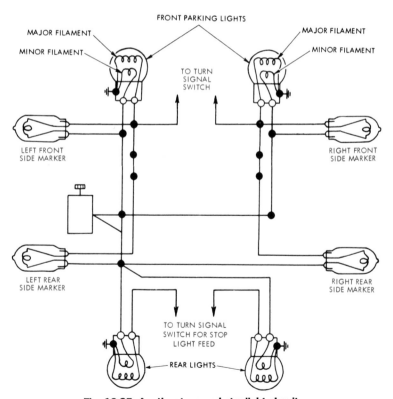

Fig. 12-35. Another turn and stoplight circuit.

This is an additional set of lamps which will be operated with the parking lights and turn signals.

Some vehicles include a cornering light which is a white lamp in the front fender. This light does not flash but is controlled by a separate wire in the turn signal switch wiring. Often a relay is used to turn the lamp on when the turn signal lever is operated rather than having a direct power source in the steering wheel. The cornering lamp is of a high candle power and draws much more current than a typical marker light. Note in particular, Fig. 12-35 which illustrates a circuit with side marker lamps which are connected in a different manner. These lamps are grounded through the filaments of the

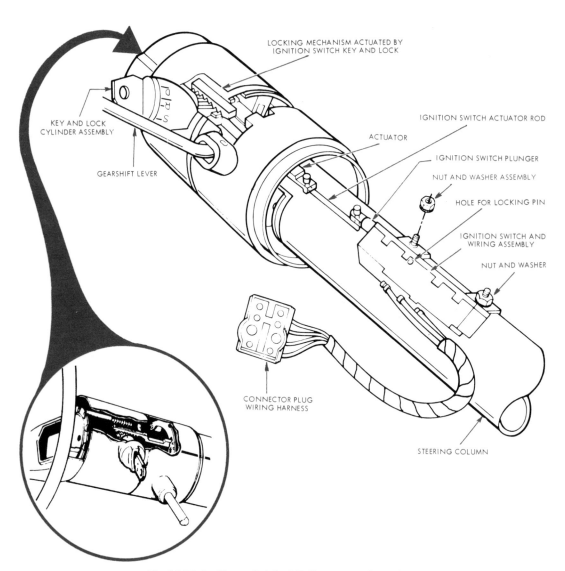

Fig. 12-36. Ignition switch installation on steering column.

parking lights. This allows for an on-off flashing sequence when the lights are turned on.

IGNITION SWITCH — STEERING WHEEL LOCK

Many cars are equipped with a new type ignition-steering switch which is mounted on the steering column. Fig. 12-36. This switch is activated by the operation of the key lock. As the key is turned to the "on" position, the steering wheel is unlocked and a rod operates the switch. The switch can be adjusted so that ignition and cranking take place properly. The switch bolts can be loosened and the switch slid up or down the steering column slightly for positioning. The older type ignition and starter switch is usually located on the dash panel. These switches are usually difficult to gain easy access to and will need to be removed for testing.

MISCELLANEOUS ACCESSORIES

Many other types of devices are used on today's vehicles. It is not possible to provide details of operation of all of these various devices in this chapter. There are many variations of similar devices which can lead to confusion. However, if a wiring diagram or shop manual is available it will often be very helpful in locating troubles.

Such devices as electric or vacuum door locks, electric seat back releases, automatic headlight dimmers, electric trunk latches, vacuum or electric headlight covers are a few of these special accessories.

Electric seat warmers, rear window defrosters, anti-skid braking systems, tilt steering wheels, folding convertible tops

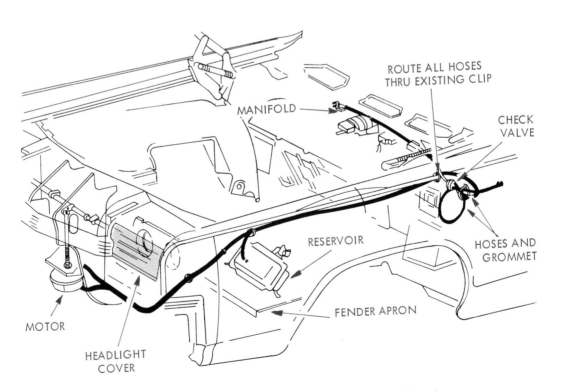

Fig. 12-37. Vacuum headlight door system. Note motor and link to doors.

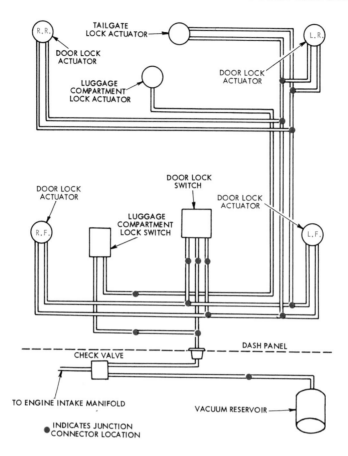

Fig. 12-38. Vacuum door lock schematic.

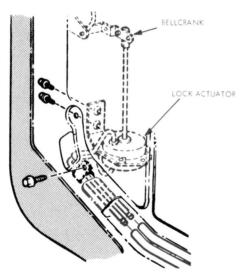

Fig. 12-39. Vacuum door lock actuator. One hose locks and the other unlocks.

and headlight shut-off delay units are more examples. Diagrams of some of these accessories are included for your information. Fig. 12-37 to 12-39.

If the basic principles of trouble shooting are followed even these accessories can be easily diagnosed. Verify what should or should not occur. Then start at the power source, to the control device, and finally the unit itself. Always be alert for the obvious broken or disconnected wire. Often a poor connection will be cleaned by simply separating the connector and reconnecting it.

TRADE COMPETENCY TEST

1. What three things are necessary for an electrical or vacuum unit to operate?

2. What is the first step in troubleshooting?

3. What kinds of troubles are typical of the windshield wipers?

4. How can washer nozzles be cleaned?

5. If the horns do not sound and the horn relay clicks, what is the likely source of trouble?

6. What is a trimmer adjustment of the radio?

7. What would be an indication that a power window motor was defective?

8. If a tailgate safety relay was out of order, what would most likely be the complaint?

9. If a power seat does not operate at all, what is likely to be the problem?

10. How does the speed control system sense vehicle speed?

11. What kinds of problems can develop in a headlight system?

12. What conditions would affect headlight aim?

13. What is indicated if no flashing occurs with a turn signal system?

14. What is a cornering light?

15. What are two locations for the ignition-starter switch?

INDEX

Bold face indicates illustration.